Stanislavsky in Focus

"Outstanding ... there are innumerable books about Stanislavsky. *Stanislavsky in Focus* is the only book worth taking seriously."

David Chambers, *Yale School of Drama, USA*

"Sharon Carnicke has single-handedly begun to demystify Stanislavsky's influence for theatre practitioners everywhere."

Anne Bogart, *SITI and Columbia University, USA*

"Carnicke's is the finest book I have read on the work of Stanislavsky in many, many years."

André Gregory, actor, director and producer

"Essential reading for every actor, whether experienced or a novice."

Ed Hooks, acting coach

Stanislavsky in Focus brilliantly examines the history and actual premises of Stanislavsky's System, separating myth from fact with forensic skill.

The first edition of this now classic study showed conclusively how the System was gradually transformed into the Method, popularized in the 1950s by Lee Strasberg and the Actors Studio. It looked at the gap between the original Russian texts and what most English-speaking practitioners still imagine to be Stanislavsky's ideas.

This thoroughly revised new edition also delves deeper into:

- The mythical depiction of Stanislavsky as a tyrannical director and teacher.
- Yoga, the mind–body–spirit continuum and its role in the "System".
- How Stanislavsky used subtexts to hide many of his ideas from Soviet censors.

The text has been updated to address all of the relevant scholarship, particularly in Russia, since the first edition was published. It also features an expanded glossary on the System's terminology and its historical exercises, more on the political context and the cognitive science in Stanislavsky's work, and the System's relation to contemporary developments in actor training. It will be a vital part of every practitioner's and historian's library.

Sharon Marie Carnicke is Professor of Theatre and Slavic Languages at the University of Southern California. She is also an actor and director, and has published numerous articles on Stanislavsky and Russian theatre.

Routledge Theatre Classics

The Routledge Theatre Classics series brings some of the theatrical world's seminal texts to a new generation. Drawn from Routledge's extensive archives, including the renowned Theatre Arts imprint, each volume has received expert editorial attention to update it for today's reader. This collection brings the theatre of the twentieth century into the spotlight of the twenty-first.

On the Art of the Theatre
Edward Gordon Craig edited by Franc Chamberlain
A prescient vision of the state of theatre from one of its great modernizers, still bearing huge influence almost a century after it was written.

Theatre Arts on Acting
Edited by Laurence Senelick
A compendium of articles from the pages of *Theatre Arts Magazine*, with contributions from John Gielgud, Michael Chekhov, Konstantin Stanislavsky and Lee Strasberg among others.

Stanislavsky in Focus (Second Edition)
Sharon M. Carnicke
A crucial exploration of one of theatre's towering figures. Dispels the misconceptions that dog his teachings and explains the truth behind the myth.

Theatre: The Rediscovery of Style and Other Writings
Michel Saint-Denis edited by Jane Baldwin
Combines Saint-Denis' two major works, moving seamlessly from theory to practice and addressing everything from actor training to the synergy of modern and classical theatre.

Stanislavsky in Focus

An Acting Master for the Twenty-first Century

Second Edition

Sharon Marie Carnicke

Aug 2009

Dear Beth
Thank you for
your interest
in Stanislavsky
Shan Carnicke

Routledge
Taylor & Francis Group

LONDON AND NEW YORK

First published 1998 by Routledge
This edition 2009 by Routledge
2 Park Square, Milton Park, Abingdon, Oxon OX14 4RN

Simultaneously published in the USA and Canada
by Routledge
270 Madison Avenue, New York, NY 10016

Routledge is an imprint of the Taylor & Francis Group, an
informa business

Typeset in Times New Roman by
Bookcraft Ltd, Stroud, Gloucestershire

Printed and bound by
The Cromwell Press, Trowbridge, Wiltshire

British Library Cataloguing in Publication Data
A catalogue record for this book is available from the British Library

Library of Congress Cataloging in Publication Data
Carnicke, Sharon Marie, 1949–
Stanislavsky in focus : an acting master for the 21st century / Sharon
Marie Carnicke. – 2d ed.
   p. cm.
   Includes bibliographical references and index.
   1. Stanislavsky, Konstantin, 1863–1938–Criticism and interpretation.
   2. Method (Acting) I. Title.
PN2728.S78C37 2008
792.02'8–dc22   2008006798

ISBN13: 978-0-415-77496-3 (hbk)
ISBN13: 978-0-415-77497-0 (pbk)

ISBN10: 0-415-77496-3 (hbk)
ISBN10: 0-415-77497-7 (pbk)

Human life is so subtle, so complex and multifaceted, that it needs an incomparably large number of new, still undiscovered "isms" to express it fully.

Stanislavsky

Contents

PART III
Transformation   127

Illustrations

Acknowledgements

For the second edition

When Talia Rodgers of Routledge suggested that I revise this book for a second edition, I felt honored, first, by the press that had acquired it in 2002 and, second, by my readers (actors, directors, students, and scholars alike) who have kept it in print for a decade. I consider the wonderful responses that I have received from my readers as my truest awards. As recently as 27 March 2007, a new reader emailed me to say that my book is "a very motivating work;" it "not only talks about the tension between praxis and theory of theatre, but demonstrates it at the same time" (Matt Foss, graduate student, Wayne State University). He puts his finger on what I most hope to do in all my work: to bridge the gap between acting practice and scholarship.

I heartily thank Talia Rodgers for her support, her staff at Routledge (especially Ben Piggott) for facilitating the editorial process, and the Taylor and Francis Editorial Board. I am deeply indebted to Anne Bogart, André Gregory, and Ed Hooks for so generously endorsing my book. In addition, I warmly thank all my readers, colleagues and friends who have contributed to this new edition: Bella Merlin and David Chambers (Yale University) for helpful comments on the revision plan; R. Andrew White (Valparaiso), Sarah Dixon, and Mary Joan Negro for reading key revisions and offering valuable suggestions; Rhonda Blair (Southern Methodist University) and Cheryl McFarren for input on the System's relationship to psychology and cognitive science; Lisa Wolford Wylam (York University) and Setrak Bronzian for encouragement; Phillip G. Bennett, director David Kaplan, Ellen Gainor (Cornell), Norman Schwartz, and two former members of the Moscow Art Theatre, Eugene Lazarev and Maria Ignatieva (Ohio State University at Lima), for valuable and pertinent conversations; Richard Kramer for his detailed corrections; and Lou Catron for promoting my book to young thespians. I also acknowledge my insightful B.A. students at the University of Southern California and the professional actors who work with me on Active Analysis in my weekly A/ACT Workshop.

This edition would not have seen the light of day without the assistance of Anatoly Smeliansky (The Moscow Art Theatre) and Ruth Wallach (University of Southern California Libraries) who obtained crucial materials for me from Russia; Azneve

Bronzian who generously volunteered to help me with bibliographic reformatting; Prakash Shirke (University of Southern California) and the wonderful staff of the New York Public Library (in both Permissions and Research Collections).

Finally, my acknowledgements from the first edition (below) are as sincerely meant today as they were in 1998.

For the first edition

My research on Stanislavsky and Strasberg was funded by the American Council of Learned Societies, the National Endowment for the Humanities, and a Rockefeller Residency Fellowship at the Wisconsin Center for Film and Theater Research (an Archive of the University of Wisconsin, Madison, and the State Historical Society of Wisconsin). During my residency in Wisconsin, Donald Crafton (Director), Maxine Fleckner Ducey (Film Archivist) and George Talbot (Curator of the Visual and Sound Archives) offered me invaluable help. The University of Southern California provided me with much needed sabbatical leave to complete the writing of this book.

The Moscow Art Theatre, the former USSR Theatre Union, and the Art Center (Moscow) facilitated visits to Moscow. I am especially grateful to Anatoly Smeliansky (The Moscow Art Theatre), Inna Solovyova (The Moscow Art Theatre School and the Russian Academy of Theatrical Arts), and Vladimir Dybovsky for sharing their research and ideas with me. I also thank Tina Andronikashvili (The International Center for Stanislavsky Studies, Moscow), playwright Aleksander Buravsky, actress Louisa Mosends, and Vladimir Prudkin (Artistic Director, Art Center) for their hospitality while I was there.

I am indebted to Michael Heim (University of California, Los Angeles) who generously allowed me access to notes he took in Moscow's archives, John von Knorring (Stylus Publishing, Inc.), Laurence Senelick (Tufts University) for his insightful comments on the typescript, Jean Benedetti (London) for his suggestions and ideas about the System and its terminology, David Hapgood, Norris Houghton and Helen Krich Chinoy for their reminiscences, Allison Comins-Richmond for her research assistance, Cynthia Baron, Ritchie Spencer, Setrak Bronzian and all my friends and colleagues for their encouragement. I acknowledge Howard Schmitt for assistance with photography, and Allen Carnicke and Kathy Lindbeck for their help with computers.

There are many others without whose inspiration and support I would never have been able to write this book: Bernard Beckerman (Columbia University), Travis Bogard (University of California, Berkeley), Aaron Frankel (Columbia University and H. B. Studios), Sam Tsikhotsky (The Moscow Art Theatre), the teachers at the Moscow Art Theatre School and the Russian Academy of Theatrical Arts (especially Natalia Zverova and Leonid Kheifets) who unhesitatingly invited me into their classes, those participants in the Americanization of Stanislavsky—Lee Strasberg, Robert Lewis, Stella Adler, Harold Clurman—whom I was fortunate to meet, and finally the actors of A/ACT in Hollywood who allow me the opportunity to experiment with acting every week.

A note on transliteration and translation

In my text, I anglicize Russian names (Stanislavsky, Tolstoy, Meyerhold, etc.) according to guidelines established by the American Association of Teachers of Slavic and East European Languages. Stanislavsky's surname is sometimes transliterated with a final -*i*, as if it were Polish, following the tradition set by his first translator Elizabeth Reynolds Hapgood. Where quotations and citations use this non-standard transliteration, I retain it in my text. Similarly, when older sources use non-standard transliterations of other names (e.g. "Nemirovitch-Dantchenko" instead of the standard "Nemirovich-Danchenko") I retain that spelling as well. For all Russian words, I use the Library of Congress system.

In my bibliography, I use established spellings of names for Russian scholars (i.e. Blyum, Smeliansky, Solovyova, etc.), who have published in English, and for émigré Russians (e.g. Michael Chekhov, Maria Ouspenskaya, etc.), whether or not the transliteration accords with scholarly standards. In all other cases, I use the Library of Congress system. Where an author's name has appeared in print in different transliterated forms, I note non-standard versions with [*sic*], but maintain the chronology of publications throughout that author's body of works.

All translations from Russian sources are mine unless otherwise specified in the citation.

Abbreviations

I use the following abbreviations for the most frequently cited sources in my book:

SS Stanislavskii, K. S. (1954–61) *Sobranie sochinenii* [*Collected Works*], 8 vols, Moscow: Iskusstvo; and Stanislavskii, K. S. (1988–1999) *Sobranie sochinenii* [*Collected Works*], 9 vols, Moscow: Iskusstvo. Vol. V of the latter edition has been divided into two books (Parts 1 and 2). In parenthetical citations, these two editions are distinguished by volume (given as a roman numeral) and publication year.

LS Lee Strasberg (1956–69) "The Actors Studio," Sound Recording No. 339A, Wisconsin Center for Film and Theater Research, An Archive of the University of Wisconsin, Madison, and the State Historical Society of Wisconsin, Madison. The individual tape number and date of recording are given in the citations.

Introduction

Stanislavsky in the twenty-first century

This book strives to set the record straight about a Russian actor and director, who was born in the nineteenth century, revolutionized actor training around the globe by the end of the twentieth, and now in the twenty-first century appears outdated. By the mid-1950s, Stanislavsky's name stood for excellence in realistic and truthful acting. By 2000, many young people who thirsted for acting careers entered my classes with either no knowledge of him or only a foggy notion that he had something to do with Method acting. As the twentieth century turned into the twenty-first, as cutting-edge theatre artists sought postmodern modes of expression, and as leading scholars began to develop the new field of performance studies, Stanislavsky began to seem less relevant. Russian director Adolf Shapiro echoes the sentiments of many today when he said that the old "psychological" methods seemed "insufficiently vivid and expressive, even boring" (Shapiro 1999:133).

I would agree that Stanislavsky's mid-twentieth century star image as a tyrannical, unforgiving director and teacher, who demands emotional vulnerability from actors as they transform themselves into their realistically-based characters, is inadequate for the new millennium. Such a persona resembles a tarnished statue of a hero, rather than a vibrant force for theatrical art. This monument registers as too patriarchal for feminist actors and theorists, too essentialist for scholars of performance studies, and too absolute for contemporary theatre artists in a multicultural, unsure age.

But this star image is not Stanislavsky. When Shapiro began to study aspects of Stanislavsky's System that fell outside the bounds of common knowledge, he experienced a jolt. "I was unexpectedly taken prisoner for life" (Shapiro 1999:135). My readers can experience exactly this jolt.

If you consider Stanislavsky too patriarchal, you might like to know that in 1937 he cast a young woman, Irina Rozanova, in the role of Hamlet. She was studying in his last Opera-Dramatic Studio and she nervously asked him for the male role. He "looked at her [...] without a smile, with no surprise on his face" and answered yes, "Hamlet will be your university" (Vinogradskaia IV 2003:386).

If you think of him as tyrannical, consider what he said to Olga Knipper, a leading actor in the Moscow Art Theatre and Stanislavsky's frequent partner on stage. She struggled to use his early System to create her episodic role in his 1907 non-realistic, symbolist production of *The Drama of Life*. As rehearsals progressed, he acknowledged her difficulties and told her, "I consider it my duty […] to renounce my rights as a director and give you full freedom in the treatment of your role" (SS VII 1995:370).

If you think of him as single-mindedly committed to Realism with its notion of cogently crafted, psychologically grounded characters, consider his notes from the 1930s about the "through-line" of a role, which I cite in full below (adding in brackets notations that make his personal shorthand clear). Here he figures out, point by point, the multiplicity of options that exist within this single technique:

> Everyone thinks that the through-line is a single line, like a cable, that extends throughout the whole play. But this is not so. There are many lines, not one, which are woven together. Let me count them:
>
> 1   The line of events, from which the story of the play takes its shape.
> 2   The line of a scene's bits, tasks, desires. [In the Method, these are called beats, objectives, motivations.]
> 3   The line of inner and outer actions.
> 4   The line of "magic" and other kinds of "ifs" [by which he means the hypothetical conditions for a production set up for the actor by the director and designers], the given circumstances, in short, the use of imagination.
> 5   The line created by the objects of attention on stage and in the role.
> 6   The line of small and large truths and beliefs. [Notice his use of plural nouns.]
> 7   The line of physical communication and spiritual communion.
> 8   The line that sends forth and receives rays of energy [a concept he derived from Yoga which posits that invisible energy emanates from and between people].
> 9   The line of adaptations [by which he means all the little details that express the actor's conception of the role].
> 10 The line of tempo-rhythm [derived in part from his study of opera as a dramatic form].
> 11 The line of *prana* and its movement [a restatement of 8 above].
> 12 The line of sound, speech, and voice.
> 13 The line of characterization.
> 14 The line of self-control as an artist.
>
> (II 1986:300)

His list includes many different aspects of the embodied art of acting, some generally familiar, like "magic if," and others generally unfamiliar, like the inclusion of *prana*. Notice that telling the story comes first, that communication is both physical (through words and bodily expression) and spiritual (through the *pranic* rays of human energy). Notice that there are technical considerations included, voice and tempo-rhythm among them. He even hints at the actor's dual consciousness when he lists "self-control" as important in the crafting of performance. Notice, too, that emotional recall and personal substitutions, so familiar from the American Method, do not appear. This list, made for his own purposes and not for publication, hints at the wide scope in his actual thinking.

In short, Stanislavsky was not what he seemed at the end of the twentieth century. This book follows the convoluted but fascinating story of how Stanislavsky's mythic image was created by enthusiastic Americans, who gravitated toward his early teachings about the importance of personal emotion in acting, and by Soviet ideologues, who insisted that his intuitions about the biological/physiological underpinnings of acting were as absolute as the laws of reflexology, discovered by the Nobel Prize winning scientist Ivan Pavlov. Thus, the "Method" in the US and the "Method of Physical Actions" in the USSR established our common, but far from complete, knowledge about him.

What Stanislavsky called the System does contain aspects of both the American Method and the Soviet Method of Physical Actions, but it also contains much more:

- Stanislavsky's sense that the moment-to-moment performance of a role is the actor's present reality and truth. This paradox, which equates "truth" with "theatricality," opens the door to non-realistic aesthetics.
- His probing of the actor's dual consciousness during creativity. This exploration puts the lie to a commonly-held assumption that "Stanislavskian" actors lose themselves in their roles and forget about their audiences.
- His insight that empathy can be a more powerful prompt to creativity than personal emotion. The 1990s' discovery of mirror neurons, which activate in the brain when a person watches another perform an action, gives new credence to his intuition that observing others is as good as observing oneself.
- His belief that great acting activates a mind–body–spirit continuum and his consequent inclusion of exercises from Yoga in the System. The recent use of Eastern practices in contemporary US actor training programs and current research on cognitive science resonate with this line of thought in the System.
- His late experimentation with Active Analysis through which actors draft performances by exploring the dynamics of human interaction through improvisation. This much misunderstood rehearsal technique best illuminates how the System can empower actors as autonomous artists.

All these topics are examined in the chapters that follow.

Such a multiplicity of interests makes the System non-dogmatic. Stanislavsky does not lay out a single right way to act. There is nothing absolute about his compendium of theory and techniques for the ephemeral art of acting that he so loved. He saw his System as offering advice to actors of different temperaments who wished to speak through different aesthetic styles. He called his System "universal" for these two reasons. Only three months before his death, he cautioned his directing students that, "One must give actors various paths" (Vinogradskaia 2000:498).

Getting beyond Stanislavsky's star image is not easy. Its cultural construction in the US and the propaganda machine in the USSR have created deep and persistent misunderstandings about his work. Many who reject him actually reject his constructed image, not his fundamental intuitions about acting. Playwright David Mamet writes that "The Stanislavsky 'Method,' and the technique of the schools derived from it, is nonsense. It is not a technique out of the practice of which one develops a skill—it is a cult" (1999:6). He is correct; cults developed around both the Method in the US and the Method of Physical Actions in the USSR. But he is correct only in regard to the mythic image of Stanislavsky, not the man who gave Shapiro a jolt. As Mamet makes his anti-Stanislavsky argument, he writes: "The actor is onstage to communicate the play to the audience" (1999:9). Stanislavsky says the same (points 1 and 7 above). Mamet writes: "The actor does not need to 'become' the character. […] There *is* no character. There are only lines upon a page" (1999:9). Stanislavsky agrees with this (points 2–4 and 12 above). In fact, he rarely uses the word "character" in Russian, preferring either "image" (*obraz*, the common Russian word for character) or "role" (by which he means the words that serve as a "score" for the actor's performance, in the same way that notes provide a "score" for musicians). Mamet writes: "Likewise, the play is designed, if correctly designed, as a series of incidents in which and through the protagonist struggles toward his or her goal" (1999:12). Again Stanislavsky would agree (points 1–3 above). Mamet is not arguing with Stanislavsky but with his statue.

Stanislavsky in Focus has been guiding students, actors, and scholars to newly relevant understandings of the System for the last decade. But the mythic image still predominates. In March 2007, on the pages of *American Theatre*, the influential director Charles Marowitz referred to Stanislavsky as the "Father of psychological realism" (57), implicitly demonstrating the need for this second revised edition.

My new edition significantly advances information about Stanislavsky and his System. I benefit from the extraordinary number of publications in Russia over the last decade that make the history of his life, culture, and ideas all the more vividly accessible. I take these volumes into account in every chapter of my updated book. In addition, I have added a new chapter on Soviet censorship, which will help you read his works as an "insider," who knows how to look between the lines for ideas that were deemed unacceptable for publication by the censor and thus find Stanislavsky's subtexts. Discussions of the key ideas behind his System have also been expanded. The first edition chapter on "Emotion and the human spirit of the role" has become two, one dedicated to the science of emotion and the other to Yoga. In the last chapter, I also clarify how the Method of Physical Actions and the more radical Active Analysis differ from one another. Finally, to guide students who have not yet practiced the elements of the System, I include in my glossary of terminology exercises taught by Stanislavsky.

As in my first edition, I avoid drowning in the ocean of competing American interpretations by confining myself to the two most extreme ends of the spectrum: Stanislavsky's writings about the theatre and Strasberg's sessions at the Actors Studio. Comparing the ideas of these two theatrical giants best uncovers the issues that transformed the Russian's System into the American's Method. Lee Strasberg participated in all the important phases of Stanislavsky's Americanization: he watched as an audience member during the Moscow Art Theatre's performances in New York, studied at the American Laboratory Theatre, co-founded the Group Theatre, and became the primary voice at the Actors Studio. Furthermore, his work has been inextricably linked to that of his famous Russian counterpart. Even Strasberg's obituary in *The New York Times* attributes the Method to Stanislavsky, and then asserts that "Mr. Strasberg adapted it to the American theatre, imposing his refinements, but always crediting Stanislavsky as his source" (18 February 1982). Ironically, this linkage robs Strasberg of the originality in his thinking, while simultaneously obscuring Stanislavsky's ideas. Examining their differences frees both from bondage.

By confining myself as I do, I limit the scope of my book in a number of ways. I examine the teachings of émigrés Richard Boleslavsky and Maria Ouspenskaya, who taught Strasberg and other members of the Group Theatre. However, I treat equally influential Russians—Michael Chekhov, Evgeny Vakhtangov, Mikhail Kedrov, Maria Knebel, etc.—and Americans—Stella Adler, Sanford Meisner, Robert Lewis, etc.—as their work impinges on Stanislavsky and Strasberg.

Gender issues are another important topic that I leave to other scholars (Ellen Gainor of Cornell, Catherine Schuler of the University of Maryland, Rhonda Blair at Southern Methodist University, Peta Tait at La Trobe University, among them). I will observe, however, that despite Stanislavsky's desire to treat women well as the quotations above demonstrate, he does at times betray his nineteenth century upbringing in the fictionalized depictions of women students in his acting manual. His female students often cry, flirt, show off on stage, respond best to scenes that feature maternal love; in short, they are drawn from stereotypical images. Of course, the men do not escape stereotypes either, even though the main narrator is an admirable actor. Others swagger around; they seem like petty, arrogant know-it-alls. The US Method also provides rich soil for gender analysis, incorporating as it does popular Freudian ideas rife with sexist attitudes. (Rose Malague, at the University of Pennsylvania, for example, argues that Stella Adler's discomfort at the Group Theatre, stemmed at least in part from Strasberg's patriarchal treatment of her.)

Conversely, there is much more to discover about a host of women—actors and others—who actively participated in the development and dissemination of the System and Method. (Maria Ignatieva of Ohio State University at Lima has uncovered fascinating information about the leading actresses at the Moscow Art Theatre.) Without Lyubov Gurevich in Russia and Elizabeth Reynolds Hapgood in the US, Stanislavsky may never have completed his books. Without Maria Knebel, the full complexity of Stanislavsky's last experiments with Active Analysis would have remained buried. (Knebel is in fact the subject of my next book.) Without Miriam Stockton and Cheryl Crawford, the American Laboratory Theatre, the Group Theatre, even the Actors Studio may not have been launched as successfully as they were.

Another topic, deserving greater attention than my inquiry allows, views the development of the Method as a direct reflection of US political relations with the Soviet Union. From the 1930s, when the Group Theatre actively admired the Soviets, to the 1950s, when widespread fear of communism resulted in the blacklisting of leading stage and screen artists, the Method responded to political climates, its acting values either dovetailing or colliding with cultural ones.

Such future inquiries, however, depend upon replacing Stanislavsky's star image with a clear-sighted look at his complex, non-dogmatic System. Bringing Stanislavsky into focus allows students, professional actors, and scholars alike, whatever their personal proclivities and individual talents, to mine the System in relevant new ways for their own purposes. In short, the second edition of this book encourages revisionist thinking and practice.

1   Demythologizing Stanislavsky

While Stanislavsky's name has dominated debates about acting in the Western world for nearly a century, most actors routinely identify his System with the Method, developed in New York during the Great Depression and popularized by Strasberg. Dynamic processes gave rise to this identification: actors of the Moscow Art Theatre inspired a generation of US actors, while they themselves struggled to survive in the political climate of post-revolutionary Russia; émigré actors taught in a foreign tongue to students whose cultural assumptions differed dramatically from their own; abridgement of Stanislavsky's books in the US and their censorship in Moscow further obscured his face; and finally, the very nature of acting practice encourages individual modifications of the System's techniques.

A map that traces the migration of Konstantin Sergeevich Stanislavsky's System throughout the world, therefore, would show two major points: New York and Moscow. In both cities, actors seized upon Stanislavsky's work as primary and essential. In both, teachers who had studied with the master passed their understanding of his practice on to the next generation of teachers. That generation in turn passed it on to our teachers, and we to our students. Both theatrical centers created tradition-bound approaches to the System that subsequently spanned the globe. From Moscow, Stanislavsky's ideas spread to Eastern Europe and Germany; from New York, they traveled to Western Europe, to Great Britain, to Scandinavia, and as far as Japan. Both traditions, however, paint retouched portraits of the historical Stanislavsky.

In the United States, conditioned by a Freudian-based, individually oriented ethos, actors privileged the psychological techniques of Stanislavsky's System over those of the physical. The Method, as it became known in New York, defined itself primarily through this one aspect of the multivariant, holistic System. Thus, the transmission of Stanislavsky's ideas to the US, their linguistic and cultural translation, and their transformation by the Method created a pervasive veil of assumptions through which we in the West commonly view Stanislavsky. While this filter has illuminated some of the System's premises (most notably those that involve psychological realism), it has also obscured others (such as those drawn from Symbolism, Formalism, and Yoga).

Stanislavskian lore, developed in Soviet Russia and claiming greater fidelity to the master's teaching, is no less suspect than the Method. In the Union of Soviet

Socialist Republics, the dictates of Marxist philosophical materialism and the collective imperative of post-revolutionary Russia exalted Stanislavsky's physical training of the actor as his most complete and scientific technique. Thus, the Russian version of the System became identified almost exclusively with yet another aspect of Stanislavsky's approach—the Method of Physical Actions. Again, some issues (action, behaviorist psychology, and Realism among them) are illuminated, but others (those from Symbolism, Formalism and Yoga) obscured.

While both centers tapped the same source, their creative readings of the System proceeded along different lines, establishing not only competing traditions but competing truths about the master's work. Neither of the two approaches found Stanislavsky's study of avant-garde and Eastern arts of more than passing interest. Neither integrated the mind and body of the actor, the corporal and the spiritual, the text and the performance as thoroughly or as insistently as did Stanislavsky himself. Both considered Stanislavsky's work in the Realist style most compelling. In short, two doctrines evolved from the same source, each gaining the force of unambiguous authority within its own culture, while the source itself receded into a vague and misty past. The real Stanislavsky was relegated to anecdotes that took on mythical rather than historical force.

When the Actors Studio in New York invited me to serve as interpreter for a visiting director of the Moscow Art Theatre (who had himself studied with one of Stanislavsky's last pupils), I watched these two traditions collide. For many months in 1978, I whispered translations of Lee Strasberg's critiques of scenes and exercises to Sam Tsikhotsky,[1] who whispered back to me critiques of his own. When the Russian directed Strasberg's protégés in a workshop production of *The Seagull*, I translated their differing interpretations about the same techniques. With Tsikhotsky's stress on action and the cast's concern with emotion, their views embodied the evolution of Stanislavsky's ideas.

Moscow's position on the map causes no surprise. Born there, Stanislavsky worked there until his death. Similarly, that the System would somehow conform to the tenets of Marxism in communist Russia raises few eyebrows. Russia has always produced arts of political engagement, and the difficult relationship between arts and government after the revolution is generally known.

But New York's competing importance in developing Stanislavsky's work bears a closer look. The historical reasons for New York's position on this map involve a passionate and mutually beneficial relationship between Stanislavsky and his American students. Despite political hostility between the USA and the USSR, this Russian actor and director left an indelible imprint upon the American imagination. After enjoying routine successes in Paris, London, Berlin, and elsewhere throughout Europe, Stanislavsky incited an especially enthusiastic and creative impulse in young American theatre professionals when he and the Moscow Art Theatre visited in 1923 and 1924. Rather than remaining passive spectators, content to enjoy the achievements of Russian theatre from the auditorium, these admirers actively sought to make Stanislavsky's theatre practice their own. Their avid adoption represents the first step in establishing New York's importance.

In 1965, when members of the Moscow Art Theatre again visited New York

City, Lee Strasberg testified to this special relationship. He greeted them as more than "honored colleagues," and explained to the Actors Studio that:

> The theatre of which they are a part [...] played a role in our lives of such value, that we can hardly think of it as a foreign theatre. ... I think, that many people in America think, that Stanislavsky must be an American. Otherwise how could he have possibly influenced the American theatre to the extent that he has?
>
> (LS A12:16 February 1965)

He echoes Stanislavsky's own 1924 assessment: "In America now, MAT is considered an American theatre" (SS IX 1999:154).

Stanislavsky's influence on US acting remains indisputable. His former students emigrated and taught in New York and Hollywood: Richard Boleslavsky, Maria Ouspenskaya, Andrius Jilinsky, Leo and Barbara Bulgakov, Vera Soloviova, Tamara Daykarhanova, and Michael Chekhov among them. The Group Theatre and the Actors Studio consciously modeled themselves upon his work. His inspiration spawned numerous acting schools and workshops throughout the country, even moving into American colleges and universities. To this day, theatre professionals tend to position themselves in relationship to him. Some, like Stella Adler and Joshua Logan, grounded careers in brief periods of study with him. Others, like Lee Strasberg and Sanford Meisner, invoked his name, even while arguing with him. Adler once said that, "The Group Theatre contributed to a standard of acting that transformed the American theatre" (Chinoy 1976:512). More precisely, this transformation occurred through Stanislavsky's inspiration, influencing three generations of actors.

Perhaps even more remarkably, Stanislavsky also captured the popular American imagination. His relationship with the general audience, too, has lasted into our own generation. The figure of Stanislavsky has become our archetypal image of the acting teacher. In the 1987 film, *Outrageous Fortune*, two would-be actresses vie for places in a highly competitive acting workshop, run by an Eastern bloc tyrannical teacher whose name sounds suspiciously like "Stanislavsky" (Dixon 1987). In *Tootsie*, Dustin Hoffman, himself a Method actor, plays a Method actor who is fired from a series of commercial jobs when he applies Stanislavsky's theories inappropriately (Gelbard and Schisgal 1982). In the Broadway musical, *A Chorus Line*, one of the auditioning performers exposes her humiliation when she feels "nothing" in distorted versions of Stanislavsky's sense memory exercises (Hamlisch and Kleban 1975). Even the android character of Data in television's *Star Trek: The Next Generation* studies the Method in his attempts to understand human emotion through acting (Lazebnick 1991). Such parodies in the popular media testify to how thoroughly Stanislavsky has entered into general discourse. Audiences do not have to be theatre specialists to get the joke.

Rarely has a culture been so riveted for so long about the technical aspects of an art. During a 1956 session at the Actors Studio, Strasberg marveled at the phenomenal public interest:

> Actors have been thought about in the past … Duse versus Bernhardt … But
> […] I think this is the first time in the history of theatre … that general people—
> the barbershop and beauty parlor attendants—are discussing the work of the
> Actors Studio […] I must say that this is unusual.
>
> (LS 2:10 April 1956)

Strasberg bemoaned the price he and members of the Actors Studio paid for
such attention. He felt that this inappropriate curiosity forced actors and teachers
to explain themselves "unnecessarily" to those who could never understand the
experience of acting. "I'm a little bit miffed, I'm a little bit disturbed, and I'm a
little bit amazed," he said (LS 2:10 April 1956). Harold Clurman, co-founder of
the Group Theatre, agreed: "The truth of the matter is that the system should never
have been made a subject of conversation, a matter of publicity, or Sunday articles,
for it does not concern the audience, or, for that matter, the critic" (1957:39).

Public curiosity was fueled by a sense of mystery surrounding the practice of
Stanislavsky's System in the United States. During the 1930s, when the Group
Theatre created a community of actors who lived as well as worked together, the
public imagined them as members of an esoteric cult from which outsiders were
excluded. Consequently, the press found them fascinating. This not altogether
sympathetic and sometimes prurient interest climaxed during the 1950s, ironically piqued by Strasberg's adamant attempts to protect his actors from the gaze
of observers while they experimented with their art. While he complained of the
public's interest, he seemed unwittingly to spur it on. On one occasion, for example,
he invited a young writer to watch an actors' session. When the guest offered a
comment, Strasberg exploded in an angry attack. "You—on the outside—here your
presence is a sufferance, it is an interruption to us, it is an interference with our
work" (LS 101A:1960).[2] While Strasberg had a real point to make—that the cumulative work of the Studio could not be understood without serious and prolonged
study—rumors of such outbursts also served to escalate interest.

Perhaps the adoption of Stanislavsky by the theatre community and public curiosity
about his methods would have been enough to insure that New York become a central
disseminating point on our map. However, Stanislavsky himself granted special
importance to the work conducted there in his name. During his 1923 and 1924 tours
he welcomed the enthusiasm of his American admirers. At home, he was castigated
by Russian avant-garde artists for old-fashioned, outmoded work and attacked by
politicos for bourgeois and capitalistic sentiments. He feared that his creativity was
flagging; he was losing confidence in his work. In New York, he unexpectedly found
new students, eager to extend his work into the future. He looked to them as saviors
of his art, which was indeed perishing in the artistic and political climate of Moscow.
While he flirted with the notion of emigration, he attempted to capitalize on the
economic opportunities the US offered him and his theatre: he toured in a grueling
schedule of performances, pursued a film contract, and turned himself into a writer.
The most lucrative of these opportunities turned out to be writing; he published his
first two major books, *My Life in Art* and *An Actor Prepares*, in the United States in
English, a language which he could neither speak nor read, before he issued them in

his native language. Money alone, however, did not prompt his unusual decision. He also hoped to evade Soviet censorship which was forcing his System into uncomfortable Marxist molds. His decision to publish in the United States resulted in commercially abridged books, but it also irrevocably granted New York its unique place on the map of migration, second only to Moscow.

Stanislavsky's influence in the US was far from cohesive or coherent. In the theatre world, obsession with his System has led to seemingly endless hostility among warring camps, each proclaiming themselves his only true disciples, like religious fanatics, turning dynamic ideas into rigid dogma. This splintering of the Stanislavsky tradition in the US began as early as 1934. Stella Adler, then a member of the Group Theatre, traveled to Paris to seek the master. She returned with new perspectives on acting and openly challenged Lee Strasberg's authority as the Group's sole acting teacher. Her words amazed the company. But rather than inspiring new collaborative experimentation with the System, her report divided them. As actress Phoebe Brand recalled, "It was like being either a Republican or a Democrat. People were staunch adherents of one side or the other" (Chinoy 1976:516). Thus, Adler insured a rift in the US theatre that exists until today. Others, like Sanford Meisner, Robert Lewis, and Elia Kazan, jumped into the fissure.

Confusion reached such a fevered pitch that in 1957, Lewis, also of the original Group, attempted to sort it out by giving a series of lectures for professional actors entitled *Method or Madness*. He spoke at the Playhouse Theatre in New York on Mondays at 11:30 p.m. after the curtains of Broadway had rung down. When the series sold out, actors without tickets tried to "crash" but were turned away. The lectures became "the hottest ticket in town" (Lewis 1984:279).[3] However, Lewis hardly stemmed the tide of debate.

Out of this extraordinary turmoil, a theatrical and cultural revolution was taking place. While Stanislavsky's ideas touched off something very deep in the American psyche, his adopted culture also transformed them. As Lewis noted, the Stanislavsky System "was slowly being distorted into the American 'Method.' [...] The 'Method Actor' was born" (Lewis 1984:279). US actors were translating and mistranslating a Russian system into English, and their creative work often lacked clarity. Moreover, while his English language books went uncensored, their abridgement added to the on-going confusion. As Lewis chided, "I have never been able to find out precisely what ['the Method Actor'] meant but, depending on which camp you're in, you hate him or you worship him" (1984:279).

Once adopted, adapted, and ultimately transformed, the Method came to dominate stage and screen in the US. Indeed, the Method's particularly strong impact on cinema acting during the 1950s significantly enlarged its sphere of influence. Stanislavsky's ideas began to loop back to Europe through an American filter (Bjornage 1989). Actors worldwide learned about Stanislavsky from Americans; even his writings were translated from the abridged English editions. Drawing a map of the System's migration throughout the world calls visual attention to this unexpected but highly charged Americanization of Stanislavsky's work.

This book examines the history and premises of the System in order to take the reader beyond common knowledge to what Stanislavsky himself had professed.

On the one hand, I lay bare the transformation of the System into the Method. With the deaths of Lee Strasberg, Stella Adler and an entire generation of US teachers who set the Method in motion, we have reached the end of an era in American theatre. It is time to dispel the Method's hegemony over the interpretation of the System in the West. On the other hand, I expose Soviet conditioning of the System. With the dissolution of the USSR and the opening of musty archives that had been sealed during Stalin's time, significant new information about Stanislavsky's life and artistic endeavor is coming to light. In the last decade of the twentieth century and the first decade of the twenty-first, the rate of publications about Stanislavsky in Russian has escalated unbelievably. These materials allow us for the first time to understand the full impact of Soviet censorship on Stanislavsky.

A fresh look at the two traditions which sprang from the same source uncovers hidden aspects of the System that contain germs for newly revitalized readings of Stanislavsky by upcoming generations of actors.

I first experienced the importance of such an inquiry when I compared Stanislavsky's English books with their Russian counterparts. I was studying with an acting teacher in New York who passionately considered himself "anti-Stanislavsky." Since I could speak Russian, he sent me to check on the original terminology. Thus, I discovered how widely Stanislavsky's Russian books vary from their standard English versions. At first glance, *An Actor Prepares*, *Building a Character*, and *Creating a Role* look one half as long as their Russian versions. Stanislavsky's attitudes toward his work and his students seemed to shift before me. His Russian *persona* had a twinkle in his eyes. He was not only the tyrannical dictator who demands iron discipline, but also a comic commentator on the foibles of acting, sparring playfully with his fictional students in endless Socratic debates.

In closer readings, I found ideas and techniques, which my teacher labeled "anti-Stanislavsky," very much part of the Russian. I noticed that the logic of an argument (hard to follow in English) became clear if long-winded. While the books often sound like obscure meditations on the art of acting in English, they struck me as highly logical, practical, and forthright in Stanislavsky's native language. Moreover, the English tends toward a more technical terminology (fostering professional jargon), rather than a direct and simple description of the actor's process, which was Stanislavsky's stated objective. As he wrote in the preface to the Russian edition, deleted from the English, "About art one must speak and write simply and clearly" (SS II 1989:42). Joshua Logan unknowingly testified to these differences when he said that, "the books Stanislavsky wrote himself are difficult to understand in English translations. His writing is nowhere as vivid as his speech" (Senelick 1981:209).

In short, reading Stanislavsky in English turned out to be a very different experience from reading him in Russian. I saw a large, ironic gap between what my teacher considered Stanislavsky's teachings to be and what they seemed to be in Russian. My work with Tsikhotsky only confirmed the existence of this gap. Our English sources together with our common knowledge about Stanislavsky dramatically diverge from sources in his native language. How could my acting teacher, who reflected Stanislavsky's ideas so perfectly, consider himself an opponent? In the classroom, we had apparently mistaken the Method for the System. Why indeed, did the Russian books look so different in English? Soviet censorship alone could not explain it. After all, why would censored books be twice the length? Wouldn't they be shorter? Apparently, the transformation of Stanislavsky's System into the Method had occurred not only metaphorically, but literally as well.

I pursued these questions further by attending classes at the Moscow Art Theatre School and GITIS (now the Russian Academy for Theatre Arts), where I began to unravel the mystery of his last studio through teachers like Natalia Zverova and directors like Leonid Kheifets. I played detective in archives located in New York and Moscow. Answers emerged through a complicated history involving the transmission and translation of Stanislavsky's ideas. In the US, acting teachers and the commercial publishing industry took part in the story; in the USSR, politics played the leading role. These are the categories of my inquiry.

The first part of my book concentrates on the transmission of Stanislavsky's ideas to the United States: the Moscow Art Theatre's tours to the US and the consequent adoption of the System by the Group Theatre and the Actors Studio. In it I examine the love affair that began in the 1920s between Stanislavsky and his US admirers. This section establishes why we need to take a second look at what might seem familiar stories.

The second part concerns cultural and linguistic translations of Stanislavsky's work: how his ideas were treated in the classrooms of émigré teachers, who taught the founders of the Method; how abridgement and translation choices altered his books in English; and how Soviet censorship forced many of his most interesting ideas into the subtexts of his Russian language books. This information provides the cultural contexts necessary to take a new look at Stanislavsky. Chapters in this section account for the ways in which acting practice impacts written theories; cope with what was deleted from the abridged English translations; and search for what remains between the lines in his more complete, but censored Russian language books.

I devote the third part to the practice of acting by examining four defining concepts from the System in their Russian and English transformations:

1 Performance itself. The System, at its best, induces a state of mind and being in the actor which Stanislavsky eccentrically calls "experiencing," and which best defines his personal understanding of theatrical art.
2 "Affective Memory," also called "Emotional Memory," a much debated technique that speaks directly to America's adoption of Stanislavsky. Here I examine Stanislavsky's psychophysical conception of emotion through the science of psychology.
3 Adaptations to acting from Yoga. Eastern practice allows Stanislavsky to move beyond the Western propensity to see mind and body as two separate realms and to establish a mind–body–spirit continuum for actors who seek to communicate the full scope of human experience through their art.
4 The concept of action. Stanislavsky explores in depth the ways in which drama speaks through action in his last Opera-Dramatic Studio. His experiments,

hidden within his home, branched into two rehearsal techniques: The Method of Physical Actions, as interpreted by Soviet Marxists, was positioned as the end point in his lifelong search for a scientific System based in the material body; the more holistic and open-ended "Active Analysis" turned into practice his deep commitment to the improvisatory state of mind necessary to performance, his promotion of acting as a discrete art, and his respect for the actor as artist.

There remain, of course, many more aspects of the System (movement and vocal training to name just two) that beg for further investigation, but the four examined in the chapters of this book provide both a conceptual and practical basis for further studies.

In all three parts, the reader will encounter an interplay of the familiar and unfamiliar. Scholars may well recognize much of the historical information, while theatre artists may nod their heads at many issues that concern acting practice. My project brings together pertinent histories, facts, theories, and assumptions from both scholarship and practice in order to weigh them against Stanislavsky's words. In the process, some common knowledge withstands close examination; some (when placed into new contexts and against new information) reveals itself as myth. In all, the book invites you to reconsider your assumptions.

Tracing the conceptual transformation of Stanislavsky's central ideas involves special difficulties. In the first place, the ideas themselves resist verbalization. As Stanislavsky himself had complained when speaking of the unconscious sources of creation, "I have to talk to you about something I feel but do not know" (1936:199). His feeling is a kind of inexpressible knowing. Metaphors, parables, and analogies must serve. In the second place, written sources about theatre must be tempered by an awareness of practice. Peter Brook amusingly recounts how he moved little cardboard figures around a model of a set before his first rehearsal of his first big production, only to find that all his work could not prepare him for the reality of three-dimensional actors on an actual stage (1968:96–7). Stanislavsky invokes the same theatrical reality when he states that his "basic method" is "to go from practice to graphic example and from my own experience to theory" (SS II 1989:368).

Studying practice presents yet more difficulties. Like performance, it is ephemeral, and can only be inferred from written sources, memoirs, tape recordings, reminiscences, etc. Moreover, it is often so personal that it varies with each individual artist, creating endless multiplicity, too great to describe in all its manifestations. Each of Stanislavsky's proponents individualizes the System in her or his own way. Examining too many permutations of this sort would only hopelessly confuse the main issues. Finally, unlike theory, practice is functional and contextual; therefore it can hold apparently contradictory principles to be equally true. At one moment, Stanislavsky writes, "There is no genuine art without truth and belief" (SS II 1989:226). At another moment, "Living truth on stage is not at all what it is in reality" (SS IV 1991:380). In one context, Strasberg sees the "foundation" of acting in "real thought, with real sensation, and therefore with real experience on stage" (LS A9:2 February 1965). In another context, he states that the actor's emotion "should never be 'really real'" (Munk 1966:197). Such contradictory statements make it possible to support or refute nearly any view of the System or the Method. Without dismissing the contradictions, I examine those ideas that most consistently define both their practices.

With these very real difficulties in mind, I step into the mine field, carefully deconstructing the System in order to construct it anew, weighing history against myth, using words to suggest a non-verbal art, and balancing theory against practice. In the following chapters, I will untangle the complicated knot of issues, which concern the transmission, translation, and transformation of the System. This project, to which my book is dedicated, is essential if the theatre is to recover hidden aspects of Stanislavsky's System. Such recovery necessitates: (a) challenging widespread and deeply fixed assumptions about Stanislavsky; (b) accessing texts and personal notebooks that have never appeared in print or been translated; (c) revisiting his printed books wearing new spectacles.

In short, I will paint a portrait of the historical man who practiced the contradictory and intractable art of theatre. I mean to demythologize Stanislavsky, and take a long hard look at his face.

Part I

Transmission

2 From Moscow to New York

The realities of the tours

Stanislavsky became part of United States history in 1923 and 1924, when he and his famous Moscow Art Theatre toured the country. His photograph, published in newspapers of the day, shows a tall, clean-shaven gentleman of 60, his shock of white hair thinning on top, his lips tensely set in a prim smile, a *pince-nez* perched on his nose. His bright eyes suggest his ability to bring life to characters on stage.

The political context into which he stepped was at best ambivalent, at worst hostile toward Soviets, and he was immediately pulled into its vortex. He and senior members of his company became the first Soviet citizens to visit the White House, nine years before the US recognized the Bolshevik government as legitimate. In 1924, when President Calvin Coolidge shook Stanislavsky's hand "with laconic and impersonal speed" (Hapgood 1963:198–9), the US government still hoped that the revolution would be a temporary upset.

Pressure to recognize the Soviet government arose from the economic sector, which saw the USSR as a new market. In July 1920, the US lifted a trade embargo against the still unrecognized government. In 1921, Lenin created the "New Economic Policy" (NEP) which allowed limited free enterprise to facilitate reconstruction of the now communist economy, ravaged by revolution and civil war. With these two decisions, trade between the US and the USSR began in earnest. The Soviet Union bought 24,000 tractors from Ford; Armand Hammer served as agent for over thirty US companies trading in the USSR; the American Relief Administration fed over eleven million starving Russians from 35,000 stations. The Soviet Union shipped furs, lumber, precious stones, and arts to the US. The Moscow Art Theatre tours unquestionably represented the best in cultural trade.

The meeting between Coolidge and the Russian actors could easily serve as a metaphor for the ambivalent political relationship between the two countries. In concession to US politicians who sought trade with the Soviet Union, the President agreed to a friendly meeting. However, the welcome was tempered by the fact that his guests were not allowed to speak. Protocol dictated that one could speak to the President only through one's ambassador, but as their government was not recognized, they did not have one.

If a silent picture of the President greeting Stanislavsky conjures up the positive side of this political ambivalence, one need not search farther than newspaper coverage to find the negative. The general press insinuated that Stanislavsky was traveling as an agent of the new Bolshevik government. He was accused of sending profits back to Soviet coffers and attempting to sway American opinion toward communism. Even purely artistic questions seemed to harbor ulterior political agendas. Stanislavsky recalled walking a fine line to avoid falling into traps set by reporters. For example, when New York journalists asked about the particular productions he had brought, they implied that he had assembled a set of plays to portray the Bolshevik version of Russian history: "as if we had brought *Tsar Fyodor* to show a weak tsar, *The Lower Depths* to show the strength of the proletariat, and Chekhov to illustrate the worthlessness of the intelligentsia and the bourgeoisie. 'We brought this repertoire, because we were asked for these very plays, and not others,' I confidently answered." Indeed, he brought the same repertory that he had used for the Theatre's first European tour in 1906, eleven years before the Revolution. As he reasoned, "America wants to see what Europe already knows" (SS VI 1994:221–2).[1]

The average US citizen remained skeptical of the company's offerings. While Russian émigrés came to the theatre to remember life left behind (Carnicke 1997:19–30), general audiences were perplexed by the exotic culture. The plays seemed strangely depressing and alien. In his *New York Times* review of *Three Sisters*, John Corbin writes: "The fact is patent, however incredible, however abhorrent, the Slavic temperament feeds upon self-depreciation, upon pessimism, and grows by what it feeds on. The plays of Chekhov, the very cornerstone upon which this admirable, this exemplary Moscow Art Theatre was builded, leave English-speaking peoples cold, and perhaps inclined to resentment." In the review of *The Cherry Orchard*, Corbin further declares that "criticism is scarcely possible, these folk and their milieu being so utterly alien and uncouth to us" (Emeljanow 1981:241, 234).

Stanislavsky's native country not only mirrored but magnified the politically suspicious atmosphere. Just as strikes and union demands in the US were seen as communist inspired, Russians took long hard looks at anyone with connections to the West. Hundreds of Soviet citizens who had worked with the American Relief Administration were arrested in 1923 for anti-Bolshevik activities. Just a few days after Stanislavsky's departure from Moscow, three hundred intellectuals and artists who sympathized with the old government were forced into emigration against their will (Archer 1975:72). Growing trade relations between the two countries did little to diminish such hostility.

Stanislavsky's very success abroad put him into jeopardy at home. He was dogged by the Soviet press during his tours, and stood accused of preserving bourgeois theatre, using Chekhov to form an alliance with capitalists, and attempting to emigrate. Stanislavsky's photograph, taken at a benefit for Russian émigré artists in New York, labeled him a "White Russian," hence counter-revolutionary (Benedetti 1990b:252). He answered the Soviet press as carefully as he had US reporters, always stressing his role as artist and cultivating an impression of political ignorance. He had not come to the United States as a communist agent, but as a proponent for theatrical art.

While he risked castigation and political ostracism at home, he stood to win artistic survival during trying post-revolutionary times. He desperately needed these tours to succeed. By 1923, the Moscow Art Theatre suffered economic peril. When Lenin introduced the NEP, the government withdrew theatrical subsidies for a time. The Moscow Art Theatre, together with its studios, required 1.5 billion rubles, and box-office receipts for completely sold-out houses totaled about 600 million. When the Theatre produced Byron's *Cain* in 1920—its only new production between 1917 and 1922—the set could not be built due to lack of funds. Stanislavsky altered the design to feature a simple black backdrop, and still he could not find enough velvet in Moscow to enclose the full stage (Benedetti 1990b:250, 244).

The tours became the Art Theatre's key financial strategy. The company split into two: one group would remain in Moscow and perform a reduced repertory; the other, headed by Stanislavsky and consisting of the company's best-known actors, would tour Europe and the US for a period of two years in order to reap Western profits.

Stanislavsky suffered personally too after the revolution. Suspected of tsarist leanings, he was arrested and interrogated by the Soviet secret police in 1918 and 1919 (Autant-Mathieu 2003:72). When his property, home and factory, were confiscated by the now state-owned conglomerate, he was transformed overnight from a wealthy Muscovite, who owned and operated the family factory that made gold thread, into a virtual pauper. He had begun to sell his possessions in order to live. "My life," he wrote, "has completely changed. I have become proletarian" (SS IX 1999:18). In 1920, the Commissar of Enlightenment pleaded with Lenin to give Stanislavsky living quarters, stressing that he was "about to sell his last pair of trousers." Lenin relented with a space that included two rooms for rehearsals. This house has since become a museum (Hecht 1989:2). Once a dapper and elegantly dressed gentleman, Stanislavsky wore shabby clothes and a torn overcoat in the US. When he reached Berlin, his first stop on the European tour, he remained in his hotel from embarrassment (Benedetti 1990b:252).

More difficulties ensued when his son contracted tuberculosis and could get treatment only in Switzerland. As Stanislavsky wrote to his family in 1923, "that costs a terrible amount of money" (SS IX 1999:110). Furthermore, that cost could best be met with foreign, not Russian, currency since the ruble had dropped in worth to almost nothing on the world market. In 1918, the dollar was worth nine rubles, in 1919, about eighty, and by 1920, 1,200 (Vernadsky 1969:316). Survival did not seem possible without Western profit.

The US with its strongly commercial theatre became the central hope for financial recovery. While still in France, Stanislavsky daydreamed of great possibilities there:

Who knows, perhaps, there in America ...
I will try ...
There dollars spill from overfilled pockets ... the streets are paved with them ...
America—the Promised Land upon which the eyes of the whole world are fastened ...

(SS VI 1994:194)

More soberly he wrote, "America is the sole audience, the sole source of money for subsidy, on which we can count" (SS IX 1999:138).

Fortunately, the artistic climate of New York into which Stanislavsky stepped was more hospitable than the political. While politics alone might have crushed the tours, the artistic world awaited his arrival with bated breath. Russian arts had already found a place in US culture. As early as 1905, Alla Nazimova had toured, agreeing to play all of Ibsen's heroines under a three-year contract with the Shuberts and finally relocating to Hollywood (Senelick 1992:9–12). The Russian revolution brought a wave of émigré artists. Some of the finest already resided and worked in the US when Stanislavsky arrived: composer Rakhmaninov; Shaliapin, whom Stanislavsky had heard sing in Moscow long before the singer's fame at the Metropolitan Opera; Baliev, who had transplanted his successful cabaret, "The Bat," to New York; painter and set designer Roerich, who founded an artists' community in an apartment building on the Upper West Side of Manhattan; and Ben-Ami, who helped make Yiddish theatre one of New York's strongest dramatic traditions. American audiences had also seen tours of Diaghelev's incredible ballet company: Pavlova, Nijinsky, and Fokine had become familiar names; fantastic sets and costumes by Benois, Golovin, Bakst, and Dobuzhinsky, several of whom had designed for the Moscow Art Theatre, were admired. Forward looking companies such as Broadway's Theatre Guild and the Guild's parent organization, the Washington Square Players, now produced Russian plays.

Moreover, Stanislavsky's reputation had preceded him. Reviews of the Art Theatre's productions and eye-witness accounts from abroad had painted his portrait as that of the ultimate theatrical artist, whose ability to create the illusion of reality on stage exceeded the usual. During his first European tour in 1906, the British *Cosmopolitan Magazine* had described him as a "man of genius" who has "an absolute reverence for truth and an inherent scorn of sham or artifice" (Emeljanow 1981:77). Another British critic had applauded the company for their creation of "a series of everyday events and discussions," specifically calling attention to "the minute details" which arouse the audience's "pleasure" (Emeljanow 1981:157). Arthur Ruhl, who had traveled to Moscow only a few months before the revolution, described a performance of Chekhov's *Three Sisters* as:

> one of the most vivid impressions I ever had in a theatre. It was the sensation (and the fact that one understood only a word here and there seemed to make no difference) not so much of getting into a play, as of getting into Russia. [...] Here it is, one felt at once. This is Russia, this is the real thing.
>
> (Emeljanow 1981:159)

In addition to such reviews, word was out that the great artists of Europe—Gordon Craig, Isadora Duncan, André Antoine and Jacques Copeau among them—not only admired Stanislavsky, but also sought collaboration with him.

The public was further primed for Stanislavsky's visit by Morris Gest, who sponsored the tours and was himself Russian born. He staged a broad and aggressive publicity campaign, plastering New York City with posters, and making sure that newspapers carried information and photographs about the troupe months before their arrival. Gest's publicity agent followed Stanislavsky on the European leg of his tours to gather material. Stanislavsky got his first taste of Gest's publicity style in Berlin. Since Stanislavsky's wife and son had been detained *en route* due to his son's illness, Gest's publicity agent insisted upon finding a substitute "wife" and "child" for the required photograph of the family's arrival (SS VI 1994:151).

Gest's overzealous approach to publicity began to backfire when Stanislavsky reached New York's shores. Gest had invited a Russian bishop to greet the troupe. The invitation promised scandal for the atheistic Soviet press. Stanislavsky was relieved when the bishop protested the Soviet Union's official adoption of atheism by refusing to come. Gest also asked the mayor of New York to present Stanislavsky with keys to the city, but mistakenly invited him for a day in advance of the company's actual arrival. Although city officials did turn up on the proper day, they impatiently piled their gifts into a waiting car and left before the long-delayed boat actually docked. Once on shore, Stanislavsky was photographed with the gifts, which then promptly vanished. He suspected that Gest had rented them as appropriate props for the occasion, turning the arrival into a "vaudeville" (Bokshanskaia 1945:518).

Gest's campaign astounded Stanislavsky and his troupe, whose approach to publicity had always been low-key. In 1917, the Russian actors had nearly offended visiting British theatre critic Ruhl by asking him to buy tickets, giving no interviews, and allowing no photographs except in a performance setting. "Their personal lives," they told him, "were their own" (Emeljanow 1981:159).

With all the publicity, both positive and negative, US audiences looked forward to judging this highly touted company, and Stanislavsky gave them ample opportunity. The Moscow Art Theatre gave 380 performances in Manhattan, Brooklyn, Newark, New Haven, Hartford, Chicago, Boston, Cleveland, Detroit, Pittsburgh, and Washington D.C. over the course of twelve months during the span of two years. US spectators were not disappointed. While they coldly resisted Russian culture, they warmly embraced Russian actors.

The mystique already surrounding the company's extraordinary acting was only heightened by their performances. Their incomprehensible language proved advantageous by focusing attention away from the texts of their plays and on to their acting. Audiences reacted to the performances as to silent movies that transcend verbal communication. As Percy Hammond wrote, "to those of us who know Russian only by hearsay, the performance is a fascinating casual motion picture" (Emeljanow 1981:231). Russell McLauchlan reminded his readers that speech is only one of the many "details of behavior" that make up performance; "an inability to understand it is no particular bar to comprehension" (n.d.). In fact, spectators responded to the productions' emotional content. During a performance of *Three Sisters*, one of the company's leading actors described catching sight of a young woman, who held the play's translation in one hand and "in the other a handkerchief. She cried, then quickly, quickly wiped away her tears, so that she would not miss a word in the book, then again more tears" (Bokshanskaia

1945:539). The Russian players even managed to touch political skeptics. A self-proclaimed "100 per cent American" marveled in doggerel:

> Just think of a bunch of low-down Bolshevicky
> That can't talk even a word of English, makin'
> A hard-boiled egg like me cry like a kid!
>
> (Weaver 1923)

As Corbin wrote: "It is the acting of Stanislavsky's company [...] that sometimes gives us what is called pause" (Emeljanow 1981:234). Kenneth MacGowan agreed. "The heart of the Moscow Art Theatre is the actor" (1923:89).

Aspects of the company's work most often praised included the actors' seamless portrayal of character, their creation of an illusion of real life without obvious theatricality but with clear artistry, and their ensemble work. Edmund Wilson touched several of these aspects when he wrote, that we:

> stood watching the family go about its business, but at the same time they bring out a whole set of aesthetic values to which we are not accustomed in the realistic theatre: the beauty and poignancy of an atmosphere, of an idea, a person, a moment are caught, and put before us without emphasis, without anything which we recognize as theatrical, but with the brightness of the highest art.
>
> (Emeljanow 1981:236)

In his review of *Three Sisters* Hammond stressed the actors' credibility:

> We liked Mr. Stanislavsky in that hopeful soliloquy which he delivered as a reverie, reclining, eyes closed, in his chair, and seeming to improvise it to its ultimate dissonance. And Mme. Chekhova when she listened and listened, as if she had not been hearing it for twenty-five years. And, in fact, all the others, when we chanced to set our eyes, if not our ears, on them. A peculiar thing about the Russian actors is that the most important of them can come into a room or leave it without theatrical emphasis. You suddenly discover that they are present or that they are absent.
>
> (Emeljanow 1981:238)

In short, the Russians became the measure against which all acting could be judged.

While the actors seemed far beyond the usual fare, the sets were a disappointment. The Moscow Art Theatre reached New York in 1923 with theatrical technology that was outdated by twenty-six years. While the characters appeared to "live" on stage, their environments smacked of artificiality. Hammond described the scenery for *The Cherry Orchard* "in the early grand opera manner" (Emeljanow 1981:231). Corbin called the sets "far below the standard of Broadway" (Emeljanow 1981:234).[2]

Ironically, the Russians' assessment of Broadway merely inverted Broadway's assessment of them. They were astounded by the technological virtuosity of the New York stage, and generally disappointed in the acting. Individual actors might impress them, as did David Warfield playing Shylock in David Belasco's production of *The Merchant of Venice*, but overall they remained unmoved. Thus, while Stanislavsky praised Warfield as "a real Russian actor" in the press (Edwards 1965:231), he told his secretary that, "Aside from the main actor, there was literally no one to watch" (Bokshanskaia 1945:534). After viewing a production of *Hamlet* with John Barrymore, the secretary similarly wrote in her journal: "I liked the external side of the production very much—the set, costumes—but the acting did not capture me at all. Barrymore was interesting in some places" (Bokshanskaia 1945:538).

Whether we can judge the tours to have succeeded as Stanislavsky so desperately hoped depends upon the measure applied. From practical and financial points of view, the tours painfully failed. A killing workload stressed the company to its limits. Not only were the repertory actors unused to playing the same role eight times a week as the US system demanded, but many rehearsals *en route* were obligatory. Because the company was split into two they were short-handed. Actors, who did not ordinarily play with the company, were recruited specifically for the tour. Richard Boleslavsky, a former company member who had emigrated from Russia four years earlier, agreed to fill in. Vera Pashennaia, a member of the rival Maly company, was conscripted. During the 1923 American tour, she played major characters: Irina in *Tsar Fyodor*, Olga in *Three Sisters*, Varya in *The Cherry Orchard*, and Vasilisa in *The Lower Depths*. Yet, she had had only a few rehearsals in Moscow, and continued to work on her roles with Stanislavsky in hotel rooms throughout Europe. When the tour began, she knew almost nothing of the System, and tried to learn the company's techniques as quickly as possible (Pashennaia 1954:134–5).[3]

In addition, illness plagued the company. Throughout their stay, many actors performed with high temperatures. Alternates replaced sick actors. Some found themselves in tears of panic upon learning that they would perform roles, which they had rehearsed only one or two times. Stanislavsky himself fell prey to the rigors of the tour. The food disagreed with him, the heavy schedule took its physical toll, and a refrain of despair pervaded his letters. "I am losing what remains of my health. My spirits are low. I'm depressed, I've almost lost heart, and at times, I think of giving it all up" (Benedetti 1990b:278).

Despite standing ovations and full houses, profit continued to elude the Theatre. The expense of transporting sets, costumes, and actors, of theatre rentals, and the required hiring of unionized stage hands and local extras consumed the earnings. Nearing the end of the 1923 tour, US taxes struck yet one more blow. Each company member had to pay 8% on income earned in the country, but few could afford to do so, since living expenses had been high. In an attempt to help, the Theatre paid taxes for those who had earned less than one hundred dollars a week, causing resentment from the others (Bokshanskaia 1945:577; Shverubovich 1990:583–6). Adding insult to injury, the management informed several members of the troupe that their services would no longer be required when they returned to Moscow. Many of these newly unemployed actors stayed in the US.

Stanislavsky's letters from the States are full of schemes to make money. He considered filming *Tsar Fyodor*, but when the company with which he was negotiating proposed rewriting the scenario to minimize the tsar's role and emphasize a secondary love plot, Stanislavsky abandoned the project in disgust (Bokshanskaia 1945:552–4; Shverubovich 1990:542–4). The publication of his first book, *My Life in Art*, in conjunction with the 1924 tour was one of his more successful money-making schemes.

Given the realities of the tours, the Moscow Art Theatre's now legendary success in the US seems a theatrical miracle. Stanislavsky arrived burdened by financial woes, stressed by a killing workload, and discouraged about the future of his art. He played to American audiences against a context of political ambiguity, and became part of that ambiguity himself. He did not find the dollars for which he had hoped so desperately, but he did find new and enthusiastic students for his System. In this audience, the tours' real success lies.

The lasting impact of the Moscow Art Theatre in the United States occurred within the theatre community, which had left the Russian actors themselves cold. The company gave special matinees on Fridays to accommodate the schedule of professional actors. Especially concerned with the opinion of this audience, Stanislavsky anxiously arranged for his best actors to play these performances. Already famous American actors applauded enthusiastically and generously. David Belasco, in an open letter to the *New York Times*, thanked Gest for bringing the Russians to the US.[4] John Barrymore reported having been shaken and intoxicated with the greatest theatrical experience of his life (Bokshanskaia 1945:526).

More importantly, the Moscow Art Theatre influenced still unknown actors and directors, who attended these matinees. The general public may have left the theatre nostalgic, perplexed, bemused, moved to tears, but this young, untried group watched as if the secret to great theatre were being offered them. They longed to learn to act in this way, to create the same kind of theatre in their own idiom. As one reviewer put it, Stanislavsky's productions "encourage us to revise our ordinary scale of dramatic and theatrical values" (Emeljanow 1981:242). The young Lee Strasberg and his contemporaries, who would ultimately transform the System into the Method, observed the work of Stanislavsky's company in awe. As Strasberg recalled:

> The first visit of the Moscow Art Theatre was for us not only an event of deep personal significance in our lives, but an event of enormous importance in our theatre. It came at the beginning of the rise of American theatre, when the American theatre was finding its voice. [...] It was therefore not simply something we appreciated or enjoyed ... I am sure that all of us feel a special bond.
>
> (LS 12A:19 January 1965)

Stanislavsky sensed this special impact, when he described opening night of the 1923 tour to his wife: "We have never, not once, had such a success, not in Moscow, not in other cities. Here they say that it is not a success, but a discovery" (SS IX 1999:69).

The ironies of the tours

Stanislavsky had found some of his most eager students on the very eve of his beloved Theatre's apparent demise. As he "confidentially" confessed to Nemirovich-Danchenko in 1923:

> We must get used to the thought that there is no longer an Art Theatre. You, of course understood this earlier than I did. All these years I flattered myself with hope and salvaged the moldering remains. During the time of our travels, it has become clearer and clearer, most precisely and definitely. No one has any *thought*, *idea*, no great *goal*. And without that, an enterprise based on ideas can not survive.
>
> (SS IX 1999:79)

Against such despair, Stanislavsky's enthusiastic reception must have been particularly gratifying. He longed to transmit what he had learned about acting: "To whom can I give that which is most important to me? I am approaching 60. Isn't it reasonable for me to dream of raising a new, young generation?" (SS IX 1999:79).

No wonder this Russian director developed such a fascinating relationship with his American admirers! Despite growing political hostility between their two countries, they needed each other. The tours might yet save Stanislavsky's art; he might yet teach a new and riveting method of acting to the West. He even seemed to consider emigration in his "Aesopian" letters to Danchenko.[5]

> He, who has been to America and felt this boundless expanse, he, who has seen the endless lines of people every day at the box office … and these lines do not end … he, who has heard the voices and the invitation from the provinces, from hundreds of cities with populations of millions, and many of these are Russian—he will understand that we can do business only in America.
>
> (SS IX 1999:80).

To nurture this new relationship, Stanislavsky allowed his former student Boleslavsky to speak in English about the System. Stanislavsky himself began to write about his approach to acting for translation and publication specifically in the United States.

There are many profound ironies in this Russian/American relationship, the first of which dates back to the founding of the Moscow Art Theatre in 1897 and 1898. Then Stanislavsky was a young man at the forefront of a timely artistic revolution; by 1923, at age 60, he was seen by younger avant-garde artists in Moscow as old-fashioned, out-dated, behind the times. As if to confirm their opinion, he toured with the Art Theatre's earliest productions. He brought a hastily prepared, under-rehearsed, twenty-five-year-old production of *Tsar Fyodor Ioannovich* by Aleksey Tolstoy that had opened the first season of the Theatre; he brought turn-of-the-century Chekhov productions; he showed Maksim Gorky's *The Lower Depths* first produced in 1902. Yet, his American admirers greeted these old productions as new and turned even their age into an advantage. "We were fortunate in seeing not productions, but works of art," Strasberg recalled. "We saw at that time […] not just the successes of that year; they brought to us the successes of their entire career. We were privileged" (LS A140:23 April 1960).

To understand the scope of this first irony, I remind you of the familiar early history of the Moscow Art Theatre. When Stanislavsky and Nemirovich-Danchenko met on 22 June 1897 to forge a program for a new theatre, both men were notable in Moscow theatre circles. At 33, Konstantin Sergeevich Alekseev had been acting for twenty years under the stage name Stanislavsky. He was a striking actor: handsome, over six feet, with prematurely white hair, a dark moustache and bushy eyebrows. In 1888, he had founded the Moscow Society of Art and Literature, which quickly became a focal point for theatre despite its amateur status. Stanislavsky's fresh talent caught Nemirovich-Danchenko's eye. At 39, Vladimir Ivanovich Nemirovich-Danchenko was a theatre critic, a member of the Repertory Committee of the Imperial Theatres, and a successful playwright. In 1891, he had become director of the only professional actor training program in Moscow, the Philharmonic Society's Drama School. Appalled by the lack of rigor in theatre, he had already introduced the scandalous practice of dress rehearsals there. In 1897, he won the prestigious Griboedov prize for the season's best play, but told the judges that *The Seagull*, a play which had premiered in St. Petersburg that same year deserved the honor (Nemirovitch-Dantchenko 1936:71). He would later plead with Anton Chekhov to allow the new, untried theatre to mount this play.

Appalled by the artificiality of professional acting, insufficient rehearsal time, poor standards of scenic design, and lack of respect for the playwright, Nemirovich-Danchenko dreamed of a way "to reconstruct [theatre's] whole life […] to change at the root the whole order of rehearsals and the preparation of plays; to subject the public itself to the regime essential to our purpose" (1936:68). He looked to Stanislavsky to help him do so. When the two men broke from their now legendary eighteen hour meeting, they had agreed to found a theatre which Stanislavsky described as nothing less than "revolutionary." Echoing Nemirovich-Danchenko's words, Stanislavsky wrote:

> We protested against the old manner of acting, against theatricality, against false pathos, declamation, against overacting, against the bad conventions of production and design, against the star system which spoils the ensemble, against the whole construct of the spectacle and against the unsubstantial repertoire of past theatres.
>
> (SS I 1988:254)

Many years later, after settling in the US, the Moscow Art Theatre actor Michael Chekhov explained to his students in Hollywood, that Stanislavsky and Nemirovich-Danchenko indeed "needed" each other. From Nemirovich-Danchenko, who saw the play's "main idea" as the "scaffolding" for a unified production, Stanislavsky learned to seek wholeness in a work of art. Thus emerged the "through-line" of actions and the "supertask" in his later System. From Stanislavsky, Nemirovich-Danchenko learned to put "human life into the scaffolding." Thus emerged the famous moods and atmospheres that became a hallmark for the Art Theatre's greatest productions (M. Chekhov 1955).

One basic attitude links all points in their program: respect for theatre as art, not mere entertainment. In this spirit, they included the audience in their program of reform. They warned spectators when the time had come to take their places by dimming the lights in the foyer. They chose seats that were not unduly comfortable to insure the spectator's alert attention. They banned anything disrespectful: irrelevant music, late arrivals, and applause that inappropriately interrupts the flow of the play.

In return, Stanislavsky and Nemirovich-Danchenko offered unified productions worthy of respect. All theatrical elements supported a central conceptual approach to the play. "Poet, actor, designer, tailor, and stage-hand all work toward one goal, set down by the poet in the foundation of the play" (SS I 1988:250). Sets were no longer assembled from furniture in stock, but were built anew for every production. Motley, unmatched assortments of clothes provided by actors were replaced with costumes designed to further the production as an integrated whole. In *The Seagull*, the actress Arkadina complains that she cannot afford to buy her son a new suit because she must provide her own costumes (A. Chekhov 1971:408). She thus alludes to one of the many realities in professional theatre, which the Moscow Art Theatre successfully reformed.

Aesthetically, Stanislavsky and Nemirovich-Danchenko translated their impulse to create serious art into Realism as an initial programmatic style. In this effort, they were tapping the best and latest trends in European theatre. Heavily influenced by Duke Georg of Saxe-Meiningen's German court theatre, which had taken advantage of the stage's perspective to produce realistic crowd scenes, Stanislavsky emphasized three-dimensional sets and historical authenticity. Two-dimensional painted backdrops were transformed into credible environments for the actor. Detailed research assured the exact reproduction of manners and style. For their first production, *Tsar Fyodor Ioannovich*, a tale of medieval Russia, the troupe combed the provinces in a private railway car to find genuine fabrics and props (Gorelik 1962:144), many of which can still be seen in Stanislavsky's house museum.

These early realistic sets and costumes were the very ones that Stanislavsky took out of moth balls and brought to the US. In short, he toured with the artistic revolution of the nineteenth century in the second decade of the twentieth. However, these productions had not kept pace with his active experimentation. His thinking, practice, and tastes had changed much since the Moscow Art Theatre's early years. Thus the tour did not adequately represent the artist who toured.

Why did this out-dated revolution strike US audiences as so exciting? As critics made abundantly clear, sets and costumes could not explain it. They pointed instead to the acting. Over and over again they agreed that the Russian troupe's ensemble work distinguished it from Broadway, and young actors linked this special talent to a rumored System for training actors.

Yet in the company's awesome acting we find the second great irony of the tours. All the productions that arrived in the US had been created without the System. The ensemble as an ideal had predated the creation of the System; it had been part of the Art Theatre's initial program: "Today—Hamlet, tomorrow—an extra, but even as an extra—an artist. [...] There are no small roles, only small actors" (SS I 1988:250). The touring productions, even Chekhov's last play *The Cherry Orchard*, had all been staged before 1906 when Stanislavsky began to formalize his System. Many of the most famous touring actors, like Olga Knipper, had resisted the System, and others hired to fill out the company, like Vera Pashennaia, knew virtually nothing about it. Furthermore, according to Stanislavsky, the acting in 1923 and 1924 was stagnant. Even the younger actors, trained exclusively in the System, disappointed him. In his opinion, they had become too settled in their acceptance of what had become a kind of dogma about their art. They had lost their spirit of experimentation. (Many of these criticized students would later become key teachers in the US.)

A second flashback to yet another familiar story—Stanislavsky's early work with actors before his creation of the System—illuminates this second irony. Just as the newly founded Art Theatre had demanded a serious approach to production overall, Stanislavsky urged respect for actors as artists. The company was formed from the most talented of Stanislavsky's amateurs and the most promising students of Nemirovich-Danchenko's 1898 class at the Moscow Philharmonic School. They included Maria Lilina (Stanislavsky's wife), Olga Knipper (who would later marry Anton Chekhov and tour the US), and Vsevolod Meyerhold (the soon-to-be leading avant-garde director). Stanislavsky insisted that every actor chosen for the new company "love art, not only themselves in art" (SS I 1988:246).

Just as the set became more three-dimensional, Stanislavsky sought a similar three-dimensionality from his actors. He saw as artificial current traditions of declamation and heroic gesture. Like the Romantic poet, he sought to make experience the subject matter of art, and nature its model. Even at the Society for Art and Literature, he had demanded truthful acting. As he recalled, "The virtue of my work then lay in the fact that I tried to be sincere and sought truth, and banished lies, especially theatrical, stock-in-trade ones. I began to hate the theatre in theatre, and sought in it living, genuine life, not ordinary life, of course, but artistic" (SS I 1988:193).

Initially, three-dimensionality in the actor was achieved through purely physical and technical means. The Art Theatre's first actors, were, after all, young and relatively inexperienced; clever directors could mask many of their faults. Stanislavsky carefully staged their movements to create an illusion of truth; he made his actors seemingly oblivious of the audience. They spoke to each other, rather than to spectators, and turned their backs on the auditorium. The Moscow Art Theatre treated audiences as eavesdroppers, peering through an invisible wall on to the lives of real people. Through these stagings, Stanislavsky was translating into Russian the latest ideas of French director André Antoine. At Le Théâtre libre, founded in 1887, where the term "fourth wall" was coined, Antoine had advanced the idea that actors should behave as if they were in a real room with one wall removed to allow the audience to watch.

Stanislavsky believed that three-dimensional sets, realistic props, and sound effects induce an actor's belief in the play. His actors therefore began using make-up and costumes as early as two months before a play opened (Nemirovitch-Dantchenko 1936:100). Furthermore, he added a great number of production details to stimulate the actors' imaginations. In his 1904 production plan for *The Cherry Orchard*, he ends Act I with a plethora of sound effects: "A shepherd plays on his pipe, the neighing of horses, the mooing of cows, the bleating of sheep and the lowing of cattle are heard" (Stanislavsky 1983:337).

Both Chekhov and Nemirovich-Danchenko objected to such apparently irrelevant details. At a rehearsal of *The Seagull* Meyerhold reported overhearing Chekhov ask: "'Why all these details?' [...] 'But it's realistic!' he heard in reply, to which Chekhov ironically remarked that a living nose taken from the model for a portrait and placed on the spot of the painted one is also realistic" (Meierkhol'd 1913:24). Annoyed, Chekhov threatened to write the following opening line for his next play: "How wonderful, how quiet! Not a bird, a dog, a cuckoo, an owl, a nightingale, or clocks, or jingling bells, not even one cricket to be heard" (Benedetti 1990b:135). Nemirovich-Danchenko specifically objected to the croaking of frogs which underscored Treplev's play-within-the-play and insisted instead upon "complete, mysterious silence." Stanislavsky countered by stating that frogs provided just that. Without them, he said, one would too easily focus on the ambient sounds of the audience coughing, turning pages, and settling in their seats which disturb the illusion of silence (Radishcheva 1997:79–80). Stanislavsky's response reminds us that he was a canny director, interested in inspiring both actors and audiences through theatrical art.

In addition to illusionist staging, lengthy rehearsals insured that actors play in sympathy with the director's concept and with each other. Sessions, in which the world of the play was microscopically examined, replaced perfunctory meetings to keep actors from bumping into one another during performance. Rehearsals at the new theatre became notoriously long. Eighty hours of work went into the 1898 production of *The Seagull*. Stanislavsky conducted twenty-four rehearsals, and Nemirovich-Danchenko nine. Three dress rehearsals were held. When the play opened, Stanislavsky still considered it under-rehearsed (Benedetti 1990b:82). In order to facilitate such painstaking work, the Theatre produced six plays during its first year, in sharp contrast to Moscow's commercial theatres which regularly opened one new production each week during the theatrical season. The acting ensemble, thereby created, set the company apart from Moscow's other theatres, just as it later did on Broadway. While fans would stand outside the stage door, waiting to catch a glimpse of a favorite star at the renowned Maly Theatre, there were no stars amidst Stanislavsky's company. As Pashennaia, wrote, the Moscow Art Theatre plays a "symphony," in which each instrument gets lost in the whole (1954:104–5).[6]

The story of the famed System begins later. Stanislavsky had always interrogated his own methods as an actor, but he did not attempt to institute them for the company until after the summer of 1906. For eight years he had worked non-stop, directing and acting in accord with the original Moscow Art Theatre agreements. He had just returned from the company's first successful tour to Europe, and he was physically and emotionally exhausted. He retreated to Finland for vacation, taking with him major tracts about acting from many centuries. He had decided to take stock. Despite the fact that he depicts himself in his autobiography as sitting on the rocks above the ocean in Byronic meditation, his wife recalls that he spent all his time in "a half-darkened room, writing, and smoking for whole days" (Vinogradskaia II 2003:33).

He began to ask himself new questions. What had happened to the "joy in creating" with which he had started his career. "Why was it that earlier I was bored whenever I didn't act, and now it's just the opposite. I am happy when free from performing?" (SS I 1988:371). How can an actor maintain spontaneity in performances repeated time and time again? How can one harness at will the ellusive moment of inspiration? How can one control a creative mood? His reading, thinking, and writing in 1906 represented his first concerted attempt to link theory with practice—in short to find a System (Radishcheva 1997:311).

When Stanislavsky returned to Moscow, he began experimenting systematically with techniques aimed at answering these nagging questions. Over the years he tested all ideas that came his way and tried any exercise from any plausible source—Yoga's relaxation and visualization, Dalcroze's eurhythmics, Duncan's approach to dance, psychological theories of emotion from France and Russia, etc. If he had lived longer he undoubtedly would have tried others. His System was never finished; it remained to the end a dynamic, ever changing experimental process. At each turn, he could not quite reach the ideal standards for acting that he envisioned as possible. No wonder he would continually criticize actors who sought to turn his System into dogma!

His own performances had, of course, served as his first laboratory. But he soon wished to experiment more widely. He applied his latest notions to rehearsals for the company's 1907 production of Knut Hamsun's Symbolist play *The Drama of Life* (*The Game of Life* in Norwegian) and then for the 1909 staging of Turgenev's *A Month in the Country*. The company's most experienced actors complied, but reluctantly. They felt they knew how to approach their roles without Stanislavsky's obsessive experimentation. Olga Knipper, playing both Hamsun's and Turgenev's leading roles, found it especially difficult to adapt. To help her better understand the new approach Stanislavsky broke Moscow Art Theatre protocol by excluding all observers from his rehearsals with her on the Turgenev play (an exclusionary practice that would later characterize Strasberg's sessions at the Actors Studio). Stanislavsky's persistence earned him the reputation of an eccentric crank among many of the actors.[7]

Moreover, using rehearsals to teach the System only incited Nemirovich-Danchenko's ire. After all, many of the actors, Knipper included, had been his students at the Philharmonic. Stanislavsky's new insistence on the centrality of action in performance seemed to threaten, as well, Nemirovich-Danchenko's belief in the centrality of the playwright. When Stanislavsky began to cut expository monologues in Turgenev's play in order to sharpen dramatic action, Nemirovich-Danchenko became incensed (Radishcheva 1999a:20–1). He began to speak of his partner's insufferable "stubbornness" and of "Stanislavskyitis," that he feared could jeopardize the Theatre's future (Nemirovich-Danchenko II 2005:294).

Stanislavsky thus turned to the charismatic Leopold Antonovich Sulerzhitsky (1872–1916) for support and collaboration. Suler, as he was known by the company, could regale a party with a song on his guitar or comfort a sick person (as he did when Stanislavsky fell deathly ill with typhus and when Michael Chekhov experienced a nervous breakdown). More significantly, Suler proved an inspired teacher, often reaching actors more surely than could Stanislavsky. Recognizing this pedagogical talent, Stanislavsky soon placed his trust in Suler as the primary teacher of the System. With his premature death, Stanislavsky lost his greatest friend and ally.

Yet, without theatrical experience, Sulerzhitsky seemed an unlikely addition to the Art Theatre family. Born the son of a Ukrainian bookbinder, he studied painting in Moscow's premier institute until he was suspended in 1894 (Poliakova 2006:28–9), presumably because he had become a staunch Tolstoyan. Lev Tolstoy had experienced a religious conversion in the latter part of his career, and those who followed the novelist's spiritual precepts were shunned by the tsarist government for rejecting the hierarchy of the Russian Orthodox Church, infusing Eastern spirituality into Christianity, and renouncing all killing (whether of human beings in war or animals for food). Sulerzhitsky had met Tolstoyans even before his arrival in Moscow; once in the capital, he became a close friend of the novelist and his family. In 1894, Suler was drafted into the navy, professed his pacifism, and, as punishment, found himself incarcerated in a psychiatric hospital for two years (Poliakova 2006:31). In 1896, he became an "adventurer" (Markov 1934:19), traveling in Central Asia, Afghanistan, and Iran "not as a criminal and not as a deserter," but finally deployed because "he never refused to work," only to kill (Poliakova 2006:37, 44).

By 1898, the year in which the Moscow Art Theatre opened, Sulerzhitsky was back in civilian life, doing odd jobs for a Tolstoyan family in the Crimea. When he learned that the novelist wanted to arrange emigration for the Dukhobors, a religious sect suffering governmental persecution for their beliefs, Sulerzhitsky offered his services. The Dukhobors (whose name means "Those who Battle for the Spirit") were communal, peasant Christians who practiced meditation and conscientious objection. As Suler told Tolstoy, "I can (even though badly) speak English; I know the sea, port life, the cost of groceries, and, I feel, with all my being, that I need to be with them" (Poliakova 2006:59). This new adventure took two years of his life.

When Sulerzhitsky returned in 1900, he settled down as husband and father in Moscow and soon became a familiar face at the Theatre. As one of Tolstoy's intimate circle, he had come to know the company's most famous playwrights, Anton Chekhov and Maksim Gorky. Thus, Suler attended rehearsals often, befriending many of the actors. As early as 1900, he had written to tell Stanislavsky that his performance of Ibsen's Dr. Stockman "penetrates to the very soul" (Stroeva 1973:192). That the two should meet seemed inevitable. Recognizing a like-minded person, Stanislavsky hired Suler in 1906 out of his own pocket as his personal assistant for *The Drama of Life* and made him an artistic confidant (Stroeva 1973:192–6). How else could Nemirovich-Danchenko greet this decision but with anger? He had been replaced as Stanislavsky's co-director by someone who had no dramatic training (Radishcheva 1997:333).

In 1911—twelve years after the Theatre's founding and eight years after Chekhov's death—Stanislavsky threatened to quit the company unless his five-year-old System were officially adopted as the troupe's working method. Its adoption, however, did not alleviate either the company's or Nemirovich-Danchenko's resistance. Therefore, in 1912 Stanislavsky established the First Studio to forge the System with actors less set in their ways. The Moscow Art Theatre's finest young talent—including Richard Boleslavsky, Evgeny Vakhtangov, Michael Chekhov, and Maria Ouspenskaya—now became his primary laboratory. He placed Suler at its head. Finally, Stanislavsky had a home base from which to launch a concerted investigation into acting as an art form.

Needless to say, neither *The Drama of Life*, nor *A Month in the Country*, nor any of the Studio's productions traveled to the US. From 1912 on, Stanislavsky sustained his experimentation by transferring his most innovative work to a series of studios, created as adjuncts to the main stage, and often personally financed. The First Studio was followed in 1918 by a Second, and then a Third, and so on. During his last years, he established his final studio in his home to work on both opera and drama. Thus, his greatest creative pleasures and his most complete and coherent attempts to teach the System always occurred outside the confines of the Art Theatre.

A third irony of the US tours emerges from the praise for the company's Realism. While Stanislavsky had indeed begun as a firm believer, by 1923 he had drifted away from the belief that an illusion of reality was sufficient measure for an actor's "truth" on stage. He insisted that his System not be associated with Realism or any other artistic style. He wanted techniques that an actor could utilize for any play in any style whether realistic, symbolist, theatricalist, absurdist, etc. "Human life," he wrote, "is so subtle, so complex and multifaceted, that it needs an incomparably large number of new, still undiscovered 'isms' to express it fully" (SS II 1989:458).

Yet a third trek into the past, some paths along it well-worn and others unfamiliar, explains this last irony. The avant-garde movement saw to it that Realism did not hold sway for long on the Russian stage. While the Moscow Art Theatre had overwhelmed audiences by creating a new level of Realism in stage production and acting, it soon provoked criticism among emerging non-realistic artists: symbolists, theatricalists, expressionists, and later, futurists and constructivists. Most of its detractors united in a shared opinion. Realism contains an innate contradiction in terms: in the attempt to present nothing but real life, it denies the essence of real art. Theatre, like all arts, depends upon a commonly accepted set of conventions, dictated by its materials. Just as painting is bound by the two-dimensional canvas, theatre is bound by its media—the actor's flesh and blood, the presence of an audience, the time and space agreed upon for the performance. As early as 1902, Symbolist poet Valery Bryusov had espoused this position in an article entitled "Unnecessary Truth." "Wherever there is art," he wrote, "there is also conventionality. [...] The stage by its very nature is conventional [...] Against the unnecessary truth of the contemporary stage, I call for conscious conventionality" (Evreinov 1955:364). Why should one seek the illusion of truth on stage, he asked, when truth may interfere with the stronger impact of art?

Stanislavsky's former actor, Meyerhold, pointed to specific contradictions between life and art in the Art Theatre's work. He reminds us that when a garland sways in the first scene of *Julius Caesar*, the audience knows that the wind is not real because the actors' cloaks remain still. The seemingly distant hills might appear convincing, but only until actors move nearer to them without shrinking in size. Anticipating New York critics, he also complained that, however "real" the bridge, chapel and ravine in Act II of *The Cherry Orchard*, the painted canvas of the sky violates the illusion. "One could cite a host of such absurdities," he concludes, "brought about by the naturalistic theatre's policy of exact representation" (Braun 1969:31). In face of such criticism, Stanislavsky's early statement that he hated "the theatre in the theatre" stuck an illogical note, as if he were willing to throw out the very essence of the art in which he worked. As the impudent director Nikolai Evreinov asked him, "why work in the theatre at all?" (Evreinov 1938:325–33).

But the mature Stanislavsky was not as bound to Realism as his critics assumed. Indeed, he too disliked Nemirovich-Danchenko's scrupulously naturalistic direction of *Julius Caesar*, preferring a more suggestive approach (Radishcheva 1997:180–9). In the early productions, Stanislavsky found realistic staging an assistance for his actors. But by 1924, in *My Life in Art*, he links the System inextricably to the active power of fantasy that lifts the actor out of "real reality." "Imagined truth" exerts greater influence over the actor than does "genuine truth," and only under its spell can "the actor begin to create" (SS I 1988:381). Because Symbolism specifically explores the realm of "imaginary truth," Stanislavsky had begun testing his acting theories on *The Drama of Life*. As early as 1905, he had embraced criticism of his theatre by opening a studio for Meyerhold with Bryusov as its literary advisor. In 1907, he draped the entire stage in black velvet for Leonid Andreev's allegorical *Life of Man*. In 1908, he co-directed with Suler Maurice Maeterlinck's fantasy, *The Bluebird*. In 1917, Stanislavsky's student Evgeny Vakhtangov, who had not yet turned to theatricality, was shocked to see characters appear from behind the audience and enter through the aisles in his teacher's re-direction of *Twelfth Night* at the First Studio (Worrall 1989:94). Stanislavsky, it seems, was more open-minded than his Theatre and sometimes more so than his students.

If the 1923 and 1924 choice of repertory, actors, and production style, however famous, did not adequately reflect Stanislavsky's current interests, then why did he bring them to the United States? Can we accept his politically careful answer— that "America wants to see what Europe already knows"? Stanislavsky's own ironic isolation within the Moscow Art Theatre suggests a more complicated answer.

Personal and political forces of equal strength had objected to key aspects of the System—its connection with forms of artistic expression other than Realism and its ever-changing, dynamic nature. These twin forces sadly pushed Stanislavsky out of his own Theatre. By 1923, the Moscow Art Theatre traded on his name, but refused his most forward-looking ideas. While US audiences hailed Stanislavsky as the company's driving force, he had virtually no administrative power and little artistic control. Decisions concerning the tour were not his, but the management's.

Nemirovich-Danchenko stood at the center of the personal whirlwind that marginalized Stanislavsky. Their estrangement had begun with their first meeting in 1897 when they had agreed that Stanislavsky would control all matters of staging, and Nemirovich-Danchenko would take charge of the repertory. This division of labor proved impossible to maintain. While Stanislavsky claimed in his autobiography that "we strongly adhered to this point of agreement" (SS I 1988:246), Nemirovich-Danchenko more frankly admits that:

> form could not be torn from content; that I, insisting on some sort of psycho-logical detail or literary image, ran the danger of running foul of their produc-tional expression, i.e. of the form; while, on the other hand, [Stanislavsky] affirming his discovered favorite form, might find himself in conflict with my literary treatment. It is precisely this point that was to become the most explosive in our future mutual relations.
>
> (1936:106).

Such conflicts emerged even in the first season. Nemirovich-Danchenko mistrusted Stanislavsky's direction of *Tsar Fyodor* and suggested that he confine himself to coaching the actors. Stanislavsky refused (Radishcheva 1997:51). In *The Seagull*, they fought over Nina and Dr. Dorn, whom Stanislavsky wanted to play. Was she an inno-cent victim (Stanislavsky's view) or something more like a heroine (Danchenko's)? Was the doctor a Don Juan (Stanislavsky's view) or a man of wisdom and insight (Danchenko's)? The quarrel led to Stanislavsky's recasting as Trigorin (Radishcheva 1997:62–8).

In 1917, their conflict reached an especially painful moment. For a year Stanis-lavsky had been preparing the character of Rostanev for *The Village of Stepan-chikova* (an adaptation from Fyodor Dostoevsky) when Danchenko insisted that his partner take another approach to the role. The retired officer Rostanev should be a "boor," not Christ-like as Stanislavsky envisioned the role. Wedded to his image of the role, Stanislavsky found he could not adjust; Danchenko reacted by removing his partner from the cast immediately after the dress rehearsal. After this incident, Stanislavsky played only those roles which he had previously prepared (Benedetti 1990b:224–30).

By the time of Stanislavsky's death, the two did not speak. They communi-cated only in letters which show their strained relationship. Perhaps Nemirovich-Danchenko came closest to the truth when he wrote: "Two bears won't get along together in one den!" (Nemirovitch-Dantchenko 1936:106). They "needed" and even "loved" each other, but they also "hated each other." In their four decades together, they had clashed in every imaginable way. The tall, handsome actor was "elegant" in his demeanor, his "every movement and how he dressed a work of art;" the short playwright was "awkward," tripping over his own feet or walking abstractedly into a chair (M. Chekhov 1955). Stanislavsky loved classical plays (Shakespeare and Gogol included), especially those that embraced the depths of human experience; Nemirovich-Danchenko preferred contemporary plays of social import (Chekhov's and Gorky's among them). Stanislavsky loved stagecraft and saw performance as that which makes theatre unique among the arts; Danchenko loved what was literary on stage. They often fought about whether the "active" or "literary" principle was most prominent in theatre. Each was jealous of the other's talents; each suspected the other of undermining his best artistic efforts (Radishcheva 1997:29, 83).

For nearly two decades, the two directors kept their quarrels private. But in 1921, in a journal article entitled "The Isolation of Stanislavsky," Meyerhold informed his readers that Stanislavsky was not what he seemed. Far from a determined supporter of worn-out bourgeois theatrical Realism, Stanislavsky had demonstrated his interest in new forms when he financed Meyerhold's first experiments in 1905. Now, the young director called the older one "a genius of theatricality." Meyerhold blamed his first teacher Nemirovich-Danchenko for Stanislavsky's "tragedy" (Radishcheva 1999b:78–9). As years passed, Meyerhold's strident criticisms always attacked the Moscow Art Theatre's main stage, not Stanislavsky's studio work. In 1922, Vladimir Volkenstein, one of the Theatre's dramaturgs, exposed more details of the quarrel; he too argued for Stanislavsky's repudiation of Realism (Radishcheva 1999b:88–9). While Meyerhold and Volkenstein may have overstated Stanislavsky's aesthetic position, they forever brought the company's dirty laundry to public attention. Even so, the complete story remained undisclosed until the late 1990s, when Russian scholar Olga Radishcheva published a three volume study, that traces in detail each twist and turn in the co-founders' complicated, soap opera relationship.

This personal history played out against political forces which tended to support Nemirovich-Danchenko's side of the argument. Firstly, Soviet policies encouraged communist-friendly arts at all times and insisted upon propagandist art when Stalin came to power. While Stanislavsky remained staunchly apolitical in his artistic views, Nemirovich-Danchenko had brought a social agenda to their mutual enterprise. He would only accept those period plays that appeared relevant (Benedetti 1990b:65). For example, in his 1903 production of Shakespeare's *Julius Caesar*, he saw Rome's angry crowds as analogous to Russia's revolutionary activists; Stanislavsky became fascinated with Roman culture on its own terms (Radishcheva 1997:182–8). Nemirovich-Danchenko feared that "if theatre dedicates itself exclusively to a classical repertoire, and does not reflect contemporary life, it risks becoming academic and dead" (Liubomudrov 1989:14). In 1906, he would call Stanislavsky's work on Griboedov's classic verse play, *Woe from Wit*, "beautiful" but "lacking the main nerve—protest" (Liubomudrov 1989:15). Danchenko's views allowed him to move into the politicized world of post-revolutionary Russia more easily than did Stanislavsky.

Secondly, Soviet policy presumed that Realism was more accessible to the proletarian masses than abstraction in the arts and, therefore, most desirable. While Stanislavsky fought artistic stagnation of any kind, even in regard to Realism, Nemirovich-Danchenko tended to preserve the realistic tradition of the theatre. Seeing Stanislavsky's experimentation as subversion of the playwright and a threat to the viability of the Theatre they had built together (Gourfinkel 1972:103–28), Danchenko became the Theatre's true champion of Realism. This bent in his thinking also resonated with the Soviet regime. The very fact that it took the Moscow Art Theatre two full years and Nemirovich-Danchenko's full persuasive powers to secure governmental permission for the US tours suggests that the tired realistic repertoire was picked in sympathy with political directives (Radishcheva 1999b:99–108). Contemporary theatre critic Anatoly Smeliansky even suspects that splitting the company in two was a political concession; by staying in Moscow with half the company, Nemirovich-Danchenko served as hostage for the return of Stanislavsky and the others (1992:50).[8]

The political forces that marginalized Stanislavsky swept through the entirety of Russian culture. By 1934, Stalin made Socialist Realism the only legally acceptable artistic style and, in the process, turned Stanislavsky into its theatrical embodiment. By the time he died, Stanislavsky was more than ever not what he seemed. Stalin's decision set in motion the most tragic part of Stanislavsky's life, when estrangement became virtual imprisonment. Soviet history tells this sad story.

Soviet control over the arts had grown gradually but steadily after the 1917 revolution. Well into the 1920s, an uneasy but tolerant relationship existed between artists and their government. The chaos wrought by revolutionary violence and by civil war had left artists relatively free; the new government needed its best energies to establish political and economic equilibrium. In this window of relative freedom, the Moscow Art Theatre had launched its tours to the US. However, the Bolshevik government, like that of the tsars, was keenly aware of the power which artists could wield over public opinion. Theatre, in particular, held special danger, since it brought audiences together in public forums. In 1917, the People's Commissariat of Education and Enlightenment (*Narkompros*) was formed in order to harness the educational potential of the arts and curb its potential hostility toward the new government. In 1919, all theatres including the Moscow Art were nationalized, and a special section was created under the *Narkompros* umbrella to take charge of them. In 1923, with Stanislavsky abroad, theatrical censorship was formalized. The newly established Central Repertory Committee (*Glavrepertkom*) obliged theatres to submit all plays and productions for clearance. The ground at home was literally shifting under Nemirovich-Danchenko's feet.

Initially, a lively debate had ensued about what kind of art would best support revolutionary ideals. Many leading artists, including newly formed proletarian groups, wanted to jettison outmoded, pre-revolutionary forms and institutions, specifically naming Stanislavsky and the Moscow Art Theatre in their attacks. Because Stanislavsky had been a member of the wealthy merchant class, he represented to them the worst kind of capitalist artist. The Association of Proletarian Writers (*RAPP*) called his spiritual and psychological approach to the actor "idealistic," a crude insult in a society committed to Marxist "materialism" ("*Zadachi Rapp na teatral'noi fronte*" 1931:2). They saw his production of Bulgakov's play *The Day of the Turbins* as "a statement by a class enemy," because it treated White Russians sympathetically (Worrall 1989:11). In the same revolutionary spirit, Meyerhold critiqued the opening of Nemirovich-Danchenko's Music Studio in the summer of 1920 by saying, "Now we know what the Moscow Art Theatre audience consists of, left-overs of the bourgeoisie who couldn't manage to get a boat out" (Benedetti 1990b:248). Another critic wrote, "The Art Theatre died a natural death on that same night [of the revolution], when a mortal blow was dealt to that class whose finest essence its magnificent productions distilled. That theatre carried the banner of Russian bourgeois theatre high until the end of its day" (Benedetti 1990b:229).

Despite such criticism, the government tended to favor nineteenth century Realism over non-representational arts. Lenin and his Commissar of Enlightenment, playwright Anatoly Lunacharsky, strove to preserve Russia's past cultural monuments, among which they counted the Art Theatre because of its commitment to Realism. At the company's thirtieth anniversary celebration in 1928, Lunacharsky quoted Lenin: "If there is a theatre which we must at all costs save and preserve from the past, it is, of course, the Art Theatre" (Mokul'skii 1957:140). With their support, the main stage continued operating, interrupted for only one month by the 1917 revolution. In 1919, under a reorganization plan, the Moscow Art Theatre was designated an official state "Academic Theatre," thus qualifying it for governmental subsidies. Furthermore, Lenin had regularly visited the Theatre in 1918 and 1919, applauding the actors' technique. While he disliked their plays, including those of Chekhov, his visits supplied fuel to those who supported Realism. He was said to have watched attentively Stanislavsky's portrayal of the general in Alexander Ostrovsky's play, *Enough Simplicity in Every Wise Man*, nodding his head in approval to his wife, laughing heartily, and exclaiming, "Excellent, excellent!" (Komar'skaia 1957:20). By the time Socialist Realism was in full swing, Lenin was remembered as having admired Stanislavsky's ability to "live his [character's] life in the minutest of details. [...] In my opinion," he supposedly said, "such truthfulness should be the art of theatre" (Skatershchikov 1976:2).[9]

This governmental support, however, encouraged the Moscow Art Theatre's earliest most realistic work and discouraged Stanislavsky's more forward looking experiments. In 1923, Nemirovich-Danchenko had read the political writing on the wall correctly in choosing their most realistic productions to send to the West.

Stanislavsky returned to Moscow only to find greater governmental control over the arts, which reached its peak four years before his death, when all writers were collected into a single professional union and Socialist Realism became its sole program. Arts were now enjoined to depict an idealized reality that viewed the establishment of communism as the logical and teleological goal of history. A newspaper writer who hailed Stanislavsky as a champion of Realism also reminded readers that "Realism can not be genuine, profound, or logical, [...] if it attempts to go against the historical tendencies of social development" (Gus 1938:3–4).

However far from nineteenth century Realism in concept, Socialist Realism looked for models in Russia's past that could be pressed into contemporary service. While Lev Tolstoy was elected as the model novelist, Stanislavsky became, willy-nilly, the official example of Socialist Realism in theatre. He was placed squarely on a pedestal. The realistic productions of his youth, Nemirovich-Danchenko's selection of socially engaged plays for him to direct, his international renown, as well as his venerable age made him the obvious choice. In sharp contrast to the insults flung at him during the 1920s, Soviet newspaper headlines of the 1930s now showered him with mythic praise. He was "Our Pride" (Iura 1938:3), "The Genius of Theatre" (Derman 1938:5), "The Creator of Realistic Theatre" (Khailov 1938:2), "A Great Master of Realism" (Grigor'ev 1938:3–4), on the front lines of "The Battle for Realism" (Gus 1938:3–4). His writing, censored to reflect Marxist doctrine (Chapter 6), was considered "a brilliant, passionate document in the battle for Realism" (Kalashnikov 1938:62). He was among the first to be honored by Stalin as a "People's Artist of the USSR." Conveniently forgotten were his eccentric experiments into other "isms." Now, his culture willfully overstated his aesthetic position.

That he himself differed from the created image mattered little. In late fall 1934, Stanislavsky went home to Leontevsky Lane and stayed there until he died in the summer of 1938. During these years, he lived in internal exile, sadly oblivious of the whirlwind of terror that Stalin had launched upon the country. Stanislavsky's startling correspondence with Stalin suggests that this confinement resulted from a policy of "isolation and preservation," reserved for internationally known, highly visible Soviet citizens (Smeliansky 1991:9). He was hermetically sealed away from the weather, in order to protect his frail body from flus, and from politics, in order to protect his public image from his private thinking. His only outings consisted of trips to a nursing home. Doctors and close associates served as his wardens and carefully controlled information from the outside world. Such isolation insured that the dynamic reality of his work need not impinge on the created image. In this way, Stalin effectively created a myth of Stanislavsky's exclusive commitment to Realism.

In the United States, pronounce the name of Stanislavsky and you evoke images similar to those developed in Soviet Russia: a grandfatherly teacher in a *pince-nez* who reveals the secrets of great acting to insecure young students; a strict disciplinarian who demands total commitment to art; a great Realist director who harnesses the truths embedded in plays and in actors' souls. This image, like the Soviet one, stems from incomplete information about his career and depends heavily on the earliest history of the Moscow Art Theatre. Little about the later development of the System and about Stanislavsky's interest in realms of knowledge other than "real reality" has seeped into our common knowledge about him. The 1923 and 1924 tours unquestionably helped paint this mythic but partial portrait for his American admirers.

3   New York adopts Stanislavsky

By visiting the US, Stanislavsky challenged young Americans to emulate the Moscow Art Theatre. His ideals—theatre as art, a permanent ensemble company, and a system by which to teach and understand acting—seeped into New York's theatrical life slowly but surely. Over the next few decades, Stanislavsky's mythic but partial portrait would come to dominate stage and screen acting throughout the country. The main highway, by which his ideas traveled, are best traced through the histories of the American Laboratory Theatre, the Group Theatre, and the Actors Studio.

In Clifford Odets' *Awake and Sing!*, staged by the Group Theatre at the height of the Depression, the Marxist-leaning grandfather, Jacob, describes the local vaudeville to which his family goes in order to escape the pressures of their lives: "Someone tells a few jokes [...] and they forget the street is filled with starving beggars" (1979:49). In contrast, he himself turns to Caruso singing "*O paradiso!*" as a hymn to the remaking of the present into a utopian future. While Caruso's recordings of opera were part of the entertainment industry of the day, Jacob sees them as a higher form of art. In this detail, Odets reflects a commonly perceived distinction in the US between escapist entertainment and meaningful art. Edith J. R. Isaacs, who would later publish Stanislavsky's *An Actor Prepares*, identifies a parallel pattern: the existence of two theatres, one central and committed to commercial entertainment, producing predominantly musicals and light comedies, and the other, existing on the fringe, dedicated to art and to plays with something to say. She calls this latter type "tributary" theatre, and says that its value lies in feeding new ideas and creativity back into commercial theatre (Fergusson 1957:6).

Utilizing this pathway, Stanislavsky's System slowly percolated from the fringes—the American Laboratory Theatre and the Group Theatre—into the center—the Actors Studio—radically changing our expectations about acting. Once retold, the stories of these three theatrical enterprises, like the history of the Moscow Art Theatre itself, set the scene for a revised understanding of the Russian System's transformation into the American Method. By the turn of the twenty-first century, the Method had become "the most popular yet controversial form of actor training in America," itself as subject to "misunderstanding" (Krasner 2000:6, 17) as had been the System from which it had sprung.

The American Laboratory Theatre

The process of assimilating Russian ideals began with Richard Boleslavsky, the first voice in the transmission of the System to young actors in the United States. His American Laboratory Theatre represents the first programmatic attempt to put Stanislavsky's ideas into practice in a serious, methodical way in New York.

Boleslavsky quite literally established himself as Stanislavsky's English-language spokesperson. On 18 January 1923, eight days after the Moscow Art Theatre opened in New York, he delivered the first of ten lectures from the stage of the Princess Theatre. Sponsored by Morris Gest (the Art Theatre's impresario) and approved by Stanislavsky, Boleslavsky enunciated principles of acting worked out at the First Studio. Audience member Miriam Kimball Stockton described these lectures "like the coming of a new religion which could liberate and awaken American culture" (Roberts 1981:108). In April 1923, while the Russian company still performed in the US, Boleslavsky published the first English-language article on the System in *Theatre Arts Magazine*.

On 29 June 1923, shortly after Stanislavsky had completed the first US tour, Boleslavsky signed a formal agreement with Stockton and other trustees, whom she had recruited, to establish a New York theatre and school (Roberts 1981:108). Significantly, in founding the American Laboratory Theatre, its backers entrusted the creation of an "art" theatre like that of Moscow's to émigrés. There until 1930, Boleslavsky and his compatriot Maria Ouspenskaya taught Stanislavsky's ideals to a generation of artists who would in turn shape the future of US theatre: Lee Strasberg, Harold Clurman, Stella Adler, and Francis Fergusson, among them. Notably, Strasberg always emphasized the central role of Boleslavsky in the transmission of the System (1987:84).

As Stanislavsky's spokesperson, Boleslavsky offered impressive credentials. In fall 1906 at age seventeen, he was one of only three actors admitted to the Moscow Art Theatre's school. Among the roles he earned was the tutor in the 1909 production of Turgenev's *A Month in the Country*, for which Stanislavsky used his developing System during rehearsals. Boleslavsky was the youngest and most inexperienced member of the cast, but the production sealed his fame as a matinee idol with Russian audiences. A founding member of the First Studio where the System was first forged, Boleslavsky participated in its creation. As one who had already worked directly with the new techniques, he became a natural leader at the Studio. Indeed, one member called him "Stanislavsky's pet" (Birman 1959:87). Here he began to direct and teach.

Although Boleslavsky fled from the Soviet Union in 1920 (three years before the Moscow Art Theatre arrived in New York), he had maintained close working ties to his former company. In 1921, he had joined the so-called "Kachalov Group"[1] in Prague, directing and acting. Headed by actor Vasily Kachalov, the troupe was comprised of half the Moscow Art Theatre's company, including some of its most stellar performers. Having been cut off from Russia in 1919 by civil war maneuvers while touring the Ukraine, the troupe performed for three years outside the Soviet Union. In their 1922 brochure, the group listed Boleslavsky as director. In that same year, however, some of the actors answered desperate pleas for them to return to Moscow. Stanislavsky needed them in order to insure a successful tour through Europe and the US. Boleslavsky chose to remain in emigration.

In 1923, Boleslavsky temporarily rejoined the Moscow Art Theatre. He had arrived in New York in October 1922 with a cabaret revue, which he had staged in Paris. When the revue closed, he waited for his former company to arrive, because he had Stanislavsky's invitation to join the tours as assistant and actor. Thus, Boleslavsky was among the émigrés who greeted Stanislavsky at New York harbor. Even though Stanislavsky had remained angry with his former protégé for having emigrated (Shverubovich 1990:489), he knew that the company, short on staff from the start, needed his services. During the tours, Boleslavsky rehearsed crowd scenes, adjusted old stagings to new theatres, and filled in for actors beset by illness, playing his former roles and alternating with Stanislavsky as Satin in Gorky's *The Lower Depths* (Roberts 1981:107).

Ironically, Stanislavsky mentioned in a letter to Nemirovich-Danchenko dated 2 December 1924 that Boleslavsky's continuing connection with the Moscow Art Theatre in emigration proved how difficult it was for Russian actors to establish themselves in the West. He saw Boleslavsky's career as a cautionary tale for young artists who might consider emigrating during the American tour (SS IX 1999:137). Perhaps he himself took counsel from it.

The collective ideals that created the Moscow Art Theatre's brilliant ensemble of actors naturally became the ruling idea behind the American Laboratory Theatre. In the school's catalogue, Boleslavsky emphasized the need to train actors as a "team" rather than as "individuals." The very nature of "living theatre" demanded this approach. Echoing Stanislavsky's motto, "There are no small parts, only small actors," the trustees enunciated their expectations for a theatre "in which each actor strives to act his part, however humble, as if it were a major part of the play, but harmonized toward a perfect ensemble" (1924–5). Boleslavsky expands upon this idea in his article for the catalogue "The Collective Education in the Art of the Theatre":

> The lot of actors is to be bound by numerous threads of interdependence, ranging from a theatric bond with the humble usher to the highly trained rapport with fellow players. This constitutes the essence of the collective method of education in the art of the theatre, or what I prefer to call *team work*. In order to get the most harmonious results, a group should be trained collectively.
>
> (1924–5)

From the first, carrying out this imported ideal proved difficult. Shortly after the founding of the Lab (1923), the actors rebelled against the trustees, demanding to be consulted in "collective" artistic decisions for this admittedly "collective" theatre. They received no satisfaction (Roberts 1981:125–6). In addition, the commercial environment of New York did little to nourish Russian artistic ideals. For all seven years of its existence, the American Laboratory Theatre struggled against financial ruin. Actors were asked to pay weekly sums to maintain solvency. Many were simply unable to do so.

Boleslavsky, himself in shaky financial straits, could not survive from his work at the Lab. Therefore, he split his attention between it and directing Broadway shows and Hollywood films. Because of his successful handling of crowd scenes, he was also hired to doctor the work of others. Commercial assignments often took him away from the Lab at crucial moments, such as in July 1927, when the Trustees attempted to move a production to Broadway before it was ready. Stockton, who later would mortgage her home to save the theatre, vented her anger with him in a letter. "It is impossible and ridiculous to attempt to build up a noble young theatre without a director. This theatre has been created for you—do you want it, do you wish to do by it as should be done—or do you not? We need to know" (Roberts 1981:192–3). Indeed, Boleslavsky was away for much of the time that Strasberg studied at the Lab, where he occasionally heard Boleslavsky lecture about acting, but consistently practiced his craft with Ouspenskaya. The American Laboratory Theatre existed for only seven years (1923–30), and that largely due to Stockton's personal and financial sacrifices. Boleslavsky was more prophetic than he realized when, in 1923, he had told Stockton that "it would be impossible to impose any foreign ideal upon American soil" (Roberts 1981:108).

The Group Theatre

Stanislavsky's ideals would need translation into the idioms of American culture in order to survive. As Joshua Logan reports, Stanislavsky himself suggested just that when he learned about the formation of the Group Theatre. He told Logan that he welcomed the Americans' emulation "as long as you keep in mind that we are different from you. We have different national goals, a different society. You like whisky, we like vodka. [...] Create a method of your own! Make your own private tradition" (1976:53). This is exactly what the Group Theatre accomplished. In 1931, the Group took the challenge out of foreign hands. Sadly, zeal for crediting Stanislavsky as their tutor often overshadows this notable accomplishment.

The new company grew from a friendship that developed in 1925 between Harold Clurman and Lee Strasberg, both young idealists, "full of piss and vinegar" as Cheryl Crawford described them (1977:53). Unlike Stanislavsky and Nemirovich-Danchenko when they met in 1897, Clurman and Strasberg had only just begun theatrical careers. They were employed by the Theatre Guild, Broadway's most intellectual and serious-minded commercial theatre.[2] Clurman was working as an extra and a sometimes stage manager; Strasberg was playing small roles.

Educated at Columbia University and the Sorbonne, Clurman had fallen in love with theatre as a child, when he saw Jacob Adler perform in Manhattan's Yiddish theatre. Later, he would also fall in love and marry Adler's daughter, Stella. As a young man in Paris, Clurman began his study of theatre with the French director Jacques Copeau who saw the actor as the living embodiment of the playwright's world. Later in 1934, Clurman would put his facility in French to use as translator for Stella when she sought Stanislavsky's help with her acting. In New York, on Strasberg's suggestion, Clurman also studied at the American Laboratory Theatre.

In contrast, Strasberg was almost totally self-educated. Although he had dropped out of high school because of financial difficulties, he read avidly about the theatre all his life. In his later, more affluent years, he lined his apartments with books, usually buying two copies of everything—one for New York and one for Los Angeles. Like Clurman, Strasberg's first theatre experiences occurred in Yiddish on Manhattan's Lower East Side. To finance a theatrical career he sold a lucrative partnership in a ladies' wig shop, where he had worked as a clerk. He had already studied at the Lab with Boleslavsky and Ouspenskaya. No wonder he impressed Clurman as being "more passionate about the theatre than I was, better informed, and already equipped with practical study and work" (1957:10).

However strong their passion, Clurman and Strasberg lacked experience in theatre's business aspects. Therefore, Clurman persuaded Cheryl Crawford to join their enterprise. A graduate of Smith College, Crawford had studied at the Theatre Guild's school and become its casting secretary. By 1925 she was working as assistant stage manager on a production for which Clurman was hired as an extra. The Guild not only valued and promoted her work, but invited her to become a member of its board at the very time when she was considering Clurman's idea for a new theatre. She proved her belief in the incipient project by turning down the Guild's guaranteed salary. Of the three, she was clearly the most experienced, and without her commitment Clurman and Strasberg's project would surely not have lasted ten years. Not only did the Group rely upon her competence as business manager, but she also functioned as mediator and peacemaker between the two strong-willed and obstinate "Old Testament Prophets," as she called her co-founders (Hirsch 1986:14).

From the first, their project would address "the truest preoccupations of an intelligent American audience," as Crawford put it (Himmelstein 1963:157). To the last, their commitment to the American context expressed itself in their choice of material. When they disbanded, they had produced only one European play, *The Case of Clyde Griffiths* by Piscator and Goldsmith, itself an adaptation of Dreiser's novel *An American Tragedy*. In 1931, when critics insisted on justly comparing the Group Theatre's first Broadway production with Chekhov, Clurman testily complained. "To speak of Russian influence, as some did, because we had learned certain things of general technical or artistic value from the best practitioners of contemporary theatre art was as pointless as it would be to view Sherwood Anderson's novels or Edgar Lee Master's verse as offshoots of Dostoevsky's work" (1957:56). When critic Arthur Ruhl saw Chekhov's plays in Moscow during 1917, he anticipated Clurman's attitude. "Of course, it is not for us to imitate the Russians' most characteristic work," he wrote. "We are a different breed, too nervous and positive, too optimistic and impatient of results. [...] We must express our own life and times in our own way" (Emeljanow 1981:161).

Could the Group Theatre do what the American Lab could not: translate foreign ideals into a form that the US audience and theatre environment could accept? Critic Gerald Weales pointed toward an answer when he aptly called the company America's "most successful failure" in the theatre (1967:67).

The Group Theatre's failures are more easily assessed than its successes. Over the course of its ten year existence (1931–41), the Group could not sustain its announced and "ultimate aim of creating a permanent acting company to maintain regular New York seasons" (Weales 1967:69). Their envisioned ensemble, grounded in Russian models, could flourish no better in the competitive American context than could Boleslavsky's company. Like the American Laboratory Theatre before it, the Group operated counter to the prevalent commercial and star-oriented theatrical structure. Unlike the Lab, the Group refused to retreat from Broadway theatres to smaller fringe venues that might have better, if more modestly, nourished them. Instead, the company idealistically endeavored to transform the very environment in which they worked. They became a focal point in American tributary theatre stubbornly performing in the commercial center. In their verve, they exceeded their model, the Moscow Art Theatre, which had originally hoped to make theatre accessible to all classes of society, but, under pre-revolutionary economic pressure, had redirected its efforts toward affluent audiences.

The Group's goal threw them into direct competition with commercial theatres for actors, plays, and places to perform. Actor Franchot Tone exemplified the company's difficulty in retaining their best actors. The lure of stardom and Hollywood money exerted too strong a pull. He, like Boleslavsky, oscillated between Hollywood and New York (Kazan 1988:75–7). As business manager, Crawford spent most of her time anxiously optioning plays, raising funds to continue production, and finding the means and places to house the Group as they rehearsed. In her diary from 1932, she wrote in exasperation, "[I] must get the money or we're washed up. Nerves jangly. We're trying to run a business like a philanthropy!" (1977:60).[3]

While the American Laboratory Theatre survived seven difficult years, the Group endured ten, ironically aided by the stock market crash of 1929. Not accidentally do the years of the Group's existence parallel the hardest of economic times. When few opportunities for gainful employment existed, the Group offered actors continuous work, if not generous salaries. As Sanford Meisner recalls, "What else was there? There was no money. There was no making a good living. Don't forget, it was the Depression. When the Depression eased up and people had somewhere to go that was more lucrative, they went" (Chinoy 1976:502).

The Depression had fostered a theatre collective as much through necessity as through idealism. With agreed upon salaries sometimes cut by as much as eighty per cent, the Group's actors could best manage by pooling their resources. Each summer the company found a retreat where they could live as well as rehearse; actors contributed toward food. Like the American Laboratory Theatre students, members often had difficulty finding funds. Robert Lewis remembers borrowing ninety dollars, calling the loan an investment in his future. When Elia Kazan joined as apprentice in 1932, he reported paying twenty dollars a week, a fortune that soon depleted his savings. His drive to remain in the Group was so strong that he arranged to pay his dues by working in the kitchen and dining room. He came to be called "Gadge" by all, because like any good gadget he made himself so useful that he could not be turned out (1988:65, 100). By 1933, the Group literally had to sing for their supper at a kosher resort—Green Mansions, New York. They provided entertainment for the guests in exchange for room and board. During free moments they rehearsed the medical drama, *Men in White*, perhaps their greatest success both artistically and financially (Chinoy 1976:449–50). During 1932 and 1933, several members, including Strasberg and his new wife Paula, Kazan and Clifford Odets, shared an apartment in New York City, parodying their emulation of the Russians by calling it "Groupstroi" (Crawford 1977:62).

Nor did the Group succeed in cultivating their envisioned national dramatic repertoire. Stanislavsky may have stood aloof from politics during the Moscow Art Theatre's tours, but his US progeny actively sought socially engaged art. While the young theatre stressed commitment to American issues, they shared Nemirovich-Danchenko's preference for plays of contemporary relevancy and gazed eastward to Soviet theatre and culture for models of expression, even for heroes. In 1935, one year after Stalin instituted Socialist Realism as the only legal style for the arts, Clurman wrote, "The theatre of the Soviet Union [is] the most *complete* in our contemporary world and [...] well on its way toward the creation of a truly modern culture" (1957:149). The Group identified with the courage of their Russian counterparts, who "had done great work under the most crucially difficult circumstances. They had been devoted, courageous and boldly creative in times that might prove either the crack of doom or the dawn of a great age. Weren't we people of the same stripe?" (Clurman 1957:85-6). The Soviet theatre, enduring the hunger and deprivation of revolution and civil war, fueled the Group's determination to endure the Depression and to express their own spirit and courage through their own art.

Like Soviet Socialist Realists, the young theatre wanted to "say something," as Clurman put it (Chinoy 1976:472). Moreover, like their Soviet counterparts, the Group's productions did not paint reality so much as propose optimistic readings of it. In an article entitled "What the Group Theatre Wants," Clurman states the goal blatantly: "A good play for us is not one which measures up to some literary standard of 'art' or 'beauty' but one which is the image or symbol" of contemporary moral and social problems, which need to be "faced with an essentially affirmative attitude, that is, in the belief that to all of them there may be some answer, an answer that should be operative for at least the humanity of our time and place" (Himmelstein 1963:156). His statement could easily be mistaken for one by a proponent of Socialist Realism.

Like Soviet censors, the Group's managers did not hesitate to ask playwrights to bring their plays into line with the desired message. They often demanded revisions that emphasized optimism but short-circuited dramatic conflicts, creating a sentimentalism that looks dated today. When Paul Green first conceived *The House of Connelly*, the Group's initial Broadway production, he envisioned a tragedy about the degeneration of class relations on a Southern estate. It ended in the murder of the landowner's young wife. "Harold, Lee, and I felt that this kind of ending was wrong for what we wanted to say," Crawford reports. "There has got to be some hope" (Chinoy 1976:492). As Clurman explained, belief "in the perfectibility of man, or at least, the inevitability of the struggle against evil [...] made us impatient with the play's violent ending" (1957:44). The Group convinced Green to give the central character a chance to redeem his land and his young wife's love, but they paid a heavy price for their intervention. The Theatre Guild, which had originally optioned the play, felt that the Group had damaged it and withdrew all financial support for its production. Similarly, the Group insisted that Odets rewrite the end of *Awake and Sing!* and change its original, more pessimistic title, *I Got the Blues*. While written by one of their own members, supported for production by the actors, and portraying struggles similar to their own (a Jewish family enduring the Depression), the play failed to convince the Group's leaders who hesitated to accept it because, in Clurman's words, "the last act I thought almost masochistically pessimistic" (1957:119). Acceding, Odets arranged for hero Ralph's conversion to social action. In so doing, however, he side-stepped Ralph's passionate and obsessive drive for money, weakened dramatic logic, and sentimentalized the story. The Group even requested a textual change in the ending of *Men in White*, adding a final telephone conversation about a recovering patient to give it an "up-beat ending" (Chinoy 1976:494).

The Group's desire to "say something" often expressed itself through leftist tendencies. In 1898, when Stanislavsky and Nemirovich-Danchenko founded a theatre to "revolutionize" Russia's theatrical system, their intention was primarily artistic. In 1931, when the Group Theatre called itself "revolutionary" their intention could be read politically as well. Given the climate of suspicion between the US and USSR, however, the founders stepped back from political labels. Crawford explicitly defined "revolutionary" as meaning "anything which breaks away from accustomed forms and sets out to accomplish something new and different." She later called *Men in White*, which features a choreographic depiction of a hospital's operating room, just as "revolutionary" as *Waiting for Lefty*, which dramatizes a taxi cab drivers' strike (Chinoy 1976:453). Clurman shrugged off charges of political intent: "Left, right, middle, a lot of meaningless words. But there was a situation in the United States. There were hungry people; there were angry people" (Chinoy 1976:475). These were the people he had hoped to address. Kazan, who had joined the Communist Party and later testified before the House Committee on Un-American Activities (HUAC) that a communist cell had existed within the Group, waffled in his assessment of Strasberg: "Lee was making an artistic revolution and knew it. [...] He'd studied other revolutions, political and artistic. He knew what was needed and he was fired up by his mission and its importance" (1988:61).

The company's engaged art did not only fail to establish an enduring body of dramatic literature, but it also hindered the company's financial stability. Promoting social messages on Broadway, where audiences expect escapist entertainment, showed boldness but also idealistic naiveté. As Crawford put it, "the people who still had money for theatre tickets did not want to be reminded of the hopeless economic conditions; they wanted to be entertained with happy endings" (1977:56–7). The Group's second play *1931* by Clair and Paul Sifton concerned unemployment directly, but those most interested could not afford tickets. During the last twelve performances, the balcony sold out, while the orchestra remained empty (Crawford 1977:56–7). All in all, the production was a financial disaster.

How would Stanislavsky have responded to Clurman's dismissal of beauty in favor of plays which projected social optimism? The Soviet press, who hailed Stanislavsky as a proto-Socialist Realist, would happily speculate that Stanislavsky would applaud Clurman. In Stanislavsky's eyes, however, beauty is absolutely essential to good art.

"Beauty lifts the soul," he wrote, "and brings out the best in us. It leaves indelible traces" (SS II 1989:178). While the Group flourished, the Moscow Art Theatre was caught in a political stranglehold that was robbing its vitality and suppressing its greatest artist. The Group could not know how far from Stanislavsky's concerns they had traveled when they emulated Russia's socially engaged art.

In idealizing Soviet theatre, the Group also accepted Stanislavsky as a hero of Socialist Realism. This created image, carefully managed and promoted by Stalinist propaganda, had already begun to obscure the real artist as early as 1923 and 1924, when he had toured the United States. By the 1930s, Stanislavsky's latest experimentation had been successfully hidden from the public's gaze through his internal exile. The Group understood that Stanislavsky stood on a pedestal as an icon of great theatre, but they interpreted his fame naively. "We read that goddamn paper they put out for American consumption, and we believed the lies they told," Kazan said in retrospect (Chinoy 1976:533).

The Group's success stands despite its failures. The company unquestionably created a new and widespread interest in the art of acting, a powerful store of theatrical legends, teachers who would continue to inspire generations of actors, and, most importantly, an influential Americanized Stanislavsky. How was the Group able to leave such an indelible imprint on the US theatre when it seemed unable to fulfill its most clearly articulated goals? The answer lies within those "certain things of general technical or artistic value" (Clurman 1957:56) that they had learned from Stanislavsky. John Paxton, in an article from 1938 entitled "The Fabulous Fanatics," illuminates the paradox of their "successful failure," when he writes: "They may lose money, and they may keep on proving over and over again the impracticality of a permanent acting company—but they will probably never give a play a poor production. Stanislavsky, faith, and talent will see them through" (Bohnen Scrapbook 1938). While the Group's idealization of Soviet culture may have led them astray, their infatuation with Stanislavsky's early work on the System (*via* Boleslavsky and Ouspenskaya) surely propelled them forward. In Moscow, Stanislavsky learned from his American translator Elizabeth Reynolds Hapgood in a letter dated 16 November 1931 that the newly founded Group "can be compared with your First Studio" (Dybovskii 1992:58).

The Group took the Moscow Art Theatre as their direct model. Clurman had seen the company while living in Paris as a young college graduate; Strasberg saw the 1923 and 1924 tours. In 1929, they first attempted to turn their theatrical ideas into reality by producing a Soviet play entitled *Red Rust*. This project betrayed their infatuation with Russian theatre in general and with Stanislavsky in particular; they called themselves "the Guild Studio," invoking the "First Studio" where their émigré teachers had studied. No matter that the "Guild Studio" lasted for only one production! The young theatre had already borrowed Russian methods and spirit.

Amazing and largely unanalyzed analogies exist between the founding of the Group Theatre in 1931 and the Moscow Art Theatre in 1898, almost as if the Group were recapitulating the early history of its model. At their inception, both companies wanted to reform commercial theatre by creating productions that could be considered serious art. For both, Realism initially seemed the appropriate stylistic path to artistic reform. In the early years of the Art Theatre a realistic stage environment, replete with the sounds of crickets, frogs, and dogs, inspired the actor's belief in the world of the play. For the Group, the actor's immersion in a character's emotional life became key. The Group's acting was seen as "startling to the audience," who "had not seen real emotion used to that extent on the stage," leaving them "flabbergasted" (Chinoy 1976:515). An audience member once remarked that "truthful emotions" on stage made seeing a Group Theatre production "like witnessing a real accident" (Chinoy 1976:485).

Central to reform for both the Group Theatre and their model was, of course, the development of an ensemble with a common approach to artistic work. The Group's chosen name proclaims their intention. Not only had Clurman and Strasberg admired such work at performances of the Moscow Art Theatre, but they had also watched Boleslavsky attempt to create an "organic group" (American Laboratory Theatre Catalogue 1924–5). However difficult to sustain in the US context, this goal expressed one of the Group's most seductive aspects, tapping a powerful psychological undercurrent among its members. Many who joined had felt like outsiders in the midst of American culture—Kazan as the child of Turkish immigrants, Strasberg from Galicia who retained a lifelong accent, Adler and Clurman, with roots in Yiddish theatre. They, like their teachers, were immigrants. In effect, they created "a society within a society" (Chinoy 1976:447) for those who felt displaced culturally as well as artistically and intellectually. Paradoxically, they did so in order to claim their place within American society by creating a national art and performing on Broadway. Strasberg's advocate David Krasner sees the "immigrant worldview" extending into the fabric of Method acting itself where "the actor experiences an inner, personal conflict" that mirrors the way in which "Method teachers, saturated in Yiddish life, saw themselves amid the conflicting passions between Old World values and New World experiences" (2000:30–1).

In order to encourage community spirit, the Group mirrored the Moscow Art Theatre's first year by seeking a summer rehearsal retreat in the country. In 1898, Stanislavsky's troupe had gone to Pushkino, near his estate outside Moscow. In the summer of 1931 the Group Theatre traveled to Brookfield Center, Connecticut, a farm where they lived, rehearsed, and studied acting before their first season. As Clurman sentimentally recalled: "Here was companionship, security, work and dreams" (1957:41). Crawford perhaps more realistically remembered it as "a stimulating but battering summer. I was unused to living in such close quarters, especially with extraordinarily volatile actors; it was like living in a goldfish bowl; it frayed my temper" (1977:54). When one conjures up a mental picture of this period, one visualizes a group of young people, outdoors, in the country, clowning and creating theatre together. While some individual faces come into focus, with features that reveal traits of their stormy personalities, the overwhelming impression remains that of community. This mental photograph, so soon to fade, catches the project's idealism. The Group may have been an uneasy collective, held together by pain and sacrifice, brought together by shared goals, and ultimately pulled apart by personality conflicts and commercial pressures, but it was a collective none the less.

In creating ensembles, both the Group and the Moscow Art Theatre actively sought to destroy the star system. How far the Group succeeded within its own ranks can be judged by Katharine Hepburn's legendary refusal to join because she was determined to become a "star" (Vineberg 1991:42). Similarly when Margaret Barker signed on, Franchot Tone cautioned her that she could become an "actress" in the Group, but not a "star" (Chinoy 1976:527). In order to succeed in this goal, both theatres needed young actors without ingrained professional habits or expectations, who could be molded to new ideals. They sought members who wanted to act and offered them, not jobs in the theatre, but commitment to art. Hence, both the Moscow Art Theatre and the Group were young, idealistic, and largely inexperienced companies at their inception. Stanislavsky's amateurs and the graduates of Nemirovich-Danchenko's acting school had comprised the Art Theatre's first ensemble. At 29, Morris Carnovsky was the oldest of the Group's twenty-eight founding members, while Stella Adler and her brother Luther—stars of the Yiddish stage—were the only seasoned actors. The youth of both theatres sustained rebellion and experimentation.[4]

The process by which Stanislavsky developed his System proves the advantage of inexperience. By 1911 the Moscow Art Theatre's actors had transformed Stanislavsky's reform of 1898 into routine and resisted his newest ideas. Only by turning to a new generation of students could Stanislavsky recapture an open attitude toward experimentation. Thus, he turned to the theatre's youngest, most inexperienced actors to create the First Studio. The Studio's members had similarly turned experimentation into routine by 1923 when Stanislavsky first visited New York. Subsequently, when the Studio's former members taught in New York, they remained ignorant of Stanislavsky's further experiments, conducted during the last years of his life with a still younger generation of students.

In reviewing the Group's history, one begins to see that its failure and success are two sides of the same coin. Collective goals were financially debilitating, yet psychologically seductive. Emulation of Russian theatre led it astray in regard to plays, while inculcating a new and productive approach to acting. Those aspects that the Group Theatre borrowed from Soviet Socialist Realism—assessment of plays, commitment to optimistic social messages—look sentimental and outdated today. Those aspects borrowed from the early years of the Moscow Art Theatre— psychological Realism as a theatrical style, the early approach to the System, respect for theatrical art, a shared approach to work in the collaborative art of theatre— survived and were handed over to the Actors Studio for further development.

The Actors Studio

The Actors Studio became the crucible in which the Russian System became the American Method, moving from the tributary fringe to the center of US film and theatre. Unlike the American Lab and the Group before it, the Studio has become a permanent part of New York's theatrical life. Over the course of its long and productive history, the Studio has significantly extended its influence by sending its members out into the commercial theatre and entertainment industry, armed with techniques borrowed from the Russians and reformulated for Americans. As Kazan ironically noted, "the rebels of the thirties and forties have become the establishment of today" (1988:142).

Kazan's words ring true even in the twenty-first century. The long running Bravo television talk show *Inside the Actors Studio*, which began in 1994 in connection with a joint graduate degree program in acting formed by the Actors Studio and the New School University (formerly the New School for Social Research) has garnered twelve nominations for the prestigious Emmy Award. The show provides a public forum for actors to discuss their careers, but many who appear are stars selling their latest films and few have directly studied the Method. Nonetheless, the show's popularity demonstrates the Studio's now institutionalized reputation as America's actor training ground.

Alumni of the Group Theatre founded the Actors Studio in 1947, seven years after the Group had disbanded. Various accounts of the Studio's inception exist. Some cite meetings in a Greek restaurant on 59th Street, nostalgically recalling Stanislavsky's and Nemirovich-Danchenko's famous eighteen hour restaurant conversation. Different opinions on who advanced the initial idea also muddy history. Was it Harold Clurman, Elia Kazan, or Robert Lewis who first suggested recreating the theatrical home lost when the Group Theatre closed? (Garfield 1980:46–7, 50). That it began with a triumvirate, like the Group, is certain—Elia Kazan (to teach beginning acting), Robert Lewis (to teach advanced classes) and Cheryl Crawford (to repeat her performance as business manager).

The Studio opened the same week that Kazan began directing Tennessee Williams' *A Streetcar Named Desire*, in which Marlon Brando's performance would come to define the Method. The first meeting occurred on Sunday, 5 October 1947 at the Old Labor Stage on West 29th Street and Broadway. Twenty-five years earlier, Boleslavsky had presented his series of lectures on the System in the same theatre (then called the Princess). Thus, by coincidence of fate, the first formulation of Stanislavsky's ideas in the US shared the stage with the organization which would adopt and transform them, prompting historian of the Actors Studio David Garfield to call the Studio Boleslavsky's "grandchild" (1980: 53). Whereas Boleslavsky had been Stanislavsky's first spokesperson, Strasberg at the Actors Studio became Stanislavsky's most famous. The Studio also proclaimed its parentage through its name, recalling both Stanislavsky's "First Studio" and the Group's earliest venture as "the Guild Studio." Twenty-six students comprised each of its two initial acting classes, almost twice the number of members in the original Group. Among these were Marlon Brando, Julie Harris, Herbert Berghof, Montgomery Clift, Mildred Dunnock, Sidney Lumet, Karl Malden, Jerome Robbins, and Beatrice Straight.

Like its predecessors, the Actors Studio was designed first and foremost to inculcate respect for the actor. In his speech for the Studio's twenty-sixth anniversary celebration on 6 December 1973, Kazan reminded its supporters that:

> No one can appreciate what the Studio means unless he can recall what the actor was in Broadway Theatre before the Studio existed, a part of a labor pool, his craft scoffed at. [...] The great body of the profession, like the long-

shoreman on the waterfront, shaped up every morning, hoped to be lucky, made the rounds, waited for a phone call, lived on the curb, had nowhere to come in out of the rain.

(Garfield 1980:46)

Kazan continued with the notion that the Studio would inspire actors with "a new sense of dignity" in an effort to get them "out of that goddamn Walgreen drugstore" waiting around to be discovered (Garfield 1980:46).

The Actors Studio extended the work of the First Studio, the American Laboratory Theatre, and the Group by experimenting with the craft of acting. Lewis explained that it was "a place where we could explore and expand our theatrical ideas" (1984:182). Within this aspiration resided a subtler and ultimately more influential goal—the forging of a common language for acting. At the Studio's opening session Kazan had said, "We want a common language, so that I can direct actors instead of coaching them" (Garfield 1980:54). Indeed, Kazan wanted actors for his productions. How simple directing could be if actors spoke the same language as their director! However, he also set a much broader mission for the Studio: to take hold of those Russian "things of general technical or artistic value," to which Clurman had alluded (1957:56), and bring them into sharp focus by means of a working vocabulary. The Actors Studio would indeed become the locus for the translation and transformation of Stanislavsky's ideas into US idioms.

Those who had studied and rehearsed with Strasberg in the Group and who had shared a common artistic approach over the years found commercial theatre frustrating; it lacks a unified approach to theatre and acting. Every production assembles a new company of actors with different training and assumptions about theatrical art. What if the Studio could create a new generation of actors who would develop common acting methods which they would then take with them whenever and wherever they worked? Reforming the theatrical system in this way could indeed be more pervasive and effective than establishing a repertory company. The Studio did not attempt to create an alternative theatre, as had the Group. Instead, it set its sights on a vast arena. Studio actors would infiltrate and transform from within the entire commercial system that had spelled the doom of the American Laboratory and Group Theatres. Thus, Stanislavsky could successfully enter into the fabric of US theatre.

This mission shaped the Studio's history. It became a special kind of club where members could perfect their acting without the pressures of production, exercise their skills and test their limits, falling on their faces without repercussion. Most importantly, it became the place where they could share acting techniques that would help them succeed in a difficult and insecure profession.

The Studio survived by strictly limiting its activities to the development of the actor's craft and avoiding commercial pressures. In its search for a common vocabulary, production would only get in the way. Although there were a few forays into producing, most notably Strasberg's staging of Chekhov's *Three Sisters* in 1964,[5] the Studio remained a workshop. Its leaders argued from time to time about the desirability of an affiliated theatre, Strasberg himself sometimes switching sides in the debate. In opposition to Kazan and Lewis, Strasberg initially had envisioned the Studio as a theatre. He wanted the fame that productions could generate. Yet, like his colleagues, he wanted to protect the Studio's spirit of experimentation, and that meant privileging the process of acting over its product in production (Garfield 1980:79). In a 1956 meeting with the Studio's board of directors, Strasberg strenuously argued for "keeping the Studio [from] being contaminated by production" (LS 7:29 May 1956).

By eschewing production, the Studio also eschewed box-office profits. Nor did it exact tuition dollars from its members. To this day membership is free, determined only by the talent of actors at auditions. In short, unlike the American Laboratory and the Group Theatres, the Studio never attempted to become self-supporting. It depended upon grants, the generosity of prosperous members (such as Paul Newman), and benefits (at times graced by such celebrities as Marilyn Monroe). Acting teachers contributed their services. In 1956, Strasberg explained that the Studio's strength lay in its very poverty: "We don't amount to anything in a sense; we don't have a nickel." And thus, the Studio "can't be bought, can't be had, can't be flirted with" even by "those people who have millions at their disposal." He then unabashedly proclaimed that, "I'm proud of that," linking his pride to the same "youthful idealism" with which he had begun the Group, and "which I've never quite overcome." The Studio, it seems, vindicated his idealism: "I sort of feel that, this way, I'm getting back at the world, to show them the value of idealism" (Hethmon 1991:60).

Ironically, Strasberg, whose name has become virtually synonymous with the Actors Studio, was initially excluded from it. Although he had been one of the Group Theatre's founders as well as its acting guru, and although the Actors Studio was admittedly an extension of the Group, he was actively shunned. Lewis reports that, "[Kazan and I] both agreed that, valuable as [Strasberg's] contribution was in starting us all off in the Group, his manner of dealing with young actors was light miles away from what we now planned and therefore, he would not be considered for the acting faculty" (1984:183). Kazan more pointedly stated that, "what we were determined to get rid of forever was Strasberg's paternalism" (1988:162).

Lewis' and Kazan's reasons were both artistic and personal. They differed from Strasberg in their approaches to actor training. While Strasberg supported psychological Realism, Lewis actively pursued stylization in his productions. While Strasberg emphasized emotion, Kazan focused on intentions behind a character's actions (Garfield 1980:80; Lewis 1984). Lewis and Kazan also knew that Strasberg brooked no such artistic disagreements and tolerated no challenge to his authority. His stubborn insistence on his own point of view had caused resentment and dissension in the past, as in 1934 when Stella Adler sought out Stanislavsky in Paris and returned to the Group with new ideas about the importance of "physical actions" (Chapter 4). Kazan and Lewis wanted a group of their own. Naturally they did not wish to subordinate their ideas.

Another major reason for Strasberg's exclusion, as Lewis said, involved his "manner." The founders of the Studio wanted to create a cordial and supportive atmosphere, a "home." Strasberg, in contrast, tested actors. He might rage, frightening and intimidating them, as readily as he might encourage or comfort them.

Many years later, while at the Studio, Strasberg recalled his violent temper during the Group theatre years:

> It took me long time [to learn the value of discussion]. When I was in the Group Theatre, I never discussed anything. If anybody dared to discuss with me, the sky wasn't too high enough, you see, for the outburst that took place. […] I was young at that time, you see.
>
> (LS A138:12 April 1968)

Many at the Studio in ensuing years would say that he still had not learned to control his famous temper. Kazan bluntly said that Strasberg had "a gift for anger and a taste for the power it brought him" (1988:61).

Given these attitudes, how did Strasberg manage to become the Studio's identity? While the Studio itself was spared the pressures of commercial theatre, its leaders were not. Lewis resigned one year after its creation over a personal and professional slight from Kazan. Lewis had asked Kazan's opinion about directing a musical which Crawford planned to produce. Kazan advised against it, and then announced himself as its director, when Lewis let the opportunity go (Garfield 1980:70). Additionally, as a highly successful Broadway director, Kazan found it increasingly difficult to volunteer at the Studio. The workshop needed someone who had free time rather than a busy career.

Strasberg had time. After the Group disbanded, his career had foundered. He had directed twelve unsuccessful plays in New York. Discouraged, he left for Hollywood where other members of the Group, such as Jack Garfield, Franchot Tone, and Elia Kazan, were flourishing. In contrast to them, Strasberg found few opportunities. He directed screen tests for Twentieth Century Fox and struggled financially. While Fox's boss Darryl Zanuck praised him as an unusually successful coach for film actors (Barthel 1975), Strasberg felt that his idealistic view of acting kept him from attaining prominence in the commercial entertainment world. "The studios used to hate me," he said, "because I taught that actors should be creative, should be allowed to think for themselves, and this challenged the studio's authority" (1978). At the worst of times he relied upon his former colleagues. For example, Crawford hired him to coach actors in her Broadway production of *Brigadoon* which Lewis was directing. By the 1940s Strasberg had begun to develop a solid reputation as an acting teacher, taking on private classes, coaching assignments, and serving on the faculties of the American Theater Wing and the Dramatic Workshop (Garfield 1980:77–9).

With Lewis' resignation and Kazan's increasing workload, Strasberg seemed the logical choice to keep the Studio going. In 1948, Strasberg joined, sharing a class with Kazan. By 1950 the Studio listed him as one of the "new guiding directorate." Because his financial situation was strained, the Studio agreed to pay him a salary, while other teachers (including Joshua Logan, David Pressman, Daniel Mann, and Sanford Meisner) continued to provide their services *gratis*. The only other paid employee was the Studio's secretary. By 1951, he assumed the title of "artistic director" and became the Studio's sole teacher. He held this position until his death in 1982 (Garfield 1980:75–6).

The Los Angeles Actors Studio founded in 1965 recapitulated the history of its New York parent. Initially, members in Los Angeles, lead by Karl Malden (a founding member of the Group), wanted to keep Strasberg out of the organization. Strasberg fought for control, never willing to delegate authority. Until his death he had final veto on the acceptance of all new members on both coasts (Hirsch 1984:235–6).

As the Actors Studio's Artistic Director, Strasberg interpreted Stanislavsky, expounded on the American Method, actively preached its efficacy, and jealously guarded it from the gaze of outsiders who could not always understand his experiential approach. From this post he inspired not only the theatrical but also the cultural imagination of the United States.

University programs

Universities began to play their part in the institutionalization of Stanislavsky relatively late in the game. When Robert Brustein took over the Yale School of Drama in 1967, he felt it "essential to create a professional model." Hence he founded the Yale Repertory Theatre, a professional regional company, with the "hope [...] to involve everybody at the School with the Theatre, and everybody at the Theatre with the School" (1984:12). Moreover, when he hired Stella Adler and Robert Lewis to teach acting, he literally linked Yale's curriculum to the Group Theatre, and hence, "accepted the preeminence, as a training method, of the Stanislavsky technique" (Brustein 1984:260).

The most extensive curriculum in Stanislavsky-based training is located at Harvard University. After leaving Yale, Brustein forged a similar link between the profession and the academy at Harvard through the American Repertory Theatre (ART). In 1997, he founded the American Repertory Theatre's Institute for Advanced Theatre Training in collaboration with the Moscow Art Theatre School. The Institute provides a two year program that culminates in a Certificate of Achievement from ART, and an MFA from the Moscow Art Theatre School. The catalogue states that, "Individually, both ART and [the Moscow Art Theatre] represent the best in theatre production and unmatched opportunities for student training and growth" (http://www.fas.harvard.edu).

While located at Harvard, training occurs primarily through the two professional venues. Students spend three months of the first year in Moscow, where they begin with "the elements of the Stanislavsky system as the primary foundation for their acting training." Russian faculty include "the second and third generation of teachers at the [Moscow Art Theatre] school" (http://www.fas.harvard.edu), thus promising a living link in the tradition that extends back to Stanislavsky himself. In effect, the program bridges the two most significant branches of the global Stanislavsky legacy. It proved so successful that the Moscow Art Theatre School began to admit American students directly and the first group of US citizens to study exclusively in Moscow graduated in May 2005.

These two graduate acting programs further demonstrate the American propensity to look to Russia for actor training. Moreover, they also suggest how professional visions about Stanislavsky traveled into the academy. One can thus find in university programs ironies as striking as those that occurred during the 1923 and 1924 tours. During Tatiana Butova's visit to Yale University in the 1970s to study American experimental theatre, she found Russian émigré teachers making their livings, much as Boleslavsky had done before them, by linking their names to Stanislavsky. Having honed their art in a nation that had "canonized and mummified" him as an icon of Socialist Realism, they had emigrated to break free of his Sovietized System; their "reaction to him could only be one of rejection." Yet, these Russians, who sought "refuge and escape from the ghost of Stanislavsky" found only the ironic "grimaces of fate" in the US. They found that "they could only feed themselves by teaching [...] the Stanislavsky System" (1997:6–7).

At times, Brustein played with the reality of this irony. During a production at the Yale Repertory Theatre, Romanian director Andrei Serban "confirmed his hatred of Stanislavsky and his suspicion of those with Stanislavsky training" by refusing to work with the repertory company's regular Method actors. To resolve the complaint, Brustein encouraged him to recast his play from the younger actors at the School, slyly admitting that, "I didn't bother to tell him that all of these actors had been grounded in Stanislavsky" (1984:158–9).

The first émigré enunciation of Stanislavsky's teachings at the American Laboratory Theatre, its adoption by US citizens at the Group Theatre, and its ultimate transformation into a working vocabulary at the Actors Studio traces the pathway by which, in Clurman's words, the Method became "part of [actors'] normal equipment, [...] no longer a peculiarity of a few offbeat or off-Broadway actors" (1958:251). As university programs linked degrees to professional venues, the Americanized Stanislavsky entered the academy as well. The love affair between American actors and Stanislavsky that began in the 1920s is still strong, with twenty-first century students traveling from New York to Moscow to get closer to their chosen mentor. This adoptive procedure, however, tells little about the transformative process, both cultural and linguistic at work in Stanislavsky's Americanization. Therefore, to examine the precise evolution of his ideas, I invite you to consider the art of translation, both from Russian to American culture (in classroom settings) and from the Russian language to English (in Stanislavsky's classic books).

Part II
Translation

4 The classroom circuit

Lore and legend of the method

American theatre practitioners, who watched the Moscow Art Theatre company in awe during the 1923 and 1924 tours, felt that Stanislavsky held a magic key to theatre. "Everybody on the stage was equally real, not equally great, but equally real," Strasberg recalled. This observation "led me to the realization that there must be something special that they do, because all the actors were doing it, not just the outstanding actors" (Chinoy 1976:545). Their stage product could tell little about their working process, however, and written information was scanty throughout the 1920s and 1930s.

Stanislavsky began to publish very late in his career. *My Life in Art* appeared in 1924, fully thirty years after the founding of the Moscow Art Theatre. Although inspirational, it merely outlines the System. He published the first practical explication of his ideas, generally known in English as *An Actor Prepares*, in 1936, five years after the Group had already adopted what they could learn of his techniques. Boleslavsky too wrote about acting late. While he had described the System in English as early as 1923, his article was all of three pages. He published his book, *Acting: The First Six Lessons*, in 1933—ten years after the Moscow Art Theatre's tours, only three years before the first publication of *An Actor Prepares*, and two years after the founding of the Group Theatre.

Because the practice of acting resists easy explanation and neat theory, most actors do not write at all. In fact, some like Maria Ouspenskaya actively shun publication. On 6 October 1947, the press reported that she had turned down $10,000 from a publisher who wanted a text on acting. "I do not believe that it is possible to learn acting from books," she said. "An actor masters his art in only two ways—first, by living, secondly, by practice" (Clippings).

Stanislavsky and Boleslavsky exemplify the typical pattern for actors who do write. They tend to publish when they come to terms with their own mortality, as if expressing a deeply felt impulse to fix into stable form their ephemeral art. Members of the Group Theatre fit the pattern as well. Sanford Meisner and Stella Adler published their first books on acting in 1987 and 1988 after more than fifty years in the profession. Lee Strasberg's book appeared posthumously in 1987, its final form heavily dependent upon editorial decisions made without his input.[1] In responding to Stanislavsky's last book, British actor Michael Redgrave faulted Stanislavsky for his impulse to write "too much," charging him with creating an illusion that he was still "an active force" in theatre (Hapgood Archive: n.d.). Clearly, Redgrave did not know of the internal exile that Stanislavsky suffered in the late 1930s, nor of his radical, but hidden, experimentation at that time.

Given the paucity of written information, émigré actors initially offered the best way to learn about the System. Since their teaching remained primarily in the classroom, an entire generation of US theatre artists necessarily embraced Stanislavsky's System as an oral tradition, which was then passed on to the next generation as lore. This oral tradition has created so powerful an environment that it continues to hold greater authority among theatre practitioners than does the written word. Even the later publication of Stanislavsky's books could not fully supplant the lore. For the same reasons that actors hesitate to write about their art, they remain suspicious of texts that theorize about acting. While most theatre students own Stanislavsky's books, few read them. Instead they place the books on their shelves as totems of great theatre. As late as 1961, Strasberg criticized critics who wanted his practice of theatre to conform to the books' content. "Our knowledge of [Stanislavsky] came not from the books, but from work with people, rightly or wrongly, people who came from the Stanislavsky background and environment … Our knowledge came from the practice, not from the books" (LS 170:15 November 1961).

Oral traditions dominated in Russia as well. In 1961, Stanislavsky's son explained to his father's English translator, that "the fate of the System in your country is apparently the same as in ours: many speak about the System, a few read it, and a very few understand it" (Hapgood Archive). Indeed, lore is the main source of information about Stanislavsky's work in his home studio during the last four painfully isolated years of his life.

The role of lore in the dissemination of Stanislavsky's ideas should not be underestimated, but oral traditions have been only looked through, not at. Indeed, lore has often provided the invisible spectacles through which Stanislavsky's books are read. Even in 1957, when Robert Lewis attempted to make sense of the Russian's ideas, he did so in a series of public lectures. Any thorough attempt to discover the System's impact, therefore, must deal as fully with lore as with books.

The oral tradition in the US began when Boleslavsky stepped onto the stage of the Princess Theatre in 1923 to give the first series of lectures about the System. With the founding of the American Laboratory Theatre hot upon the heels of the Moscow Art Theatre's successful tour, Boleslavsky's lectures and Ouspenskaya's classes[2] influenced those who would shape US theatre from the 1930s until the present. To Strasberg, they were always "my teachers" (1987:84).

Émigrés were limited in their ability to speak for Stanislavsky in a number of ways, the first of which involves the very medium in which they taught. They communicated in an acquired language and thus began the process of linguistic and cultural transformation of the System into the Method. Boleslavsky's personal history presents a fascinating example of how language conditioned the oral transmission of Stanislavsky's ideas in the US. Boleslavsky may have sowed the ideals of Russian theatre from New York to Hollywood, yet his cultural loyalties were not only Russian; he was a Pole, hence a double émigré. He had relocated to Moscow in his teens, but he remained intimately bound to his native land, despite the fact that it did not exist as a separate country at the time of his birth. As he explained to a close friend, "You can say whatever you want about Poland, but you can not remake me, being a Pole. [...] Whatever I did was tinted very strongly by that only passion in me [...] Inside, I am just a Goddamned, obstinate Pole" (Roberts 1981:4). He had learned to speak standard Muscovite Russian as an actor. In fact, he acquired such flawless Russian, and used it so consistently, that even his wife did not know that he spoke another language until they were fleeing across the border to Poland with Soviet bullets in literal pursuit of them. Boleslavsky cried out to the border guards for protection in Polish (Roberts 1981:80–1).

As the first spokesperson for Stanislavsky in the US, Boleslavsky functioned in his third language, but he never spoke English fluently. J. W. Roberts speculates that he had good command, but had not developed sensitivity to its nuances (1981:186). A student at the Lab in 1926, Francis Fergusson, had a more pessimistic view. "His English was pretty terrible, but he would act out whatever he wanted to say, and that was good. He would act out almost everything he talked about" (Roberts 1981:149). His accent functioned creatively to help cause the infamous confusion between "affective" memory (referring to the emotions) and what his students understood as "effective" memory. (It did, indeed, work well!) Similarly, the "bits" of each scene, strung together like "beads" on a string all became musical "beats" when pronounced with his accent.

The émigré teachers' second limitation is of much greater complexity than their accents. Linguistic translation always involves simultaneous cultural translation, which, more often than not transforms ideas into hybrids. Even when we think we understand a translated word, we may still not comprehend its underlying cultural assumptions. This process of cultural displacement played a significant part in the oral transmission of Stanislavsky's System. Listeners in the United States actively filtered Russian ideas through their own social expectations and backgrounds, with cultural contexts sometimes transcending individual interpretation. This subtle form of miscommunication turned Stanislavsky's System into Strasberg's Method even more dynamically than the linguistic barriers of awkward English.

The centrality of emotion in the Method is a case in point. American popular interest in Freud made the subconscious and introspective aspects of Stanislavsky's work most intriguing. Students at the American Laboratory Theatre seized actively upon these, and paid less attention to other issues, such as action.[3] Clurman explained that, "the American, who, being part of an extroverted society which makes the world of *things* outside himself the focus of his hourly concern, seems to find in the technique of affective memory a revelation" (1958:256). In short, Boleslavsky's students listened selectively.

By the 1950s, the Method mirrored America's obsession with the Freudian model of the mind by employing therapeutic techniques meant to free the inhibited actor from long-lived repressions. Many members of the Studio visited therapists as regularly as acting classes and Strasberg naturally adapted to his students' experience (Krasner in McFarren 2003:195). Affective Memory (the recall of emotional moments in one's personal past) became the Method's corner-stone (Chapter 8). Stanislavsky may have taught that if the given circumstances in the play are clear, if the actor's senses and imagination are working, then "all the actor needs is action," but Strasberg disagreed. "Well, I say, if all these things are there, I can afford the luxury of not having the action" (LS 2:10 April 1956). Sessions at the Actors Studio probed members' private inhibitions and their inti-mate feelings. Indeed, actors must confront their deepest fears as they learn to act, Strasberg explained in 1962, because these fears arouse their most powerful reactions; "they 'oil' the entire instrument" (LS 169:2 January 1962). Strasberg's Private Moment exercise, in which actors recreate behavior they would normally never do in front of others, like taking a shower, further facilitated his psychoana-lytic approach. While Strasberg was accused in the press of practicing psycho-therapy without a license, his attitudes reveal a specifically American reading of Boleslavsky's teaching. Strasberg's sometimes cruel attempts to break down actors' inhibitions seem a far cry from Stanislavsky's own belief that Affective Memory serves as a gentle "lure" (SS II 1989:318) for the creative imagination, and an even further cry from Stanislavsky's later Method of Physical Actions or Active Analysis.

The process, by which this shift in emphasis occurred, depended as much upon what Boleslavsky's students expected to hear, as it did upon what Boleslavsky himself actually had to say. Reception changes meaning. In a lecture given at the Lab in 1925 Boleslavsky expressed his deep frustration with this dynamic particu-larly in regard to the use of emotion:

> It seems to me that I shall have to speak once more—and again try to make myself clear—on a certain part of the method. From what I hear and from a couple of letters that I have received from you, some minds do not seem to catch the point. I do not think it is the fault of my English, or my words, or of the way I explain. It is probably something much deeper. For me, the question is clear, but you do not understand ... You do not [...] understand the way of using the feelings.
>
> (Roberts 1981:165–6)

Clearly he understood how culture affected his words.

Boleslavsky's students turned the oral transmission of knowledge into an art itself. The creation of lore pervades the entire history of the Group Theatre. In 1930, Harold Clurman and Lee Strasberg began holding meetings for actors interested in banding together to revolutionize theatre. They met every Friday night after the theatres closed, and exhorted actors to love art and to embrace the ideals of the Moscow Art Theatre. Clurman would philosophize for hours. Many listeners recall his talks as "inspirational." The young designer Boris Aronson quipped that "if he wouldn't have been the director of the Group Theatre, he would have been Father Divine," the Depression era's most famous preacher (Chinoy 1976:485). Another recalls that Clurman "would tell marve-lous stories about Stanislavsky," analyze every conceivable aspect of theatre, "and, you know, he can go on forever" (Chinoy 1976:538). Clurman's talent as a speaker brought loyal converts into the fold. As Kazan put it:

> Harold was able to make us believe that a Group Theatre was the only course that would give our lives worth. [… He] railed in the manner of a visionary, calling into being what does not exist. I believed that a great theatre had been born and that it would be unlike any other that existed in this country. When he was through, I was an altered man.
>
> (1988:62)

These recollections echo those of Stockton, who had described Boleslavsky's 1923 lectures "like the coming of a new religion which could liberate and awaken American culture" (Roberts 1981:108).

Beginning with Clurman's lectures, which mesmerized his listeners, filling them with messianic fervor, and continuing with Strasberg's classes during the first summer of rehearsals, orality shaped the Group Theatre. Lectures, anecdotes, and harangues dominated the training of its actors. Even when the Group sought written sources to buttress what they had learned from their émigré teachers, they turned texts into oral experiences. Their cook, Mark Schmidt, who knew Russian, translated material written by Stanislavsky's foremost students (Evgeny Vakhtangov's diaries, Michael Chekhov's notes, etc.) and by Russian theatre scholars (Pavel Markov's history of the First Studio, Nikolai Volkov's biography of Meyerhold, etc.) (Garfield 1980:30).[4] After rehearsals, the actors and directors would gather together and listen with "romantic awe" as Schmidt would read to them (Clurman 1957:85).

One of the major legends of the Method dates back to 1934. Unhappy with Strasberg's emphasis on emotion at the Group Theatre, Stella Adler had travelled to Paris to meet Stanislavsky in order to test Strasberg's word against the master's (Clurman 1957:129–31; Vinogradskaia IV 2003:288–9).[5] Adler's and Stanislavsky's memories of this now mythological meeting vary greatly.

Adler describes it as accidental, and herself as uncharacteristically "reticent" in the presence of such an overwhelming and influential person (1988:119). In contrast, Stanislavsky recalls her as "a completely panic-stricken woman," who sought him out purposefully. "Frightened to death, she rushed off in pursuit of me. She went to Nice, did not find me there, and eventually caught up with me in Paris" (Filippov 1977:59). In Adler's account, Stanislavsky gently persuaded her to confide in him: "'Young lady, everybody has spoken to me but you.' That was the moment that I looked at him, eye to eye, we were together. I heard myself saying, 'Mr. Stanislavski, I loved the theatre until you came along, and now I hate it!'" (1988:120). Stanislavsky recalled a different emotional tenor: "She clutched me and cried, 'You've destroyed me! You must save me!'" (Filippov 1977:59). He agreed to work with her on a scene which she was preparing from John Howard Lawson's *The Gentlewoman*. "Stanislavsky knew America," Adler wrote. "He was very anxious to get some kind of clarity about his work through me" (Chinoy 1976:508). He too felt that his System was somehow at stake: "They say my method is being introduced in America, yet suddenly this talented actress who has studied my system 'withers away' before everyone's eyes. I had to take her on, if only to restore the reputation of my system. I wasted a whole month on it" (Filippov 1977:59).

However recalled, this meeting was fateful in the emigration of Stanislavsky's ideas to the United States, and further added to the oral tradition surrounding Stanislavsky's name. When Adler spoke to the Group Theatre that summer on then unfamiliar aspects of the System, she challenged Strasberg's sole authority. Meisner recalled that she specifically opposed Strasberg's take on Affective Memory with new information on how the play's "given circumstances" shape character, the power of the actor's imagination, and what would come to be known as the Method of Physical Actions (Chinoy 1976:119–20). Lewis reports, that Strasberg reacted by calling a counter meeting on the next day to announce that "he taught the Strasberg Method, not the Stanislavski System." He particularly defended his emphasis on emotion, saying "that we used the practice of Affective Memory in our own way, for our own results" (1984:71). On that day Strasberg described both the gulf that had opened between the American and Russian evolutionary branches of Stanislavsky's work, and a rift in the American theatre that continues to exist into the twenty-first century. Internet subscription lists for actors and directors show that Adler's and Strasberg's debate remains as provocative as it was in 1934 (Carnicke 2001).

The conflict between Adler and Strasberg not only set into motion endless debates about acting, but also betrays two more essential aspects of the oral transmission of Stanislavsky's System. In the first case, their argument dramatizes how intimately actor training is driven by personality. Strasberg and Adler ultimately emphasized elements of the System which suited their own needs best. As all actors do, they chose tools that compensated for their individual strengths and weaknesses. Strasberg was a distant, unemotional person, famous for not greeting people as he passed them in the halls. Kazan wrote that "unyielding remoteness was habitual with Lee" (1988:61). Adler deemed him a "fanatical, unsocial personality—untheatrical" (Chinoy 1976:508). Geraldine Page more kindly called him "pathologically shy" (Munk 1966:256). As recently as 2001, he was remembered as "volatile and aloof" (Schiffman 2001:4). Recall of personal emotions and Private Moment exercises were clearly necessary to Strasberg in his own work on himself. Adler, in contrast, exhibited an extravagant personality, entering rooms with her entourage in tow, clearly enjoying attention. As she herself put it, "I had a flair" (Chinoy 1976:507). Strasberg describes her as having "a very full, vivid emotion, but one which frankly rubbed me the wrong way" (Chinoy 1976:550). He felt that she needed reining in. For Adler, emotional risibility did not present an acting problem. She needed, instead, structure and craft to temper her. Thus, she naturally found Stanislavsky's work on the play's given circumstances and actions helpful.

In the second case, the very nature of the System made it difficult to speak accurately for Stanislavsky and encouraged debates. Stanislavsky had never envisioned his System as complete. He suggested no final answers, only various experiments. As he cautioned, "There is no System. There is only nature. My life-long concern has been how to get ever closer to what is called 'the System,' that is, to get ever closer to the nature of creativity" (SS III 1990:371). He had progressed through many stages in his quest. He explored the power of imagination and fantasy ("magic if"); he studied Yoga (relaxation, visualization, communication by means of rays of energy); he looked into the psychology of emotion (Affective Memory) and behaviorism (the Method of Physical Actions); he asked how the actor could better work with the play's text (Active Analysis).

In the 1934 debate, Strasberg emphasized Stanislavsky's early concerns. After all, Strasberg had been a student of Boleslavsky and Ouspenskaya; they had encountered the System in its earliest stages of development as members of Stanislavsky's First Studio. At the American Laboratory Theatre, they had continued to teach Sense Memory (remembering the smell of coffee or the taste of lemons) and exercises based in Yoga. In contrast, Adler's report featured aspects of Stanislavsky's later work. When she met him in Paris, he was in the process of developing a method of physical actions, which suggests that the emotional life of a character results from the actors' physical behavior more directly than from Affective Memory. Thus, she brought back his later focus on scoring (or listing) a character's physical activities over the course of the play. Taken together, Strasberg and Adler—the one reflecting early and the other later Stanislavsky—do not represent a radical change in the System as is often assumed, but rather a cross-section of the master's continuing experiments.

When Stanislavsky worked with Adler, he had felt that her understanding of the System was not so much incorrect as incomplete (Filippov 1977:59). She had taken one piece of the puzzle for the whole. She was not alone. All teachers of the System necessarily reflect whatever stage of Stanislavsky's work they had learned. As Jean Benedetti explains, teachers in the West understood Stanislavsky's ideas differently depending on "*when* they were taught" (1982:72). Similarly, Polish born director Jerzy Grotowski acknowledges that, "During the numerous years of research, [Stanislavsky's] method evolved, but not his disciples." Moreover, Grotowski sees in this fact, the source of conflicts like that between Adler and Strasberg. "Stanislavsky had disciples for each of his periods and each disciple is limited to his particular period; from that came discussions like those of theology" (1968:206). Neither were Russian actors and teachers immune. Stanislavsky's last assistant noted that each group of his students took a different part of what he gave and created from it a "secret cult of knowledge" (Knebel' 1968:46).

In contrast, Stanislavsky remained all-embracing. He could count each technique important without discounting the necessity of others, even when they seemed somehow logically contradictory. He could see both Strasberg and Adler as right, while they bitterly argued with each other.

Undoubtedly, the most persistent and influential voice in the creation of the Method's oral tradition was that of Lee Strasberg, whose teaching had begun with the founding of the Group Theatre in 1931 and continued until his death in 1982. Like his teachers, Strasberg too was an émigré and taught in an acquired language. He had arrived in the United States in 1909, an emigrant child from Galicia, then part of the Austro-Hungarian Empire. He lived with his uncle, a rabbinical teacher, attended the local Hebrew School, and learned English relatively late. Until his death he retained not only an accent and faulty grammar, but a "Talmudic" (Lewis 1984:42) speaking style that reflected his roots.

Audio-tape recordings of Strasberg's sessions at the Actors Studio from 1956 to 1969[6] captured the powerful rhetoric by which he introduced three generations of actors to Stanislavsky. His critiques were recorded in order that actors could study his comments in depth. Consequently, the recording machine, which was snapped on at the end of each scene or exercise, sadly relegated the actors' work to oblivion, but fortunately preserved the idiosyncratic and colorful language, which distinguished Strasberg's voice from those of others who participated in the development of the Method's lore.

Strasberg spoke in "serpentine wanderings" (Hirsch 1984:153–4) that could seem crystal clear to those in touch with his basic assumptions about acting, while utterly unintelligible to others. He would often begin a sentence, run on and on, until like a wind-up mechanism, he would eventually come to a stop.[7] He knew how confusing his speech could seem. In speaking to Studio member, Viveca Lindfors, about the actor's "peculiar logic of work," he said:

> It sounds so weird when you put it, "Should I be she, should I be me," and so on. I don't know, people listening—I sometimes wonder. She... Me... Because we ourselves get confused, yet we know what we're talking about. [...] I'm sure that people coming here say, "What the hell is this, what is this kind of existentialist talk?" ... if they were philosophic. If they weren't, they'd say, "They're utterly crazy, I think those people are nuts. I thought acting is acting. You get up on the stage, you've got the author's words, my God, you've got a director, he tells you where to stand. What the hell more do you want?" Well, we know that it isn't quite so simple, so easy.
>
> (LS 167:19 December 1961)

His rhetoric could indeed appear muddled and self-contradictory.

Nonetheless, he could also brilliantly marshal ellipses and parallel constructions to inspire actors, as he did when he told Studio members that acting "demands a greater application, not less, a greater logic, not less, a greater definition, not less. Otherwise, we are left only with the desire to do and not knowing how" (LS A31:27 December 1957). Such a passage exposes his ability to speak forcefully. That he manipulated language consciously was obvious. In a humorous mood, Strasberg admitted to using "philosophic" words "because they're impressive and therefore make you think, you know, that I'm saying something" (LS A31:20 December 1957).

His listeners either despised or loved his convoluted speech. In an apparent parody of Strasberg's own doublespeak, one critic wrote that in Strasberg's prose "the obvious presence of thought does little to hide the absence of thinking" (Munk 1966:265). Actress Madeleine Thornton Sherwood studied Strasberg's comments on her scene, only to complain, "I can't understand what you're saying. I went and listened to the damned tape and I heard it three times" (LS A88 10 January 1967). Her frustration did not lessen with time. In a later interview, she explained that after joining the Actors

Studio, "I soon realized that I didn't know what [Lee] was talking about" (Hirsch 1984:153).

In contrast, most members felt that his teaching changed their lives, that he spoke not only to their minds but to their hearts. Crawford recalled, "The actors responded to Lee's teaching the way hungry people respond to bread. It fed them" (1977:222). Those who best understood him thought of his words as verbal reflections of what they experienced in performance. As Shelley Winters said: "You have to do it. Nothing here can be understood—you experience what takes place" (LS A88:10 January 1967). Robert Hethmon, who transcribed many of the recordings, agreed: "Sometimes *what* [Strasberg] says, taken literally, does not make sense. Only when it is understood that he is making his point through a total response to what the actor has done, through a *total* communication, can one detect his purpose" (1991:17). More simply put by Geraldine Page, "Lee's very Zen in the way he teaches" (Munk 1966:256). At an international symposium in Paris in 1988, some of Strasberg's most famous students refused to answer questions about the Method, invoking its experiential level (*L'Actors Studio*: 4 November 1989). Foster Hirsch eloquently describes the paradox of Strasberg's language: "For all his verbal foibles, he was a powerful wielder of words, employing them with remarkable skill to wound, and to cure, to strike and to soften, to goad, galvanize, berate, to arouse, and to silence. [...] Yes, he was a terrible speaker and a great one" (1984:153–4).

However confusing Strasberg might seem, he rarely bored his audience. He peppered his speech with metaphors drawn from the most sophisticated to the most mundane of spheres in an attempt to express the inexpressible art of acting. In one breath, he might eloquently say that "the technique with which we play the piece of modern music is the same technique with which we play a piece of Tchaikovsky" (LS A1:26 November 1963), that "the actor is at once the piano and the pianist" (Strasberg 1974:59), or that "paint is not yet a painting" (LS A5:5 January 1965). In the next breath, he might draw upon less lofty associations. "If I give you a baseball bat, you still have to know what to do with it to hit the ball" (LS A62:10 April 1965). To an actor, who cannot relax enough to perform properly, he might say, "When a car stalls, you turn the key, push the pedal down to turn it over. [...] If the motor doesn't turn over and you proceed as if the car is working, you're fooling no one but yourself" (LS A150-1:20 October 1960).

Many of his most humorous metaphors involve food. Responding to an actor's unexpected or poor performance, he might say that "a whole apple is better than half a pear—especially if you want an orange" (Lewis 1984:42) or that "the stove has only pretended to cook" (LS A150-1:29 October 1968). Adding water to frozen orange juice concentrate, he taught, is like adding emotion to the words of a play (LS 45:14 February 1958). Echoing Stanislavsky's device for explaining how, like a roast turkey, a role can be carved into smaller bits and made especially tasty with an Affective Memory sauce, Strasberg advises that "If you have a tough piece of meat and you have to serve it to guests tonight, and you ask 'What can I do with this?' I'll tell you, 'Use a sauce.' That doesn't mean I don't prefer you to buy better meat" (LS A67:31 May 1966).

Metaphors drawn from medicine, perhaps inspired by his success with the medical drama *Men in White* at the Group Theatre, are among his most startling. Critiquing an actor's work is like a doctor diagnosing an ailment: "I could make a mistake on my prescription, just as a doctor can make a misdiagnosis, but that doesn't mean that surgery itself should be criticized" (LS 2:10 April 1956). Working at the Actors Studio, he tells its members, is like dissecting a corpse in medical school; actors need a place to work on "dead bodies" without worrying about whether "the patient lives" (LS 39:21 January 1958). Reading a script is like reading an X-ray: "A doctor looks at an X-ray and sees things in it that you don't see. Why? Because he's a doctor. When an actor looks at a script he sees things in it as an actor" (LS 39:21 January 1958).

The recordings also capture Strasberg, the gifted story-teller. At the Actors Studio, he functioned as an informal professor of theatre history, the Studio becoming his university. He lectured about major figures from history, among them Eleonora Duse, David Garrick, and Edmund Kean, as well as Stanislavsky. He formulated history into stories, culled from his voracious reading and from his own study with Russian émigrés. These stories became legends, repeated so often that members of the audience could recite them along with him, much as grandchildren might repeat often told family stories. He told of Sarah Siddons frightening herself in the attic while studying the role of Lady Macbeth, and thus finding her way into the mad scene. He related how Stanislavsky once kept the key to a locked cabinet in the pocket of his costume, despite the fact that he never opened the cabinet during performance, thus inducing in himself belief in the reality of his role. He described Duse's famous blush on stage. He even turned the experience of his students into stories about how psychological blocks in acting could be overcome. These anecdotes are the very substance of the oral tradition of acting.

As professor *cum* story-teller, Strasberg highlights yet another problem inherent in the oral transmission of Stanislavsky's ideas. Many of his stories revolve around Stanislavsky. Strasberg quotes the master, recounts his performances, analyzes, and criticizes his theories in almost every session. Despite Strasberg's great erudition, however, he was not a scholar who supplies footnotes. He misquotes sources and attributes suspect intentions to artists. Most of his stories are difficult at best to document. They become mythic rather than historical, to be taken on faith or rejected.

When such orally transmitted myths find their way into printed books about Stanislavsky, as they so often have, they can lead to confusion, even muddling what is irrefutable in the historical record. For example, the deeply ingrained but inaccurate myths that confine Stanislavsky's work to Psychological Realism are passed from generation to generation of actors despite irrefutable historical evidence that proves his turning away from this style as early as 1907. While books alone may be an imperfect way to understand an art based largely on tacit knowledge, practice without reference to documentation proves equally imperfect in transmitting acting theories to future generations of practitioners. The complex interplay between lore and written records thus becomes critical in disentangling Stanislavsky's thoughts from those of his protégés.

The Actors Studio tapes do more than capture Strasberg's unique speaking style and record his mythic stories. They literally embody the history of oral transmission that promoted and transformed Stanislavsky's ideas in the US. Strasberg's vocabulary about acting reveals his primary source of knowledge. Rather than words adopted from the later polished English translations of Stanislavsky's books, Strasberg uses terms he learned from "his teachers." For example, Strasberg does not use "objective" (as *zadacha* was translated by Hapgood) but the standard "problem" and "task" (Chapter 5).

More tellingly, Strasberg uses raw calques of the original Russian words: root-by-root translations which reflect Russian etymology. Thus, he regularly refers to the actor's "living through" of the role on stage, an awkward translation that was in the air in émigré circles and that literally mirrors the Russian roots in the word for "experiencing" (*perezhivanie*) (Chapter 7). Émigré Aleksandr Arnoldovich Koiransky, who served as interpreter for Stanislavsky in the US and taught design at Boleslavsky's school, regularly translated *perezhivanie* as "living through" (Senelick 1983:127–30). Recalling Stanislavsky's attempt to distinguish his unique type of theatre (*teatr perezhivaniia*) from that of others, Strasberg also speaks of someone trained in the System as "the actor of experience." Similarly, Strasberg discusses the actor's "self-feeling," reflecting the roots of the Russian word for a sense of self (*samochuvstvie*) (LS A62:15 April 1966).

Far from accurate translations, these calques clearly distort Stanislavsky's meaning. In *perezhivanie*, Stanislavsky invokes the experiential nature of acting, not naturalistic acting. In *teatr perezhivaniia*, he does not refer to actors with a lot of experience under their belts, but rather actors who are fully present on stage. In *samochuvstvie*, he labels the creative state of mind necessary for performance. These awkward translations persuasively testify to Strasberg's reliance on interpreters of Stanislavsky's ideas rather than on books. They directly reflect the vocabulary of his teachers, who created new words and bent their newly acquired language to suit their purposes whenever they did not know a standard English word that would do.

In sum, while embellishing the lore with his own unique style and personality, Strasberg passed along a specific oral tradition about the System, which had originated just after the Moscow Art Theatre's tours to the United States, was grounded in Boleslavsky's vocabulary, emphasized Stanislavsky's early work, and finally was modified through the linguistic and cultural dynamics of emigration. By the 1950s, Strasberg had become the living embodiment of this Stanislavskian tradition, with all its authority, charms, and limitations.

Practice as theory in the system

As those critics, who faulted Strasberg for not following Stanislavsky's books, could sense, the Method's lore had diverged from the System. Orally transmitted information is notoriously slippery. Like a game of telephone, in which whispered information gets distorted as it passes from one person to another, oral transmission surely transformed the master's unique ideas. Yet, oral tradition also goes to the heart of theatre practice. Stanislavsky too participated in the creation of lore by teaching. His Russian students too amended and modified his ideas according to their propensities (Chapters 6, 8 and 10).

In examining various modes of inquiry that have affected the teaching of writing, Stephen M. North distinguishes the activity of "practitioners," who operate on prescriptive, pragmatic knowledge, from "scholars," who depend upon published descriptive theory. Rather than assuming the usual relationship—that scholars "make knowledge" while practitioners "apply it"—North sees practice itself as generating new and legitimate knowledge (1987:20–6).

Actors, like writers, are practitioners, not theorists. As Peter Brook so aptly notes, theatrical "aesthetics are practical," based upon an assumed and often unexamined "working system," which constantly prompts "value-judgements." "A chair is moved up or down stage, because it's 'better so.' Two columns are wrong, but adding a third makes them 'right'—the words 'better,' 'worse,' 'not so good,' 'bad,' are [used] day after day, but these words which rule decisions carry no moral sense whatever" (1968:89–90). As Strasberg similarly quipped, an idea may be theoretically wrong, but if it helps the actor, it is good; if it is theoretically right, but does not help the actor, it is not good. "I never do anything because anybody else said so, because Stanislavsky said so. I do something because I think it works" (LS 162:14 November 1961; Hethmon 1991:40).

Strasberg's disdain for scholars, who deign to discuss theatre, reveals his ultimate reliance upon lore. Despite avid reading, he felt that only "theatre people" who have direct experience of performance, can speak effectively about acting and its history. As he said in 1956, "All this discussion, all these theories, all this thing about wanting to solve something by having an opinion, I think you're right and you're wrong, it's crazy. It is suicidal in the theatre. And the only thing that counts is what you see" (LS 9:29 October 1956). In short, effective practice is more important to artists than accurate understanding of theory. This is no less true for Stanislavsky. "I am a practitioner," the Russian observes, "and it is not through words but through work that I can help you know, that is feel, artistic truth" (SS II 1989:273).

Knowledge generated by practice becomes shared in lore more satisfactorily than in theoretical books. In the first place, practice escapes verbal boundaries. It taps an experiential realm called the "tacit dimension" by philosopher Michael Polanyi (1966:3–25). Actors know more than they can say. Acting, like riding a bicycle, is easier to do than to explain. Strasberg's apparently incomprehensible language spoke so powerfully to generations of actors, because it communicated despite the words. Oral tradition that allows for verbal approximations, subtle restatements, parables, and metaphors encodes "tacit knowledge" better than clear expository prose.

Secondly, as a pragmatic system, theatre knowledge can contain mutually contradictory ideas as theory cannot; it can evolve and shift dynamically from day to day as need demands, with each practitioner tinkering and adjusting it to suit the moment. North visualizes "The House of Lore" as "a rambling [...] delightful old manse, wing branching off from wing, addition tacked to addition, in all sorts of materials—brick, wood, canvas, sheet metal, and spires, spiral staircases, rope ladders, pitons, dungeons, secret passageways" (1987:27). Passed from generation to generation amended and modified by each actor and teacher who adopted it, the oral tradition about Stanislavsky in the US perfectly resembles this house. In Russia, a separate house was built. While encompassing the messy reality of practice, such houses are nonetheless solid structures, based upon a consistent attitude toward the actor's work and a solid core of information which informs the whole. Lore may appear to be "random," North reminds us, but all its various elements are indeed "connected."

Written theory, which demands neat and selective editing, is often not as flexible as lore. Practitioners, North observes, seldom turn their work into theory. Practice tends toward routine, adapts old solutions to new problems, and remains a conservative form of knowledge (1987:33–6). Stanislavsky's enduring importance to the theatrical world thus rests upon a rare project: to exploit practice in order to generate theory. His obsessive journals, his study of how great actors work, and his dissection of his own performances, all testify to his use of practice as inquiry. Had his project remained in the classroom or rehearsal hall, Stanislavsky's career would have differed little from that of other fine actors and directors who taught. But he took his project one step further, paradoxically using oral tradition to generate a written one. "I believe that all masters of the arts need to write," he said, "to try and systematize their art" (Filippov 1977:58).

Stanislavsky knew how difficult it would be to accomplish his goal when he wrote to his translator on 2 February 1937. While he felt that he had found "sufficient words" for his autobiography, which "speaks of facts and events in my life," he struggled "to convey the subtleties of creative work. And I can not," he stressed, "I can not satisfy myself." Capturing the practice of acting in words demanded a new kind of creativity. "For art and psychology, one needs to think up more and more new words," he wrote in 1937. "Without them, one has to take evasive action, to choose a form, a mood, employ comparisons, juxtapositions, examples, whole scenes, and that's very hard, and takes a great deal of time" (SS IX 1999:671). In this list, Stanislavsky enumerates the many rhetorical strategies, that he uses in his acting manuals, and that Strasberg would use later, to describe "the tacit dimension" of acting.

As early as 1923, Stanislavsky had decided upon a form that would allow him to incorporate lore directly into his acting manuals. In a letter home, written between the two US tours, he called his planned book "'the system' in a novel" (SS IX 1999:99). By creating a fictional classroom, he mirrors the oral dimension of acting classes and minimizes the need for neat theory in expository prose. He portrays, rather than explains, the process and practice of acting, thus maintaining an "experiential structure," in North's terminology (1987:23). His Russian editor found this "half-fictional form [...] very well suited to its content" (Dybovskii 1992:110). In this form, however, Stanislavsky also permitted himself multiple examples and restatements of each idea, a style which was condemned for apparent redundancy by his US publishers.

In his imagined classroom, Stanislavsky casts himself in two roles. As the naive and overanxious young student, Nazvanov, whose name means "the chosen one" and whose journal becomes the fictional conceit of the book, Stanislavsky depicts his own lifelong obsessive desire to record experiments into acting. In this younger portrait of himself, Stanislavsky also borrows traits from one of his favourite students, Evgeny Vakhtangov who knew shorthand. As Tortsov, the famous and experienced master before whom Nazvanov stands in awe, Stanislavsky depicts himself in his later years, confidently teaching some aspects of the System ("magic if," the centrality of action, "given circumstances" in the play, etc.), while humbly seeking to gain a greater understanding of others (such as the "ocean of the subconscious"). In an earlier draft, Stanislavsky had named his fictional teacher Tvortsov, which means "Creator," thus stressing the fact that the System seeks the secret to creativity itself (SS IV 1991:175–261). As Nazvanov and Tortsov interact in the System's novel, "the elder Stanislavski meets the young actor he once was" (Benedetti 1982:55).

Stanislavsky further endows Tortsov's students with personalities that depict the types of people attracted to acting, and their various attitudes; in some cases he unfortunately relies upon obvious stereotypes. The handsome, arrogant Govorkov, whose name means "the talker," debates continuously with Tortsov. The blond, vain Velyamin ova, whose name signifies her intensity, tends to love herself in art more than art in herself. The insightful Shustov forms a direct genealogical link to nineteenth century traditions of acting, since he has learned much from his uncle who is a famous actor of the old school. This character was originally named "Chuvstvov," the word for "feelings" in Russian thus betokening his "sensitive" and "emotional" nature. The shy and vulnerable young actress, Maloletkova (meaning "of tender years"), combines humility, innate talent, and enthusiasm for learning with a tendency to get upset. Stanislavsky creates arguments, conflicts, and alliances among these characters. They challenge each other and their teacher; support each other with suggestions and critiques. They get confused, lose their way, but occasionally break through to a viable understanding of acting. In short, Stanislavsky creates his own fictional version of the System's lore.

Stanislavsky's success in suggesting the dynamic processes of acting can be judged by his imitators. His example inspired an entire genre of acting texts that utilize fictional frames. Boleslavsky presents *Acting: the First Six Lessons* as if it were a dialogue between an older, wiser teacher and a young, talented, but naive actress, its form mirroring that of a play. While Sanford Meisner does not change his name and *persona* in his 1987 book, he follows Stanislavsky's lead by portraying the classroom rather than expounding upon theories of acting. Meisner explicitly admits that he had written an earlier, theoretical book. But he was "bitterly disappointed" with the "confessional mode," because theatre is "an arena where human personalities interlock in the reality of doing." He further explains that, "In [this book], I appear […] as I am: a teacher, surrounded by gifted students, of a difficult and ultimately mysterious art, that of acting" (Meisner and Longwell 1987: xviii). Meisner's reasoning recapitulates Stanislavsky's own; Meisner too wishes to expose the practice of acting.

Unlike oral tradition of real classrooms, Stanislavsky's fictional lore is modified by the very act of writing. Despite the fact that Stanislavsky successfully approximates the oral dimension of actor training in his books, he necessarily bends to the demand of the written word. While the books remain a mirror of the practice from which they spring, they also suffer from the enormous problems inherent in describing dynamic but tacit knowledge verbally. He simplifies and categorizes as he writes. He turns messy practice into neat theory. He makes cogent prose from often contradictory experiences. He stops his process of experimentation long enough to fix it into words. His legendary dissatisfaction with draft after draft and his notorious reliance upon editors both in the USSR and in the US testify to his belief that the very words he wrote robbed his ideas of their vitality. "What does it mean to write a book about the System?" he asked his translator in 1936. "It does not mean describing something that's complete and ready-made. The System lives within me, but in an unformed state. When you begin to seek a form for it, only then does the System become established and defined" (SS IX 1999:658–9).

By fictionalizing his books, Stanislavsky admits the necessity of lore for actors. By writing, he acknowledges the need for definitive statements on the many facets of the System. Thus, in his books Stanislavsky reproduces the tension between oral and written sources about acting, each type vying for greater authority and credibility. A similar tension between the authoritative voice in the classroom and a search for accurate information about the System characterized the atmospheres at the American Laboratory Theatre, the Group Theatre, and the Actors Studio.

By placing the Method's oral tradition (embodied in the words of Strasberg) next to the System's lore (as encoded by Stanislavsky in his books) the distance between them can be measured (Chapters 7–10). However, before this measurement can be considered accurate, the publication history of Stanislavsky's books also must be weighed, specifically their abridgement in the US (Chapter 5) and censorship in the USSR (Chapter 6).

5　The US publication maze

Stanislavsky abridged

The given circumstances[1]

The long anticipated publication of *An Actor Prepares* in 1936 appeared to offer a definitive English-language source of information for theatre practitioners, who had searched avidly for rules of the System in a charged atmosphere of disagreement. Couldn't American theatre people now test lore against the written word? But this book did not answer questions so much as raise new ones.

As early as 1954, Henry Schnitzler discovered discrepancies between *An Actor Prepares* and its Russian counterpart when he read an alternative but unpublished English translation. He then compared both *An Actor Prepares* and *Building a Character* to unauthorized German translations in order to confirm his feeling that the former is not the complete System, and the latter shows "a surprising lack of editorial care" (1954:13). Theatre Arts Books saw Schnitzler's article on these discrepancies as an attack. In response, the books' translator, Elizabeth Reynolds Hapgood, asked her friend, the former Moscow Art Theatre actress Varvara Bulgakova, to write a reply. Bulgakova vouched for Hapgood's accurate representation of the System. Additionally, the publisher arranged for a comparison of the Russian and English versions, resulting in a notarized statement that nothing substantial had been eliminated in the editorial process (Hapgood Archive; Munk 1966:181).

Time and time again the differences between the two editions were dismissed as either unimportant or the necessary polishing of Stanislavsky's long-winded prose. Hapgood certainly saw the latter as her primary job. In her introduction to *Creating a Role* she writes: "I have carried out once more the task entrusted to me by Stanislavski himself, to eliminate duplications and cut whatever was meaningless for non-Russian actors" (1961:ix). Russian scholar and translator David Magarshack suggests the same: "The main fault of this American edition of Stanislavsky's great work is that it leaves out a great deal of the original book" (1980:27 n.). As recently as 1989, Mel Gordon called any criticism of the Hapgood books a "shibboleth" because, in his estimation, Stanislavsky is a poor writer who uses unclear neologisms (45–6).

But many who could read either Russian or German found the differences significant. While Magarshack equivocated publicly, he complained bitterly in private about the inadequacy of the English versions for scholarly purposes (Theatre Arts

Books Archive). Critic Eric Bentley preferred the German translations as "admirably complete," specifically noting that references to Théodule Ribot, the psychologist from whom Stanislavsky took the term "affective memory," do not appear in English. "Mystery is created," he laments, "when a translator decides to leave out so much that is of interest." Like Magarshack, Bentley felt that such deletions deterred serious study (1962:128).[2]

Suspicions about the English books percolated from the scholarly community into the professional theatre world. In 1969, Strasberg warned that Stanislavsky's "books give a wrong impression." He laid blame at Hapgood's feet: "The American editions are edited […] not by Stanislavsky, but by the translator, who has made herself responsible […] for the presentation of the Stanislavsky material in a form that she considers to be suitable" (LS:15 January 1961). He too relied upon the German, explaining in a letter to the editor of the *Tulane Drama Review* that "for those unable to consult [the] Russian […] valuable discussions of the Stanislavski system can be consulted in German translations. I am surprised that so little attention has been paid to them by all the American experts" (1966:239). He lists the German books in his *Encyclopaedia Britannica* article on "Acting" as "essential for serious study" (1974:63).

To understand how these detectable differences came about, we must examine the "given circumstances" under which Stanislavsky decided to publish *An Actor Prepares* first in English, a language he could neither speak nor read. Three specific circumstances must be disentangled: his attitude towards writing, the commercial pressures of American publishing, and the Soviet political context that prompted him to make such an unusual decision.

First, Stanislavsky had long resisted publishing anything about the actor's art, fearing that print would turn experimental attitudes into dogma. He had obsessively kept personal notes on acting since age fourteen. But publication threatened to fix his ever-changing ideas into unalterable forms. Just as compulsively as he revised and perfected his System did he alter and expand his writing. All his texts are works in progress. As Jean Benedetti, Stanislavsky's first postmodern translator, writes, "A notion of a fixed, once-for-all text is entirely alien to [his] spirit of enquiry and research" (1982:300).

Stanislavsky devoted nearly half his life to writing a publishable acting manual. As early as 1899, he identified the need for an actor's "grammar." In 1904 he drafted one, but two years later he completely rethought its rules. In 1908, he organized his massive accumulation of notes into discrete topics in preparation for a book. In 1909, with his System already in use as a rehearsal technique, he tentatively introduced some of its most famous and infamous terms in yet another manuscript. During 1910 he generated dozens of drafts and potential titles.

Stanislavsky was so slow to finalize anything that others beat him to the punch. Director Fyodor Komissarzhevsky published *The Actor's Creativity and the Stanislavsky Theory* in 1917. Stanislavsky wrote "Lies!" in the margins of his copy (SS VII 1960:737). In 1919, actor Michael Chekhov published a two part journal article based upon work at the First Studio (M. Chekhov 1995 II:31–58). Chekhov's friend and Stanislavsky's protégé Evgeny Vakhtangov responded publicly. He attacked Komis-

sarzhevsky for producing a description entirely unrecognizable to those who practiced the System and criticized Chekhov for laying out its elements without providing
sufficient theoretical context. "It seems to me," Vakhtangov writes in defense of his
mentor, "that only the person who created this method is capable of giving a 'complete
and detailed presentation'" (Vendrovskaya and Kaptereva 1982:126).

While these publications spurred Stanislavsky's desire to complete an acting
manual, he abandoned yet another version drafted during the US tours to write more
saleable memoirs (Bancroft Typescript). Only in 1928, after a serious heart attack
forced him to stop acting, did he focus squarely on the project. By November 1930
he appeared to have a finished typescript, but one so long that he reluctantly split it
into two volumes; and still he continued to work. After several deadline extensions,
Yale University Press lost patience and dropped their contract with him (Dybovskii
1992:92). In 1935, he finally let go of one version of the first volume, sending it to
Hapgood for publication and labeling it "definitive for America." *An Actor Prepares*
is a significantly abridged translation of this version. Stanislavsky continued to
expand, rewrite, and modify chapter after chapter. His labor ended only with his
death in 1938. His last and most complete draft, *An Actor's Work on Himself, Part I*,[3]
appeared in the USSR following significant censorship (Chapter 6).

Part II became further dissociated from *Part I*. The vagaries of war delayed its
publication on both sides of the Atlantic. In Russia, *An Actor's Work on Himself,
Part II* first appeared in 1948. The English variant, *Building a Character*, appeared
in 1949, a full thirteen years after *An Actor Prepares*. Thus, for more than a decade
half of the System appeared to be the whole. The effect of this delay was less
detrimental in Moscow, since the Russian title suggests a sequel. In contrast, the
commercially appealing English title sounds more self-contained.

If *An Actor Prepares* differs from the Russian *Part I, Building A Character* differs
even more from *Part II*. Stanislavsky had left his second volume incomplete; as a
consequence Hapgood and the Russian editors used different drafts to assemble their
books. Therefore, the two versions vary so greatly that even sequences of material do
not always match. At his death, Stanislavsky also left a myriad of unfinished drafts
for his projected third volume. These drafts too were edited and ordered differently,
appearing in Russia as *An Actor's Work on the Role* in 1957 and in the US as *Creating
a Role* in 1961.

Stanislavsky clearly felt unable to express himself in a way that matched his
internal understanding of the actor's experience. He struggled to get what he knew
on paper, only to go over and over the same territory. His inability to say exactly
what he meant and his consequent frustration can be traced in correspondence
with his long time friend and editor Lyubov Yakovlevna Gurevich (1866–1940).
He punctuates a long letter from 1930 with sentences like: "*I can not arrange my
enormous amount of material and I'm drowning in it.*" "You are afraid to change
my face. But the pity is I myself don't know my own face." "Promise me that
you'll believe me when I say that I have absolutely no *literary ambition*." "I know
that I am not a writer. What should I do, when I consider myself obliged to set
down what I can't manage" (SS IX 1999:437–41).

In frustration, he often delegated responsibility for finishing his texts to others.

My Life in Art is an amusing case in point. Stanislavsky was "in a panic" when the publishers threatened to drop the project if he could not deliver a complete manuscript in two weeks. He turned to Aleksandr Arnoldovich Koiransky, for help. A theatre critic and poet who had resettled in the US shortly after the revolution and taught at the American Laboratory Theatre, Koiransky was serving as Stanislavsky's interpreter and guide during the US tours. Koiransky recounts:

> I sat down and, then and there, wrote the only passage I had contributed to the book, the one beginning with "There is no art that does not demand virtuosity …" In it I quoted Degas. When I read it to Stanislavsky he asked: "Who is Degas?" and added the last lines which conclude the book. That night we had dinner at Michel Fokine's. The host asked Stanislavsky how his book was coming. Stanislavsky looked unhappily at me across the table and said: "Well, Koiransky says that it is finished."
> (Letter accompanying Stanislavsky's Bancroft Typescript: 17 November 1960; Senelick 1983:203–4)

Koiransky was only first in a series of editors who helped Stanislavsky deliver final manuscripts to publishers. Gurevich encouraged him to write, then critiqued and assembled his books in Russia; Hapgood did so in the West; before his death Stanislavsky appointed yet another, a young student Grigory Kristi; and still later an entire Soviet commission took charge. During the 1930s, Stanislavsky asked anyone who visited him to take a look at drafts (Zon 1955), even sending a copy to the scientist Ivan Petrovich Pavlov (Chapter 8). Stanislavsky's letters to Gurevich dramatically testify to his growing reliance on others. In 1930 he writes: "Change, mark up, cross out everything that I have written. I give you *carte blanche*. I trust your knowledge completely." "You can tell me anything, you can do anything with my writing." "For every comment—I am grateful; to every change—I agree." "Do with the book what you like" (SS IX 1999:440–1). Again in 1931 he writes, "Truly, I have no one but you. Only you, and that's why I trust you more and more and beg you one more time to do with my book, whatever you wish" (SS IX 1999:465–6). Similar refrains echo in letters to Hapgood. "I trust your tact, taste, care," he writes. "Fix, cross out what is difficult to understand. Do everything that you think necessary" (Vinogradskaia IV 2003:368). In short, editors' tastes, talents and views need consideration when working with his books.

Of his many editorial relationships, his reliance on Gurevich was the most long-lived, extending more than thirty years. She had been publisher and chief editor for a leading Russian Symbolist journal before she became involved with the Moscow Art Theatre as literary advisor (Gurevich 1972). Because Stanislavsky had not finished school when he took over his father's business, he never felt well-educated and adopted her as his personal scholar. When he left for Finland in 1906, she assembled a reading list about acting for him. This reading became crucial in his creation of the System. While he toured Europe and America, she made sense of his piles of personal notebooks, so that he could better organize his book when he returned (SS IX 1999:123). In January 1930, he instructed his secretary that nothing of his could be printed without Gurevich's approval, including all Western editions (SS IX 1999:384). Over the years, Gurevich prodded him to finish his books, reassured him of their value, and nursed him through the entire trying process.

Stanislavsky's decision to publish *An Actor Prepares* in the US rather than in the USSR generated the second "given circumstance" that directly contributed to variations in his books. This decision was his most successful money-making scheme during the tours, because US and international copyright law insured that he earn immediate money on all translations and that future royalties go to his family. Under Soviet law, Stanislavsky could secure neither copyrights nor royalties. He explained to his co-director:

> You can't make a living in the theatre, I must never forget that, never. I have had to search out other ways, writing a book [for example]. You probably suspect that I'm doing this for pleasure. But you know my relationship to pens and paper. I am doing this only from the most extreme and heavy necessity.
>
> (SS IX 1999:136)

During the 1930s, when he could no longer act, US publication became an even more essential way to earn money. The American Laboratory Theatre in New York had offered him a stipend to teach, but his frail health and his decision to remain in Russia made such opportunities impractical.

Having tested the waters of Western publication in 1924 with *My Life in Art*, Stanislavsky formalized arrangements for all his books in 1930. While in France recuperating from his heart attack, he signed a legal agreement with US citizen Elizabeth Reynolds Hapgood (1894–1974), giving her power-of-attorney over all publications and translations into any language for his current and future books. The agreement was all encompassing, even including recording and movie rights (Theatre Arts Books Archive). This extraordinary agreement secured full copyright protection for his writings, whenever and wherever he finished them.

Stanislavsky had first befriended Hapgood in 1924; she had served as interpreter for him and his company when they were presented to Calvin Coolidge at the White House. She and her husband, theatre critic Norman Hapgood, worked diligently on his behalf for many years afterward. Although Soviet authorities permitted Stanislavsky to stay abroad in 1929 and 1930 to hasten recovery of his health, he struggled with living expenses. Responding to his near destitute state, the Hapgoods created a fund for him to which they and other friends contributed. The Hapgoods made it easy for Stanislavsky to accept the charity gracefully by telling him that a "stranger" had paid an advance for his book. When he summered in Badenweiler (Germany) in 1930, the Hapgoods stayed nearby, visiting him almost daily and helping him write as well as edit (Hobgood 1986:156–7). After the 1930 agreement until her death in 1974, Elizabeth functioned as "attorney-in-fact" of the Stanislavsky estate. In this capacity, she negotiated with Western translators and publishers for rights to his books, protected his financial and legal interests, and publicized his importance throughout the US and the world. Without her efforts, Stanislavsky's writings would certainly have taken much longer to be known outside Russia.

However smart from financial and legal points of view, Stanislavsky's decision to publish in the US had an ironic outcome. Copyright law protected problematic versions of his books into the twenty-first century.[4]

When Little, Brown and Co. rejected Stanislavsky's early draft of an acting "grammar" (Bancroft Typescript), requesting instead more commercially viable memoirs, he wrote *My Life in Art* hastily, so that it could appear during the second US tour. He worked, he said, "like a convict with only a few days left to live" (SS VIII 1961:87). He was unhappy with the results. "The contents," he wrote, "are not up to the [physical] book. I didn't think it would come out so ostentatiously. Of course, everything is made a hash of, there are absurd omissions, but there my inexperience is to blame. I hope to publish it in other languages as edited by me" (SS IX 1999:152). When he returned to Moscow, he completely revised the book, and at his death considered the Russian version definitive.[5]

Other publishers too found his beloved "grammar" about acting uncommercial. When Yale University Press rejected it, Theatre Arts Books agreed only on condition that Hapgood make significant cuts and modify obscure Russian references. Editor Edith Isaacs explained to Hapgood that the book appeared to her "practically useless to publish in this form," because it would not be accessible to "Anglo-Saxon" readers (Hobgood 1986:159).

Remembering his experience with *My Life in Art*, Stanislavsky had tried to insure against variations between the English and Russian "grammars" but to no avail. A Soviet lawyer advised him to retain the characters' exact names as a touchstone for comparison, but complicated Russian names were among the first changes demanded by Theatre Arts Books. Hapgood thus uses nicknames, rather than the formal names that appear in Russian. In the end, Stanislavsky reluctantly conceded to reality: the two editions would differ (SS IX 1999:643–6; Dybovskii 1992: 86, 101).

His signed agreement with Hapgood preserved her abridged versions. Since *An Actor Prepares* was published two years earlier than its Russian variant, it became the legal original protected by US and international copyright. To insure this protection, Hapgood and her husband registered and renewed the copyright for *An Actor Prepares* with the US Library of Congress as co-authors based upon the work that they had done with Stanislavsky in Badenweiler.

Any competing translation from Russian could threaten this clever legal ruse. Therefore, Hapgood staunchly defended her version, even though she herself had initially protested the requested cuts. When arrangements were made to translate it into other languages, as Stanislavsky's "attorney-in-fact" Hapgood naturally insisted that all publications follow her edition. Translations made from her English include editions in Italian (Bari 1963), Spanish (Madrid 1975 and Mexico City 1954), Dutch (Amsterdam 1985), Portuguese (Rio de Janeiro n.d.), and French (Paris 1958). Her right to do so was upheld by the Italian courts, when Theatre Arts Books challenged a 1956 translation made from Russian in Bari by Editori Laterza. The Italian translation in dispute was pulled from production, and a new one made from *An Actor Prepares*.

A few unauthorized translations from Russian slipped past Theatre Arts Books. Argentina produced a Spanish translation (Buenos Aires 1954). Others appeared in Denmark (Copenhagen 1940), Finland (Helsinki 1946, 1951), and Sweden (Stockholm 1944). The 1940 translation in East Berlin,[6] which gained authority among US theatre practitioners and scholars, fell outside international copyright protection and thus could not be contested in the courts. After abortive attempts to publish translations from Russian in Japan (1951), authorized versions from English followed.

As correspondence proves, Hapgood also regularly reviewed translations of terminology into other languages, and sometimes even chose translators, as she did for the French edition of *An Actor Prepares* (Hapgood Archive; Benedetti 1990a). While she gave Olivier Perrin translation rights in 1952, she did not approve the resulting translation, and the rights lapsed. When the French edition of *La Formation de l'acteur* appeared in 1958, Hapgood had selected Elizabeth Janvier whose translation is still in print (Paris: Petite Bibliothèque Payot, 2001). In addition, Theatre Arts Books vigilantly protected Hapgood's versions however threatened. For example, when in 1967 Penguin Books printed *An Actor Prepares* in England and credited the Russian title in the copyright notice, Theatre Arts Books objected. Hapgood's version was, after all, the legal original. Penguin changed their note (Theatre Arts Books Archive).

In sum, the commercial pressure that retouched Stanislavsky's books in the US extended throughout most of the West and even into Asia through Japan, wherever translations were made from English. This publication and translation history means that Hapgood's choices in terminology and style together with the publisher's editorial decisions determined the dominant form for Stanislavsky's ideas outside Russia, with the result that *An Actor Prepares*, *Building a Character* and *Creating a Role*—the "ABC's" of acting—became definitive editions. Furthermore, because Hapgood's decisions also entered the lore of acting, the "ABC's" continue to shape Western assumptions about the System. For example, contemporary actors recognize "objective" (her translation of *zadacha*) even though Strasberg actually used the more standard translations of "problem" and "task" (Chapter 4). Her usage has become actors' common coin. As US scholar Burnet Hobgood succinctly put it, we have suffered from an "English language curtain" (Hobgood 1973:158).

Lastly, Stanislavsky's decision to give control of his books to Hapgood sprang, at least in part, from the third "given circumstance," Stalin's mobilization of control over the arts. Stanislavsky's decision, indeed his ability to publish in the US involves his and his theatre's relationship to Stalin. While the dictator eliminated politically independent artists like Meyerhold (who suffered torture and execution in 1940), Stalin used others like Stanislavsky to support his programs (Chapters 2, 6). Without doubt, Stanislavsky's decision to publish abroad represented more than a financial strategy; he also sought to protect his System from appropriation by communist ideologues. No other reason could have inspired the apparently nonsensical and clearly unenforceable clause in the 1930 agreement with Hapgood that gives her authority over Russian, as well as Western, publication of his books.

In December 1924, when Evgeny Zamyatin's banned anti-utopian novel *We* appeared in New York, Soviet authorities paid little attention. Similarly, the 1924 US publication of *My Life in Art* raised few eyebrows in Moscow. By 1927, however, things had changed. *We* again appeared abroad, ostensibly without Zamyatin's consent, but this time the All-Russian Writers Union castigated the author (Guerney 1960:164–5). When novelist Boris Pilnyak published abroad in 1929, he was expelled from all Soviet literary organizations (Slonim 1967:87–8; 64). Moscow's attitudes toward publication abroad had calcified. By 1934, with the establishment of Socialist Realism, Stalin completely controlled the arts. Two years later, when *An Actor Prepares* appeared in New York, the Soviet regime mysteriously ignored the event.

Why could Stanislavsky get away with what others could not? Why could he openly sign contracts and translation agreements in the West, when others, who had denied complicity in the publication of their works abroad, were ostracized? Correspondence shows that he worried about the ramifications of his decision. While recuperating from his heart attack, he marveled at his continued permission to stay abroad while writing. He lay awake at night, agonizing over whether his foreign connections would be seen as "disloyal" at home. He imagined that his drafts and notes would be confiscated upon his return to Moscow. Knowing that his book would be published in the US allowed him to continue writing; but he doubted that it would ever appear in Moscow (Dybovskii 1992:25, 23–4, 42). While his extraordinary international reputation protected him from the egregious disappearances that decimated Russia's artistic community, only Stalin's unique relationship with the Moscow Art Theatre fully explains Soviet leniency toward him.

Stanislavsky had greeted the 1917 revolution with ambiguous optimism. In March, he wrote of "the great and joyous events of recent days" (SS VIII 1998:464); by August, he spoke more soberly: "A revolution is a revolution. A dangerous disease. It will not vanish like a wonderful dream. Horrors and atrocities are inevitable" (SS VIII 1998:473–4). When the Red Army vandalized the Maly Theatre, he advised forgiveness. "We must be wise! The savagery of people who have not received the blessings of culture should not offend us. […] Patience, endurance and calm reason are the only arms which we should bear" (SS VIII 1998:473–4).

As the Soviet government seized more and more control over the arts, he reacted paradoxically. On the one hand, he boldly supported ostracized artists in whom he believed. He appealed urgently, if unsuccessfully, to authorities to allow productions of Mikhail Bulgakov's phantasmagoric depiction of Russian émigrés in *Flight* and Nikolai's Erdman's acerbic satire, *The Suicide*. In a 1931 letter to Stalin, Stanislavsky praised Erdman's already prohibited play as "one of the most significant works of our epoch" (Ermolaev 1997:23). Stanislavsky even offered Meyerhold a job, at a time when people crossed the street in order to avoid being seen in proximity to his house.[7] On the other hand, Stanislavsky also mistakenly trusted Stalin's artistic sensibility and his good intentions. "We, actors," Stanislavsky wrote, "do not defend genuine art ourselves, but leave it to the Party and to the government" (SS VI 1959:353). Neither "a forced exaggeration," nor "a deliberate lie," his statement merely demonstrates his "surreal interpretation of the world outside the walls of his home" (Smeliansky 1996:43). In his seventies, he looked inappropriately to the younger Stalin for "fatherly" protection (Smeliansky 1991:12).

Stanislavsky's handling of two of the Moscow Art Theatre's political advisors exemplifies his misreading of Soviet reality. In 1929, Mikhail Geits was appointed to the Theatre as the company's communist watchdog. Stanislavsky saw advantages in such an appointment:

> A good manager in such a position could offer the theatre a great deal of help. [...] We know how important it is to have communists, who understand the theatre's nature, and who solicitously fight for that which must be lovingly saved and preserved.
>
> (SS IX 1999:354)

He expected Geits to take charge only of the administrative and financial health of the theatre, paying no attention to "stage direction, to aesthetics, to repertory, to literary choices, and generally, to the artistic and acting areas in the life of the theatre" (SS IX 1999:355). Predictably however, Geits encouraged plays with socialist ideals; that these plays were mediocre was beside the point. In line with Stalin's first Five Year Plan that focused on quantity in industrial production, Geits also increased the repertory, disturbing the company's slow and careful rehearsal process.

Stanislavsky protested to Stalin in 1931, complaining that political advisors "force us to give the audience potboilers and they imagine that in such a way we can educate the new audience. No, that's not true." Stanislavsky argues that culture cannot grow by bureaucratic interference and directives. He then pointedly reminds Stalin of the many offers to emigrate that he had turned down. "I decided to give my strength to my country, and to take part in its new structuring." He suggests that such loyalty deserves Stalin's help. "I do not say, that the Art Theatre has already been destroyed, and that there are no means by which to resurrect it, but I do say that it is on the eve of catastrophe. [...] My child is perishing." He concludes by demanding the removal of the "red manager" and suggesting that his theatre report instead to the highest governmental organs. Stanislavsky assumes that the greater the personage, the less mediocre his understanding of art (SS VI 1994:339–50). Stalin granted Stanislavsky a pyrrhic victory. Geits was removed and the Theatre now answered directly to the government's Central Executive Committee.

In 1935, Stanislavsky wrote to Stalin, suggesting that Mikhail Arkadiev take over as the Art Theatre's ideological advisor. Knowing Arkadiev's work with *Narkompros* (the People's Commissariat of Education and Enlightenment), Stanislavsky thought him "an experienced, cultured communist manager who will help Vl. I. Nemirovich-Danchenko and me to repair our mutual relations." Stanislavsky weds this practical request to undaunted idealism: "Our theatre can and must become the foremost theatre in our country through its ability to theatrically reflect the full, inner spiritual life of the worker, who is now positioned as the earth's proprietor" (SS IX 1999:631–3; translated by Carnicke 2003). His language shows his paradoxical view of politics; his mixture of spirituality with the proletarian rhetoric of work was patently untenable in the atheistic Soviet state. Yet, again Stalin agreed to Stanislavsky's request. Only two short years later in June 1937, Stalin executed Arkadiev for his mishandling of the Art Theatre's tour to Paris (Autant-Mathieu 2003:74).

Under Stalin, Stanislavsky and his company garnered extraordinary privileges denied to others: extended stays abroad, apartments, unusually generous subsidies and stipends, prestigious awards, and the willingness to overlook publication in the West. Such indulgences followed upon Stalin's decision to promote the Theatre's interest in nineteenth century realism as the model for twentieth century Socialist Realism (Chapter 2) and Stanislavsky's System as the official curriculum for all Soviet theatrical institutes. These privileges, however, entailed high costs: the return of loyalty, unquestioning adherence to Stalinist ideals, loss of autonomy, and, in Stanislavsky's case, internal exile during his last years. As long as Stanislavsky's politically incorrect appeals could remain hidden behind a politically managed public mask, Stalin could afford generosity.

The Moscow Art Theatre had walked a tightrope in the early years after the revolution, balancing severe criticism of its bourgeois repertory against insidious governmental support which threatened to stifle free, artistic expression. Stanislavsky stood precariously on this rope while he toured the US. The out-dated repertoire for the Theatre's US tours suggest that the company had begun to lose its balance in the 1920s. By the late 1920s, the company's ultimate fate could be predicted in the Party's forthright statement:

> Given the dictatorship of the proletariat, when theatres are the property of the Soviet government and when the means to regulate and direct theatrical life are in our hands, like governmental subsidies and *Glavrepertkom* [the state committee for theatrical oversight], all theatres can sooner or later develop a socialist direction, and can and must undergo ideological–political reconstruction.
>
> (Solovyova 2007:551).

Stanislavsky's decision to publish *An Actor Prepares* in the US suggests that he was still struggling to maintain his balance during the early 1930s, but by 1938—the year of his death—both the company and he had irrevocably fallen. The Moscow Art Theatre had become the Soviet "showpiece of theatrical policy" (Autant-Mathieu 2003:74) and Stanislavsky the officially sanctioned acting and directing teacher. At the company's fortieth anniversary celebration in 1938, actor Leonid Leonidov, who had played Othello in Stanislavsky's 1930 production, spoke the following panegyric words: "Stalin is in our every thought; Stalin is in all our hearts; Stalin is in all our songs; your life seethes in our work and in our battles; Stalin, you are my sun, thank you!" His ode expresses the utter capitulation to Stalin, an act tantamount to "artistic suicide" (Smeliansky 1989a:345).

If *An Actor Prepares* resulted in part from Stanislavsky's decision to protect his System from communist appropriation, then his encounter with the US commercial pressures detailed above seems all the more ironic. Was the abridged version of *An Actor Prepares* (analyzed below) a compromise worth making to avoid censorship (Chapter 6)?

An Actor Prepares

Given all three circumstances behind the publication of Stanislavsky's books, it is nearly impossible to establish canonical texts for the System; multiple drafts and discrepancies among different published versions make it seem true that, "Like the Bible, Stanislavsky's basic texts on acting can be quoted to any purpose" (Strasberg 1987:42). Yet Stanislavsky's work has been promoted so widely through the Hapgood editions, that comparing his *persona* in her versions with his Russian counterpart makes sense despite textual confusion and new translations. In fact, without such examination, his ideas remain hopelessly entangled with those of his interpreters. I take the Russian texts as my baseline for comparison because they contain more of Stanislavsky's drafts and the System's terminology in his native language.

I also take variants of *An Actor's Work on Himself, Part I* as my primary object of attention. First, since this volume was the only one which Stanislavsky finished before his death, it represents the most definitive text. Stanislavsky himself had approved all three of its incarnations: he initialed every page of the 1935 typescript, which he sent to Hapgood for translation; he saw the proofs of her abridged 1936 English translation; he considered the later 1938 Russian variant, edited by the Soviet Commission, complete (SS III 1990:18).[8] Second, *An Actor Prepares* holds a special place in the transformative adoption of the System, since it predates *Part II* by thirteen years and was consequently mistaken for the whole. In summary, study of *Part I* can help better appraise how the publication maze affected an American sense of Stanislavsky.

The most striking difference between the two published variants is length. While *An Actor's Work on Himself, Part I* is 575 pages, *An Actor Prepares* numbers 295 pages of much larger typeface, set from a typescript of approximately 700 pages. Even allowing for variation in syntax, word length, typeface and Stanislavsky's own obsessive revisions, the numbers suggest how drastic are the differences between the two published editions. The abridgement, demanded by Theatre Arts Books, resulted in an English version about one half as long as the Russian.

Faced with the daunting task of condensing Stanislavsky's *chef d'oeuvre* in order to insure its publication, Hapgood did indeed "eliminate duplication" as she intended. Stanislavsky the writer often repeats phrases instead of substituting pronouns, uses two or three apparently synonymous adjectives when one might do, and runs on in long convoluted sentences. Hapgood does the obvious job of substituting pronouns, choosing one adjective from among many, and condensing long unwieldy sentences. Most of these changes do little to alter Stanislavsky's portrait. For example, in one passage Tortsov asks a student to "Cut 95 percent of that tenseness!" In Russian he repeats the demand four times, and Hapgood merely cuts the repetition in half [Typescript Chapter XVI:11–14; English:270–2].

Such minor cuts could not comply fully enough with the publisher's conditions. To reduce the length further, Hapgood looked for "whatever was meaningless for non-Russian actors," as she put it: paragraphs here and there containing details and student reactions that enliven the book, restatements of ideas in modified forms, and examples that include obscure Russian references. All these areas relate to Stanislavsky's strategies for writing about lore. Hence, with this set of deletions, the book begins to shift in style.

In the first chapter, Stanislavsky describes how his protagonist, Nazvanov, selects, rehearses, and performs a scene from *Othello*. While Hapgood retains all the key points in the story, she edits out several comic moments. The reason that our hero chooses Shakespeare is merely because he happens to own a copy. At home, while practicing a tiger-like gait for Othello, he suddenly pounces upon a pillow, which he then imaginatively transforms into his beloved Desdemona; the attack becomes an embrace. After working for several hours dressed in a makeshift tunic with his face darkened by melted chocolate, he catches sight of himself in a mirror only to discover how ridiculous he looks. Having arrived at the theatre, Nazvanov finds an ally: a tall, lean make-up artist, resembling Don Quixote, who rescues him from his feeble attempts to apply color to his face. Nazvanov also discovers an enemy: a muttering prompter, who maliciously sabotages his performance [Typescript Chapter I:3–6, 21, 16; Russian:46–8, 54–5].

Of more import are deletions of student reactions. Gone are the fears and anxieties when their teacher requests that they perform scenes to show their talents. While Hapgood retains Tortsov's stern reprimand of Nazvanov for arriving late to rehearsal, she leaves out the peer pressure that follows [Typescript Chapter I:3, 8; Russian:46, 49]. When Tortsov introduces the idea that the subconscious affects performance, Hapgood cuts Nazvanov's nervous confusion together with another student's contrasting, ecstatic welcome of the idea [Typescript Chapter XVI:3, 27]. In exploring the power of the "magic if," Stanislavsky includes a concrete example of what he means: Tortsov hands one of his students a glass of water, telling her it is poison; she "instinctively" recoils in horror. While Hapgood deletes this example in *An Actor Prepares*, Stanislavsky expands upon it in the 1938 edition. Here, Tortsov also hands around a glass ashtray as if it were a frog and a chamois glove as if it were a mouse, thereby further dramatizing the fictional life of the classroom. [Typescript Chapter III:25–6; Russian:99–100].

Deleting such interactions has two effects. In the first place, it diminishes the give and take between student and teacher. While Stanislavsky's Socratic style adds little new factual information, it creates an attitude that is experimental and open to argument. Undercutting this style turns Tortsov from a workshop leader into a lecturer. In the second place, preserving expository passages while eliminating practical examples of applicability makes the English seem a more theoretical book.

Of even more import are cuts that affect content. Determining what is redundant or "meaningless for non-Russian actors" is far from easy. What sometimes appears repetitive, may in fact add subtle nuances. When the stated artistic goal, "to create the human life of the spirit of the role," becomes in English simply "to create the life of a human spirit," and when "the human being/actor" becomes a mere "human being," the person of the actor begins to overshadow the play, opening the door for the common misconception that an actor deals primarily in self-expression [Russian:51; Typescript Chapter II:9; English: 15–16]. When

Stanislavsky explicitly includes the work of directors, designers, and technicians along with the playwright in the "given circumstances" with which actors must cope in performance, he acknowledges the collaborative and cooperative nature of theatrical art. When Hapgood deletes these details, we lose a sense of how the actor fits into a collective [Typescript Chapter III: 25–6; Russian:99–100].

This level of abridgement also affects the book's clarity. Although Stanislavsky's own prose is florid and repetitive, the English sometimes seems illogical or cryptic. Such disruption of logic can be found in the discussion of how an actor's "objective" relates to an "action."

In both the Russian typescript and publication, Stanislavsky clearly outlines a logical process of analysis for each segment of the play: the actor first examines the "given circumstances" in order to describe the character's situation. The situation poses a "problem" (*zadacha*, in Hapgood's translation "objective") which the character must solve through the choice of an "action." By carefully defining the "problem," the actor discovers the character's specific "action" for that segment of the play. During performance, the actor places his or her full attention on carrying out the required action, with the character's emotions arising as a natural result of the action. By focusing solely on action, the actor experiences something akin to the role's emotional life as a subsidiary effect. Stanislavsky concludes: "If our preparatory work is right, the results will take care of themselves." He finishes the passage by warning that actors make a common mistake when they worry about the result, rather than the action [Typescript Chapter VII:12–14; Russian:212–14].

In English, the entire two-page passage reads: "'The objective will be the light that shows the right way,' explained the Director. 'The mistake most actors make is that they think about the result instead of the action that must prepare it'" [110]. The argument jumps from a definition of "objective" (*zadacha* or "problem") to a conclusion without explanation. The reader either does not follow the illogical jump, or confuses "objective" with "action," a common American misreading of the text. The logical step-by-step process described in Russian has not been conveyed.

In sum, abridgement necessitated by Theatre Arts Books does indeed change the effect of the book, both stylistically and conceptually. No wonder Stanislavsky's wife, Maria Lilina, herself a leading actress of the Moscow Art Theatre, objected to Hapgood's blue pencil, claiming that it damaged communication with the actor! (Hobgood 1986:157; Vinogradskaia IV 2003:399).

Hapgood had never intended to change Stanislavsky's theoretical framework and strongly objected to many of the deep cuts requested by the publisher. Moreover, when comparing the 1935 typescript with the later Russian edition, one sees clearly that not all variations between *An Actor Prepares* and its 1938 counterpart can be laid at her door. Some, of course, result from compromises with the Soviet censor (Chapter 6); others stem from Stanislavsky's own obsessive writing. As he continued to revise his book, he shuffled and reshuffled topics and paragraphs like a deck of cards. Since his ideas are so tightly interrelated, he sometimes questions and rethinks the order in which he should present them. Such reorganization becomes more and more frequent in the last chapters of the book. Topics move fluidly from context to context. In one passage, Tortsov explains that human beings/actors, who wish to express joy through art, have set a lofty goal for themselves. Stanislavsky first places this passage in Chapter XVI and relates it to the actor's subconscious life. In 1938, he transfers it to Chapter XV calling this goal a personal "super-supertask" [Typescript Chapter XVI:51–2; Russian:420; the passage does not appear in English]. Similarly, he moves a synopsis of the entire System, complete with diagram, from the end of *Part I* into the delayed *Part II* [Typescript ChapterXVI:22–3; SS III 1990:308–11].

While variation in editing is the first point of comparison among the variants of Stanislavsky's acting manual, the choice and usage of terminology is the second. In his foreword to the Russian edition (translated by Hobgood 1991:219–32), Stanislavsky discusses the nature of language necessary to describe the actor's work. He claims that his students invented the terminology, thus proving it to be a natural outgrowth of practice, not a predetermined theoretical vocabulary. He adds that, aside from a few commonly used psychological terms like "intuition" and "subconscious," his words are without "scientific roots," come from daily language, and are not meant to establish a professional jargon. This simplicity is important, he says, because acting, which is an art and not a science, must have a practical and concrete vocabulary that appeals not to the intellect but to the "heart" [Russian:41–2].

His claims look somewhat disingenuous. In the first place, while Stanislavsky tells us that his language was invented by his students and denies complicity in its creation, he also frequently imposes labels—however simple they may be—calling them "our actor's jargon" [Russian:132]. Moreover, he sometimes uses a common Russian word eccentrically enough so that it begins to take on the force of a term. For example, the word *vymysel* simply means an idea, a conception, a thought. His usage makes it a term, "the creative idea." It comes to signify any fictional element in a scene that actors invent to spark their imaginative work. Indeed, actors at the Moscow Art Theatre often bristled at Stanislavsky's imposition of words and labels.

In the second place, despite claims to the contrary, he often uses science to give special credibility to his ideas. He consistently invokes "organic" laws of human nature, both psychological and physical, as the basis for his System. In discussing the need for logic in acting, he assumes that "in nature, everything is consistent and logical" [Russian:125]. In examining Affective Memory, he asserts that "nature alone can control" aspects of our psyches over which we have no conscious control [Russian:284]. In teaching his students how to look out at the audience from the stage as if looking at the horizon, he warns them to use their eyes "as our nature demands;" no one in the audience, he tells them, will believe an actor who breaks with physical laws [Russian:174]. Such reliance upon "natural laws" is tremendously appealing to insecure actors. Using science inspires confidence in the ability of the teacher to teach an intractable art and the student's ability to learn. In calling Stanislavsky's work "a systematic science," Boleslavsky helped foster such confidence in the US (Boleslawski 1923:74). Invocations to science and the physical world also assuaged Soviet censors, who required a materialistic basis for ideas in the book (Chapter 8).

But Stanislavsky's apparently disingenuous claims also contain grains of truth. On the first count, Stanislavsky does indeed draw terms from commonly used, simple

Russian words; "magic if," "concentration," and "action" are far from mysterious. On the second count, while he uses science when it suits him, he often flagrantly disregards it in favor of artistic intuition. In 1935, in a letter to his son, he admits to "illiteracy" in psychology and philosophy (Dybovskii 1992:90). Like any artist, Stanislavsky incorporates science only when it inspires his imagination. Despite Gurevich's constant requests that he meet with Soviet scientists to hone his terminology, his reluctance to do so proves that his own creativity was ultimately his most important resource. In this sense, his preface is truthful.

However one finally interprets Stanislavsky's preface, the Method certainly adopted a professional and quasi-scientific vocabulary, separating Method from non-Method actors. As Robert Lewis explained: "Another fetish that has been made from the Method in some quarters is the one about terminology. It has created a kind of dogma out of what should have been a freeing principle" (1958:69).

While the English translation does not create the Method's jargon, it sets the tone for its establishment. Consider Hapgood's rendering of "objective" for *zadacha*. The Russian word is a simple one, used commonly in everyday speech. As above, it can be translated "problem," and Stanislavsky in fact associates it with a child's arithmetic problem to clarify his idea [Typescript ChapterVII:13; Russian:212]. Such a "problem" implies a logical solution; and for the actor, Stanislavsky says, the solution lies in action. The Russian word is also commonly translated as "task," which demands fulfillment through action.

By choosing to translate *zadacha* as "objective," Hapgood shifts the focus of Stanislavsky's concept. Webster defines "objective" as "something aimed at or striven for," in short, a goal. Thus, "objective" stands at the opposite pole of meaning from that of *zadacha* by implying not an impulse toward action but rather the action's outcome, and hence further confusing the path from "problem" to "action" as described by Stanislavsky. In short, "objective" can easily become a professional term, as it has, clear to those who use it and slightly mysterious to the general populace.

One result of Hapgood's translation of *zadacha* has been an identification of "objective" with "action." Even Lewis, in his classic attempt to straighten out confusions between the Method and the System, writes: "This word 'Action' as used here in 1934 was the term employed in the Group Theatre, too. (Of course it means *inner action*—not physical action.) If you have read the books, you know it is translated by Mrs. Hapgood as 'Objective'" (1958:29). This is not the case at all. "Objective" clearly translates the word *zadacha*, not *deistvie* ("action"). Here again, the English text supports a common misreading, examined above in connection with editing and now supported through word choice.

Taken together, the concepts of "problem" (*zadacha*) and "action" (*deistvie*) comprise the heart of Stanislavsky's System. Therefore, drawing a distinction between the two is important. By defining a problem, which originates in the circumstances of the play, the actor logically discovers his or her action. By placing attention on actions, the actor gains focus and confidence on stage. Harking back to Aristotle, Stanislavsky points out that action distinguishes drama from other forms of art. In the Russian edition, he traces the origin of the word "drama" (cognates in Russian and English) to the Greek word *dran* ("to do") in order to enforce this idea. He takes this etymology as his reason for choosing *deistvie*, derived from the root "to do" in Russian, to describe what an actor does on stage [Russian:88]. Unfortunately, Hapgood cut this passage. As Francis Fergusson muses, "I cannot discover whether Stanislavsky and Nemirovich-Dantchenko got their concept of action from Aristotle or not" (1949:253). This deletion offers precisely the evidence that Fergusson sought.

Deistvie is one term in an interlocking series of Russian words with which Stanis-lavsky expresses various nuances within the basic concept of "action." The clearer the distinction among these, the clearer "action" as a concrete concept emerges. The major distinctions are as follows. Stanislavsky distinguishes the word *igrat'* ("to play" and commonly translated as "to act") from the Russian words *delat'* and *deistvovat'* ("to do" and "to take action"). He rejects the traditional word for acting, *igrat'*, because it implies pretense. He claims that to act one must do something as if it were real; one must take action on stage, not play. The word for "action" (*deistvie*) derives from the roots of *delat'* and *deistvovat'*. From this derivation one can easily understand Stan-islavsky's insistence on using active verbs to describe "actions." Stanislavsky further distinguishes *deistvie* from the more abstract Russian word *aktivnost'*, "the state of being in action" or "dynamism." *Aktivnost'* describes a general propensity for action on stage as compared with *deistvie*, which suggests purposeful action aimed at solving a specific problem. While actors must indeed possess this propensity, they must focus it into specific actions while performing. Stanislavsky gives several examples of how to do this. Merely opening a door will not suffice, while opening a door in order to find out if an intruder stands outside is *deistvie*. Sitting on stage for its own sake is too general; sitting on stage in order to await instruction is a specific and acceptable action [Typescript Chapter III:5–7; Russian:88–9].

Because English does not have a similar root system, any translator would find it impossible to make all these distinctions clearly with word choice alone. Hapgood's inconsistency of usage, however, confuses the issue more than necessary. Take as example the following passage. The dialogue concerns an exercise in which an actress has been asked to sit on stage awaiting further instructions from her teacher. Before giving any directions, however, the teacher declares the exercise finished success-fully, much to the surprise of the actress who feels that she has done nothing. The Russian words, and a consistent English choice for each, are included in brackets for the sake of comparison.

"How do you feel?" the Director asked as they returned to their places in the auditorium.

"I? Why? Did we act?" [*igrat'*/act]

"Of course."

"Oh! But I thought […] I was just sitting and waiting until you found your place in the book, and would tell me what to do [*delat'*/do]. Why, I didn't act [*igrat'*/act] anything."

Then he turned to the rest of us. "Which struck you as more interesting?" he asked. "To sit on the stage and show off your small feet, as Sonya did, or your whole figure, like Grisha, or to sit for a specific purpose [*delat'*/in order to do something] even so simple a one as waiting for something to happen? It may not be of intrinsic interest in itself, but it is life, whereas showing yourself off takes you out of the realm of living art."

"On the stage, you must always be enacting something [*deistvovat'*/taking action]; acting [*deistvie*/action], motion [*aktivnost'*/the state of being in action] is the basis of the art of the actor." [Here is deleted the passage on the etymology of the word "drama."]

"But," Grisha broke in, "you have just said that acting [*deistvovat'*/taking action] is necessary, and that showing off your feet or your figure, as I did, is not action. [No direct word is translated here. This is a paraphrase.] Why is it action [*deistvie*/action] to sit in a chair, as you did, without moving a finger? To me it looked like a complete lack of action" [*bezdeistvie*/inaction] [...]

"You may sit without a motion and at the same time be in full action [*deistvovat'*/taking action]. Nor is that all. Frequently physical immobility is the direct result of inner intensity" [*deistvie*/action].

"On the stage it is necessary to act [*deistvovat'*/to take action], either outwardly or inwardly."

(English:34–5; Russian:88–9)

Leaving aside consideration of deletions, one can easily see how inconsistent Hapgood's usage is by comparing her English choices with the Russian words. While she initially sets up a clear distinction between *igrat'* (to "act") and *deistvovat'* (to "enact"), nicely playing upon the English root system, she does not maintain these choices. By the end of the passage, however, when she translates *deistvovat'* with the word "to act," she has lost the initial distinction. In English, therefore, the passage implies a nonsensical conclusion: the main thing on stage is not to act but to act. The Russian leads to the more logical conclusion: the main thing is not to act but to take action.

With similar inconsistency, Hapgood does not use her initial choice for *deistvovat'* (to "enact") in Grisha's question. She again substitutes the word "to act." In Russian, the student clearly asks his teacher for a clarification of terms, carefully repeating his teacher's words. Without this repetition in English, he appears either inattentive or not very bright. In Russian his question is far from rhetorical.

Finally, Hapgood sometimes translates *deistvie* ("action") with another concept altogether, as she does when she renders *deistvie* with "inner intensity." This choice places undue emphasis on the emotional work of the actor. The intensity or emotional content of the scene, as Stanislavsky explains, is the result of the action and not the action itself. The distinction between emotional life and "action" is blurred, allowing members of the Group Theatre to find support for their emphasis on the actor's internal work. In short, the inconsistency of terminology erases specific distinctions in Russian and makes the logic of Stanislavsky's argument harder to trace. The fact is ironic given Stanislavsky's own insistence on the logical building of actions upon the circumstances of the play.

This analysis suggests some of the major differences between Hapgood's English and the Russian versions of Stanislavsky's books and how these differences can affect interpretations of the System: deletions change the style and disrupt the logic of the text, sometimes shifting the overall emphasis or focus of a passage, and inconsistent translations of vocabulary or inexact word choice confuse distinctions between similar but different concepts.

The next chapter turns a spotlight on the operations of Soviet censorship and the consequent culture of reading between the lines in Stanislavsky's native land. These topics lay the last stones in the historical mosaic that made definitive texts of the System hard to find and painted imperfect and incomplete portraits of its creator.

6   The USSR publication maze

The System in the subtext

In the 1960s Russian director Adolf Shapiro decided to study with Maria Osipovna
Knebel (1898–1985), one of Stanislavsky's last assistants, in order to prove that the
master's ideas were no longer valuable. In Shapiro's view, Stanislavsky's "nause-
ating" approach to psychological and Socialist Realism was "insufficiently vivid
and expressive; it was boring. [...] Yes, I went to study with Knebel deliberately
with my own ruse in mind." But, she turned Shapiro's ruse inside out. "I went to
[her] like a spy, in order to worm out of her my opponent's secrets so that I could
use them against him. But, in the end, unexpectedly for me, I was taken prisoner
for life" (1999:133–5).

Shapiro's assumptions had come from his knowledge of the "official" Stanislavsky, manufactured by Stalin in the late 1930s, promoted by authoritative
Marxist practitioners and scholars during most of the twentieth century, and taught
in the Soviet theatrical institutes. In turning the private Stanislavsky into a public
icon for Socialist Realism (Chapter 2), the Soviet propaganda machine had done
its work well. By the end of World War II, his name dominated the Soviet art scene.
According to art historian Matthew Cullern Bown, even painters claimed to use the
actor's System. "No representative of Soviet culture received more praise, exegesis
and column-space" than Stanislavsky (1998:265). When a politically liberal journal
sought permission to print Mikhail Bulgakov's comic novel about the Moscow Art
Theatre in 1963, the censors cautioned the editors to avoid a "lampoon" of their
artistic hero (Ermolaev 1997:146).

Unfortunately, one can easily find the boring, paternalistic master that Soviet
culture had made of Stanislavsky in his Russian books. Censorship made sure of
that. Only months before his death, Stanislavsky read the first published excerpt
from *An Actor's Work on Himself* in a Soviet journal, and reacted as so many soon
would. To his wife he said, "How uninteresting this is!" (Smeliansky 1996:45).

In 1932, the Soviet regime had decided to create a model acting school as adjunct
to the Moscow Art Theatre. Consequently, *An Actor's Work on Himself*, over which
Stanislavsky then agonized, became no longer his private endeavor. The government saw it as the school's primary textbook and appointed a commission to bring it
into line with dialectical materialism, which, in Stanislavsky's words, had become
the philosophy "required of all" (SS IX 1999:475). As expressed in communist
Russia, this Marxist philosophy single-mindedly saw all aspects of the world as

materially and economically caused. It also rejected any other explanations with the pejorative label, "idealistic." When Stanislavsky's book finally appeared in print, Marxism seemed to have robbed the System of its rich complexity.

What excited Shapiro, however, still lies beneath the surface: a multi-pronged System that aims to trigger the actor's artistry through mind, body, and soul. Like subtext in a play, the richness of Stanislavsky's ideas can be found only by reading between the lines, an accommodation made necessary by the culture of Soviet censorship. As émigré novelist Anatoly Kuznetsov starkly observes, "When we read Soviet literature as published, we have [...] to make enormous allowances for what the censorship has done" (Dewhirst and Farrell 1973:89). Stanislavsky's books and those written about him in the USSR are no exception.

Soviet censorship did more than ban books; it also prescribed what could be said and written. Censors became educators and enforcers of politically correct content, form and style, giving writers to understand that "everything is forbidden; what is permitted is obligatory" (Blyum 2003:10, 15). Therefore, a high stakes game developed between those who crafted and those who censored words. The writer's goal was, as author Arkady Belinkov put it, "to get round [...] the censor" (Dewhirst and Farrell 1973:9). Thus, authors learned to hint at what could not be said. They began to use "metaphoric insurrections, allegoric disguises, hidden ciphers, cryptic symbols, ambiguity, paradox, enigma, esotericism, and illicit changes in signs," to borrow Sue Curry Jansen's list of writing strategies. Such ploys allowed writers "to tell deadly serious jokes, to say one thing and mean another, to use praise to blame or blame to praise" (1988:192). The censor, in turn, strove to block as many of the writer's moves as possible, the more deletions the better (Ermolaev 1997:57).

Stanislavsky began to play this game during the 1930s when all the cards were marked in favor of the censors. He was finalizing his acting manual while Stalin was terrorizing the country. In 1934 (when Socialist Realism became the only sanctioned style for art and home confinement Stanislavsky's only option), Party boss Sergei Kirov was assassinated under circumstances that suggested Stalin's direct involvement. In 1936 (when Stanislavsky published *An Actor Prepares* in the US), Stalin began his infamous mass purges with a show trial for Kirov's alleged murderers. A single statistic exposes the extent of the era's growing terror: on 12 December 1938 (four short months after Stanislavsky's natural death), Stalin signed execution orders for 3,167 people (Ermolaev 1997:51). Stanislavsky felt the terror personally in 1930 when his nephew and his nephew's wife and sister-in-law were arrested for political resistance. At first, Stanislavsky pleaded for their release; nine months later he hopelessly pleaded for their lives (Solovyova 2007:535–6).

Stanislavsky found the post-revolutionary political rules difficult to absorb. While he had side-stepped controversy during his tours to the US by giving interviews of studied neutrality (Chapter 2) he betrayed an utter lack of political instinct in 1928 when he spoke at the thirtieth anniversary celebration of the now Soviet Moscow Art Theatre. Before an exclusively communist audience, Stanislavsky praised "our beloved" Sava Morozov (SS VI 1994:297), the wealthy capitalist who had contributed to the company in its Russian years. A barrage of vicious attacks in the press followed on the next day, triggering the severe heart attack that ended Stanislavsky's acting career (Autant-Mathieu 2003:73). In a 1936 letter to Hapgood, Stanislavsky acknowledges how distant he felt from Soviet values by pointing to the young people around him. Having grown up in difficult circumstances that inculcated in them radically different attitudes from his own, they are, the old man marvels, "actually new people" (SS IX 1999:656). In publishing his books, he had to deal with this new, inscrutable society.

Censors modified everything that Stanislavsky said and published in Soviet Russia, from 1917 to 1938 and posthumously. With the fall of the USSR in 1991, the archives were emptied of all his personal writings, including those that the censor had disallowed. A host of post-Soviet publications have since made these previously unpublished drafts, notes, and letters available. This previously hidden information informs every chapter of the book you now read. But the censorship of his Russian-language publications could not be undone. *My Life in Art*, *An Actor's Work on Himself*, *Parts I* and *II*, and *An Actor's Work on the Role* will forever bear the censor's marks. While the most recent edition of his *Collected Works* (SS 1988–99) includes previously suppressed materials, the basic books are reprinted as previously approved by the censors.

If we theatre practitioners and scholars hope to recover the vibrancy of the System that Shapiro unexpectedly found through Knebel, we must look the Soviet censor squarely in the face. To replace our boring, but maddeningly persistent image of Stanislavsky as the tyrannical "Father of psychological realism" (Marowitz 2007:59) with clear-sighted depictions of his open-minded, multivalent System we, like Knebel, must read between the lines of his books to find their subtexts. An examination of Soviet censorship provides the necessary corrective lens through which to read not only Stanislavsky's Russian texts, but also those of his Russian-language interpreters.

The leading expert on Soviet censorship, Arlen V. Blyum, describes its history as a classical play with an unexpected sixth Act. Acts I and II (1917–29) trace the unprecedented introduction and administration of prescriptive censorship (1994:16). In Act I, Stanislavsky tours the US, securing the international fame that would soon protect him from the fates suffered by other artists under Stalin. Yet, the growing power of censorship has already insured that the Art Theatre take only their most realistic productions abroad (Chapter 2). Thus, the tours begin to craft a distorted image of Stanislavsky. By the end of Act II, Stanislavsky learns how strident censorship had become when his politically incorrect speech at the Theatre's thirtieth anniversary elicited verbal assaults of a magnitude previously unknown to him.

Act III (1930–53) moves inexorably through the total terror of Stalin's regime when punishment for infractions smaller than Stanislavsky's speech insured imprisonment or execution (Blyum 1994:16). The first eight years of Act III dramatically juxtapose Stanislavsky's private thinking with Stalin's aggressive public campaign to turn the old man into a model for Socialist Realism. Thus, while others perish, Stanislavsky remains in his home, ill and frail, but still pursuing his art. As Act III opens Stanislavsky eludes the censor by arranging for US publication of *An Actor's Work on Himself*, only to see *Part I* of his acting manual drastically cut to suit American commercial tastes (Chapter 5). As Act III continues, Stanislavsky dies, struggling to say what he means about his System despite ideological pressures to change his book to suit Soviet exigencies. As the Act closes, censorship has bled his words of their spiritual and artistic complexity.

Acts IV and V (1954–84) follow the story through Khrushchev's "thaw," Brezhnev's period of "stagnation," and Gorbachev's "openness" (Blyum 1994:16). Censors remained vigilant, but now only books, not their authors, risked death (Dewhirst and Farrell 1973:8). During the falling action of these two acts, critics take over for Stanislavsky in defining the parameters of his System. But a conflict appears between those who hold to the Party line and those who encourage readers to find Stanislavsky's subtexts. This conflict can be found in the pages of Stanislavsky's mid-century *Collected Works* (SS 1954–61). The Soviet commission, headed by Mikhail Kedrov (see below), insured that only politically correct materials be included. The editorial team, headed by Grigory Kristi, wrote tantalizing footnotes about the System's subversive elements (such as Yoga) by slipping information past censors as criticism of Stanislavsky's adolescent, but now outgrown, errors.[1]

The unexpected sixth Act (1985–91) in the drama about Soviet censorship culminates in the surprised shock among Western journalists who witnessed the stringent censorship that immediately followed the fall of the Soviet Union. For Russians, Blyum wryly notes, "there was, however, nothing strange in this; [...] the new dictators were walking in the trodden path" (1994:16). Notably, the first four volumes of the complete *Collected Works* (SS 1988–99) appear during this Act and reprint the four standard (hence censored) versions of his books. The volumes that fortuitously appear after 1991 publish all the previously suppressed materials. No doubt, had these volumes appeared before the fall of the USSR, they too would still be incomplete.

Outlining the changing forces that shaped the Soviet publication of Michael Chekhov's writings gives insight into Stanislavsky's own publication history by analogy. In *Life and Encounters* Chekhov tells of an imminent warrant for his arrest that led him to flee his country in July 1928, the year of Stanislavsky's fateful speech at the Moscow Art Theatre. Chekhov was under suspicion for his belief in Rudolf Steiner's Anthroposophy, a spiritual and artistic system outlawed by the atheistic state. "Resistance was becoming futile," Chekhov admits (2005:136). He recounts an incident just before his emigration that brings to life the era's atmosphere of fear. Two apparently enthusiastic actors had joined Chekhov's classes, where he utilized, but carefully avoided naming, Steiner's methods. Later, Chekhov discovered that the two actors' enthusiasm masked a darker intent; they had been spying for *Narkompros* (The People's Commissariat of Education and Enlightenment). A deceitfully friendly letter from the Commissariat directed Chekhov to cease teaching Steiner. In this letter, verbatim quotations from Chekhov's classes were placed next to "the relevant quotations from Steiner's works." The actors, Chekhov now realized, had been "hiding behind the door curtains" in order to record "the phrases that to their mind were suspect" (2005:135–6).

Still hoping against hope that he might return to Moscow, Chekhov wrote a long, detailed response to *Narkompros* in October 1928, boldly stating that he had been "expelled" from both his country and "the Russian theatrical life which I so love," the only discernible reason being the "unbearable fact" that "senselessness" has overtaken "our theatrical life" (I 1995:342). Chekhov received no answer and never returned.

During the next several decades, not only Chekhov but the Russian theatre community suffered the consequences of his emigration; he had become an enemy of the Soviet people for the duration of his natural life, a fate shared by all émigrés, Strasberg's teachers among them. Since the only proper response to enemies in Stalinist Russia was annihilation of one sort or another, Chekhov's name became anathema in his native land with his emigration in 1928, remained so for the duration of his natural life which ended in 1955, and found rehabilitation only in the late 1980s. As Solovyova explains:

> For most of the people who stayed in Russia those who had gone abroad actually did cease to exist. All ties were severed. There was no way of finding out whether an émigré was alive or dead. Historians of the arts had to fight for the right to mention that émigrés had actually existed even before their departure: the inroads of official propaganda went that far.
>
> (Senelick1992:70)

Chekhov was as good as dead to Soviet theatre history until a decade after his physical death when Khrushchev's "thaw" in the arts made a few articles about him possible, including a full chapter by one of his first students, Maria Knebel (1967:52–134), whose teaching about Stanislavsky would later surprise Shapiro (above).

Flash forward to the 1980s, during the sixth Act of censorship's drama, when Knebel made it her mission to publish a first, groundbreaking, but still censored edition of Chekhov's *Literary Heritage* in his native land. While compiling the materials, her editorial team read "in secret" those passages proscribed by the censor. "It was painfully bitter to read them," Knebel's editor recalls. "The stupidity of the institution of censorship was obvious to all of us" (Liadov 1998:56). This 1986 edition serves as a touchstone for what was still politically incorrect during the most liberal years of the Soviet Union. Censors required both small and large deletions throughout, especially with regard to passages that concern Chekhov's emigration and his religious beliefs, which partly grew from the Yoga that he had learned in Stanislavsky's First Studio and later blossomed into the banned Anthroposophy. His letter to the head of *Narkompros* too was disallowed. These materials would appear in Russian only after the fall of the Soviet Union, when a second, uncensored edition of his works (1995) could restore what had been excised in 1986.

In addition to cuts, Knebel also realized that she had to provide in her introduction politically acceptable explanations for Chekhov's deviations from the official Stanislavsky. We can see Knebel playing the censorship game deftly when she reminds her readers that in 1919 Stanislavsky had said, "Study the system via Misha Chekhov" (1967:28), and when she explains that Chekhov's "path to theory [may have been] different" from Stanislavsky's, but "its roots in the analysis of self were similar"(M. Chekhov II 1995:6). By linking Chekhov to Stalin's chosen theatrical icon for Socialist Realism, Knebel made the émigré safe for the censors and available to Soviet readers.

Stanislavsky may not have mastered the censorship game, but his protégé Knebel had. She put her savvy to work for both her teachers, as Shapiro's experience with the

System warrants. Her awareness of what one might write under changing political circumstances can be made visible simply by comparing how she describes the same politically suspect information about Chekhov's belief in Anthroposophy at different times. Consider, for example, her description of a 1923 studio which she joined on Steiner's eurhythmy (a movement system that makes poetry visible through dance). In her 1967 autobiography, published during the years of "stagnation" in Soviet arts, she notes that the poet and Anthroposophist Andrei Bely visited the workshop often and read poetry for the participants, but she does not say that Bely had become Chekhov's spiritual guide (124). No doubt she was protecting Bely, who remained in the Soviet Union after Chekhov had fled. For the 1986 edition published during Gorbachev's government, she identifies this studio as Bely's and Chekhov as his best student; she even risks mentioning her own visit to Steiner's school in Switzerland (I 1986:18–9).

Stanislavsky's spoken words

In turning to the specific ways in which censorship shaped and reshaped Stanislavsky's words, analysis best begins with a consideration of a series of private conversations. In 1928 when Stanislavsky spoke from the stage of the Art Theatre and Chekhov saw his own classroom words quoted back to him in a governmental letter, both men realized that censorship concerned the spoken as well as the written word. No wonder Soviet citizens worried about listeners who might monitor what was said and report any violations of political etiquette to the Party! So too did Stanislavsky.

Transcripts of his rehearsals and conversations with director Boris V. Zon from 1933 to 1938 provide excellent examples of how censorship could affect the lore of acting. In an opera rehearsal from 1933, Stanislavsky carefully couches remarks that touch upon his abiding interest in Yoga (Chapter 9). "Reach your hand out to Olga," he tells a singer. "Completely. So that your hand calls to her, so that it radiates the call." He then names the Sanskrit term behind his assumption that a hand can radiate, but with an implicit criticism of it. "Earlier we naively called this *prana*" (Zon 1955:445). "Naively" alerts his listeners to his suspect source without admitting any present fault.

In a subsequent conversation with Zon about the rehearsal, Stanislavsky further implies his continuing interest in Yoga by mixing together a verbal dismissal, an unattributed citation, and a physical demonstration of *prana*. The dismissal comes when he makes light of the term "radiation" as merely shorthand "in our actors' jargon." Then, when he describes how the physical energy of radiation moves through the body like "mercury," he refers to a recurrent image for *prana* from the books on Yoga that he studied. Finally, he makes the concept concrete as a "distinctive kind of gymnastics." "Now all my energy is in my shoulder! Now further down in my elbow! My wrist! In the hand! The fingers! And now it reverses direction!" (Zon 1955:446). Stanislavsky uses dismissals (e.g. SS II 1989:132) and unidentified references to banned books in *An Actor's Work on Himself* as well.

Zon's transcripts also suggest how Soviet watchdogs, witnessing conversations silently, added undercurrents of tension to otherwise apparently casual communications. Playing this shadowy role in Zon's chats with Stanislavsky is the young actor Mikhail Nikolaevich Kedrov (1893–1972), an assistant at Stanislavsky's last home studio and the major promoter of a Sovietized Method of Physical Actions (Chapter 10) during the 1940s and 1950s. It is as if, Kedrov has already been appointed by unseen authorities to become Stanislavsky's official Marxist interpreter.

A flash forward to the 1940s explains how Kedrov's apparently innocent presence can be interpreted as sinister. When Stanislavsky died, Kedrov actively donned the mantle of true heir by staging Stanislavsky's last rehearsals of Molière's *Tartuffe*. After Nemirovich-Danchenko's death, Kedrov became artistic director of the Moscow Art Theatre with the government's assent. Kedrov thus became Stanislavsky's posthumous public voice.

But Kedrov told a radically different story about Stanislavsky's experiments during his last years than did Knebel, also an assistant in the home Studio. Whereas Kedrov taught that Stanislavsky had moved beyond his early errors to arrive in his last years at a scientifically accurate "Method of Physical Actions," Knebel stressed how the multi-dimensional (physical, spiritual and psychological) scope of their mentor's last work built upon the foundation of his earlier experiments. She would later call Stanislavsky's last rehearsal technique "Active Analysis" in order to differentiate it from Kedrov's Marxist intervention.

To rid the Art Theatre of her dissident view, Kedrov abruptly fired Knebel in a manner that mirrored Stalin's ironfisted leadership. At the end of the 1949 season, a minor theatre administrator officially informed Knebel that Kedrov would work only with those who considered themselves his "students," and as she observes, being "the same age, his comrade, his colleague" she could not (1967:477). When she arrived for work the next season, she found that all the productions in which she was scheduled to perform, even Chekhov's *The Cherry Orchard* in which she played Charlotta, were pulled from the repertory.

With this future history in mind, Kedrov's presence in Zon's notes registers differently than it might otherwise. Kedrov first appears in the transcripts in 1934, the year in which Stanislavsky's confinement to his home began in earnest. Moreover, Kedrov arrives in the middle of a conversation about "radiation." He had arrived early, Stanislavsky explains, for an appointment to review drafts of *An Actor's Work on Himself* (Zon 1955:466–7). Was Kedrov listening at the door so that he could enter if and when the discussion became too seditious? Did his appointment betoken the early on-going censorship of Stanislavsky's writings? Was the young man monitoring Stanislavsky's conversations for the authorities? Such paranoid questions arise from the atmosphere of the times, which was affecting Stanislavsky, too; he "speaks loudly and strongly, as if trying to destroy an invisible enemy" (1955:445).

Kedrov then joins Stanislavsky and Zon on an automobile drive through Moscow for pleasure (1955:468). That Stanislavsky (stricken by poverty after the revolution and in need of the Hapgoods' charity to support himself abroad) would have access to a luxurious automobile and use it for an outing of this sort is strikingly out of the ordinary. Was the automobile one of those perks provided by Stalin to keep the old man compliant (Chapter 5)? And did Kedrov accompany the party to make sure that the now internally exiled Stanislavsky behave himself? While Stanislavsky treats him as a talented young student, nothing more, Kedrov's presence brings to mind Michael Chekhov's enthusiastic student spies.

When Zon next mentions Kedrov, the young actor arrives at an especially critical moment and explicitly voices communist ideology. It is August 1934 and Stanislavsky has just learned that the USSR has ratified Socialist Realism as its official artistic style. The "main task of the Soviet writer," he muses, "is to show the soul of the new people." Kedrov strenuously objects: "The soul is a figure of speech." Stanislavsky pushes back in precisely the same way as he will soon do with the editors of his books. "Think up an equivalent word," he dares the young man, "and I will happily use it." But Kedrov cannot (Zon 1955:468). So too will Stanislavsky's spiritually unacceptable word resonate in his censored acting manuals.

Finally, Zon's conversations with Stanislavsky suggest how the pressures of censorship were already shaping his manual. In 1933, Zon reports that Stanislavsky expressed fear that his books might not accurately convey the fact that "my new method is a development of what has come before." In these words, Stanislavsky seems to endorse Knebel's future teachings over that of Kedrov's point of view. Does he already anticipate Marxist distortions of his System? He appears desperate as he asks Zon "in complete seriousness" to "tell actors, tell students…. Please…. Tell them, explain to them, try without fail, and then tell me what comes of it. This is for me terribly important" (1955:453–4). By 1934, however, when Zon tries to turn their conversation back to the dangers of misinterpretation, Stanislavsky avoids the topic, by "pointing to Kedrov who was standing to the side" and saying "it is the work of the young to elucidate everything" (1955:471). Was Stanislavsky aware that he could not speak freely in front of Kedrov? Does he actually expect clarity from Kedrov? In either case, Kedrov's presence foretells the Sovietization of the System, which, like its Americanization, drops the very elements that can best propel it into the postmodern world.

The painful effects of censorship are everywhere palpable in Zon's transcriptions both in their spoken conversations and in Stanislavsky's anxieties for his writing project.

An Actor's Work on Himself

If ostensibly private conversations could be so conditioned by the prescriptions of Soviet censorship, one can easily imagine how much more so were texts intended for public dissemination. Stanislavsky's Russian books may be unabridged in comparison with the classic Hapgood translations, but they are censored. In 1929, 1930, and 1931, when Lyubov Gurevich read drafts of *An Actor's Work on Himself*, she warned her friend of the "dangers" in his work which "frighten her." She tells him that he is living "locked away in the world of your art" (Dybovskii 1992:49, 13, 39). She cautions him to bury his unacceptable thinking in approved language in order to escape the dangers. Where he takes her advice, he begins to write between the lines,[2] as most Soviet authors would learn to do or perish. Where he refuses, he pushes back against her and the censors, as he did with Kedrov, by arguing that no other language will do. An author without Stanislavsky's international fame to protect him might well have seen his book perish in the resistance.

Two major aspects of Stanislavsky's drafts rankled with the powers-that-be. On the one hand, many of his examples and exercises recall a bygone era of capitalism and bourgeois values. As such, they were perceived as offensive to Soviet youth. On the other hand, his System itself—based upon the premise that there is an indissoluble link between mind and body, spirit and flesh—violated the required materialistic philosophy. Body and flesh were acceptable, mind questionable (if it meant the subconscious), and spirit unacceptable.

The first of these criticisms makes sense when seen in light of the realities of a country torn apart by revolution and civil war, still suffering wide-spread economic depression and material deprivation. In an acting exercise, Stanislavsky's fictional *persona*, Tortsov, asks his student Maloletkova to search for a diamond brooch, lost somewhere in her apartment. He tells her that by finding it, she can insure her continued study at school. Its value will pay for her classes. In another exercise, Stanislavsky uses a scene from a play in which a character inherits a fortune. In Soviet Russia, such examples that depend upon owning jewels and capital did offend. In a recurrent exercise—the improvisation of the "burned money"—a clerk has brought a large amount of cash home from his office to count, but his handicapped brother-in-law playfully burns it (SS II 1989:89, 146). The physical reality of handling, counting, and burning money strikes a particularly disturbing note in view of the poverty of the times. These examples are especially striking when one considers that after the revolution Stanislavsky himself had lost the family business and fortune, wore threadbare clothes, and struggled to find hard currency to pay for medical treatment for his son's tubercular condition.

Suggesting self-censorship, Gurevich urges him to find other examples. He answers that he can think of no others, and resists the pressure to contemporize his ideas. He wants to write about universal truths, he says, calling his system a "psychotechnique for all times" (SS VIII 1961:271), not only for these times. His original examples remain in the published text. If we take Stanislavsky at his word, he believes that Soviet references will date the book and narrow its scope. No doubt he was correct, given that Theatre Arts Books objected to even classical Russian references as obscure. But his resistance registers as especially ironic in the twenty-first century, given that postmodern scholars react to his references as limiting the book to either Romantic or Realist aesthetics.

The second area of concern—the linking of body to mind and flesh to soul—interrogates the System's terminology. In 1929 Gurevich warns her friend about terms such as "affective memory" which do not conform to predominant trends in Soviet psychology. She repeatedly asks him to seek out scientists to gain a better understanding of current communist thought (Dybovskii 1992:13). In 1931, she warns that terms like "the life of the human spirit," "the soul," and the "magic if" (for which she suggests substituting "creative if") invite "Marxist scissors" because they invoke non-material ideas (Dybovskii 1992:49). Kedrov's reaction to Stanislavsky's use of "soul" in 1934 bears out Gurevich's instinct. And indeed in 1936, the Central Committee of the Communist Party writes to Stanislavsky, objecting to these terms as "hazy" and adding "intuition" and "subconscious" to the list (Dybovskii 1992:101).

Stanislavsky may have compromised his theatre to Stalin, but he defended his book in much the same way that he had defended his use of "soul" to Kedrov. All the concepts attacked by dialectical materialism go to the heart of his System. He saw them as essential components of artistic creativity and defended suspect words like "soul" and "subconscious" in his response to the Central Committee (Benedetti 1990b:346–7). The Party, like Kedrov, had no substitutes to suggest and thus insisted that Stanislavsky "concretely" uncover their "realistic" content in his texts. (Dybovskii 1992:101). These conditions are significant when one compares the Party's sanctioned definition of Socialist Realism as the form that "*demands* of the artist the truthful, historically concrete representation of reality in its revolutionary development" (Jansen 1988:110).

Compromises were made on both sides. Some passages and phrases, such as the "ocean of the subconscious" and Yoga's *prana* appear in the 1935 typescript of *An Actor's Work on Himself, Part I* [Typescript Chapters XVI, X; English:267, 14], but disappear in the 1938 edition; other sections were adjusted in ways that would not exclude essential ideas, but would be palatable to the authorities. In both versions, Stanislavsky includes a passage that speaks of "psychotechnique" in engineering metaphors [Typescript II; English:187; SS II 1989:61], echoing Stalin's invocation of the artist as "the engineer of the soul" (Ermolaev 1997:53). In the 1938 edition, Stanislavsky compares the spark that arises from the subconscious to a chemical, hence material, reaction [Russian:440], a comparison absent in his 1935 draft. Similarly, whenever Stanislavsky mentions the emotions, he always connects them with the body thus stressing their material, hence "concrete," basis.

By making such concessions to materialism, Stanislavsky made safe for the censors what his Soviet critics called "idealistic" in the System. In other words, he made the immaterial psyche and soul "concretely realistic," as he had been asked to do by the authorities. Because he was able to side-step the censor in these ways, his Russian books still serve as keys to his actual concerns about art. As he had told Gurevich, changing words is one thing, changing concepts and ideas is another (SS IX 1999:452). In this regard, he published a remarkable book given the conditions of the times.

With the System touted as "the only method for reaching Socialist Realism in the theatre" (Mokul'skii 1957:137) censorship alone would not suffice to force it into Marxist molds; interpretive criticism now came into play. With so much of the soul and subconscious left in the book, Soviet critics made the content more acceptable to Marxism than the text itself. The Byelorussian scholar Anthony Adamovich coined the term "censorial criticism" because Soviet scholarship "acts as a watchdog for the [censorship] system, sniffing around and pouncing on anything the censor has missed or let through" (Dewhirst and Farrell 1973:41). Thus, Soviet interpretations of the System emphasized its physical aspects, privileging the materialist version of the Method of Physical Actions over other experimental techniques for the actor. Reading for Stanislavsky's subtexts, therefore, gets harder, not easier when we begin to read what others in the USSR wrote about the System.

Reading the system between the lines

If Western theatre artists intend to look for Stanislavsky's System, they must learn to read between the lines as did Russian readers. While writers (Stanislavsky among them) made compromises with censors, readers came to mistrust surface meanings in books. They knew that authors used multiple strategies to insure publication, and thus Russians "in their early childhood" turned reading skills into "a fine art" (Dewhirst and Farrell 1973:33). As Blyum observes:

> The ability to discover the hidden, inner, second sense of a work and interpret it has always been an essential feature of the shared creativity of the [Russian and Soviet] writer and the reader. The author addresses his "reader-friend," counting on him to participate in the creative process and conjures up parallels relevant to the realities of Soviet life.
>
> (2003:6)

To read Russian-language publications by and about Stanislavsky in this Soviet way means deconstructing the strategies writers used to accommodate the culture of censorship. In the words of the science writer Leonid Finkelstein, who spent five years in Stalin's labor camps, "the Western [reader] must not only be familiar with the [cultural] picture from the outside but also with what is going on internally, below the surface" (Dewhirst and Farrel 1973:146). A reader must weigh a book's contents against its context and also consider the author's ideological point of view. In short, reading between the lines can only succeed if one reads as an "insider" (Dewhirst and Farrell 1973:146).

I admit that I read about the System in this way. Of course, I weigh Stanislavsky's ideas and techniques against my experience in acting and directing, as I expect you, my readers, to do as well. But I also use my expertise in Russian studies to decipher Stanislavsky's subtext for those of you who may be unfamiliar with the forces of history that impacted him. This book comes from this sort of reading. Moreover, in the next few pages, I offer you, my "reader-friend," a guide to reading in this way yourself. By learning even a few rules of the censorship game played in the USSR, any reader can begin to read between the lines for the subtexts that lie beneath the rhetorical garb of Socialist Realism and Marxist ideology, making revised understandings of Stanislavsky and his System possible.

Censorship in the USSR proceeded as a multi-layered process; a manuscript passed from author to editors and finally to the government's censors. Every time an author or editor made a change, however small or large, including those required by the censor, the text would be resubmitted to the authorities. Few texts passed without censors reading them at least three times (Blyum 2003:2). This system applied to books, journals, exhibitions, public speeches, performances, everything (Ermolaev 1997:1–10).

The so-called *Glavlit* (a stable acronym for the often changing name of Moscow's main administrative center for censorship) was founded in 1922, reorganized in 1931, and disbanded in 1991 when the USSR fell. Starting in 1925 the Communist

Party issued to *Glavlit* heavy tomes entitled *The Secret List* that laid out what was acceptable and unacceptable. Regular updates were circulated in additional "directives," so frequent that censors held regularly scheduled staff meetings to keep abreast of changes. During the worst years of Stalinism, rules could change daily and hourly, often appearing nonsensical when what was acceptable yesterday is banned today. Everyone was kept off balance all the time. Moreover, censors were not exempt from breathing this atmosphere of confusion. They too could be imprisoned, tortured, and executed for their mistakes, however inadvertent. Thus, they tended to err on the side of caution, banning anything that fell into gray areas.

As the rules of censorship kept changing, writers employed a host of different strategies to get their books into print. They freely used the so-called "Aesopian language" to suggest subtextual ideas in the same way that Aesop taught lessons through parable. By placing a story in another place or time, authors might comment on contemporary issues; the reign of Ivan the Terrible, for example, could stand in for Stalin's regime. Some ploys to get around the censor seem petty but were nonetheless consequential. Writers might consciously mistype dates to make controversial items appear to have occurred before the revolution; they would then count on readers to understand the willful error (Dewhirst and Farrell 1973:10). Authors sometimes used page lay-outs to suggest something that they could not say. A word conveniently hyphenated at the end of a printed line, "anti-capitalism" for example, could appear as its opposite if the reader assumes the start of the next line carries the author's true intent (Plamper 2001:535). Similarly, the juxtaposition of image and text might carry weight. For example, a journalist placed the obituary of the Nobel Prize winning Boris Pasternak (maligned by the government for having published abroad) next to an appropriate headline—*A Magician of Poetry*—for another article about a minor poet (Dewhirst and Farrell 1973:61).

Such strategies to circumvent the censor (too many for full consideration here) not only worked, but became recognizable enough to make reading between the lines possible. Three in particular apply directly to the Stanislavsky tradition: self-censorship, a forced rhetoric of Realism, and quotations from communist philosophy.

An author's first line of defense was, unsurprisingly, to avoid anything to which the censor might object. In the 1930s, when Stanislavsky was finishing *An Actor's Work on Himself*, such self-censorship "gradually entered the flesh and blood of the majority of writers, stifling them" (Blyum 2000:14). When Gurevich advises Stanislavsky to jettison pre-revolutionary references and to replace vaguely non-materialist terms like "magic if" and "subconscious" with more concrete words, she suggests precisely this type of self-defense. Perhaps Stanislavsky's growing reliance upon editors as different as Hapgood, Gurevich, and Kedrov testifies to his inability to handle self-censorship as evidenced by his disastrous speech in 1928. Identifying self-censorship entails comparing published works to archival records (Stanislavsky's letters to Gurevich and Hapgood, alternative drafts of his books like the 1935 version he sent to Hapgood, and the Bancroft Typescript, etc.).

The second strategy—using the rhetoric of Realism to make all sorts of ideas acceptable to Soviet ideology—is by far the most crucially important to the Stanislavsky tradition and only cultural context can expose such language as strategic.

Blyum sees the use of ideologically inflected writing as the propping up of a text on "Marxist crutches" (2000:39). Literary critic Aleksey Yakushev observes that "by making Soviet terminology a vehicle for other ideas" an author can "undermin[e] the official ideology" (Dewhirst and Farrell 1973:74). Readers who take Stanislavsky at his word without seeking his deeper subtext can easily mistake his texts as singularly interested in Psychological Realism.

Stanislavsky demonstrates the simplest use of this ploy when he adopts engineering metaphors to evoke Stalin's famous rhetorical flourish that made the artist into an "engineer of the soul." More significantly, he uses this second strategy with extreme subtlety whenever he speaks of "realism," "reality," "nature," "sincerity," "belief," and "truth" to suggest that true art, in all its manifestations, communicates human experience. While such words register on the surface as an apology for Realism (hence Socialist Realism), Stanislavsky actually redefines them for his own purposes. In his view, these words do not specify any particular theatrical style but denote instead the deep human communication possible in theatre of the highest order in any aesthetic style. As Russian scholar Boris Zingerman writes, "Creative fantasy and adherence to life's truth do not contradict each other in [Stanislavsky's] view." He could find reality in non-realistic stagings as long as they communicated felt experience. "Stanislavsky's position was [...] fantastic: truthfulness was the same as theatricality." Zingerman continues with an anecdote from an opera rehearsal in the early 1930s. Stanislavsky astonished the cast by announcing that because "truth takes us to the limits" of imagination, "the more truthful [a production] the more theatrical" (Vinogradskaia 2000:5).

Stanislavsky's oxymoron—real theatricality—is precisely the kind of paradoxical language that censorship provoked in writers. "Equivocation," after all, "empowers alternative interpretations" (Jansen 1988:198). As Blyum suggests, using the rhetoric of Realism to speak of theatricalism is much like George Orwell's depiction of *Newspeak* in his novel *Nineteen Eighty-Four*; in the USSR words sometimes could indeed mean their opposite (Blyum 1994:2). In fact, the label "Socialist Realism" itself is *Newspeak*, since it required the writer to idealize the communist state and optimistically ignore painful aspects of reality. As novelist Konstantin Fedin said, "All talk of realism in such a situation is hypocrisy" (Volkov 2004:203). Without understanding the System's central oxymoron (examined fully in Chapter 7), one cannot get beyond the mythic portrait of Stanislavsky as an exclusively realistic artist.

But was Stanislavsky's use of "truth" for "theatricality" a conscious strategy for writing between the lines or merely fortuitous? It is difficult to say. He had grown up in a world that aspired to sincere and truthful art, and he may very well have used familiar words to say what he meant, much as he had used pre-revolutionary examples to illustrate his ideas. As Zingerman observes, "Nature and truth in life had always fed his imagination;" it was natural to him to see truth and imagination as extensions of one another (Vinogradskaia 2003:5). Could he guess that his nineteenth-century language would be willfully misread? If Zon is correct about Stanislavsky's anxious concern for his books, then, yes, he knew what could happen.

When putting Stanislavsky into focus, this second strategy in the censorship game (using the rhetoric of Realism for theatricalist modes of thought) deserves serious attention, not only in terms of Stanislavsky's own books, but also for those by his

Russian-language interpreters. Soviet practitioners and scholars alike, from Kedrov to Knebel, used Stanislavsky's rhetoric of sincerity to gain the censor's trust.

Shortly after Stanislavsky's death, self-censorship and *Newspeak* alone became insufficient measures, however. Authors were now expected, indeed required, to cite key communist thinkers (Marx, Engels, Lenin, Stalin) to demonstrate ideological loyalty. This third strategy in the censorship game was used, not by Stanislavsky, but by his proponents. Moreover, like the rhetoric of Realism, quotations from the four major ideologues could be used to support any idea, even the subversive. Thus, to read past such citations, one must know something about the author's views. Consider, for example, two major Soviet interpreters of Stanislavsky, Pavel Simonov and Maria Knebel. They both use the same communist philosophy to argue opposite opinions of the System, again demonstrating how words, without contextual understanding, can mislead.

The Marxist scientist and psychologist, Simonov, set out to prove that the System was founded exclusively on behaviorist psychology, a science in sympathy with Marxism and opposed to Freud's non-materialistic views. Thus, Simonov appropriately begins his *Method of K. S. Stanislavsky and the Physiology of Emotions* with an epigraph from Marx that links humans to the animal kingdom (1962:5) Quotations from the communist leaders pepper the entire book as Simonov works hard to prove his main premise:

> In the realms of theory and the practice of scenic art, Stanislavsky emerged as a logical materialist. [Thus...], Soviet socialist reality, the world view of the Communist Party of the Soviet Union, and the classic tomes of Marxism–Leninism have enormous meaning in Stanislavsky's creative work.
>
> (1962:7)

In light of Stanislavsky's proven naiveté in reading political winds, Simonov's idea is patently absurd.

Knebel strove to preserve the System's full continuum of mind, body and soul. She fought against what she called the Marxist "vulgarization" of Stanislavsky's last technique (1971:79; 121–3). Therefore, when she quotes Marx, she does so to insure that her competing story get told. Like Simonov, she begins her book, *About the Active Analysis of Plays and Roles*, with a statement from Marx. She uses his quotation, "ideas do not exist independently of language," to substantiate Stanislavsky's notion that words on stage always imply action (1982:4). Moreover, despite the fact that Knebel's overall thesis contradicts Simonov's, she like him peppers her book with the required quotations from the major Marxists. She even draws many of her examples of acting techniques from Nikolai Pogodin's play, *The Chimes of the Kremlin*, in which Lenin appears as the leading character. Moreover, as she develops her thesis, she, like Stanislavsky before her, uses the rhetoric of Realism to make her ideas safe for publication.

To see through Knebel's ruse, the reader must, in some sense come to know her as had Shapiro. The context of her life and career provide the necessary clues to her actual thinking. First, Knebel saw the terrors of Stalinism first hand. In 1940 her brother Nikolai was inexplicably arrested in front of his family while they were on vacation. His branding as an enemy of the state meant that she too for a time became dangerous company. "In the corridors of the Moscow Art Theatre people would avoid meeting her, so that they would not be obliged to say hello," recalled one of her students from those years (Liadov 1998:100). Knebel knew the potential costs of speaking too honestly in her books. Second, her directorial career proves that she thought outside the Soviet aesthetic box. For example, when she staged the Chinese fairy tale *The Magic Flower* (1958), she broke away from the stricture of Socialist Realism. The actors wrote the text through improvisations. They used the stylized physical vocabulary of Chinese theatrical dance, taught to them by a specialist in the form. As they worked, they created "bolder and more varied forms of expression" (1967:508–9). When *The Magic Flower* premiered, it astonished audiences with its unique stylistic combination of language, dance, and pantomime. As critic Pavel Markov wrote, "theatrical stylization became fairy tale reality" (Vladimirova 1991:133).

Among Soviet writers the use of political quotations became so pervasive that sometimes the strategy emigrated along with its authors. For example, exchanging Marx for the US President, émigré Sonia Moore[3] begins *The Stanislavski System* with an epigraph from John F. Kennedy: "Art establishes the basic human truths which must serve as the touchstones of our judgment." Not only does she choose a quotation that supports the Soviet truism that the best art is truthful (hence realistic), but she also adds yet another familiar Soviet notion, that art should edify the populace: "President Kennedy's views about art echo those of Konstantin Sergeevitch Stanislavki [... for whom] theater is an institution of cultural and moral education" (1965:19).

This brief guide to reading between the lines would remain incomplete without a glance at how the highly educated people who censored publications fought back against the writers with an all-embracing strategy of their own, "the abolition of ambiguity in language." Censors knew very well how subtext can emerge from willfully "hazy" and paradoxical language, and so "onemeaningness" became a key requirement for publication (Plamper 2001). They scrutinized texts for anything that might be read in more than one unambiguous way. How terrible for the System which Stanislavsky saw as multivalent! He wanted to provide more than one path for actors, because in the end, as a practitioner himself, he knew that people with different personalities might need to work in different ways (Chapter 4). No wonder Soviet interpreters like Kedrov and Simonov sought to make the System's multiplicity appear univalent (Chapter 10). To borrow Knebel's words, when "we dismiss that which is complex" in favor of "simplicity," that which is complex risks "being reduced to simplicity, and quite often loses its true scope" (M. Chekhov II 1995:21).

Soviet censorship, in the final analysis, stripped the surface layer in both acting lore and Stanislavsky's books of richness. A Soviet joke says it all: "What is a telegraph pole? An edited pine tree" (Dewhirst and Farrell 1973:107). As the limbs of the tree are cut to make the pole, so too was Stanislavsky's transcendent understanding of art cut from the trunk of his early realism. Only in the subtexts of both lore and books can one find the limbs and leaves of the System intact.

All the fragments of history in the first two sections of this book—the realities and ironies of Stanislavsky's tours to the US, the American enterprises and lore that emanated from the tours, the abridgement of his books in English, and their censorship in Russian—create the necessary cultural context from which Stanislavsky can emerge on his own terms and inform acting practice in the twenty-first century. The next section of this book examines three key tenets of the System by weighing practice and lore, separating his actual work from his publicly managed *persona*, comparing different drafts of the same texts, referring to uncensored archival records, and sorting out which of his witnesses and interpreters can best be trusted, in short by reading between the lines.

Figure 1 A formal portrait of Stanislavsky at age 60, taken at the White photographic studio in New York during the Moscow Art Theatre tours to the United States. Stanislavsky and his company rarely posed in their street clothes. Russian publicity focused on the artistic work of actors, not their personal lives. Stanislavsky was especially hesitant to appear out of costume in the 1920s because his worn clothing testified to the financial losses he had suffered following the Russian revolution.

Figure 2 Stanislavsky and his wife, actress Maria Lilina, on 14 September 1922 as they boarded the ocean liner *Majestic* to sail to the United States via Europe. Shortly after this photograph was taken, their son, Igor, fell ill and Lilina remained in Europe to care for him. Stanislavsky continued on with the company, and when he arrived in New York, the tour's impresario, Morris Gest, arranged for another woman to "stand in" for Lilina in photographs. Thus, Stanislavsky learned about the American publicity machine.

Figure 3 The Russian-born impresario Morris Gest shakes Stanislavsky's hand, while Olga Knipper-Chekhova and the rest of the Moscow Art Theatre company look on in New York, 1923. Gest's aggressive publicity campaign surprised and shocked the Russian actors, who regularly refused to give interviews about their personal lives at home.

Figure 4 Fund-raising prospectus by Morris Gest for the 1924 Moscow Art Theatre Tour to the United States. The artistic success of the 1923 tour convinced Gest that a second tour could be more profitable. In 1925 and 1926, he would also bring Nemirovich-Danchenko's Musical Theatre to New York for a tour.

Figure 5 The Moscow Art Theatre troupe outside the White House after meeting Calvin Coolidge, Washington DC, March 1924. This group represents the first Soviet citizens to shake the hand of a US President. From left to right: actors Evgenia Rayevskaya, Lydia Koreneva, and Aleksandr Vishnevsky; US theatre critic Norman Hapgood; actors Olga Knipper-Chekhova, Ivan Moskvin, and Stanislavsky; translator Elizabeth Reynolds Hapgood; actors Vasily Luzhsky and Nikolai Podgorny; translator Sergei Bertenson; Morris Gest's representative Mr. Spink; and the leading actor Vasily Kachalov.

Figure 6 Stanislavsky sitting beside Rudolph Valentino on the set of the film, *Monsieur Beaucaire*, at the Famous Players Studio in Astoria, New York, 1924. For a time, Stanislavsky considered filming the Moscow Art Theatre production of *Tsar Fyodor*. He changed his mind when he learned that Studio executives would rewrite the play to emphasize romance over history.

Figure 7 The co-founders of the Moscow Art Theatre. Notice that Nemirovich-Danchenko is standing on a step in order to match Stanislavsky's height. Their artistic collaboration made theatre history, but differences in taste, sensibility, and values made their personal relationship stormy from the first. They respected, loved, hated, needed and envied each other for more than four decades.

Figure 8 Stanislavsky's Realism in Chekhov's *Three Sisters*, 1903, Act IV. On the left, Vershinin (Stanislavsky) bids a painful goodbye to Masha (Olga Knipper-Chekhova), while, on the right, Olga (Margarita Savitskaia) and Irina (Nina Litovtseva) turn away to give the two lovers privacy. Notice the illusionistic set, full of the details of daily life. Staged before the System, the cast could not then imagine Stanislavsky's future impact on actor training.

«СИНЯЯ ПТИЦА» М. МЕТЕРЛИНКА.   Моск. Худож. Театръ.

Figure 9 Stanislavsky's Symbolism in Maeterlinck's *The Blue Bird*, 1908. The masked figure of "Time" (Nikolai Znamensky) is surrounded by the "Souls of the Unborn." Notice the abstract costumes, sculptural grouping of figures, and the absence of a set. This production was staged when Stanislavsky first began to grapple with the principles of his System. The production ran continuously throughout the twentieth century, and over time, became a fairy-tale for children rather than a statement of Symbolist aesthetics.

Figure 10 Leopold Sulerzhitsky, Stanislavsky's assistant, friend, and confidant in the early development of the System. "Suler" was the heart of the First Studio, created specifically to investigate the principles of acting. As a follower of Tolstoy's religious beliefs, "Suler" believed in the spiritual power of art. As a former sailor and adventurer, he inspired his students to think experimentally about theatre.

Figure 11 A cartoon (1907) of Stanislavsky's Symbolist production, *The Drama of Life* by Hamsun. Depicted are the tall Stanislavsky (Kareno) and his frequent acting partner, Olga Knipper-Chekhova (Teresita). Sitting on the infinite shore of the ocean, the idealist Kareno reaches his head above the clouds, while the earthy Teresita tries to entice him back to reality. In this production, Stanislavsky stripped the stage of all props and set pieces and emphasized the actors' ability to bring imagination to life.

Figure 12 A cartoon (c. 1909) lampooning Stanislavsky's search for the natural laws of acting. The founding members of the Moscow Art Theatre found their director's innovative acting exercises extraneous and his obsessive experimentation with acting a distraction from rehearsals. He became known as an eccentric throughout the company. The cartoon captures this early twentieth century view of Stanislavsky.

Figure 13 Stanislavsky and Elizabeth Reynolds Hapgood, Badenweiler, Germany, 1930. They met in Washington, DC, at the White House when she translated for him and President Coolidge. This photograph dates from the year in which Stanislavsky gave Hapgood all rights to his books and she became his "attorney-in-fact," translating, editing and protecting his rights throughout the world.

Figure 14 Stanislavsky at work on his acting manual in the late 1930s. Notice the Soviet medal on his lapel, showing that he is a People's Artist of the USSR. In September 1936, the Communist Party created this new award for those in the forefront of Soviet arts. The first People's Artists were Stanislavsky, Nemirovich-Danchenko and two Moscow Art Theatre actors, Vasily Kachalov and Ivan Moskvin.

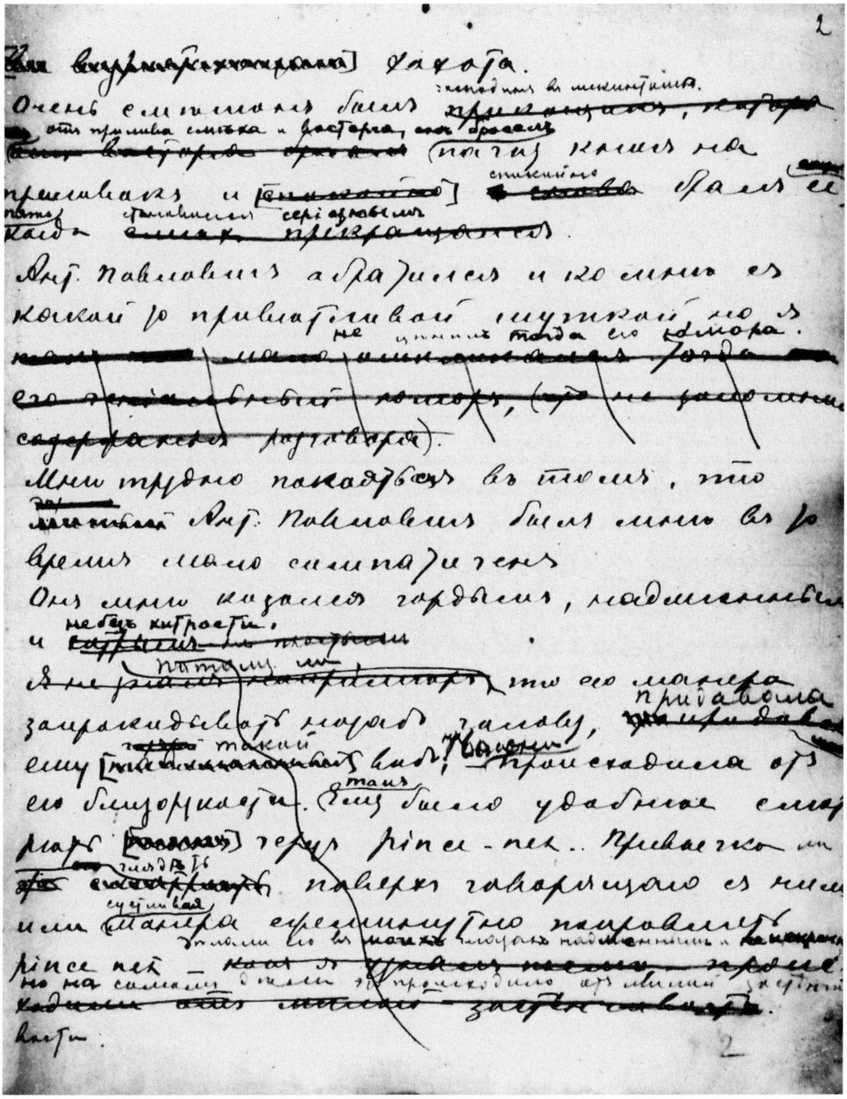

Figure 15 A tortured manuscript page from Stanislavsky's *An Actor's Work on Himself*. Stanislavsky wrote obsessively about acting since the age of fourteen, but, as this page demonstrates, describing an actor's tacit knowledge in words is a difficult endeavor.

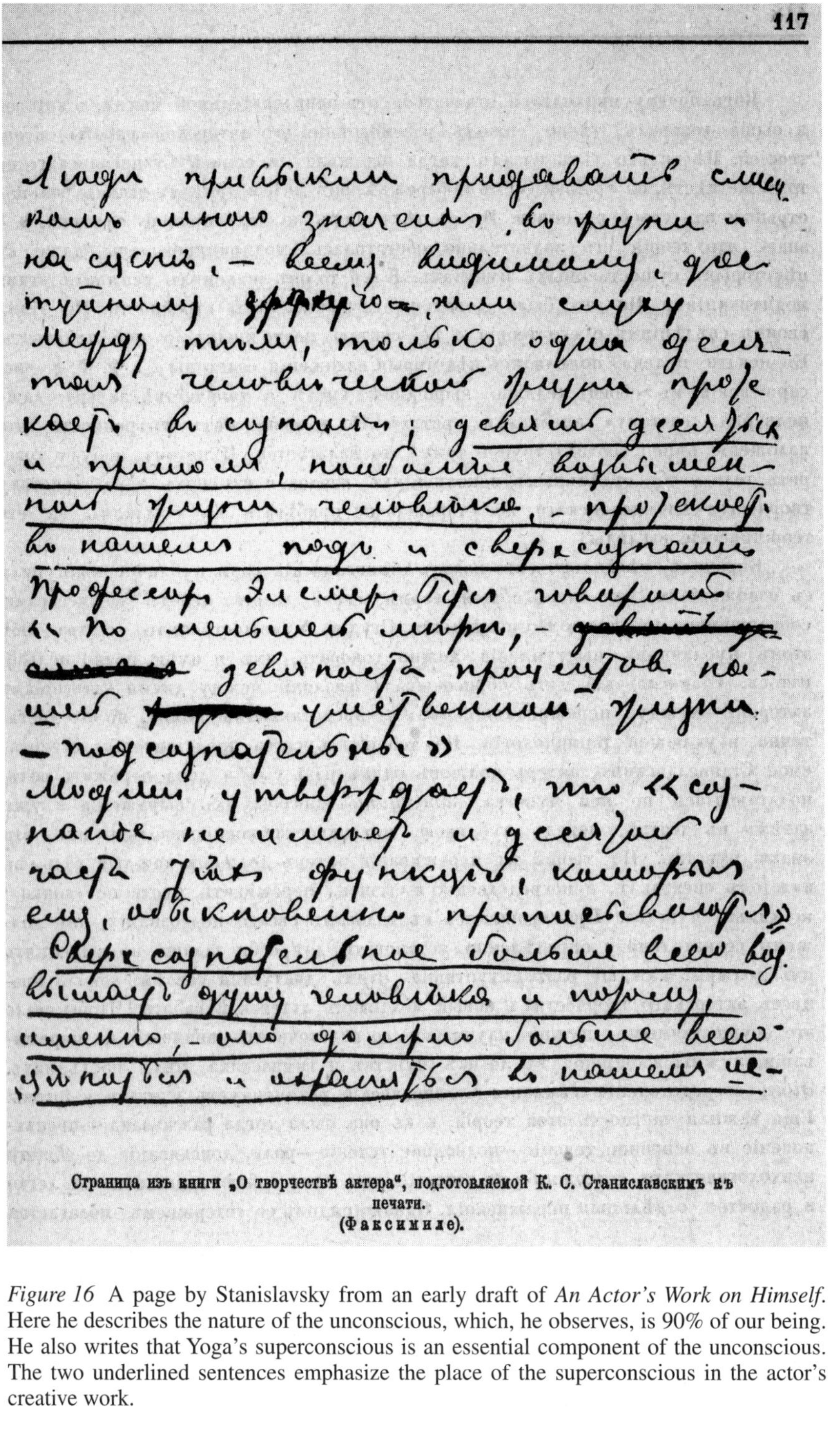
117

Люди привыкли придавать слишкомъ много значенія, въ жизни и на сценѣ, — всему видимому, доступному зрѣнію или слуху. Между тѣмъ, только одна десятая человѣческой жизни протекаетъ въ сознаніи; девять десятыхъ и притомъ, наиболѣе важной части жизни человѣка, — протекаетъ въ нашемъ подъ и сверхсознаніи. Профессоръ Элмеръ Гетсъ говоритъ: «По меньшей мѣрѣ, — девяносто процентовъ нашей умственной жизни — подсознательны». Модсли утверждаетъ, что «сознаніе не имѣетъ и десятой части тѣхъ функцій, которыя ему обыкновенно приписываютъ». Сверхсознательное больше всего возвышаетъ душу человѣка и потому, именно, — оно должно больше всего цѣниться и охраняться въ нашемъ ис-

Страница изъ книги „О творчествѣ актера", подготовляемой К. С. Станиславскимъ къ печати.
(Факсимиле).

Figure 16 A page by Stanislavsky from an early draft of *An Actor's Work on Himself*. Here he describes the nature of the unconscious, which, he observes, is 90% of our being. He also writes that Yoga's superconscious is an essential component of the unconscious. The two underlined sentences emphasize the place of the superconscious in the actor's creative work.

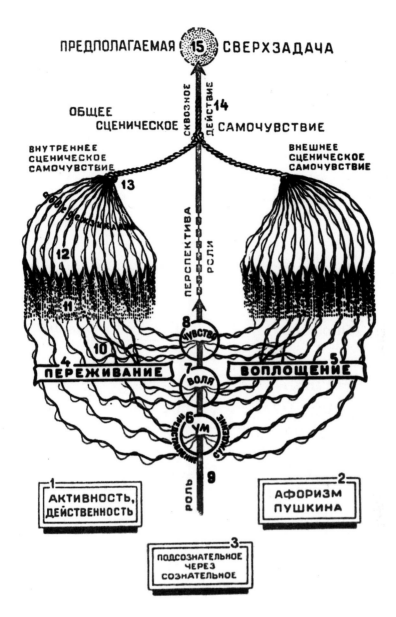

Figure 17 Stanislavsky's drawing of the System. From bottom to top: 1. "Dynamism";
2. "Pushkin's Aphorism" (i.e. Given Circumstances); 3. "The Subconscious by means of
the Conscious"; 4. "Experiencing"; 5. "Embodiment"; 6. "Mind"; 7. "Will"; 8. "Feeling";
9. "The Role"; Running along the line. "Perspective of the Role" and "Through Action";
Between 12 and 13. "abcdefghijk" (i.e. subtle reference to all the lures and techniques in the
System); Either side of 14. "General Theatrical Sense of Self"; Left of 14. "Inner Theatrical
Sense of Self"; Right of 14. "Outer Theatrical Sense of Self"; 15. "Proposed Supertask".
Notice that the drawing looks like lungs, suggesting the rhythmic breathing exercises from
Yoga that Stanislavsky adapted for actors.

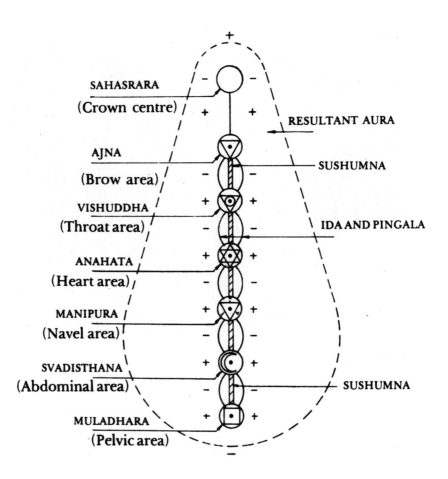

Figure 18 The chakras of Yoga, which are the psychic centers of energy that lie along the body's spine. Comparing Stanislavsky's drawing of the System (above) to this one, Stanislavsky's psychic initiators ("Mind", "Will", "Feeling", nos. 6-8) become the actor's chakras.

Figure 19 Stanislavsky rehearsing Molière's *Tartuffe* in his Moscow home, 1937. To his left at the table sits the young actor Mikhail Kedrov. Notice, as well, that to Kedrov's left is a blank space. Taken during the time of Stalin's terror, it is likely that a person, who fell out of favor with the government, has been removed from the photograph.

Figure 20 Stanislavsky's books. The first Russian edition of *An Actor's Work on Himself* sits in the center of the bottom row. Surrounding it on all sides are translations of *My Life in Art* and other of his writings. Notice that the spelling of his name appears in a number of different transliterations: Stanislavsky, Stanislavski, Stanislavskij, Stanislawski, etc.

Part III
Transformation

7   Stanislavsky's lost term

Chapter Two of Stanislavsky's *An Actor Prepares* in Hapgood's translation begins with a critique. Tortsov's new students have just performed a series of scenes to acquaint him with their talents, and he identifies only two "instances" when "you who were playing, and we who were watching, gave ourselves up completely to what was happening on the stage. Such successful moments, by themselves we can recognize as belonging to the art of living a part" (1936:12).[1] The Russian word, "experiencing" (*perezhivanie*), which Hapgood renders here as "living a part," is crucial to Stanislavsky.

His System for the actor balances theory and practice. It is at once an aesthetic model, or, as Stanislavsky writes, "an entire culture in which one must grow up and be raised over the course of many years" (SS III 1990:372) and teachable techniques embedded in "an entire series of exercises" (SS I 1988:474). No single aspect of the System captures this precarious balance as completely as Stanislavsky's discussions of "experiencing," the term he chooses to describe what actors feel when the exercises successfully release their full creative potentials. Nor does Stanislavsky give to any other aspect of the System such weight. In short, experiencing becomes the means by which he turns his System into a theory of artistic creation and a practical way to distinguish actor as artist from actor as entertainer.

Experiencing, in short, is the *sine qua non* of the System. Stanislavsky persistently uses it to set his own brand of theatre apart. In the Russian version of the above passage, he baldly states that this special kind of art "is cultivated in our theatre and is mastered here in its school" (SS II 1989:59). Yet, however important, experiencing remains Stanislavsky's most elusive concept.

In the first place, it does not name anything concrete that can be described and learned, but rather identifies a creative state that the System can, with luck, foster. Throughout his writings, Stanislavsky relates "experiencing" to states of mind and being that seem more familiar: "inspiration," "creating," "creative moods," the activation of the "subconscious." He also compares it to the sensation of existing fully within the immediate moment—what he calls "I am" (*Ia esm'*) and what American actors generally call "moment-to-moment" work.[2]

In the second place, experiencing expresses a totality that cannot be broken down into component parts. After a rehearsal with Boleslavsky in preparation for the 1909 production of *A Month in the Country*, Stanislavsky records in his diary a detailed technical analysis of the scene on which they had worked that day, but, he muses, such deconstruction in and of itself means little. "Dramatic experiencing is the composite whole" (SS V Part 1 1993:480).

In the third place, experiencing resides within the tacit dimension; it can be known but not expressed. Stanislavsky primarily speaks of it from the actor's point of view, and the concept remains stubbornly subjective. All his attempts to pin it down sound equally abstract, metaphorical, and finally unsatisfying, despite the fact that most actors can know in their bones what this lost term means.

So then, what is "experiencing"? Stanislavsky describes this state as "happy" but "rare," when the actor is "seized" by the role (SS V Part 2 1994:363). At such a moment, the artist feels something akin to that of a yogi who has reached a higher state of consciousness; there is an "all-perceptive" sharpening of the senses, an "intense awareness," an "oceanic joy," and "bliss" (Yogananda 1993:166–7). Michael Chekhov, who experimented with the System at the First Studio, writes that, when an actor reaches this state:

> Everything changes for him at this happy moment. As the creator of his character, he becomes inwardly free of his own creation and becomes the observer of his own work. […] He has given to his image his flesh and blood, his ability to move and speak, to feel, to wish, and now the image disappears from the mind's eye and exists within him and acts upon his means of expression from inside him.
>
> (1991:155)

Contemporary jargon calls this state "flow," a term coined by US psychologist Mihaly Csikszentmihalyi who studies subjective accounts by athletes and artists at peak performance. As Mozart had said of composing centuries earlier, "My ideas flow, and I cannot say whence or how they come" (Ramacharaka 1906:110).

The testimonies of Stanislavsky, Chekhov, and Mozart resonate closely with each other and with the findings of Csikszentmihalyi, making clear that all are struggling to verbalize the same piece of tacit knowledge. Like Stanislavsky who points out that the creative state provokes a sense of totality, Mozart too experienced his music as an indivisible whole. "I do not hear in my imagination the parts successively, but I hear them, as it were, all at once" (Ramacharaka 1906: 110). Like Chekhov who describes the character he has crafted as simultaneously inside and outside of himself, Mozart too hears his music in his imagination but already externalized enough for transcription. "The rest is merely an attempt to reproduce what I have heard" (Ramacharaka 1906:110).

Another composer, interviewed by Csikszentmihalyi, echoes Chekhov's words even more closely than does Mozart:

> You yourself are in an ecstatic state to such a point that you feel as though you almost don't exist. I've experienced this time and time again. My hand seems devoid of myself and I have nothing to do with what is happening. I just sit there watching in a state of awe and wonderment. And it just flows out by itself.
>
> (Goleman 1995:90)

Chekhov expresses the same joy and freedom, along with the same eerie disso-
ciation from one's body that results in the observation of oneself as other. All of
this mirrors Stanislavsky's personal notes from 1909, where he similarly equates
"aesthetic experiencing" with "ecstasy" (SS V Part 2 1994:348).

Psychologist Daniel Goleman observes that "flow represents the ultimate in
harnessing the emotions in the service of performance and learning. In flow,
the emotions are not just contained and channeled, but positive, energized, and
aligned with the task at hand" (Goleman 1995:90). Stanislavsky would, no
doubt, nod his head in agreement and add that, for the actor, the "task at hand"
is the creation of "the life of the human spirit of the role."

The elusive, subjective concept of experiencing serves a highly practical function
within the System. It gives actors a way to evaluate their work in an art form which
precludes the artist from seeing objectively his or her own creation. Actors, after all,
cannot watch themselves while they perform; even film denies the actor this experience
during the process of working. At the American Laboratory Theatre, Maria Ouspenskaya taught her students that judging oneself during performance does not help and
indeed hinders one from the artistic tasks at hand. As she recounted, "Sometimes
Stanislavsky would come from the stage all excited saying 'Oh, tonight was good!'
And Nemirovitch-Danchenko would [...] say to Stanislavsky, 'What was the matter
with you tonight?'" (January 1955:3–4). At the First Studio, her teacher Leopold
Sulerzhitsky had stressed that actors must treat those who watch—teachers, directors, audiences, and critics—as "mirrors" for their work (Sulerzhitskii 1970:306–8).
The ability to recognize a subjective state of experiencing in oneself ultimately offers
the only direct means of appraising one's acting. If I feel this "happy moment," I can
infer that the System has worked for me.

Examining the word "experiencing" in its Russian associations and Stanislavsky's self-contradictory conceptions of it aids us in seeing the System through its
creator's eyes.

The word

Despite its centrality, "experiencing" remains the most obscure of all the System's terms.
Although *perezhivanie* is a common Russian word, Stanislavsky uses it so idiosyncrati-
cally that *The Dictionary of Contemporary Russian Literary Language* attributes one
of its many meanings to him alone: "the genuine penetration of a psychic state in a
represented character" (Hobgood 1973:149). In Russia, actors and scholars genuinely
puzzle over Stanislavsky's usage of the word, sometimes substituting less ambiguous
alternatives.[3] In the West, at the turn of the twenty-first century, most writers and practitioners remain ignorant of it, merely and erroneously assuming that the System's main
thrust is toward truth and realism in theatrical style with a concomitant desire for the
psychological fusion of actor with character in performance.[4]

In Hapgood's classic English translations, the force and pervasiveness of Stanislavsky's central term gets lost. Not only is the Russian subtitle of the first volume of
his acting manual, *The Creative Process of Experiencing*, dropped from the more
commercially appealing *An Actor Prepares*, but within Hapgood's rendition, no

single word or phrase emerges as a consistent equivalent. She translates the term variously in order to encompass its many meanings and nuances. In so doing, however, she makes readers unable to see it as a discrete concept, which Stanislavsky struggles to establish and define. Depending upon context she chooses: "the art of living a part" [15], "to live the scene" [121], "sensations" [172], "living and experiencing" [15], "experience" (1961: 44), "emotional experience" (1961:44), and finally "creation" (1961:44). Additionally, Hapgood aligns the term with "emotions" and "sensations" when she translates *perezhivanie* as "the capacity to feel" [170], and when she renders *chuvstvovaniia* ("feelings") as "experiences" [166]; both derivative verbs (*perezhit'* and *chuvstvovat'*) become the single "to feel" [277]. Ironically, while Western practitioners turned other ideas into heatedly debated jargon—emotional/affective memory, objectives, motivations, etc.—Stanislavsky's own definition of his System disappeared from the polemics.

Given the proliferation of translation options, "one feels a need to establish an English equivalent for [*perezhivanie*] in critical discussion," Burnet Hobgood rightly observes (1973:149). The Russian word generally translates as "experience," and Hobgood further argues that "experience" is the best translation for acting as well.[5] In this book, I use "experiencing" in order to convey Stanislavsky's process-oriented understanding of acting and his eccentric usage.

English language interpreters of Stanislavsky have shied away from the usual, preferring options that use the Russian derivation of the word from the verb "to live" (*zhit'*). As a consequence, many translators incorporate this root, as does Hapgood. In fact, she may have adopted "living a part" from J. J. Robbins, who used it in his 1924 translation of *My Life in Art* (Hobgood 1973:149). Moreover, this awkward translation was in the air at that time. After visiting the Moscow Art Theatre, critic Arthur Ruhl reported being told that Stanislavsky's actors "live into" their roles (Emeljanow 1981:161).

Accounting for the word's prefix, émigré teachers spoke about actors who "re-live" and "live through" their roles every time they step on stage (Strasberg 1987:103), thus coining calques that entered into the Method's oral tradition (Chapter 4). Such translations play with two of the many possible nuances, and help adjust "living" to "performing."

In one sense, *pere-* ("re-") simply suggests that the action of its verb is repeated, and thus reflects Stanislavsky's concern with repetition as a distinguishing feature of live stage performance. At the Moscow Art Theatre actors often performed the same roles over the course of many years. In *An Actor's Work on Himself, Part I*, Tortsov enters the classroom to find his students frantically searching for a lost purse. When he starts class, he asks them to repeat this search on stage. They cannot do so. From their failure, Tortsov concludes that only the ability to repeat what has been "lived" can turn reality into art (SS II 1989:224–5). By drawing attention to repetition, the prefix also anticipates two later developments in acting theories: Sanford Meisner's Repetition Exercise that teaches actors to attend closely to their partners as they repeat each other's exact words and intonations; and Richard Schechner's paradigmatic shift in the definition of performance as "restored behavior" or "twice-behaved behaviors" (2006:28–36).

In another sense, *pere-* ("through-") makes the verb persistent, continuing through to the very end of the action. As a Russian maxim states: "Living through (*pere-zhit'*) one's life is not like crossing through a field."[6] Invoking this level of meaning, Stanislavsky uses "experiencing" to describe an actor's unbroken concentration on the events of the play during performance. When the actor is totally "gripped by the play," experiencing is "natural" (*estestvennoe*) (SS II 1989:60) and "correct" (*pravilnoe*) (SS III 1990:166, 185). Many Western critics saw such focused attention as a hallmark of Stanislavsky's company. One critic wrote, the actors "are wholly concentrated on their job and their acting is sustained the whole time the curtain is up, whether they are taking the stage or temporarily withdrawn from the limelight in some obscure corner" (Emeljanow 1981:330).

However literal, translations that merely mirror the Russian roots do not capture the complexity with which Stanislavsky endows this vexed term. That he directly, if eccentrically, appropriated the word itself from Lev Tolstoy, whose hatred of theatre was infamous, provides a significant clue to Stanislavsky's usage of it.[7] In the 1897 tract, *What is Art?*, Tolstoy argues that art communicates experiencing, rather than knowledge. "Art begins," Tolstoy explains, "when a person, whose goal is to convey to other people a feeling which he has experienced (*perezhil*), calls it up in himself and expresses it through recognizable external signs" (Tolstoi 1964:85–6). For Tolstoy, art entails a self-expressive act, impelled by a memory of emotion, with the artist's experience as central. He thus forges inseparable links between the work of art and its creator and between the communicated content and its expressive medium.

These notions—self-expression, the recall of emotion, and the artist's use of personal experience—inform the System, as well. "Actors can experience only their own emotions," Stanislavsky explains. "They can understand, empathize, put themselves in their characters' shoes, and begin to act as their characters do. This creative action calls forth experiences analogous with the role" (SS II 1989:293). Moreover, Stanislavsky sees the link between creator and art as especially pronounced in acting where the artist is the medium. "The actor creates the life of the human spirit of the role from his own living soul," he explains, "and incarnates it in his own living body. There is no other material for the creation of a role" (Bancroft Typescript[8]:171). In more pedestrian language, he writes, "You never lose yourself on stage. You always act in your own person as artist. There's no walking away from yourself" (SS II 1989:294) As Strasberg succinctly puts it, "The actor is at once the piano and the pianist" (Strasberg 1974:59).

Tolstoy furthers his definition of art when he describes a young boy, who has been frightened by a wolf, telling his tale. "If the boy experiences once again during his story what he felt then, and infects his listeners—makes them experience all that he, the storyteller, has experienced—that is art" (1964:85). In these words, he makes clear that without an audience self-expression is for naught, because art's greater function is to communicate to others. Tolstoy puts it this way: "People being infected with the feelings of other people is the fundamental operation of art" (1964:86).[9]

Stanislavsky too uses the verb "to infect" precisely in Tolstoy's sense. Like those who listen to the boy's tale about the wolf, the spectator at the theatre "takes silent part in [the actors'] communication, sees, recognizes, understands, and is infected with their experiencing" (SS II 1989:322). "Real art," Stanislavsky explains, "is based on the infectiousness of genuine feelings and experiences" (SS VI 1994:58). Given the fact that so many interpreters of the System stress the actor's need for "public solitude" and envision the characters that Stanislavsky created as acting behind an invisible fourth wall, the fact that he specifically draws attention to how audiences complete the communication link in a theatre of experiencing bears special emphasis. For Stanislavsky, the actor needs the audience.

Stanislavsky willfully adapts Tolstoy's theories to an art form for which Tolstoy himself had little respect. In *War and Peace* he pointedly arranged for his heroine, Natasha Rostova, to be seduced at the theatre during the performance of an opera. The very setting insures her moral fall from grace (see Part VIII, Chapter 9). He dismissed Shakespeare as a bad writer with a snide wave of the hand and saw contemporary drama as "petty and immoral entertainment for a petty and immoral crowd" (1964:345). Tolstoy called Stanislavsky's production of *Uncle Vanya* "nonsense" (Nemirovitch-Dantchenko 1936:335).

Yet, despite this disdainful attitude, Stanislavsky had long been infatuated with Tolstoy's aesthetic and moral philosophy. Stanislavsky first directed a Tolstoy play, *The Fruits of Enlightenment*, in 1891 for the Moscow Society of Art and Literature. He brought *The Power of Darkness* to the Moscow Art Theatre's stage in 1902. When he hired Tolstoyan, Leopold Sulerzhitsky, as his assistant in 1906 and placed him at the head of the First Studio in 1911, Stanislavsky turned fascination with Tolstoy into appropriation (Stroeva 1973:97).

In fact, Stanislavsky cleverly uses Tolstoy's ideas to encourage respect for theatrical art through an implied tautology. If art infects its audiences with the artist's experiencing, and if acting does the same, then acting must be a legitimate art. Conversely, acting that most consistently embodies experiencing must be the most successful form of theatrical art. How fitting that this respect for acting in part would insure Stanislavsky's influence among his US students! Yet, how ironic as well that Stanislavsky and Tolstoy, who both turned away from strict Realism as they matured, would both be appropriated by Stalin as icons of Socialist Realism (Chapters 2, 6), in part because of their shared conception of art as experiencing! Tolstoy's concept of *perezhivanie* ultimately leads Stanislavsky to his paradoxical redefinition of "truth" as "theatricality."

The concept

Two recurring contexts in which Stanislavsky uses the term "experiencing" serve as further clues to his deeper meaning. The first of these constructs a neat theoretical model. In it, having incorporated Tolstoy's notion of art as the communication of genuine personal experience, Stanislavsky must logically reject Diderot's classical formulation of the actor's dual consciousness as inauthentic. In this context, which was adopted by the American Method, the actor seems indistinguishable from the character.

The second context places "experiencing" into the messy, self-contradictory world of theatrical practice, where "flow" often induces a sensation of watching oneself and where Stanislavsky can thus embrace both Tolstoy and Diderot at the same time. In this context, the actor creates a character as a work of art distinguishable from the self. Philosopher R. I. G. Hughes observes that the term *perezhivanie* easily allows for the apparently contradictory premise, that "Even when the artist and artwork both inhabit the same body, the distinction between them still persists. […] The relation between the two can be charted in many ways, as the contrast between Brecht and Stanislavski attests" (1993:41). In short, *perezhivanie* carries with it the possibility that a Stanislavskian actor, using the self as artist, can maintain objectivity, a distance clearly necessary in practice when controlling one's performance. Despite the Method's call for loss of self in character, Hapgood points American theatre practitioners in this generally overlooked direction when she includes the following passage in *Building A Character*:

> Our art […] requires that an actor experience the agony of his role, and weep his heart out at home or in rehearsals, that he then calm himself, get rid of every sentiment alien or obstructive to his part. He then comes out on the stage to convey to the audience in clear, pregnant, deeply felt, intelligible and eloquent terms what he has been through. At this point the spectators will be more affected than the actor, and he will conserve all his forces in order to direct them where he needs them most of all: in reproducing the inner life of the character he is portraying.
>
> (Stanislavski 1949:70)

Consider the theory first. As early as 1909, Stanislavsky had begun to work out his theoretical model in a book that establishes "experiencing" as the primary label for his brand of theatre. When offered the opportunity to publish in the United States, he immediately returned to this early project, and produced a draft that is far more theoretical than either his memoirs or his later acting manuals. He abandoned this draft when his Boston publisher requested something more commercially attractive, but as late as 1930 he still planned to return to the project (SS IX 1999:438).

In theory, Stanislavsky distinguishes "the theatre of experiencing" from two other theatrical forms, "craftsmanship" (*remeslo*) and "representation" (*predstavlenie*).[10] He judges each by its relative success in creating "the life of the human spirit of the role," his overarching goal for the art of acting. He ranks them in clear hierarchical progression, with the Moscow Art Theatre's commitment to "experiencing" near the pinnacle. This same schema informs Tortsov's critique cited above.

"Craftsmanship" occupies the lowest rung in Stanislavsky's hierarchy. In his US draft he cruelly dismisses it. "There are things about which one cannot speak seriously; for me 'craftsmanship' is one of these. I fear that I cannot keep from laughing and smirking when I speak of it, even though my book has no pretension to wit" (Bancroft Typescript:67). This type of theatre relies upon what Stanislavsky calls "clichés," silly tricks-of-the-trade that may have been vital and communicative at some time in the past, but have lost all connection to "the life of the human spirit;" they present form without content "like a shell without the nut" (Bancroft

Typescript:11, 49, 21). American actors call such empty conventional signs "indicating," that is to say, an actor "indicates" looking without really seeing, or drinking
without ever tasting. Stanislavsky gives several examples: "A black dress, powdered
face, sorrowful nodding of the head, nose blowing, and wiping of dry eyes" portray
grief. "Pressing a telling finger to the lips and a solemn stealthy walk" telegraph
secretiveness. "Clutching one's chest or tearing at the collar of one's shirt" indicates
death. He adds parenthetically, that "Craftsmanship recognizes only two kinds of
death, that from heart failure or asphyxiation" (SS VI 1994:51).

These tricks have calcified into an arsenal of ready-made theatrical signs, which
actors learn mechanically by imitating other actors. Such "craftsmen" become mere
technicians, who "only know how to report a role from the stage, e.g. to recite it
by heart, grammatically" and "to perform only mechanical gymnastics" (Bancroft
Typescript:36). In summary, Stanislavsky categorically refuses to recognize such
technical acting as art; it remains mere craft.

In large part Stanislavsky blames audiences for sustaining this form of theatre.
Spectators who actively seek lavish effects prod theatres to concentrate upon
telling the playwright's story in as striking a way as possible, and thus to subordinate acting to stage effect (Bancroft Typescript:21, 6). Moreover, audiences who
demand variety make it lucrative for theatres to produce new plays in haste. Consequently, actors, who must learn countless new roles each season with only three
or four rehearsals per role, have no choice but to rely upon short-hand clichés. As
Stanislavsky laments, "Hurried work is a dangerous obstacle to creativity and art"
(Bancroft Typescript:52).

In notes from 1909, Stanislavsky imagines the actor's subjective state of mind
during performances that primarily strive to entertain as radically different from
the creative state (or "flow") that his System seeks to induce:

> The main difference involves the object of attention. The technician is concerned
> about the public and the audience. He wants to convince them, not the actor
> who stands speaking with him on stage. [...] For the actor who is in the process
> of experiencing [the role], the object of attention is himself and what surrounds
> him on the stage. Such an actor convinces the person to whom he is speaking.
> He does not pay [conscious] attention to the audience, but plays for himself.
>
> (SS V Part 1 1993:444)

By placing one's primary attention on the audience, the actor distorts the truer type of
communication demanded by art. In the one case, the people on stage curry favor by
drawing attention to themselves. In the other case, the actors on stage as an ensemble
convey the content of the story they tell.

The indictments of both audiences who expect mere entertainment and pandering
actors bring to mind the spirit of reform with which Stanislavsky and Nemirovich-
Danchenko had founded the Moscow Art Theatre. These indictments also anticipate director Peter Brook's critique of "deadly theatre" which, he observes, is often
mistaken by audiences for great (1968:9–37). In our own century, instances of
"deadly" craftsmanship, in which an empty shell is offered up as nourishment, can

still be found. One need only look, for example, at televised soap operas to understand how talented actors need clichés when hurried in their work.

The theatre of "representation" occupies the next rung in Stanislavsky's hierarchy. He explicitly takes the label from the great French actor Coquelin the Elder (1841–1909), who deemed his art that of "representation." In his eloquent description of his working method, Coquelin compares the preparation of a role to the painting of a portrait which reveals the inner life of the subject through the careful selection and crafting of telling details.

For Coquelin, as for the Moscow Art Theatre company, the preparation of a role begins with the play. He writes, the actor "must read the play carefully over many times, until he has grasped the intention of the author." This leads to "a clear understanding of his personage [such that the actor] *sees* him as he ought to be." Drawing upon the portrait metaphor, Coquelin notes, that "When [the actor] has attained to this [mental image] he has his model." Now, whereas the painter puts the model's image on canvas, the actor must use the self as the artistic medium. Thus, Coquelin explains, the actor juggles both a "first self" (the artist) and a "second self" (the canvas); in acting, the first self shapes the second. The actor "sees Tartuffe in a certain costume, he wears it; he feels he has a certain face, he assumes it." In short, the actor "recasts his own individuality till the critic which is his first self declares he is satisfied and finds that the result is really Tartuffe." The actor now completes the portrait by placing it on stage within the picture frame of the proscenium arch (Cole and Chinoy 1970:192–3).

This theatrical approach elicits Stanislavsky's respect. In the first place, the theatre of representation seeks to communicate genuine feelings, and therefore invokes experiencing to some measure. Unlike the technician who adopts ready-made theatrical vocabularies, the representational actor "concentrates on the inner essence of the role." He or she looks beyond the externals of the story to its emotional content. With Tolstoyan flair, Stanislavsky writes, "These actors are not interested in *how* the characters come and go, marry or divorce, but in *what* they feel under these circumstances, how they *rejoice*, and *suffer*, how they *hope*, *become disillusioned*, *love* and *hate*" (Bancroft Typescript:68, 108). If "feelings" are "the essence of all art" as Stanislavsky (following Tolstoy's lead) insists, then these actors are true artists.

In the second place, the theatre of representation places the actor at the creative nexus of theatrical production, and thus values the actor as much as Stanislavsky does. "Actors are everything in such theatre," Stanislavsky explains, and its stars, like Sarah Bernhardt (1844–1923) who toured Russia in 1881, 1891, and 1908 to wide acclaim, sometimes reach admirable heights of virtuosity (Bancroft Typescript:21, 96).

Yet, "representation" also resonates as a theatrical pejorative. Tolstoy uses precisely this word to debunk theatrical convention when he describes what Natasha Rostova sees on stage at the opera just before her seduction in *War and Peace*. In "representation," Stanislavsky detects a betrayal of art through its skewed emphasis on the person of the actor as star. "We love the individuality and art of these actors more than we do their creations" (Bancroft Typescript:110). Personality and charisma threaten to outweigh the play, and thus detract from the basic function of art (the communication of experience). In this critique, he again recalls the Moscow Art Theatre's reforms, specifically its reliance on an ensemble of equally important players. There are, for Stanislavsky, no small parts, only small actors. In our own era, one need only think of Hollywood to understand that stars continue to attract audiences as much, and often more so, than the material they embody.

For Stanislavsky, this misplaced emphasis on the star results from an unsatisfactory use of experiencing during the creative process. In the theatre of representation, the creative state occurs only once or twice during the preparatory phase of the work. At such times, imagination projects the actor into the circumstances of the play, and creates an experience of the role. This is what Coquelin means when he says he "sees" his personage. In 1923, Stanislavsky describes such moments as follows:

> While daydreaming, the actor visualizes the circumstances and conditions of the life of his role in all its most trivial details. [...] He feels himself at the center of this created world; in the very thick of the role's life. It disturbs him, makes him happy, or frightens him. He wants to enjoy it or to run away. [...] He is activated. He becomes the main character. This action—even if only in his mind's eye—is already motion, life. This action, which is analogous to that of the role, is already a little piece of the role's life, already an experiencing of it. Dreaming—we act; acting—we experience.
>
> (Bancroft Typescript:191)

Of key import in this passage is the relationship between imagined "action" and "the life of the role," for without "action" there can be neither drama nor experiencing.

While Stanislavsky embraces this use of imagination in his System, he criticizes representational actors for leaving it behind in the rehearsal room when they step out on stage. They do not present their fantasies to the audience. Rather they transform what they have visualized into dispassionate, objectified "images of passions" (Bancroft Typescript:103), beautiful but no longer active, hence no longer essentially dramatic. Implicitly referring to Coquelin, Stanislavsky continues, "At first, the actor daydreamed himself into a character who takes action; he was active at that time. But then the actor becomes a spectator, taking a passive role. Having divorced himself from the dream, he watches himself, thus becoming his own critic, director, and the sculptor of his own body" (Bancroft Typescript:134). These now passive images take center stage.

With the delineation of this process, Stanislavsky unmistakably joins the debate about the role of sensibility in acting instigated by Denis Diderot (1713–84). Stanislavsky had read *The Paradox of the Actor* when he retreated to Finland in 1906 to contemplate the art of acting. In 1912, he wrote to tell his friend and editor, Lyubov Gurevich, that he now felt he had to contend with Diderot when considering the theoretical history of acting (SS VIII 1998:304).

Stanislavsky's depiction of the representational actor's work exactly parallels Diderot's depiction of actress Clairon working on the role of Agrippina:

> As it will happen in dreams, her head touches the clouds, her hands stretch to grasp the horizon on both sides; she is the informing soul of a huge figure,

which is her outward casing, and in which her efforts have enclosed her. As she lies careless and still on a sofa with folded arms and closed eyes she can, following her memory's dream, hear herself, see herself, judge herself, and judge also the effects she will produce. In such a vision she has a double personality; that of the little Clairon and that of the great Agrippina.

(1957:16)

Stanislavsky's "images of the passions" also recall Diderot's notion that Clairon, like Coquelin, uses a painterly metaphor as she constructs in her imagination a *modèle idéal* ("type") for Agrippina. As Diderot writes, "To conform to this type has been her first thought." Moreover, her model is "ideal" because she heightens and refines it to "the highest, the greatest, the most perfect type her imagination could compass."

This type [...] which she has borrowed from history, or created as [...] some vast spectre in her own mind, is not herself. Were it indeed bounded by her own dimensions, how paltry, how feeble would be her playing!

(1957:16)

Compare what Stanislavsky says of the characters created by representational actors: "The spectator immediately sees that these are not just ordinary people whom we meet in life, but personages, whom we see in paintings and about whom we read in books" (Bancroft Typescript:96). In short, Stanislavsky unambiguously places Diderot's conception of the actor's art into his theoretical model as a description of "representation."

Within Stanislavsky's model, therefore, Diderot's vision of theatre extends only halfway to the most vital kind of art; its actors may "experience" their roles during rehearsal, but they merely reproduce planned images on stage. As Coquelin puts it, "There must be the conception by the first self and the reproduction by the second" (Cole and Chinoy 1970:193). Like poets who, when caught in private by a moment of creativity, produce poems which then become fixed objects, representational actors turn performances into "objective," reproducible, and fixed works of art. While Stanislavsky concedes that representational actors can sometimes create powerful moments of experiencing, he faults them for their inability to do so throughout entire performances. "The effect of this art can be keen, but not sustained. It surprises more than convinces us" (Bancroft Typescript:145).

By rejecting "craftsmanship" and criticizing the use of experiencing in the theatre of "representation," Stanislavsky has all but defined his ideal as that form of theatre which presents the actor's active imagining directly to the audience. The theatre of experiencing "is itself a genuine, conscious process; it is itself the life of the human spirit of the role in accordance with the laws of creative nature" (Bancroft Typescript:116). Unlike poets and representational actors who need to experience a moment of creativity only privately, experiential actors summon a dynamic creative process every time they perform in public. Their art cannot be turned into fixed forms (as are printed poems and pre-formulated gestures), because their performances embody the ephemeral and improvisational creative act itself. The theatre of experiencing thus encompasses the moment, described by Tolstoy, in which a boy, who had been frightened by a wolf, remembers and relates his emotion to his audience. In this sense, however fixed a play's text and blocking may be, its performance remains deeply improvisatory and of the moment.

Whereas Bernhardt, Coquelin and Clairon stood for the best in the "theatre of representation," Stanislavsky found "experiencing" in performances of the Italian Tomasso Salvini (1829–1955) and the First Studio actor Michael Chekhov (1891–1955). Salvini's portrayal of Othello struck the young Stanislavsky as awe-inspiring: "Since I saw Salvini, the dream of playing Othello has lived within me" (SS I 1988:225). Later, Michael Chekhov's performance in Nikolai Gogol's grotesque comedy *The Inspector General* showed an uncanny ability to improvise continually without changing a movement of blocking or a word of text. Chekhov demonstrated "the improvisatory state of mind and body within the rigid framework of first-class dramatic material" (Knebel' 1967:276). Stanislavsky sought to induce this very state via the System. These actors and roles thus provide Stanislavsky with multiple examples of "experiencing" in his manual.

In summary, Stanislavsky uses his theoretical model to set forth the actor's immediate communication of felt experience as his notion of true art. This usage of "experiencing" can be read as a propensity toward Romanticism, as does William W. Worthen. From Stanislavsky's Byronic posture on the cliffs of Finland, contemplating the nature of acting in *My Life in Art*, to his expression of "an authentic sense of being through acting," Worthen sees the Stanislavskian actor as "principally committed to self-discovery." He summarizes "Stanislavsky's project [...] as an attempt to accommodate the theatre to the prevailing attitudes of Romantic art, mainly through a redefinition of the actor as a Romantic artist" (1983:33, 38).

While Romanticism in Russian literary history is a topic fraught with argument, Stanislavsky is indeed Romantic in so far as he rejects classical, archetypical "images of passion" and the heightened poeticism of the theatre of representation. His ideal actor does not seek a *modèle idéal*, but something more familiar. Stanislavsky regularly uses words such as "intimate," "meaningful," and "convincing" to describe the audience reaction he seeks to induce, much as Tolstoy does when he concludes his 1897 tract by calling for art to "unite" all people in a common "brotherhood." When seen through an Anglo-American, rather than a Russian, cultural filter, Stanislavsky's actors reach out to an audience of their peers, just as the poet became "a man speaking to men," as Wordsworth put it. Of course, Stanislavsky the director initially used scenic Realism (as in his touring productions) to create this illusion of Romantic familiarity, but he soon turned to more expressive, less naturalistic forms of storytelling (as in Turgenev's *A Month in the Country*, Symbolist plays, and opera) to do so.

Stanislavsky also invokes the Romantic rhetoric of "sincerity" as an evaluative measure for art, as did Tolstoy who asked the artist to feel genuinely what he proposed to communicate. In *An Actor's Work on Himself, Part I*, Tortsov asserts that, "Scenic truth is necessary to the actor in the moment of his creation. There is no genuine art without truth and belief!" (SS II 1989:226). In assessing his most successful moment on stage, Nazvanov speculates that, "Perhaps I felt in these words the offended soul of a trusting man and sincerely pitied him" (SS II 1989:57). Stanislavsky's famous criticism, "I don't believe you," ringing out from the auditorium seals the case. The actor's "truth" and "belief" banish the "lies" and "falsehood" of theatrical clichés. As Douglas Clayton suggests, "Like Tolstoi's theoretical attack on convention," Stanislavsky's insistence on sincerity and truth makes the "contract" between stage and audience "which creates theatrical convention […] immoral, because convention is a lie" (1993:47).[11]

The oxymoron of theatrical truth

Now, turn to the messy world of practice. Stanislavsky's eccentric and ambiguous use of "experiencing" cannot be fully explained by his neat theoretical model. Within the second important context through which he defines "experiencing," that of practice, the model's three types of theatre never occur in pure forms. Only in theory can he separate and analyze them. In practice, the most talented and well-trained actor may succumb to clichés, while the most amateur, untried performer may reach unexpected moments of creative flight.

In *An Actor's Work on Himself, Part I*, when our narrator, Nazvanov, struggles to transform himself into Othello, he makes every conceivable acting mistake. He declaims at top voice, then murmurs for fear of disturbing his neighbors. He dresses himself in royal robes fashioned from a towel and blanket, and stalks around his room like a jungle cat. When he works on stage, he reproduces the image he created at home, but then he throws it away and improvises. His experimentation goes on and on. At each turn, he thinks he has found the "secret" to acting; at each turn he is foiled. Finally in his performance before Tortsov, he stumbles accidentally into a moment of experiencing. "The famous line, 'Blood, Iago, blood!' burst from me. It was the cry of a man in torment. How it came out of me I don't know. […] I had the impression that the audience pricked up its ears for a moment, and a rustle went through the crowd like wind through treetops" (SS II 1989:57). Thus, we follow Nazvanov's adoption of acting clichés, his reproduction of planned images, and his discovery of the creative moment on stage, as if he were recapitulating the evolution of theatrical art.

Even more problematic is the theoretical demand for sincere self-expression. While poets may use their own feelings unalloyed, actors may not, and in practice Stanislavsky never forgot that actors play their roles, not themselves. As semiotician Eli Rozik writes, "actors inscribe images of human behavior, including speech, into their own bodies" in order to "deflect references from themselves to the characters who are supposed to produce them" (2002:23). To resolve the tension between a desire for sincerity and the need to deflect reference from themselves to their characters, actors face a tough practical choice. They must either align their feelings with those of a playwright,[12] or superimpose their own texts onto the author's. Such choices, which continue to confront actors today, lead Worthen to define the position of the Stanislavskian actor on stage as "unremittingly ironic," since "the actor can only *be* as the other" (1983:37).

Work at the First Studio, Stanislavsky's most Tolstoyan period, brought this irony into sharp focus, and proved to Stanislavsky that self-expression in the theatre was, at best, problematic. Even as the Studio's young actors sought sincere fusion with their characters, they "did not do away with the falsehood of *performing*," according to Pavel Markov.

> By rousing his affective emotion, this method aimed to fuse the actor with the character [but instead …] it enveloped the actor with a mass of detailed and particularized perceptions; it overflooded the actor. The actor was forced not only to dissemble and be outwardly, but to embrace alien feelings and perceptions. He had to *dissemble* inwardly. Or he had to put the content of his own daily life in place of […] the experience of the character.
>
> (1934:57–8)

In short, the First Studio proved that the actor's fusion with character could not work in practice, however seductive in theory. Ironically, it did not bring greater sincerity, but greater falsehood.

In descriptions of the actor's creative state during performance, Stanislavsky addresses this irony, and in so doing finds himself appropriating Diderot for the theatre of experiencing rather than rejecting him. Relegating Diderot's model to representational acting had made good theoretical sense. Because Clairon's work includes a dual vision of herself and her role, it seems to violate Stanislavsky's ideal of an integrated performance in which the actor "knows a role spiritually and physically" (Bancroft Typescript:113). Because her paradoxical double consciousness entails a passive component in which she "split herself into her own spectator" (Bancroft Typescript:181), it seems to oppose Stanislavsky's notion of action as central to drama.

In practice, however, Diderot's model squares with Stanislavsky's personal experience on stage. Clairon's duality as actor and character supports rather than denies his own sensations while performing. Indeed, most accounts of "flow" report sensations of dual consciousness. The composer, cited above, "just sit[s] there watching" himself compose "in a state of awe and wonderment" (Goleman 1995:90). Michael Chekhov, too, had "become the observer of his own work," adding that the creative state induces a "divided consciousness" (1991:155).

Stanislavsky also invokes dual consciousness in *An Actor's Work on Himself, Part II*, when he describes the performer's "sense of self" (*samochuvstvie*) as comprising two equally important perspectives—being on stage and being within the role. He had identified this division in Salvini's Othello, a role he considered most challenging. Quoting Salvini, Stanislavsky writes: "While I act, I live a double life, I laugh and cry, and still I analyze my tears and my laughter, in order that they can affect more strongly the hearts of those I want to touch." He concludes that "this dividing of oneself does not interfere with inspiration. On the contrary, one helps the other" (SS III 1990:150). As he baldly states in his artistic notes, "I have two wills on stage, not one" (SS V Part 2 1994: 379).[13] Even more tellingly, he uses hyphens to yoke the "human being" with the "actor" (*chelovek-akter*) and the "actor" with the "character" (*artisto-rol'*), typographically connecting the experience of the performing actor with that of the person and role.

Thus, theory parts company with practice, and Stanislavsky seems to reverse his position on Diderot. Dual consciousness, no longer merely a signal for the theatre of representation, becomes part of the System.

Reluctant to give up entirely on the Tolstoyan notion of genuine experiencing, Stanislavsky now redefines the very idea of "genuine." Dual consciousness itself becomes "sincere," and not only on stage. "We also divide ourselves in real life," he writes, "and that does not interfere with our vital and strong feelings" (SS III 1990:150). As if he were anticipating sociologists of the 1960s like Erving Goffman (who examine social behavior as a form of performative role-playing) and performance scholars of the 1990s like Richard Schechner (who find performative elements virtually everywhere in human activities from art and ritual to the expression of personal identity), Stanislavsky suggests that we experience something like performance in social situations, when he describes a practical joke played on Tortsov near the end of *An Actor's Work on Himself, Part I*.

At a party the guests decide to play hospital and operate on him. Like a performer, Tortsov as "patient" becomes the natural focus of attention. His friends wheel in two tables, one for him, the other for the "medical equipment." They bind his eyes and proceed with their work. When they take off his blindfold, he finds one of his arms wrapped in swaddling clothes, a face painted on his hand, and himself the proud "mother" of a new infant. As he describes Tortsov's perceptions during the experience, Stanislavsky alternates between realistic enjoyment of the joke and irrational fear, as if the operation were real. "This so confused me, that I did not know how to behave: to laugh or to cry. A stupid thought even occurred to me: 'What if they suddenly begin to cut for real?'" (SS II 1989:433). He further compares this alternation of perceptions with the actual experience of a patient facing a serious operation. Like a photographic plate of Tortsov's experience, a patient oscillates between realistic worry and incredulity.

Tortsov concludes that this alternating sense of reality and fiction is necessary and healthy. It allows both actor and patient to "endure," to "suffer" the experience, yet two more possible translations for the Russian verb *perezhit'*. "If this were not so," he explains, "the spiritual and physical human organism could not withstand the kind of work which produces art" (SS II 1989:434–5).[14]

Experimental director Joseph Chaikin (1935–2003), who became a leading voice in the US avant-garde of the 1960s, provides unexpected but persuasive confirmation of Stanislavsky's analysis. Chaikin describes undergoing a diagnostic heart operation under local anesthetic, during which "I broke down. My body was throbbing and sobbing and screaming." When given a sedative, his perception changed:

> I felt then, in the clearest way I have ever felt, something that I think goes on all the time. I felt it then especially because my body was pinned down: it was the sense of the two extreme ends of me, the person as terrified as I

ever remember being, and the performer making the right words and trying to
form the responses that would register in that room.

(1987:123–6)[15]

Chaikin's experience of being a "real" patient confirms Tortsov's conclusion, that
both performance and reality incorporate dual consciousness.

Diderot's philosophy need not turn the actor into an inauthentic personality after
all. In the striking metaphor that compares the actor to someone undergoing an operation, Stanislavsky reinterprets Diderot's model, transforming the active/passive
dichotomy (which he cannot accept) into one of belief/disbelief (which he can). In
it, he also recasts the problem of the actor's fusion with character that arose at the
First Studio into one of alternating perceptions between artist and role. By so doing,
he begins to think of the theatrical event itself as the source of the actor's genuine
experience.

Stanislavsky now equates "to experience" (*perezhivat'*) with "to create" (*tvorit'*)
(SS II 1989:28). He thus identifies the actor's time on stage with real time, hence
life experience. In *An Actor's Work on Himself, Part I*, Stanislavsky defines "experiencing" by turning Coquelin the Elder's words inside out. As an exemplar of
representational acting, Coquelin had said that "the actor does not live, but acts"
(Cole and Chinoy 1970:193). In contrast, Stanislavsky's apparently anti-theatrical
actor "does not act, but lives" (SS II 1989:71–2).

While Stanislavsky's clever rhetorical trick can be used to prove his commitment
to Socialist Realism in the USSR, to argue his Romanticism in the US, and hence to
support translations of *perezhivanie* that feature the Russian root "to live," it actually embraces a subtler, postmodern notion: actors "live" on stage, because they
"create" on stage. In this sense, experiencing invokes the immediacy of performance and the actor's "presence," to borrow the title of Chaikin's book. Performing
becomes the sincere reality of creative process. "Truth" itself is consequently rede-
fined. "Living truth on stage is not at all what it is in reality," Stanislavsky writes
in one of his notebooks. "On stage truth is whatever you believe and in life truth is
what actually is" (SS VI 1994:81–2). Moreover, "the actor's experiencing on stage
is not at all the same as it is in life," where feelings occur, not according to plan, but
"accidentally" (SS IV 1991:380).

One of the company's main actors, Vasily Vasilievich Luzhsky, observed that
this conception of truth distinguished Stanislavsky's approach to theatre from the
Moscow Art Theatre's co-founder. For Nemirovich-Danchenko, "both on stage
and in life," Luzhsky wrote, "there was a single 'truth.' For [Stanislavsky], 'truth'
in life and on the stage was only a means […] that must be used to attain one's
goals" (Radishcheva 1997:306). In short, the experiential actor conveys theatrical
"truth" whenever the performative actor, in whatever aesthetic style, activates a
state of "flow." Boleslavsky also witnesses this strand in Stanislavsky's thinking
when he seeks to comfort his student, who has just discovered the inherent duality
of performance. "The theatre exists to show things which do not exist actually," he
tells her. "When you love on the stage, do you really love? Be logical: you substitute creation for the real thing. The creation must be real, but that is the only reality

that should be there. Your experience of double-feeling was a fortunate accident" (1933:41). Timothy Wiles correctly suggests, that for Stanislavsky "what is essentially 'real' about theatrical Realism lies as much in the reality of performance itself as in the true-to-life quality of the play's details" (1980:14). Russian theatre scholar Olga Radishcheva concurs, when she writes, "Stanislavsky did not in any circumstance equate experiencing on stage with experiencing in life" (1999a:14).

Stanislavsky's redefinition of "truth" as whatever happens in performance can best open the System up to the many different dramatic styles that fall outside the realm of Psychological Realism. Dennis Beck demonstrates this new possibility when he uses Stanislavsky's lost term to trace the System's influence on the largely non-realistic theatrical work of Eastern Europe (Krasner 2000:261–82).

In sum, Stanislavsky uses "experiencing" in two senses. On the one theoretical hand, art communicates the artist's personal experience; in this sense, he travels toward Tolstoy, bringing to mind Romantic notions of sincere self-expression and the fusion of actor and character. On the other practical hand, acting generates its own experiential dimension in performance; here Stanislavsky accepts the alternation of actor and character. When Stanislavsky suggests evaluating performance on its own terms and seeing "truth" as relative to the play, he travels away from Tolstoy and anticipates developments in modernism that embrace the formal media of art: visual artists who create abstract art by drawing attention to paint and canvas, theatricalists who destroy realistic illusion unabashedly to show an actor on a stage, etc. Janus-like Stanislavsky looks backward to nineteenth century traditions in art and forward to the late twentieth century and beyond.

The US tradition has tended to see Stanislavsky's backward glance as more genuinely and authentically his. Thus, Strasberg invokes English Romantic poets, especially Wordsworth, to prove "the link between affective memory and creativity" (1987:36). Many teachers in Strasberg's wake have taken Stanislavsky's concern with sincerity and self-expression as a ruling aspect for actor training, encouraging confessional and psychologically therapeutic behavior. Similarly, many scholars read his words on sincerity unambiguously and see the so-called "Stanislavskian actor" as functioning best in realistic dramas with psychologically rounded characters.

Adopted in the Method's lore and in published translations, calques, that rely heavily on the Russian root "to live," have helped foster this US inclination by stressing Stanislavsky's anti-theatrical usage, by masking his performance-oriented concerns, and overlooking his paradoxical redefinition of "truth." Strasberg does so when he explains that Stanislavsky trains the actor to "have the belief, faith and imagination to create on the stage the 'living through' that is demanded of the performer." Indeed, Strasberg underlines his point of view, when he adds, "This remains my own major emphasis" (1987:123). While Hapgood correctly reflects many of the nuances of "experiencing" in *An Actor Prepares*, she tends to favor emotional colorations over those that foreground experiential dimensions of performance. Only with choices such as "experience," "sensation," and "creation" does she accurately point toward the performer's work on stage as theatrical reality. But these translations are relatively rare within the overall text, and often lose their appropriate ambiguity when modified by added adjectives such as "emotional." In short, while Hapgood translates Stanislavsky's words as

"There can be no true art without living" [23], Hobgood properly asserts that if Stanislavsky had meant that an actor lives the role, he would have said so (1973:149).

The process by which this selective emphasis occurred in the US was not always unconscious. Strasberg knew of Stanislavsky's reinterpretation and acceptance of Diderot. Moreover, Strasberg's explanation of Stanislavsky's view to members of the Actors Studio in 1960 brings to mind Brecht's Alienation Effect which Strasberg also rejected: "As Stanislavsky defines it, the actor goes on stage and the character does this and therefore you see both the character and the actor on stage, almost standing apart." Strasberg actively rejects this dual consciousness. Taking the First Studio as his model, he "prefer[s] a fusion, where there is seemingly no difference between the actor and the character" (LS 129:8 November 1960). In this preference, Strasberg claims to adopt Evgeny Vakhtangov's (1883–1922) early reformulations of Stanislavsky. Consider, for example, Strasberg's take on the "magic if," which he attributes to Vakhtangov. Whereas Stanislavsky asked the actor to behave as if in the imagined given circumstances of the play, Strasberg "reformulates" the basic question in order to allow the actor to personalize the play. "The circumstances of the scene indicate that the character must behave in a particular way; what would motivate you, the actor, to behave in that particular way?" (1987:83). This reformulation, which better allows for personal substitutions, positions the actor's dual consciousness as something to be avoided.

Vakhtangov, one of Stanislavsky's most talented students, traversed a directing career that began at the First Studio with an exaggerated demand for realistic illusion and culminated with the theatricalist gem, his production of Carlo Gozzi's *Princess Turandot* (Worral 1989:97). Strasberg's information about Vakhtangov's approach to the System comes from Pavel Markov's history of the First Studio, which Mark Schmidt had translated specifically for the use of the Group Theatre. Markov emphasizes Vakhtangov's interest in the Romantic notion of self-expression through acting: "Vakhtangov went to the very essence of the actor as a man and found that there was no duality" only "monism." Furthermore, "he gave the right of priority to the personality of the actor" (1934:57–8). By preferring "fusion" of actor with character to an alternating consciousness of both, Strasberg reduces the concept of experiencing to self-expression.

By the late twentieth century, when relativity had become a key value in a multicultural world, when phenomenology had reduced our idea of "truth" to one of opinion, the critical stance that judges art on its relationship to absolute truth seemed outmoded. As Lionel Trilling wrote, the word "*sincerity* has lost most of its high dignity. When we hear it, we are conscious of the anachronism which touches it with quaintness. If we speak it, we are likely to do so with either discomfort or irony" (1972:6). More and more we came to understand that even science does not encode indisputable truths, but rather relies on paradigmatic thinking. No wonder the Method's reductive view of *perezhivanie* seemed old hat!

Returning to the full complexity in Stanislavsky's lost term can best propel his System into the twenty-first century. In 1993, Sarah Beckwith reminded us that "the nature of the theatrical medium [is] to foreground the human body through the mechanism of the actor as at once image and physical presence, at once representation and experience" (1993:61). She unknowingly reminds us of the power of Stanislavsky's thinking about Diderot that places the notion of dual consciousness at once in the camp of "representation" and in the theatre of "experiencing." This more paradoxical definition of experiencing as that which happens on stage makes it possible for experimental theatre artists as diverse as Jerzy Grotowski and Anatoly Vasiliev to call themselves Stanislavsky's students. Looking beyond the conventional view of Stanislavsky as unambiguously in favor of sincere self-expression places him within reach of contemporary theatrical scholars as well. If genuine experiencing is indeed the experience of performance itself and if this creative state allows for the alternation of contradictory states of mind, then by recovering Stanislavsky's lost term we can easily revisit his System from a postmodern angle and bring renewed vigor and relevance to his techniques. Recovering Stanislavsky's lost term, *perezhivanie*, unequivocally breaks the assumed but inaccurate link between the multivalent training System and the aesthetic style of Psychological Realism. Stanislavsky's redefinition of truth as whatever happens during performance can take the contemporary actor into any dramatic style, including those yet to be invented.

8 Emotion and the human spirit of the role

Psychology

The US bias

In Stanislavsky's eyes, experiencing may represent the ultimate goal for the actor, but in New York emotion took precedence. In so far as experiencing leads to the communication of emotion through art, the two notions are linked. However, as the Western branch of the System evolved, "experiencing" went unrecognized as a discrete concept. The Method's hallmark became the discrete technique of Affective Memory (recalling an emotion from one's past, analogous to the emotional life of one's character), which, in turn, prompted other now familiar acting tools such as the Personal Substitution (replacing the character's logic and emotion with something from one's own past).

However central, no other acting technique in the United States has roused such charged arguments, such heated advocates, such angry opponents as has Stanislavsky's proposal on affective memory. In the 1920s, American students listened to Boleslavsky and Ouspenskaya speak about emotion, passed their remarks through a popular Freudian filter, and set the scene for turmoil. In 1934, Stella Adler expressed discontent with Strasberg's use of emotion at the Group Theatre, sought an alternative approach, and established the debate's polarities. While Strasberg's ardent advocates see the recall of past emotional experiences as the most effective technique for powerful acting, his equally ardent opponents call it an unhealthy invasion of the actor's psyche.

Even the term causes controversy. Stanislavsky thought of "affective" memory (an adjective borrowed from psychologist Théodule Ribot) as older, superseded by the less scientific "emotional" memory (SS II 1989:279). American scholar Eric Bentley contested this chronology (1962:128–9). Strasberg in turn defined "affective memory" as a broad category containing both "sense" memory and "emotional" memory (1987:69). The latter, he states, "pertains specifically to the more intense reactions of an emotional response" (1987:111). Contemporary science clarifies the distinction between "emotion" as the unconscious biological and chemical responses in the body and "feeling" as our subjective awareness of emotion (Damasio 1999:42–3). In *An Actor Prepares* (1936), Hapgood translates the term as "emotion" memory.[1] I use "the memory of emotion," and "affective memory" interchangeably to discuss the psychophysical continuum that links subjective mind to objective body because in practice Stanislavsky did the same.

If anything, the debate about the place of emotion in the actor's arsenal has only intensified in the first decade of the twenty-first century. On one side are those like the prominent Los Angeles teacher, who recasts Affective Memory into post-Freudian terms by modeling her "Twelve Step [Ivana] Chubbuck Technique" on contemporary recovery programs. She echoes Strasberg's opinions on emotion without directly quoting him whenever she asks the actors "to use their own personal pain to win their character's goal." Her version of Strasberg's "substitution" helps actors use "your dark side, your beliefs, your priorities, your fears, what drives your ego, what makes you feel shame, and what initiates your pride" as "your colors, your paints to draw as an actor" (Chubbuck 2004:ix, 2).

On the other side are those, like Benjamin Lloyd, who continue to see psychological and therapeutic models for acting as pernicious. Lloyd argues that the widespread use of "substitution, as well as the general mid-twentieth century American tendency to make the actor's life and personal experience the centre of his creative journey, alike play into narcissistic disorder. [...] 'Substitution'," he concludes, "is an empty promise" (2006:72).

Strasberg countered such criticism in his own time with an insidious argument that drew upon his adoption of the psychoanalytical thinking that had engulfed American culture in the 1950s. He claimed that all great actors use Affective Memory whether they admit it or not. Any actor who rejects its efficacy is merely in denial (LS A10:2 February 1965). He criticized even Stanislavsky because "he did not stress [it] theoretically enough" (LS 45:14 February 1958). No other debate so typifies the Americanization of Stanislavsky's ideas. "Emotion" has become both a consummation devotedly to be wished and a dirty word.

When I ask Russian colleagues about their attitudes toward affective memory, they invariably avoid the terms of the US debate. While affirming its importance, they describe instead exercises on concentration, relaxation, imagination, and communication, which Americans generally do not connect with the memory of emotion. The Russians even relate affective memory to script analysis—an intellectual process which Method actors sometimes fear will damage their instinctive responses to their roles. In short, Russians see emotion inextricably entangled with the whole development of the actor and the actor's development of the role.

Two articles that seem like mirror images of each other—one published in the US and the other in Russia—dramatically portray this cultural difference in attitude. American Lee Norvelle lists nine "rules" for Stanislavsky's System; one of them is "emotional memory" (1962). Russian Vasily Sakhnovsky also lists nine "rules," but subsumes affective memory under various aspects of the System, including "communication," "the through line of action," and "creative ideas," categories not identified by Norvelle. Sakhnovsky does not list emotion as a discrete category (1988).

Stanislavsky's writing easily supports the Russian point of view. A knot of concepts forms around affective memory. Stanislavsky links it to the logical stringing together of small physical activities (eating, writing a letter, or getting dressed), inner actions bereft of motion (contemplating suicide or awaiting a verdict), the actor's empathy with the character, intuition, the subconscious, and spirituality. All aspects of successful acting radiate out from a central core of emotion, which Stanislavsky sees as the essence of all art, its very content.

Invoking Tolstoy, Stanislavsky assumes that we choose to act, because we desire to communicate emotion through the creative process. Tolstoy's formulation—"Art begins when a person, whose goal is to convey to other people a feeling which he has experienced, calls it up in himself and expresses it through recognizable external signs" (1964:85–6)—translates into Stanislavsky's recurrent definition—acting uses "emotional material" to forge "the life of the human spirit of the role" into "artistic stage forms" (SS II 1989:64, 182). From this point of view, Stanislavsky would agree with Strasberg, that "affective memory is the basic material [...] for the creation of real experience on the stage" (1987:113). Additionally, Tolstoy's suggestion that something akin to affective memory takes place during the creative state ("experiencing") also sets the stage for Stanislavsky's interest in the recollection of emotion and Strasberg's adoption of it as a tool for the actor's creativity.

As theatre's very content, emotion naturally infuses all aspects of the System equally. Stanislavsky always resists the temptation to associate emotion with any single technique, and maintains a multivariant approach expressed through a central metaphor. He compares the actor to a hunter and the memory of emotion to a shy bird.

> If the bird will not fly to [the hunter] by herself, then nothing will bring her from the leafy thicket. There is nothing else to do but entice the wildfowl out of the forest with the help of special whistles, called "lures."
>
> (SS II 1989:313)

He never pursues this pervasive metaphor to its logical conclusion, trapping and killing the prey. Rather, he uses it to stress the gentleness with which the actor must tread. The hunter must never "force," only "attract" prey (SS II 1989:92, 118). Strasberg approaches the mood of Stanislavsky's metaphor by turning "lure" into "lollipop." "Coax [a little child] to take a lollipop, but if you demand it take the lollipop, it runs away" (Hethmon 1991:112–13).

Stanislavsky continually sought new "lures" to rouse the memory of emotion. The first reading of a play can induce an emotional response and so Stanislavsky teaches actors to read with open minds and hearts. External realities of the stage—blocking, set, lights, costumes, stage properties, etc.—represent one kind of lure. A bright, sunny yellow light might induce happiness; placing a photograph of one's late grandmother on stage might incur nostalgia. Stanislavsky used such means to great advantage in his realistic stagings of Chekhov's and Gorky's plays, designing his often ridiculed sound effects not so much for the audience, but primarily for the actors, to entice them into the world of the play. Through these external details, he encouraged his actors to attend closely to what surrounded them, hence to focus outward. Later Stanislavsky added physical activities to his stock of lures. How it feels in the body to lift a heavy sword or level a small pistol, to walk to the door calmly or in hasty anger, to hug another in fear or in supportive comfort can induce an actor's emotional understanding of a role. Through the varying tempos and rhythms of such physical motions the emotional content of performances can emerge.

More complex psychophysical techniques represent yet another kind of lure. Relaxation and concentration, incentives that spark the imagination ("magic ifs," "creative ideas," "visualizations" of another time and place, personal associations with the play, etc.), examination of the play's actions and given circumstances—all of these are still more "lures" to incite the actor's memory of emotion. As Stanislavsky explored these more inwardly directed, meditative lures, he helped actors focus on their characters' states of mind by eliminating anything distracting from the stage environment. Now, mentally visualizing key moments in the character's life might replace yellow lights and grandmother's photographs. In sharp contrast to his earlier productions, Stanislavsky created an atmosphere of stasis for Turgenev's *A Month in the Country* in 1909. By keeping gesture and detail to a minimum, he encouraged the actors to focus inwardly.

In short, the System becomes his compendium of "lures," both physical and mental, both external and internal.

In sharp contrast, the Method transforms the System's multifaceted understanding of emotion into sure-fire technique—the Affective Memory exercise. By recalling all the sensory details surrounding an emotional moment from one's past, the actor can theoretically learn to revive feelings at will. Remembering the time of day, the weather, how the sun felt on her face, how his shirt clung to him, the actor revives the grief she felt at her mother's funeral, the anger that flared when his wife left him. With practice, the actor can become more and more adept, reducing the necessary time to just "one minute" (Strasberg 1987:112). By careful selection of emotional material analogous to the play, the actor can mine personal experience in the creation of character.

A number of rules of thumb developed in the Method's lore to support the use of this recall technique: You "should go to the most traumatic thing [from your past] that is similar [...] to the play" (Shelley Winters in LS A151:29 October 1968); a personal experience which is used as the basis of an Affective Memory should be at least seven years old (LS A43:18 January 1966); if the same experience can be successfully recalled three times in a row, it will be a good "emotional source" (Lewis 1962:55–6); indeed, such a memory can be used in long runs on Broadway because it "does not fade" (LS A10:2 February 1965). Stanislavsky would probably find such rules patently absurd, yet they can offer security to insecure actors. Follow these rules, and surely you will act well. As actor Shelley Winters once said, "I've always thought it was effective memory because it is so effective" (Hull 1985:102).[2] Like those who calcify complex theology into sets of dogmatic rules, many US proponents of the System simplify and codify Stanislavsky's complex conception of emotion.

The Method's originality specifically rests in this creative interpretation. Strasberg explicitly stakes out the control and expression of emotion as his special territory. In responding to Stanislavsky's vision of the unconscious as a large storehouse with many places in which to hide a precious jeweled "bead" of emotion (SS II 1989:290), Strasberg explains that, in his opinion, finding this bead is the actor's "true task." Moreover, he states, "this was the task I was to devote myself to in establishing the Method" (1987:60).

At the Group Theatre, Strasberg had already made emotion his primary criterion for acting. As actress Margaret Barker said, "Strasberg was so intent on what he called 'real emotion' that he reduced us to a pulp" (Chinoy 1976:523). When Sanford Meisner resisted performing an Affective Memory exercise in preparation for a role, Strasberg told him that he would be left "without total emotion" and snidely added "if you want to settle for that, that's fine" (Chinoy 1976:546). Many years later, he told members of the Actors Studio that they needed to build "a fence of technique" to "fight the terrible desire to settle" (LS 129:8 November 1960).

By the mid-1950s, Strasberg had created other exercises to buttress the central one, with Personal Substitution only the first among these. In the Private Moment an actor performs in public an activity so private, that "we shouldn't see or be witness to it." Actors take imaginary showers on stage; they sit as if at home contemplating their navels. Strasberg recommended this exercise to people who had difficulty with affective recall and "who couldn't really let go" (LS A160:24 December 1968). In the Song and Dance Strasberg attempts to forge a link between emotion and its expression. At his command, the actor sings a song in unusual ways—separating each syllable, changing tempo and pitch, and adding physical movements. "Mary Had a Little Lamb" becomes unrecognizable as the actor slows down, speeds up, jerks her limbs, and twists her neck, etc. By means of uncomfortable and awkward demands, the exercise affects the actor in some way, perhaps inducing anger or embarrassment. When the actor can no longer suppress emotion, when the actor explodes in raw reaction, the exercise is complete.

In these exercises, Strasberg reveals his ingenuity. He takes elements he had learned at the American Laboratory Theatre and pushes them as far as they will go. He begins with a foundation that, in his words, was "confined to the area of analytic memory," by which he means sense memory (recalling the taste of tea or the scent of a favorite flower) and manipulation of imaginary objects (putting on invisible shoes and socks or pouring invisible vodka). He then admittedly extends the scope "in my own work" to "exercises with *emotional memory*" (1987:75). Further testifying to this approach, he explains the genesis of the Private Moment. "I haven't heard of such an exercise in Stanislavsky, but it seems so natural an extension for his phrase 'private in public,' that I'm surprised I haven't thought of it before" (1987:144).

Despite Stanislavsky's view that acting expresses emotion, his writing does not readily support the Method's technical orientation. In the first place, he refuses to offer security through rules. One of Tortsov's students expresses great frustration with his teacher's equivocation. "But how?" he persists. "I passionately want to learn how […] to rouse my memory of emotion." Tortsov will not answer. He merely reiterates that everything in the study of acting will be brought to bear upon the question (SS II 1989:313). Moreover, he adds, continual exposure to literature, art, people, cultures, and history, in short a firm and continuous liberal education, an "infinitely wide range of interests," will do much good (SS II 1989:316). If there is, indeed, one piece of advice that Stanislavsky consistently offers in regard to emotion, it is his insistence on broadening one's knowledge as a way to expand one's store of affective memory (SS IV 1994:144).

In the second place, although Stanislavsky reminds actors throughout his book that analogous experiences help create characters, he does not advise the use of personal memories in a direct way. He may write that every time you perform a role you must "experience feelings analogous with your own" (SS II 1989:63), that "your own sentiments" must be "analogous" to the character's and that, "thanks to the analogies between your sentiments and the character's, many places in the role will come to life easily and quickly in you" (SS II 1989:377), but he also reminds you that "analogies spring from recollections gleaned from your reading and from stories about other people" as readily as from your personal life (SS II 1989:312), in short from empathy with others.

Tolstoyan Sulerzhitsky fostered the direct use of emotion more zealously than had Stanislavsky himself by stressing the need for "fusion of one's personal life with the character's life" (1970:307). He frequently emphasizes the need for an actor to develop a rich "affective life," "affective feelings" and a sense of "public solitude" (1970:307–8, 314). In notes from 1908 Stanislavsky credits Sulerzhitsky with the amazing discovery that in searching for analogous feelings one's own life could serve (SS V Part 1 1993:443). Suler transmitted this personalized focus to the US through his work at the First Studio with émigré teachers Richard Boleslavsky and Maria Ouspenskaya. Boleslavsky certainly taught actors to supplement work on a role with personal experience; he suggests this approach unambivalently in his book (1933:39–40).

While most theatre practitioners assume that Stanislavsky used affective memory liberally in his early work on the System, he actually did not. His concern for actors' privacy and their "mental hygiene" as well as his own modesty prohibited him from asking actors to perform affective recall in front of others. Stanislavsky told Joshua Logan, "We never ask anyone to practice my method in public" (1976:53).[3]

Stanislavsky also worried that personal associations could threaten the actor's focus on the play and confuse acting with playing oneself, a criticism often leveled at Method actors. Whenever personal stories would derail rehearsals at the First Studio, Stanislavsky would shift attention to sources for emotional experience in empathy and imagination. Even so, he found that "to restrain the actors from dropping into pathology was very difficult" (Markov 1934:16, 23). After cautious experiments with personal feelings triggered a nervous breakdown in his talented protégé Michael Chekhov, Stanislavsky recognized "the limitations" of such work (Kirrillov in M. Chekhov 2005:4). Emotion's strongest advocate, Sulerzhitsky, now also warned against "stage hysteria," which conveys only "the sick nerves of the actor and not the hero's" (Markov 1934:16). Thus, Stanislavsky never advocated that the actor use personal emotion as directly as Strasberg later would.

There is only one instance of a Method-like Affective Memory recall in Stanislavsky's acting manual (SS II 1989:450–4). It is both accidental and disturbing. Tortsov asks a young woman, Dymkova, to perform an étude in which she cradles and protects an imaginary child. From the narrator, we learn that, unbeknownst to her teacher, a rumor has been circulating among the students that Dymkova's own baby had recently died. From her performance of the exercise, Nazvanov concludes that the rumor must be true. Her tears flow freely, and she moves the entire audience with her performance. When Tortsov asks her to repeat the exercise, he cautions her to focus her memory on the physical details of her performance. "You can't hold on to feelings. Like water they run through your fingers." But she ignores his advice and places faith in her empathy with the character. Her second performance fails. All the subtle movements that she had unconsciously used to create an illusion of the child—the careful caressing of tiny hands and feet, her gentle kiss, and her gaze of admiration—are lost. Personal association alone, it seems, is not sufficient for successful acting.

After Dymkova can remember and repeat her physical actions, Tortsov asks her to perform the exercise yet again adding a new circumstance to stimulate her imagination further: what if she were to discover that the child she holds has unexpectedly died. The narrator reacts in horror to his teacher's innocent suggestion, and hurriedly whispers in his ear the rumor about Dymkova's baby. Tortsov clutches at his heart and runs to the stage to stop her. Dymkova, however, has already begun the exercise, and completes it successfully. Her success, Tortsov concludes, stems from her ability to separate improvised fiction from the reality of her life. This incident stands out as a rare and ambiguous intrusion into the personal life of an actor. While the accidental affective memory helps Dymkova, Tortsov does not encourage it.

Within the framework of Stanislavsky's book, this example shocks the reader with its extreme and delicate nature. Within the framework of the Method, such exercises became part of normal creative activity. Unlike Dymkova's experience, which is accidental and rare, Affective Memory was encouraged and expected in New York, even when a person's analogous experiences seemed to trivialize extreme situations in dramas. One need only think of Boleslavsky's example of swatting a mosquito as a suitable analogy for murder (1933:44).

Stanislavsky drew upon two sources as he explored how emotion informs acting. He looked to the science of psychology (examined below) and the practice of Yoga (Chapter 9). In light of his infrequent citation of sources, his quotations from the French psychologist Ribot and the American metaphysician Yogi Ramacharaka stand as impressive testimony to their equal influence on the System. First, consider the science.[4]

Affective memory

The genealogy of affective memory can be most productively traced to Théodule Ribot, the psychologist from whom Stanislavsky borrows the term. In his search to discover whether or not people possess the ability to recall emotion, Ribot tells an anecdote about a person who had nearly died by drowning. As he stood on a cliff watching the waves below him, he recalled the circumstances of his accident, but felt little. Ribot then speculates that others might feel a slight shiver at the thought of such an accident, while a few especially sensitive people would "recall the circumstances *plus* the revived conditions of feeling" (1897:152–3).

Stanislavsky cites this anecdote in *Part I* of his acting manual, further dramatizing it. He envisions two travelers who stop at a precipice overlooking the sea. As they look down at the foamy water, one of them recalls all the details of a near-drowning, "how, where, why." The other recalls the same incident but more generally. Stanislavsky then adds a still more dramatic, Proustian example of affective recall: he tells how two men, upon hearing a familiar polka, try to remember where they had heard it before. One recalls sitting near a column, the other sat to his left. We were eating fish, he reminds his friend, as the smell of perfume wafted by. Suddenly the memories of these two scents remind them of being drunk and their bitter quarrel that night (SS II 1989:284–5).

The Method turns these anecdotes into models for its central exercise: recalling circumstances and sensations, the actor ends with emotion. What starts as a mere example of the range of emotional recall in Ribot results in the means by which to ensure its arousal in the Method.

Appointed professor of the College of France in 1888, Théodule Armand Ribot (1839–1916) became director of the College's first psychology laboratory and there founded French experimental psychology. He stands among the first scientists to study the elusive subject of emotion, anticipating other psychophysical theories such as that of William James and Carl Lange. While Freudian psychology took hold of the American popular imagination, Ribot gained authority in Russia. As early as 1896, Ribot had caught Russia's interest through his monograph on Schopenhauer, the German philosopher who influenced many early twentieth century Russian artists. Later, Ribot's espousal of physical methodologies (seen as sympathetic to Marxist materialism) made him acceptable in post-revolutionary Russia as well. Ribot's differential impact on the two societies is embodied in the fact that his name was dropped from the *Encyclopaedia Britannica* after 1911, but remained through the 1970s in the *Bolshoi Soviet Encyclopedia*. Ribot's major books were translated into Russian within two years of their publications in Paris.

Stanislavsky's interest in psychology mirrored that of his native culture to some extent. He owned six of Ribot's books, read them voraciously and filled them with marginal notes (SS II 1989:502). The Russian responded to the Frenchman because they both sought to define a psychophysical continuum between mind and body. By contrast, Stanislavsky seemed uninterested in Freud's work. Translated into Russian in 1910, Freud was recommended to Stanislavsky in 1911, but there is no evidence that he took the suggestion (SS V Part 2 1993:358). After the revolution, Freud's works were banned for their non-materialist teachings about the structure of the personality. Where in the body can you locate the *id, ego* and *superego*? Where is the *subconscious*? While such questions did not bother Stanislavsky, he too felt that Freud only attended to the mental half of the continuum.

In the work which most captured Stanislavsky's imagination, Ribot set out to discover whether human beings possess a memory of emotion. He did so by experimental inquiry of approximately sixty subjects, who were asked to describe their recollections of pain, pleasure, taste, smell, etc. His anecdote of a man, recalling an experience of near-drowning, exemplifies his methodology. By contemporary standards, Ribot's method lacks rigor and his sample is ludicrously small. However, like Stanislavsky, he understood that subjectivity must be taken into account when studying the biological basis of emotion. At the end of the twentieth century, neuroscientist Antonio Damasio honors Ribot's point of view:

> We [scientists] must not fall into the trap of attempting to study consciousness exclusively from an external vantage point based on the fear that the internal vantage point is hopelessly flawed. The study of human consciousness requires both internal and external views.
>
> (1999:82)

Stanislavsky would say the same about acting. In adapting Ribot to the System, Stanislavsky relied upon both perspectives.

In searching for evidence of affective memory, Ribot distinguishes between "concrete" recollections, which involve the total psychophysical being, and "abstract" memories, which do not. A "concrete" memory is "felt" in the body as surely as the original emotion. Ribot discounts any recollection that does not have a physiological component. "An emotion which does not vibrate through the whole body is nothing but a purely intellectual state" (1897:163). "The false or abstract memory of feeling is only a sign, a simulacrum, a substitute for the real occurrence, an intellectualized state added to the purely intellectual elements of the impression, and nothing more" (1897:161). Stanislavsky picks up this distinction in *An Actor's Work on Himself, Part II* when he describes the analytical process most appropriate to art: "If the result of scholarly and scientific analysis is *thought*, then the result of artistic analysis should be *physical sensation*. In art, not reason but feeling prompts artistic creation" (SS IV 1991:53; 1961:91). In these words, he melds Tolstoy (who positioned emotion as the content of art) with Ribot (who saw emotion as physically experienced).

Many years later, Strasberg would imply a similar distinction when he repeatedly upbraided actors for "mental thinking" in sessions at the Actors Studio (LS 12:26 October 1956; LS 162:14 November 1961; LS A37:21 December 1965; LS A142:14 May 1958), no doubt intending to discourage what Ribot would call "abstract" memories. In his concern about intellect contaminating emotion, Ribot thus anticipates much of the anti-intellectualism that has engulfed Method acting.

From his studies, Ribot observes that memory of emotion does indeed exist, but that it is rare and highly evanescent. He noticed that his subjects often mistook "abstract" recollections for "concrete" ones, which needed much time and prompting to activate. Concrete memories arise very slowly and infrequently. He is especially struck with how seldom extreme experiences such as childbirth can be concretely recalled, explaining this phenomenon as a psychological coping mechanism and speculating that few women would have more than one child if they could recall their first experience fully. Although he identifies a few subjects who possess an especially sharp memory, and whom he terms "affective types," the vast majority exhibit little if any true affective memory. He concludes, "The emotional memory is *nil* in the majority of people" (1897:160).

Stanislavsky seizes upon Ribot's memory of emotion as undisputed fact. For him, it becomes one of the many personal qualities that actors possess simply because they are human. Like sight, smell, taste, touch, and hearing, feelings can be recalled, and thus, affective memory, albeit a "most rare phenomenon" (SS II 1989:280), can be used to create the "life of the human spirit of the role." Stanislavsky underlines the comparison with sense memory by using the Russian word, *chuvstva*, which refers simultaneously to "feelings" and the five "senses." "Once you can grow pale or blush at the memory of something you have experienced," Stanislavsky writes, "once you are frightened to think about something unhappy that you lived through long ago, you have a memory for *chuvstva* (feelings, senses) or a memory for emotion" (SS II 1989:281).

In fact, Stanislavsky expects actors not only to possess this sixth sense, but also to sharpen it. He dismisses Ribot's conclusion by writing, "Affective memory is weak, because it is never developed" (SS V Part 2 1993:364). He implicitly categorizes the successful actor as one of Ribot's "affective types," and thus again betrays an affinity with Romanticism, which portrays the artist as an especially sensitive individual.

To prove the importance of affective memory to acting, Tortsov asks his students to repeat an exercise, which they had earlier played successfully. In this étude, they imagine that a man who has escaped from a mental institution is trying to break in at the front door. In their first performance, the logic of the circumstances had roused in them genuine behavior: they hid, blockaded the door with furniture, looked for any means of self-defense. Without consciously trying to do so, they were able to simulate the normal working of the human organism under fictional circumstances; in short, they had used both their emotional and physical resources on behalf of the scene. When they repeat the exercise, however, the students remember only the physical form of their behavior, not its emotional content. While they repeat movements, postures, gestures, and vocal inflections, they do so without tapping their memories of emotion. Tortsov concludes that successful acting demands more than the activation of muscle memory and the five physical senses; it demands the sixth affective sense (SS II 1989:276–9).

In his System, Stanislavsky significantly extends his belief in the existence of affective memory to the audience. If, as Tolstoy insists, art must "infect" others with the artist's experience (1964:86), then, as Stanislavsky eloquently puts it, "Spectators create the soul's acoustics. They take from us and like a resonator they return to us our vital human sentiments" (SS II 1989:329). In his 1915–16 notebooks, Stanislavsky calls the audience the "third artist" in theatre, the first two being author and actor. For a performance to be successful, he muses, "the spectators, just like the actors, must carry traces of their feelings in their memories" (SS V Part 2 1993:463). In other words, the audience too must activate their sixth sense. This notion corrects the widespread misconception in the US that Stanislavsky taught actors to ignore the audience. As a form of communication, theatre needs spectators (Chapter 7).

Despite finding that organically experienced memories can indeed be induced, Ribot remains perplexed by two questions. First, why should a "concrete" recollection be considered a memory at all? If the subject experiences something physically in the present, why not call it a valid new experience merely based in the past? Even more problematically, Ribot asks whether concrete memories can be distinguished from pathological hallucinations. In both, the subject reacts organically to imaginary stimuli. Ultimately Ribot could not answer these questions (1897:48–9), leaving the notion of affective memory arguable.

However, what disturbs Ribot the scientist is easily assimilated by Stanislavsky the artist and later becomes Strasberg's very definition of acting, "the ability to react to imaginary stimuli" (1974:58). As practicing artists, Stanislavsky and Strasberg simply accept what they need for their art and reject what they do not. While Ribot finds it hard to distinguish between an emotion and its concrete recollection, Stanislavsky assumes not only a difference, but one crucial to stage acting, a performing art that demands repetition. He draws a line between "first time" or "primary" (*pervichnyi*) and "repeated" or "secondary" (*povtornyi*) experiences, thereby effectively brushing aside Ribot's questions, and minimizing the distinction between "concrete" and "abstract" memories.

Contemporary scientific studies on emotion take the difference between primary and secondary emotions as given, and add a third category of background emotions that provide the context against which other momentary experiences unfold (Damasio 1999:51–3). This addition strikes a familiar chord with Michael Chekhov's insight that "atmospheres" of scenes can do much to prompt the actor's work.

For Stanislavsky, primary feelings are "spontaneous, strong, highly colored" and occur rarely. "It's annoying: we do not control moments of primary experience; they control us." Like a bolt of lightning, they may suddenly and dramatically illuminate an actor's understanding of a character, but they are also dangerous. As Tortsov warns, an actor playing Hamlet, who feels blood lust for the "first time" during a performance, may inadvertently harm his partner! Thus, Stanislavsky sees the avoidance of primary feeling on stage as a matter of "mental hygiene." After Nazvanov's first exhilarating performance, Tortsov asks, "Do you feel capable and strong enough, mentally and physically, to play all five, huge acts of *Othello* with the same exaltation that you played accidentally this one short scene?" (SS II 1989:66; 1936:17). Obviously not.

While actors welcome primary experiences for the insights they offer, they must learn to summon secondary feelings during performances. These "more accessible," repeatable feelings "prompt our memory of emotion" and create the illusion of first time experiences, not their reality (SS II 1989:292). Memory safely filters and controls emotion, maintaining artistic distance between the actor and the event portrayed. It is the "crucible," Stanislavsky writes, in which emotion is transformed into art (SS II 1989:290). When asked by his Russian editor to clarify this aspect of the System, he explained that affective memory "washes feelings clean of all that is superfluous. It results in the quintessence of all similar feelings," and hence, "it is stronger than genuine real-life feeling" (SS IX 1999:450). Nazvanov demonstrates how this crucible of memory works when he witnesses a terrible accident on the street. He then traces how his recollection of it changes over time, becoming all the more imaginative and aesthetically powerful (SS II 1989:185–291).

Stanislavsky also uses the distinction between primary and secondary feelings to address Ribot's question about hallucinations. Nazvanov asks whether Dymkova "hallucinated" when she used the death of her baby as her "magic if." Tortsov takes her success as proof that she did not. In his eyes, she successfully maintained an aesthetic distance from her own experience. Dymkova used personal associations as a key to unlock emotional content, but never lost sight of the fact that she held empty swaddling clothes in her arms. She does not mistake her personal life for art (SS II 1989:450–4). Instead, she experiences something like the alternation of consciousness that Stanislavsky explored when he revisited Diderot's paradox of the actor in terms of his own experience as an actor (Chapter 7). Secondary emotions, in short, are never mistaken for the "real thing;" the actor remains aware of their fictional level and, as an artist, in control of them.

Stanislavsky's "magic if" helps insure this distance. Tortsov reminds his students, that he never asked them to hallucinate a madman breaking in at the front door; they were only to imagine what they would do if someone dangerous were there. "Hallucination" would have undermined their performances (SS II 1989:453–4). As Stanislavsky writes elsewhere, beginning actors often needlessly "expend all their energy" on pointless efforts "to hallucinate," ruining their ability "to concentrate on stage" (SS II 1989:102, 327). Strasberg reports that Boleslavsky's teaching was in consonance with this idea. In his notes from 1925, Strasberg quotes Boleslavsky as saying, "The aim of affective memory is not really to feel or see or touch something—that is hallucination—but to remember the mood when doing that" (1987:69).

In all this discussion, Stanislavsky never gives a firm description of how a secondary emotion actually differs from the first time it occurs except that it is more controllable. Yet, when Tortsov's students experience one, they not only recognize it but also act well (according to the values and standards set for them by their teacher). Have we entered a realm of tacit knowledge? I think so. Since lore embraces verbal contradictions that denote tacit knowledge, Strasberg too suggests that we have indeed entered the experiential dimension of acting. He had demanded "real emotion" from the Group Theatre members in the 1930s, and yet he also warned that the actor's emotion "should never be 'really real'. It should be only remembered emotion" (Munk 1966:197). Strasberg thus accepts and incorporates Stanislavsky's point of view, even though he mistakenly attributes the idea of "remembered" emotion to Stanislavsky's protégé Vakhtangov (LS 45:14 February 1958). No doubt, the role of affective memory in acting has generated heated debates precisely because it pertains to practice, with theory offering only partial and unsatisfactory explanations.

That Stanislavsky and Strasberg do not share the same basic assumptions about psychology can be best exposed by comparing their differing conceptions of the subconscious. Placing Stanislavsky's gentle understanding of it next to Strasberg's frightening vision reveals much about the transformation of the System in the US.

Stanislavsky places his extended discussion of the subconscious at the end of *An Actor's Work on Himself, Part I*; Nazvanov's first year of study culminates in its activation (Chapter XVI in SS II 1989:429–60). In his preface, Stanislavsky had emphasized the importance of this chapter by asking readers to "pay exceptional attention, since it contains the essence of creativity and the whole *system*"

(SS II 1989:42). Now, near the end of the volume, as he lists the conscious lures by means of which the actor might awaken the subconscious, the reader notices that not only are they the same ones proposed for trapping emotion, but that they recapitulate the book's chapter titles and, true to his initial promise, Stanislavsky has encompassed the System as set forth so far.

Stanislavsky begins his analysis of the subconscious with the repetition of an already familiar, although highly melodramatic, Dostoevskian étude. A young man is counting his company's money at home. His wife calls him into the next room to admire their newborn. When he leaves, his mentally handicapped brother-in-law becomes fascinated with the pretty colored bills and begins to burn the money in the fire-place. Returning to the room, the young man rushes to save whatever he can from the flames, but in his haste, he accidentally strikes a fatal blow to his brother-in-law.

Nazvanov consciously works through a familiar process: relaxing, concentrating on, and evaluating the given circumstances of the exercise, identifying problems, and attempting to solve them through actions. In short, he proceeds exactly as he has done before. This time, however, he experiences something new: the circumstances of the étude become especially dear to him. He imagines himself the sole support of a family of five. He then imagines that his job is on the line, due to a special audit scheduled for the next day. As he envisions a possible deficit, he plays distractedly with a paper band that had wrapped the bills. He must run to the office, he reasons, and make sure that his books are in order. His watch tells him that it is four, but he cannot fathom whether it is four in the afternoon or in the morning with the office locked. Before his wife enters, he sits immobile in his chair, absorbed in his thoughts.

"I lost myself in the role," Nazvanov explains, and labels the experience "inspiration." Tortsov, however, resists his student's analysis. For Stanislavsky, the word "inspiration" implies a force from without; recalling the word's etymology with its Latin connection to "breath," inspiration is Apollo breathing life into the artist. But Stanislavsky wants to empower actors and banish ideas that displace them as the nexus of creativity. For him, the subconscious is inner "poetry" that the actor consciously organizes through the "grammar" of technique (1936:266). Traditional ideas of "inspiration" have no place in the System. If the goal of acting is to tap the subconscious through conscious means, as Tortsov often reiterates, then Nazvanov has successfully done so. And if the whole System fosters experiencing, then Nazvanov now understands this special creative state. Merely activating the subconscious, which is within us, Tortsov contends, should not be confused with divine inspiration that comes from without. Tortsov thereby reverses Nazvanov's formulation: "You found yourself in the role and the role in yourself" (SS II 1989:432–3). In short, activating the subconscious induces experiencing.

For Stanislavsky, the subconscious accompanies us continuously in our daily lives. Like affective memory, it is simply part of human make up. In his eyes, "we are great friends with our subconscious" (SS II 1989:434–6).[5] It is a normal part of daily life that should become a normal part of our creative lives as well; it provides an infinite source for our imaginations. To prove his point, Tortsov asks several students to mention objects not present in the room. Their answers—a shaft, a pineapple—are random and dispassionate, yet Tortsov sees them as springing from their subconscious minds. Tortsov then asks another to describe what he is thinking. Before answering, the student mechanically wipes his hands against his trousers, pulls out a piece of paper from his pocket and folds and unfolds it. After his answer, Tortsov asks him to repeat his physical actions, but he cannot remember doing anything. His actions too demonstrate how easily the subconscious works in normal life.

In contrast, Strasberg treats the subconscious as the actor's foe. For him, it is the frightful, mysterious, uncontrollable place that popular Freudian tradition pictures. He sees it as interfering with creativity more readily than fostering it. He assumes that actors, being normal people, have neurotic "habits of expression" engendered by painful childhood and traumatic social experiences which they have repressed. These "habits" inhibit their ability to act, creating a "veil" that obscures them (1987:95). Because a person "is conditioned to express his feelings and emotions not by the nature, character, and strength of his emotional responses, but by what society or environment will permit," the actor cannot "use himself fully" unless "he rid himself of that interference" (LS 149:2 January 1962).

Strasberg's view suggests a therapeutic approach to acting: the person who wishes to act must confront and overcome blocks and repressions in the psyche in order to free the means of expression (1987:95; LS 43-1:18 January 1966). "That's why we often need to be concerned with an actor's personal problems—because they affect the behavior of the actor on stage" (LS 169:2 January 1962). For example, Strasberg tells of one actress who could not relax her neck, "an area," he adds, that "some psychiatrists believe retains certain types of traumatic emotional experiences." Her sister, who had shared her bed during childhood, threatened to beat her whenever she tossed and turned restlessly in her sleep. In true pop psychoanalytical fashion, once the actress can recall this autobiographical fact, she can relax her neck (1987:98–9). In Strasberg's eyes, one of the main advantages of the Affective Memory exercise involves its ability to lift the "veil" of interference from the actor. In a session at the Actors Studio in 1965, Strasberg prompted an actor through the exercise by telling him that "better acting" should not be his primary goal, since his "acting is not bad." Rather, he should focus his full attention on himself as a person: "All we want is more of you to begin with on the stage. [...] The foundation is you: with your thoughts, with your reactions, with your behavior, with real thought, with real sensation, and therefore with real experience on stage" (LS A9:2 February 1965).

In American lore, Stanislavsky's conception of the friendly subconscious has been lost. Chubbuck exemplifies how Strasberg's darker conception and thera-peutic approach continues to resonate in the postmodern age: "Every actor knows that discovering and understanding your personal pain is an inherent part of the acting process." When she then adds, "This has been true since Stanislavski," she also brings the Method's misconception of the Russian's views into the present (2004:vii). Not only does her technique grow "out of my search to overcome my own personal traumas" (2004:viii), but it will teach "even a non-actor [...] to learn how to use your pain and win your goals" (2004:x).

Politically correct psychology

When Tortsov reminds his students that "Each stage of the program we have undergone brings with it a new lure (or stimulus) for the memory of emotion and for the repetition of feelings" (SS II 1989:313), Stanislavsky links his ideas to behaviorism, the school of psychology that sees human behavior as physiological responses to stimuli. Of course, he had embraced Ribot because he saw emotion as dependent upon a psychophysical connection that struck Stanislavsky as correct. He also found this connection in Yoga (Chapter 9). But, Ribot's reputation as a behaviorist was welcome. By adding the word "stimuli" and connecting Ribot's quest for physicalized affect to behaviorism, Stanislavsky could satisfy the Soviet censors' demand that he make "concrete" such incorporeal notions as "soul" and "subconscious" (Chapter 6). In short, by associating the System with the material science of behaviorism Stanislavsky insured publication of his books in the USSR.

Begun in Russia when Ivan Mikhailovich Sechenov (1829–1905) discovered that neural activity originates from electrical currents and chemical reactions in the brain, behaviorism suited the Soviet mindset. Sechenov's physiological model for the brain was censored by the tsarist government for challenging the immaterial soul but embraced in the USSR for dispelling such spiritual notions. The Nobel Prize winning Ivan Petrovich Pavlov (1849–1936) built upon Sechenov's work by proving the existence of conditioned reflexes in experiments with salivating dogs. In their experiments, both scientists aggressively valued the "external vantage point" over the "internal," to borrow Damasio's words cited above (1999:82).

Ribot was contemporary with Sechenov, and like him, the Frenchman envisioned immaterial aspects of human experience as springing from the material body. As John J. Sullivan points out, French psychology bases the term "subconscious" on "an analogy with the organization of the central nervous system." Higher mental processes take place in the cerebrum and the emotions in the brainstem, hence the subconscious is "topographically" below the higher functions. Thus, as for Stanislavsky, there is nothing hidden or mysterious in Ribot's subconscious (Munk 1966:103–4). Unlike Sechenov, however, Ribot also trusted subjectivity in his work, relying upon the autobiographical narratives of those he studied. Thus, as for Stanislavsky, "external and internal" perception together prompt discovery of "truths" (SS II 1989:244).

The archival record clearly reveals that Stanislavsky's interest in strict behaviorism is one of convenience. While Stanislavsky read virtually everything that Ribot wrote, there is scant evidence to suggest such curiosity about Sechenov and Pavlov. During the 1880s, the Maly actor Fyodor Kommissarzhevsky recommended Sechenov's first book on the brain to Stanislavsky, but he did not read it until 1930 (Vinogradskaia IV 2003:65,125). The date suggests that he was dutifully following Gurevich's advice to consult Soviet scientists (Chapter 6).

Stanislavsky turned to Pavlov four years later. In October 1934, the head of the All-Russian Theatrical Union told Stanislavsky that Pavlov had asked to read the latest draft of *An Actor's Work on Himself*. Stanislavsky sent a typescript in the hope that the famous scientist would vet the System's terminology in advance of the book's submission to the censor. Had the head of the Union arranged for this reading in order to protect the manual by associating it with Pavlov? Or was he arranging for a round of actual, but surreptitious censorship unbeknownst to its author? Stanislavsky's letter to Pavlov tellingly combines great respect with extreme caution, especially in regard to the politically suspect plan to publish in the US (Chapter 5). "I send you my heartfelt gratitude for your attention to my work," Stanislavsky writes. "I am especially moved that you, knowing of my agreement with an American publisher, personally suggested that I entrust my materials to you" (SS IX 1999:612).

These few references to Sechenov and Pavlov comprise the entire body of evidence that links Stanislavsky to Soviet psychology. The Russian archives reveal nothing else.

Following Stanislavsky's death, however, those aspects of Ribot's work that link him to Yoga were willfully ignored in the USSR, while those that anticipate behaviorism were studied more deeply than the records warrant. Soviet scholars and practitioners were fulfilling expectations by providing politically correct readings of Stanislavsky. They used the scant evidence to manufacture a deep connection between Pavlovian behaviorism and the System. A group of scientists wrote a formal letter to the Marxist Kedrov in 1949—the year in which he became the new head of the Moscow Art Theatre and fired Knebel for her multivalent understanding of the System (Chapter 6). The scientists stated the required ideological position unequivocally:

> The goals of I. P. Pavlov and K. S. Stanislavsky coincided. The object of their mutual interest was the living human being. Specifically, these two inspired researchers, one through art and the other through science, both sought the truth about the human central nervous system and its governing laws. If Ivan Petrovich Pavlov approached his goal logically by studying the basic forms of the nervous system beginning with the lowest organisms, then Konstantin Sergeevich Stanislavsky walked toward the great physiologist from the other direction, by studying and discovering the laws which govern the highest processes, human artistic creation.
>
> (Vinogradskaia IV 2003:462)

In 1952, Soviet scientist Pavel Simonov positioned Sechenov and Pavlov at the heart of the System. By 1963, actor Aleksei Popov accepted Stanislavsky as "a natural materialist [who] walked hand in hand with the great physiologist I. P. Pavlov" (Vinogradskaia IV 2003:465). In short, Russia's acting lore promoted the System's overstated link to behaviorism as common coin. The force of this linkage was so persuasive that the Method too assumes that this scientific heritage is accurate. The notion that recall of emotion can become easier with repetition amounts to self-conditioning on the part of the actor. "That's how we're trained," Strasberg said, "not from Freud, but from Pavlov" (Munk 1966:198).[6]

Beyond Affective Memory and behaviorism

In a speech to theatre directors on 30 November 1935, Stanislavsky said: "The subconscious is still little studied, especially by people in creative professions like actors." Nodding to cultural expectations, he adds, "The scientist Pavlov is now taking first steps in this area, but his work has not yet led to any definitive results" (SS VI 1994:514). As the twentieth century turned into the twenty-first, scientific advances in psychology and neuroscience have still not unlocked the mysteries of the mind, but they are shedding new light on Stanislavsky's conception of emotion. For example, experiments by Susana Bloch and Paul Ekman prove the physical connections between emotion and its expression. Bloch conducts research on the relationship of breathing patterns to emotional expression at the *Institute de Neurosciences* in Paris; she has adapted her findings into an actor training program called "Alba Emoting" (Chabora in Krasner 2000). Paul Ekman has proven that primary emotions result in biologically driven facial gestures that are universally recognized across gender and culture (1980:73–101; 2007), a discovery that is being used by computer scientists to create virtual actors for virtual reality environments (Marsella *et al.* 2006).

While scientific developments like these are too numerous to list here, two areas of research particularly illuminate the topics of this chapter: findings on Post-Traumatic Stress Disorder (PTSD) challenge the Method's Affective Memory exercise and discoveries in neuroscience support Stanislavsky's assumption that emotion is experienced as a psychophysical continuum. Both areas point to ways in which actors can take Stanislavsky's understanding of "experiencing" as the ground for performance into the future.

In *Rethinking Affective Memory* actor and educator Cheryl McFarren describes her complex reaction to a teacher who saw extreme emotional vulnerability as a hallmark of success. "I had been obedient to my teacher in the pursuit of art," she writes, "and I was traumatized by the Affective Memory exercise" (2003:13). Years later this formative experience prompted her to examine Strasberg's central technique in light of PTSD, a condition officially recognized by the American Psychiatric Association in 1980. Symptoms of PTSD include physiological flashbacks to traumatic events, in which the brain and body respond to a trigger as to the original trauma. Scientific literature suggests strong similarity between the operations of PTSD and the "concrete" physicalized recall of emotion that Ribot had sought. In fact, one might say that PTSD answers affirmatively Ribot's question about the pathology of such memories. As McFarren writes, "The Affective Memory exercise, through its focus on sensory details [...] often calls forth traumatic experience" (2003:188). In fact, Strasberg felt that traumatic moments actually provide the best material for the exercise (above). In short, an Affective Memory exercise might trigger a flashback "in those who have survived trauma" (2003:188).

McFarren addresses two other important facts. First, prolonged or repeated trauma changes functions and structures in the brain. Therefore, should an actor reexperience a traumatic event during an Affective Memory exercise, real harm may be done. Second, PTSD is extremely prevalent in the US. Therefore, teachers might unknowingly welcome into their classes students who may "unwittingly elicit memories of experiences that are far from benign" (2003:174). McFarren thus advocates that the theatrical profession take seriously the quip that acting teachers practice therapy without a license (Martel 1988). "The psychotherapist has important resources that the theatre practitioner does not," she observes, "tools that make explicit the goal of preserving the client/patient's best interest in the interpersonal transaction between them" (2003:184).

Through contemporary psychology, McFarren returns to an overlooked aspect of Stanislavsky's writings: ethics. He had promoted ethical examination of the actor's profession from the first, observing that in order "to create a wholesome atmosphere [for work] the actor must first of all know what conditions have a destructive effect on him" (1984:104). The challenge posed by the prevalence of PTSD to the Affective Memory exercise leads McFarren to call for a code of ethics in the teaching of acting that begins with the cardinal rule of the medical profession: first do no harm.

McFarren's work suggests precisely how contemporary American psychiatry can reinvent Stanislavsky's cautious work on personal emotion and encourage, as he does, alternative sources for artistic material in imagination and empathy. In fact, the discovery in the 1990s of mirror neurons seems to prove Stanislavsky's insightful notion that empathy with others is as powerful as personal experience. These neurons fire in the brain in exactly the same way whether a person performs or observes an action, leading scientists to posit that empathy is at base the physiological mirroring of another's experience (Winerman 2005). In short, empathy might be personal too.

Actor/director Rhonda Blair harnesses a range of contemporary research on the brain for theatrical practice. Underlying her considerable work in this direction (2006, 2007) lies Stanislavsky's key assumption that acting as an embodied art necessarily relies upon a psychophysical continuum. She observes that, "Cognitive scientists, neurophysiologists and psychologists are proving that Stanislavsky, seventy five years ago, began intuiting something fundamental about how we, as human beings and as actors, work" (Krasner 2000:204).

One need read only a few pages of any of Damasio's eloquent books to prove Blair's statement. Consider, for example, pages eight and nine of *The Feeling of What Happens in the Body: Body and Emotion in the Making of Consciousness*. As Damasio discusses the issues that prompted him to study consciousness, he writes, "I had come up against the obstacle of self, for something like a sense of self was needed to make the signals that constitute the feeling of emotion known to the organism having the emotion" (1999:8). Similarly, Stanislavsky has written that because the System makes the actor consciously aware of the unconscious underpinnings of artistic creation, it fosters "a sense of self" (*samochuvstvie*). "You can never lose yourself on stage. [...] There's no walking away from yourself" (SS II 1989:294). To do so would mean falling into unconsciousness.

Damasio then proceeds to tackle the elusive "problem of consciousness" by asking "how the brain inside the human organism engenders the mental patterns we call, for lack of a better term, the images of an object." As he defines his terms, he even more clearly echoes Stanislavsky's vocabulary. "By *object* I mean entities as diverse as a person, a play, a melody, a toothache, a state of bliss; by *image* I mean a mental pattern in any of the sensory modalities, e. g., a sound image, a tactile image, the image of a state of well-being" (1999:9). Stanislavsky too calls "objects of attention" anything that demands the actor's focus during performance, whether partner or prop (SS II 1989:149), and "images" those sensory details that emerge from actors' visualization exercises (Chapter 9). Blair finds cognitive research on image formation, Damasio's "movie-in-the-brain" (1999:9), especially valuable in acting (Blair 2006:182); Stanislavsky had called the same process the actor's mental "filmstrip."

I would add that Russian uses the word "image" (*obraz*) even more extensively than does Damasio. "Image" is the common Russian word for "character," which for Stanislavsky is no less a "mental pattern" than the imaginary image of a tree. In this sense, "character" as "image" registers as radically different from the psychologically coherent personality that postmodern artists and scholars generally assume to be Stanislavskian. Rather, the wide-ranging stylistic possibility in the mental images of characters allows actors to treat any type of theatrical performance as "truth" (Chapter 7).

Twenty-first century science allows contemporary artists to redefine "truth" as "theatricality" in terms more familiar than those that Stanislavsky had borrowed from Tolstoy (Chapter 7). As Blair observes, discovering about how the brain works

> frees us from conventional notions of affective and sense memory as "retrievals of past truths" and objective notions of the self, since it allows the actor to work from the perspective that there is no "objective" authentic self, past or other, to emerge but only the self-in-the-now of the rehearsal or performance.
>
> (2006:181)

In other words, science helps break the stranglehold that the rhetoric of truth, sincerity, and realism has placed on the System.

Furthermore, postmodern science gives new credence to Stanislavsky's insight that acting, like human experience, is at once corporeal and incorporeal. As Blair puts it, "The neuroscientific perspective critiques twentieth-century approaches that compartmentalize different aspects of the actor's being, e.g., separating acting from voice, voice from movement, and all of this from research and critical thinking" (2006:180). In other words, contemporary inquiry makes way for Stanislavsky's second source on human emotion, Yoga, which also does away with compartmentalization.

9 Emotion and the human spirit of the role: Yoga

The system at the crossroads of East and West

When Strasberg writes that for Stanislavsky "the actor's internal means [...]" was still called at that time the 'soul'" (1987:67), we understand that Strasberg wishes to replace "soul" with "subconscious," reflecting his own assumptions about acting as grounded in popular psychology. Stanislavsky, however, would not equate the two words. While he uses Ribot's psychology as a jumping off point, he also incorporates transcendental ideas of emotion in his System. When Stanislavsky asserts that acting should embody "the life of the human spirit of the role," he does indeed mean the psyche as "soul."

In the 1935 manuscript that Stanislavsky sent to Hapgood for publication in the West, he provides an image that was deleted from the 1938 Soviet version by the censors, no doubt because of its clear spiritual tonality. As Nazvanov works through his étude about the burned money, he stands on the shore of an "ocean of the subconscious" as the tide rolls in. Tortsov now metaphorically contradicts an earlier rejection of inspiration as an externally felt influence; he measures each stage of his student's success by the externally rising tide that engulfs him. As Nazvanov unconsciously plays with the wrapper from the money, Tortsov sees his student "on the threshold;" as Nazvanov looks at his watch, Tortsov identifies "a big wave;" as Nazvanov contemplates his company's deficit, Tortsov comments that the water has reached up to the waist; when Nazvanov reaches a state of immobility, Tortsov whispers, "He is out in the ocean of the subconscious now" (Chapter XVI 1935; 1936:274–5).

In the Western context, this image easily calls to mind Freud's analysis of religiosity as an "oceanic feeling," and, in fact, the connection to religious sentiment is apt. While Stanislavsky would reject a dark, Freudian view of the subconscious, he would embrace this spiritual association. Tolstoyan "experiencing" as the desired state of the actor in performance shares much with Eastern spirituality; recall Yogananda's description of his meditative moment as "oceanic joy" (1993:167). The actor, like the yogi, engulfed by the creative state of mind, undergoes something akin, when mind, body, and soul unite in communion, not only with each other, but also with others on stage and those present in the audience.

One of the most remarkable aspects of Ribot's essays on emotion involves his critique of the very language in which he writes. Anticipating late twentieth century studies in semiotics, he complains that Western languages create an arbitrary opposition of mind and body through verbal signs, thus making it nearly impossible in his culture to formulate a holistic view of human feelings. Yet, in his view, emotion is a monistic phenomenon, a total psychophysical event with no causal relationship between mind and body. In necessary compliance with his native language, Ribot reluctantly bisects this event into internal (or "organic") and external (or "motor") functions. He concedes, that "this somewhat arbitrary distinction is desirable for the sake of clearness in exposition," but compensates by avoiding any suggestion of causality (1897:113).

By disputing the usual Western Cartesian assumption of mind imposing order on the physical world, Ribot sets himself apart from psychologists like James and Lange, and behaviorists like Sechenov and Pavlov, whose theories maintain either that mental impulses cause bodily responses or vice versa. Moreover, by rejecting a causal assumption, Ribot anticipates twenty-first century developments in cognitive science and brain chemistry that investigate the seamless interdependence of physical and mental operations

Stanislavsky, too, presupposes an indissoluble link between mind and body. Echoing Ribot's assertion that "a disembodied emotion is a non-existent one" (1897:95), Stanislavsky insists that, "In every physical action there is something psychological, and in the psychological, something physical" (SS II 1989:258). The physical churning of one's stomach cannot be divorced from the emotional sensation of anger. He puts this monistic, psychophysical view of human experience at his System's heart.

Actor Bella Merlin, who studied in Moscow, defines this "continuum" well. "In a nutshell, the basis of psycho-physical acting is that *inner feeling* and *outer expression* happen at the same time" (2001:27). Such acting addresses precisely what Strasberg had identified in 1948 as "a central problem." He found that, through an Affective Memory exercise "an actor could experience and yet not be able to express an emotion" (1987:94). Addressing this dichotomy lead him to develop more physically based exercises ("Song and Dance," "The Private Moment," etc.) as complements to the memory of emotion. The need for such exercises best testifies to the Cartesian dualism implicit in the Method, as distinct from the System. In contrast, the psychophysically trained Russian actor does not perceive the same gulf between emotion and its expression. As Merlin puts its, "when we're playing a character, the inner/outer dialogue takes place truthfully and simultaneously. Then and only then, will an audience really understand what's going on before their eyes" (2001:27–8).

Russian offers Stanislavsky an easier entrée into monistic thinking than French allows Ribot or English Strasberg. Not only does the noun, *chuvstva*, apply equally to the five physical "senses" and to emotional "feelings," but its verb, *chuvstvovat'*, is remarkably extensive in its possible meanings: "to feel," "to have sensation," "to be aware of," "to understand." As Martin Kurtén, a Finnish actor who has translated Stanislavsky for Scandinavia, exclaims, "This is sensational: a verb which can mean anything from feel to understand [...]! In a calm, everyday situation the two [opposites, 'emotion and reason,'] walk gently hand in hand" (1989).

Unfortunately, English like French is less accommodating; the simultaneous physical and emotional associations implicit in *chuvstva* invariably get lost in English translations. With its every appearance in a text, translators must choose from its multiple and contradictory nuances. Indeed, the Hapgood versions of Stanislavsky's books generally privilege its emotional layers, supporting the Americanization of the System.

But for Stanislavsky, the psychophysical connection is not yet sufficient for art, which for him, as for Tolstoy, must go beyond the rational and communicate the ineffable about human experience. Thus, Stanislavsky pushes the psychophysical contention further into a physiospiritual realm, if I may coin another awkward adjective. The "organic connection between body and soul" is so strong, he insists, that artificial respiration revives not only flesh but also "the life of the human spirit" (SS II 1989:349).[1] In short, Stanislavsky may have rejected the Western "breath" of inspiration, but he embraces the Eastern view of breath as a means to control the energy of life (*prana* in Sanskrit). In the organic continuum of body and soul, Stanislavsky betrays his interest in Yoga, which views the physical as a threshold into the spiritual.

Through this wider physiospiritual connection one can find the clear lineage between Stanislavsky and his protégé Michael Chekhov, who, as a Christian, could not fully accept Yoga and turned instead to Rudolf Steiner's "anthroposophy" (M. Chekhov 2005:133–5). Like Stanislavsky, Chekhov was interested in communicating transcendental human experience through art.

Additionally, through the physiospiritual link, one can find synergy between Stanislavsky's notions of psychology and twenty-first century neurobiology. Consider the following words by cognitive scientist Antonio Damasio:

> To discover that a particular feeling depends on activity in a number of specific brain systems interacting with a number of body organs does not diminish the state of that feeling as a human phenomenon. Neither anguish nor the elation that love or art can bring about are devalued by understanding some of the myriad biological processes that make them what they are. Precisely the opposite should be true: Our sense of wonder should increase before the intricate mechanisms that make such magic possible. Feelings form the base for what humans have described for millennia as the human soul or spirit.
>
> (1994:xx)

Finally, the seamless continuum of body and soul links the System to contemporary performance scholarship as well. In 1918, Stanislavsky uses exactly this liminal image: "My System must serve as a threshold into the creative state, and one must learn to open, not close, the door" (SS II 1986:193). Unaware of this yogic notion in Stanislavsky, performance scholars, who sought to examine this threshold state of being in performances of many different kinds, turned to anthropologist Victor Turner's studies of "liminality" in ritual activity (Schechner 2006:66–73).

The mind, body and spirit continuum is the ocean in which Nazvanov swims. When Tortsov tells Nazvanov that he has found the spirit of the role within himself, he invokes the key idea in Yoga: that we reach God by finding the god within. The image of an outer "ocean of subconscious" engulfing the actor expresses the yogic sense that the inner and the outer are absolutely continuous. In fact, Stanislavsky takes both his primary images of the subconscious, a "friend in our own mind" and an "ocean of life, pulsating, moving, thinking, living" around us, directly from a book on Yoga that he owned (Ramacharaka 1906:37, 147).

Additionally, when Stanislavsky uses "I am" (*Ia esm'*) as a synonym for experiencing, he further betrays the yogic influence on his thinking. On one hand, *Ia esm'* is not Russian but Old Church Slavonic, a language created for the Eastern Orthodox liturgy. (Russian itself has no first-person present tense for the verb "to be.") Therefore, his usage is already enough to imply spiritual overtones. On the other hand, "I am" also names the state of mind in which a yogi becomes aware of a deep "relationship to, and intouchness with all life, expressed and unexpressed," to quote Ramacharaka whom Stanislavsky read. This "I am" is far removed from our usual sense of "I" as an individual abiding in quotidian reality (Ramacharaka 1906:1–2).[2] The same Eastern notion (that the "Self is not personality") also influenced the performance work of director and theorist Jerzy Grotowski (Schechner and Wolford 1997:481), making clear why he had always called Stanislavsky his teacher despite critics' desire to put him at an opposite aesthetic pole. Moreover, because the "self as spirit" breaks away from a sense of "self as individual," so too does the System break away from psychologically-based conceptions of character.

When Stanislavsky writes that you must use yourself fully in acting, "all of yourself, from your soul to your body, from your feet to your head" (SS II 1989:200), he means this not only psychologically, as would Strasberg, but also holistically. The prism of Yoga best allows us to see Stanislavsky's recurrent phrase, "the human spirit of the role," as far from rhetorical flourish; he means "spirit" quite literally. If, as Ramacharaka writes, "All of life—is a manifestation of the Spirit" (1904:239), then for Stanislavsky, all of the actor's art—is a manifestation of the human spirit of the role.

The sources

In July 1911, while Stanislavsky was vacationing with his family in France, his son's new tutor, Nikolai Vasilievich Demidov (1884–1953),[3] a young medical student, made a helpful suggestion. "Why invent exercises yourself, and why look for words to name that which has already been named?" he asked. "I'll give you these books. Read *Hatha Yoga* and *Raja Yoga*. They will interest you because many of your thoughts coincide with what's written here" (Vinogradskaia II 2003:294). Indeed, Stanislavsky became absorbed in these books by Yogi Ramacharaka and borrows from them as explicitly as he borrows the term "affective memory" from Ribot. Stanislavsky writes:

> Having worked wonders in the realms of sub- and super-conscious, Yogis give much practical advice in these areas. They also approach the unconscious through

conscious, preparatory devices, from the body to the soul, from the real to the *unreal*, from naturalism to abstraction. And we, actors, must do the same.

(SS IV 1991:142)

Many years later, he continues to marvel, that "a thousand years ago, [the Hindus] sought exactly the same things we are seeking" (1919–20:79).

While Tolstoy and Diderot offered Stanislavsky ways to describe the creative state, Ribot and Ramacharaka suggested concrete and practical approaches for the process of creative work. In fact, Ramacharaka might have welcomed the collaboration. Not only does he quote Ribot directly, (1906:117), but he also observes that "The Theory of the East, wedded to the practice of the West will produce worthy offspring" (1904:103).

The transcendent layer of Stanislavsky's thinking reverberates with aspects of Russian culture that had long envisioned Moscow as a crossroad where Western religion (represented by Rome) could combine with Eastern Orthodoxy (represented by Constantinople). In the early twentieth century, interest in the Orient surged. Tolstoy had corresponded for many years with the Indian leader Mahatma Ghandi, and is thought to have affected Ghandi's approach to civil disobedience (Zaechner 1968:176–9). Russian Symbolists became fascinated with the occult. Avant-garde artists of the day sought reality beyond the world of the actual and embraced Eastern models. Such interests made the Ramacharaka books especially popular in the 1890s and through the 1910s in Russia (Poliakova 2006:184). Stanislavsky's protégé, director Vsevolod Meyerhold experimented equally with European circus and Japanese Kabuki and Noh. Both Michael Chekhov and Maria Ouspenskaya, members of Stanislavsky's First Studio and émigré teachers in the US, pursued Eastern religious practice in emigration, he through Rudolf Steiner's Anthroposophy[4] and she through Yogananda's Self-Realization Fellowship (White 2006:80). As the abstract painter Mikhail Larionov wrote in 1913: "Hail beautiful Orient! We unite ourselves with contemporary Oriental artists for communal work. [...] We are against the West vulgarizing our Oriental forms, and rendering everything valueless" (Gray 1962:136–7).

Stanislavsky began to think in yogic terms as early as 1906. Evidence exists from that year that he was already using exercises on relaxation and concentration that resembled Yoga in the on-going production of Anton Chekhov's *Uncle Vanya* (White 2006:78). Moreover, by 1906 he also felt that both he and his theatre had reached "a dead end" with European theatrical Realism; "the old [paths] had been destroyed," he mourned. "My God, are we stage artists really doomed because of our material bodies to serve eternally and portray only crude realism?" (SS I 1988:354–6). Why not look for "new paths" in the same direction as his culture and his artistic peers— to the East? Stanislavsky's search for a System of actor training coincided with his desire for artistic forms that transcend Realism, and both quests significantly coincided with his discovery of Yoga. This search first led to his funding Meyerhold's 1905 studio, dedicated to the production of Symbolist plays. It then led to his hiring of the Tolstoyan Leopold Sulerzhitsky (Chapter 2) to assist with a series of allegorical and mystically inflected productions at the Moscow Art Theatre: in 1907

The Drama of Life (Hamsun) and *The Life of Man* (Andreev), and in 1908 *The Blue Bird* (Maeterlinck).

Sulerzhitsky advocated Meyerhold's studio and "stood up for the right to produce 'mystical theatre,' [... and] for experiments in the field of theatrical symbolism" (Poliakova 2006:111). No doubt, Suler (as he was called by friends and students) also encouraged an Eastern orientation. Not only had he adopted Tolstoyan spiritual values, but he also witnessed meditation as practiced by the "Dukhobors," the Christian sect whom he had resettled to Canada at Tolstoy's request (Poliakova 2006:54–102). In fact, Stanislavsky invited Suler into the Moscow Art Theatre after reading his account of this two year mission (Sulerzhitskii 1970:42–7).

His non-theatrical background made him especially valuable to Stanislavsky. As one of Suler's students would later too romantically recall, "Having sat in the evenings over philosophical and spiritual books" the Tolstoyan "did not well know why the Art Theatre needed him and what he would do there" (Sulerzhitskii 1970:57). Since Sulerzhitsky was well known to the company, the inaccurate recollection still registers as true when one considers the fact that Stanislavsky relied on Suler precisely because of this reading. He "brought with him to the theatre baggage filled with fresh and vital spiritual material," Stanislavsky observed, making the Tolstoyan able to eschew conventional "words such as naturalism, realism, impressionism, romanticism." He used instead "other words: beautiful and not beautiful, base and sublime, sincere and insincere, life and affectation, good and bad." Thus, without theatre training *per se* "he could do instinctively [...] what we were now avidly striving to do" (SS V Part 1 1993:183–4), a comment that parallels precisely what Stanislavsky has also said of yogis.

By far, Stanislavsky's most important source of information about Yoga was the several books that he owned on Hatha Yoga (the physical discipline) and Raja Yoga (mental training that teaches concentration and meditation). Both schools of practice approach spiritual understanding through biology, hence, Stanislavsky's famous insistence on the "organic" foundations of acting.[5] Specifically, his library contained Russian translations of several books by William Walker Atkinson (1862–1932), who wrote under the pen-name Yogi Ramacharaka. Among these were those given to him by Demidov, *Hatha Yoga: or The Yogi Philosophy of Physical Well-Being* and *Raja Yoga: or Mental Development*, as well as *Teachings of Yoga about the Mental World of the Person* (SS IV 1957:496–7).

Atkinson was an American lawyer, who turned his passion for Eastern metaphysics into a series of twelve books that were published by the Yogi Publication Society of Chicago between 1903 and 1907; these remain in print in English. He intended that his books introduce Yoga to the Western world, and indeed they found a wide readership not only in the US but internationally (White 2006:81–2).[6] Thus he took pains to explain Eastern philosophy through the lens of more familiar thinkers, like Ribot, wherever he could (Ramacharaka 1906:120–1). His books were translated into Russian in the 1910s.

Stanislavsky quotes liberally from the Ramacharaka books. Many of the System's images and catch phrases can be found there. For example, both writers call the subconscious a "friend" who assists in our mental and creative work (Ramacharaka 1906:145, 148; SS II 1989:436). Both astound their readers with the fact that this friend occupies ninety percent of our being (Ramacharaka 1906:93, 107, 109, 123; SS II 1989:140). For both, the entire point of training lies in learning how to use "the subconscious mind, under orders of the conscious mind," as Ramacharaka writes (1906:139; also 113, 140, 141; SS II 1989:61, 427, 437). Additionally both describe the memory as a "store-house" from which to retrieve "bits" of human experience (Ramacharaka 1906:83, 144; SS II 1989:290). Moreover, both see "truth, not as it had appeared before," to quote Ramacharaka (1906:51) and "not at all what it is in reality," to cite Stanislavsky (SS IV 1991:380).

However quaint the 1910s' style of the Ramacharaka books might strike the postmodern reader, examining them with Stanislavsky's System in mind prompts little shocks of recognition page after page. These sources clearly provided Stanislavsky with more than conceptual notions and practical exercises; they provided a structural model for what he most passionately wanted: to assist actors in harnessing the creative state. Overall, his System teaches this control in much the same way that "the Science of Raja Yoga [...] teaches as its basic principle the Control of the Mind" (Ramacharaka 1906:50).

First, Ramacharaka lays out a structured program that, like the System's books, moves from work on the self outward. Both programs of training "hold that the internal world must be conquered before the outer world is attacked" and that "the first knowledge for the Candidate is the knowledge of the Self" (1906:2). Stanislavsky's titles for his manuals *An Actor's Work on Himself, Parts I and II* and the planned *Part III, An Actor's Work on the Role*, make this same progression obvious. Moreover, the crucial word "work" also echoes in Ramacharaka. "Do not forget that all that we know we have 'worked for.' There is nothing that comes to the idler, or shirker" (1906:79). No wonder discipline was emphasized at the First Studio (White 2006:78) and became a hallmark for the System at any of its stages of development! Using an image suited to the late 1930s Soviet context, Suler's fictional stand-in, Rakhmanov, reminds Tortsov's students, that "the actor, like the soldier, demands ironclad discipline" (SS II 1989:48).

Second, Ramacharaka suggests much of the basic vocabulary for Stanislavsky's project. Consider the very word "system," which is, as Jonathan Pitches notes, "polysemic" because it allows for "a sense of fluidity, of receptivity to local, national and international influences" and for "an interrogative attitude to performance" (1999:112). Just as Ramacharaka lays out "a system of exercises, drills, etc." in *Raja Yoga* (1906:88), so too does Stanislavsky create a "System" that includes "exercises and drills" (*trening i mushtry* in Russian). Like Ramacharaka, Stanislavsky reminds his students that this "system" should be treated as a "guide," not as a set of hard and fast rules (SS III 1990:371). Modeling himself on "Yogi teachers [who] are constantly leading the Candidates toward [their] goal [...] first by this path and then by that one, [...] until finally the student finds a path best suited for his feet" (Ramacharaka 1906:35), Stanislavsky tells his directing students three months before his death that, "One must give actors various paths. One of these is the path of [physical] action. But there is also another path [... that starts from] feeling" (Vinogradskaia 2000:498). Pitches is clear on how "system" can accommodate all paths, in contrast to the more limiting word "method:" "A system can draw upon a range of methods to achieve its overall aim, but the reverse does not hold true" (1999:112).

Other words from Ramacharaka also echo in Stanislavsky's terminology. The yogi grounds his work in mental "tasks" (Ramacharaka 1906:14); so too does the actor have "tasks" (*zadachi*), or in more common parlance "objectives" (Hapgood's loose translation). Thoughts as well as plays can be handled more easily when broken into component "bits" of information (Ramacharaka 1906:149), or *kuski* (translated as "units" by Hapgood and transformed into "beats" in US lore). Absorption in the "object of the examination and consideration" which Ramacharaka deems critical to successful concentration (1906:23) finds its place in the actor's arsenal as "objects of attention." Like a tree growing in a crevice, which, through the "principle of accommodation," adjusts its shape to fit, so too does the actor use "adaptation" (*prisposoblenie*) to adjust to the given circumstances of the play and production (Ramacharaka 1904:26). If "the 'want' [*khotenie* in Russian] is not sufficiently strong" neither a person, nor a character as developed through the early System can attain his or her goals (Ramacharaka 1906:151).

Stanislavsky's quest for terminology, no matter how problematic, is far from a trivial pursuit. As Ramacharaka writes regarding the value of "word images" in meditation, "It is difficult for the mind to build itself around an idea, unless that idea be expressed in words" (1906:165). Language counts as well for Ribot on the monistic phenomenon of emotion and for Stanislavsky on the actor's tacit knowledge. In Stanislavsky's later work on Active Analysis (Chapter 10), the words of a play, like notes in music, encode performance, and thus take on even greater significance as "verbal action." Perhaps the simultaneous difficulty and importance of naming tacit knowledge is the source for the terminology wars that often characterize the various camps that developed in American Method acting (Pitches 1999:6–8). As semioticians would later agree, words, however imperfect, do more than describe; they create ideas.

Ironically, as US theatrical culture would later adopt and adapt the Russian's System, so too did Stanislavsky adopt and adapt an Americanized view of the East! Because Atkinson as Ramacharaka wrote for Western readers, he gives an overview rather than "favor[ing] one specific school or philosophy of Yoga over another, as an actual Yogi might" (White 2006:82). Atkinson explains in *Hatha Yoga* that, "To go into the minute details of the Yogi theory would be foreign to the purpose of this work, and we must rest content with the general statement here given" (Ramacharaka 1904:62). Similarly, the practice that the Ramacharaka books encourage is easier to follow than would be the stricter disciplines of true Yoga. Hence, Stanislavsky's key published sources are, as it were, "second-hand information" (White 2006:82), leading some to see Stanislavsky's use of Yoga as "curiously watered-down" (Hobgood in White 2006:83).

Ramacharaka's books, however, were not Stanislavsky's only source of information on Yoga. In 1916, the Moscow Art Theatre considered producing two plays that further extended Stanislavsky's knowledge of Eastern spirituality. The first was *The Romantics*, a new play about the Russian intelligentsia by the Symbolist poet Dmitry Merezhkovsky, a leader in Moscow's occult movement and co-founder of the Religious-Philosophical Society. The second was *The King of the Dark Chamber* by Rabindranath Tagore, the Bengali author who had received the Nobel Prize in 1913. This dramatic allegory about spiritual enlightenment concerns a mysterious, perhaps divine king who only appears to his subjects under cover of darkness; thus he can be known to them only through faith. Both plays became embroiled in the company's debate about whether their theatre should move away from Realism toward Symbolist and theatricalist styles. Nemirovich-Danchenko pursued these productions in a spirit of reconciliation, hoping through them to forge a "new link" with his estranged partner's methods (Radischeva 1999a:262; Senelick 2997:47).

Stanislavsky's greater enthusiasm and unequivocal regard for Tagore's play is palpable in his letter of 11 August 1916 to his partner. For the Merezhkovsky play, "there is hope" because it could be "of interest to the actors;" but "Rabindranath" is "the genuine article" (SS VIII 1998:448–9). In this instance, the two partners agree. Nemirovich-Danchenko describes Tagore's play as "charming" and, in comparison with Merezhkovsky's "immeasurably more in terms of its clarity, religiosity, and beauty" (II 2003:483, 494). The company ultimately chose only to proceed with Tagore's play, and Nemirovich-Danchenko began rehearsing a cast that included actors from the First Studio. While the production never opened to the public, fragments were shown to the company in December 1918 (Nemirovich-Danchenko II 2003:762; SS VIII 1994:544).

In conjunction with these rehearsals, Nemirovich-Danchenko had arranged for an Indian to lecture on Hindu philosophy (Stroeva 1973:19; 1977:330), and clearly both Tagore's play and the lectures contributed to Stanislavsky's respect for and knowledge of Yoga. Even the atheistic Soviet editors ventured the opinion that Stanislavsky had "valued the great Indian writer extraordinarily" (SS VI 1959:386). That the lectures had an impact on Stanislavsky is best demonstrated by the fact that on 9 March 1919, during a conversation with the Moscow Art Theatre actors about new theatrical forms, he suggested that they again invite Tagore's translator and the Indian to speak with them further (SS VI 1994:488).[7]

The practice

While one often accepts Stanislavsky's near-religious devotion to acting and his belief that a theatre should be treated with the reverence accorded a temple (an idea he had borrowed from the great nineteenth century actor Mikhail Shchepkin), one rarely casts such spirituality in other than Western terms. Yet, Eastern thought offered him different and in ways more satisfying models for the mind/body relationship than science alone could offer. These models he found not only theoretically but, more to the point, practically useful. By 1912, at the First Studio, he and Sulerzhitsky were regularly using exercises based in Yoga and taken, in many cases, directly from Ramacharaka's books.

However bastardized the Ramacharaka books might seem to true disciples of Yoga, Stanislavsky and the members of his First Studio found them exceedingly valuable. Demidov, in fact, became the Studio's yogic "mentor" (Poliakova 2006: 184). In 1915, Evgeny Vakhtangov, one of Stanislavsky's most talented students, testified to Ramacharaka's continuing value when he wrote the following instruction to the members of his own newly created studio. "Please take one rouble from the cash-register on my account. Buy Ramacharaka's *Hatha Yoga* and present it to [the actress] Ekzemplyarskaya as a gift from me. She should read it attentively and she must perform the exercises in the section on breathing and on *prana* this summer" (Vendrovskaya and Kaptereva 1982:65–6). Especially interesting, in view of the fact that Demidov had been a medical student, was Vakhtangov's added note that these exercises would boost Ekzemplyarskaya's health. Michael Chekhov too speaks of studying Yoga at the First Studio (SS I 1995:152).

Indeed, Ramacharaka's Westernized approach actually proved fortuitous to the System. Compare, for example, Stanislavsky's easy appropriation of Ramacharaka with the difficulty encountered by Grotowski. He had followed Stanislavsky's lead in the study of Yoga but found that strict adherence deters theatrical work.

> This [type of yogic] concentration destroys all expression: it's an internal sleep, an inexpressive equilibrium: a great rest which ends all actions. This should have been obvious because the goal of yoga is to stop [...] all life processes [... and to find] fullness and fulfillment in conscious death.
>
> (Schechner and Wolford 1997:44)

While Ramacharaka, too, sees Yoga as directed toward an inward turning state of mind that would seem to contradict the System's primary artistic goal of communicating felt experience outward, Stanislavsky was able to turn "the idea [...] that you should be able to abstract yourself, so far as is possible from distracting impressions" (1906:8) into a useable state of attentiveness during performance.

The difficulty with adapting Yoga to acting did not mean, however, that Grotowski saw no benefits in it for actors. On one count, the physical "positions help very much the natural reactions of the spinal column; they lead to a sureness of one's body, a natural adaptation to space," and on another count, "these paradoxical positions go beyond the limits of naturalism." With this in mind, Grotowski asks, "Why get rid of them? Just change all their currents" (Schechner and Wolford 1997:45).[8] Change the "currents" Stanislavsky did! If one considers how many people now practice modified versions of Hatha Yoga and meditation primarily for physical exercise and stress reduction, one can better understand how Stanislavsky could redirect Ramacharaka's inward techniques outward and use his principles to escape realistic and naturalistic boundaries in artistic expression.

From *Hatha Yoga*, Stanislavsky adopts relaxation and breathing techniques, along with the belief that rays of vital energy (*prana*) can be consciously manipulated. While he takes the book's suggestions in the first two instances without modification, he uses the manipulation of *prana* to increase the effectiveness of communication (detailed below). Émigré actress Vera Soloviova recalls exercises at the First Studio in which actors send and receive rays of *prana*, not words (Munk 1966:211). Like Ramacharaka who does not describe the familiar physical postures from Hatha Yoga (White 2006:83), Stanislavsky expresses great admiration for the Yogi's ability to retain the center of gravity and hence to balance in any pose without describing any specific yogic movements (SS V Part 2 1933:379).[9]

From *Raja Yoga*, Stanislavsky takes conceptual ideas about the creative state, the nature of the unconscious, and discrete ways to sharpen concentration, attention, and observation. Among his adaptations are the use of circles and objects of attention. Soloviova specifically cites exercises on concentration, which she called "getting into the circle" (Munk 1966:219). Stanislavsky explicitly uses meditation techniques from Ramacharaka as a way to tap the subconscious through the conscious mind. In rehearsal notes from 1916, Stanislavsky writes: "On the advice of Hindus, we attentively examine each thought [...] and strive to admire it" (Vinogradskaia 2000:58). In *An Actor's Work on the Role*, he paraphrases *Raja Yoga*, when he suggests that the actor "throw" a "bundle of thoughts" into "a kind of mental trap-door" and "tell your unconscious mind" that "I wish this question to be thoroughly analyzed, arranged, classified (and whatever else is desired) and the results handed back to me" (Ramacharaka 1906:166; SS IV 1991:144 or 1961:82).[10]

Another of the System's specific meditation techniques—visualization—may have been sparked by the lectures surrounding the Tagore play.[11] As adapted for the System, this technique exercises the actor's capacity for imagination and builds affective memory by using the inner eye to form eidetic images (*videniia*) of circumstances and predicaments that lie outside the actor's personal experience.

An often cited visualization exercise occurs in *An Actor's Work on Himself, Part I*, when Tortsov asks his students to imagine themselves as trees. By specifically envisioning the species, the shape and color of the leaves, the age, and the environment, the students project themselves into a world they could not otherwise know. As they work, they add more imaginary senses to their visions: the tactile feel of the roots buried deep into the earth, of the branches reaching toward the sky, and of the bark's exposure to the weather; the sounds and smells of this specific place and time. Finally the sixth sense, emotion, is aroused by visualizing a narrative that occurs at the base of the tree: a battle, a romantic tryst, a picnic (SS II 1989:133–6; 1936:61–3). The choice of Tortsov's subject in this visualization relates it directly to Yoga, which seeks to make humans aware of "the interpenetration of our being into all objects." As Tagore writes:

> In the West the prevalent feeling is that nature belongs exclusively to inanimate things and to beasts, that there is a sudden unaccountable break where human nature begins. [...] But the Indian mind never has any hesitation in acknowledging its kinship with nature, its unbroken relation with all.
>
> (2004:2, 4)

Tortsov takes the visualization exercise into the rehearsal hall by teaching his students to create a "filmstrip" of mental images from their characters' lives. Each image projects a vision of a key moment and helps focus the mind of the actor during performance (SS II 1989:130). This notion directly anticipates contemporary neuroscientific findings. In asking how one can understand the process by which the mind "engenders the mental patterns we call [...] the images of objects," Damasio writes:

Quite candidly, this first problem of consciousness is the problem of how we get a "movie-in-the-brain," provided we realize that in this rough metaphor the movie has as many sensory tracks as our nervous system has sensory portals—sight, sound, taste, and olfaction, touch, inner senses, and so on.

(1999:9)

Stanislavsky would find emotional memory implicit in this list of senses as well.

Additionally, Stanislavsky's study of Yoga supplied him with a multitude of parables for his teaching, one of which, that proves the need for concentration, appears in *An Actor Prepares*. A maharajah tests potential ministers by asking candidates to carry a pitcher of milk around the city without spilling a drop. He who is undeterred by the city's bustle wins the position (1936:81). Again, Stanislavsky's description of the concentrated creative state emulates the meditative state of "I am." Compare, for example, Yogananda's anecdote about a young man who reaches this state in the middle of noisy Calcutta, and thus finds himself suddenly enveloped in "a transforming silence" somewhat akin to the sense of public solitude that the System attempts to induce in the performing actor. "Pedestrians as well as the passing trolley cars, automobiles, bullock carts, and iron-heeled hackney carriages were all in noiseless transit" (1993:94–5).

Two Hindu concepts, *prana* and the *superconscious*, particularly fascinated Stanislavsky and bear closer examination.

Stanislavsky accurately defines *prana* as "the vital energy [...] which gives life to our body" (Chapter X 1935:1; 1936:187).[12] He saturates his rehearsal notes from 1919 and 1920 with references to it that closely parallel words in Ramacharaka's *Hatha Yoga*. Perhaps taking notes while reading, Stanislavsky takes time and space to describe this force in great detail:

> a.) *Prana*—vital energy—is taken from breath, food, the sun, water, and human auras. b.) When a person dies, *prana* goes into the earth through maggots, into microorganisms. c.) "The Self"—"I am"—is not *prana*, but that which brings all *prana* together into one. [...] e.) Pay attention to the movement of *prana*. f.) *Prana* moves, and is experienced like mercury, like a snake, from your hands to your fingertips, from your thighs to your toes. [...] g.) The movement of *prana* creates, in my opinion, inner rhythm.
>
> (II 1986:220–1; Ramacharaka 1904:149–50)

Palpable but invisible rays of *prana* ground Stanislavsky's analysis of communication in theatre. In a successful performance, he explains, *prana* rays (*luchi*) pass between actors and their partners and between actors and their audiences, thus becoming the vehicle for infecting others with the emotional content of the performance (SS II 1989:318–52). Like other communicative vehicles such as speech and song, *prana* too can be manipulated and controlled through the breath. The "Pranic Exercises" given in *Hatha Yoga* are largely concerned with rhythmic breathing (Ramacharaka 1904:159–68; see White 2006:83–5).

No wonder the 1918 invitation to teach his System to the opera singers of the Bolshoi Theatre so excited him and developed into an interest that persisted for the rest of his life!

In *Hatha Yoga*, Stanislavsky read that a person can both store and actively radiate *prana* (Ramacharaka 1904:154, 231). Learning to control such radiation became especially important in the First Studio, as Soloviova above notes. Imagining that psychic rays travel much like radio waves from transmitter to receiver, Stanislavsky developed exercises that train actors in the "emanation" or sending (*izluchenie*; also *lucheispuskanie* or "radiation") and the "imanation" or receiving (*vluchenie*; also *luchevospriiatie* or "irradiation") of silent signals (SS II 1989:338, 340). Stanislavsky's Soviet editors identify Ribot as a source for these terms (SS II 1954:507). Radiation is one of the System's tenets that Michael Chekhov would retain and later develop in his own evolving approach to acting.

Moreover, because communication is central to the function of art, Stanislavsky sees the control of *prana* as essential to acting. He draws a schema of his System in the form of human lungs, visually referring to techniques of Yoga that radiate *prana* through the body using rhythmic breathing. Even Yoga's *chakras* (or wheels of concentrated psychic energy that lie along the length of the spine) find corollaries along the center line of Stanislavsky's chart as circles that represent the actor's "mind," "will," and "feelings" (SS III 1990:309).[13]

Stanislavsky's interest in rays of energy continues to inform exercises in communication at Moscow's leading acting schools. I first witnessed their use in 1989, at the Russian Academy of Theatrical Arts. One male student, standing just in front of another female student in single file, went from stasis to motion when he received the invisible rays that she, standing out of his view, transmitted to him mentally. He went to the piano, as she followed. He picked up a flower lying there and presented it with an elaborate bow to one of the spectators. Stasis again, and then he ran to the window, slamming it shut. In this exercise, he was not to move until he felt her unspoken order. Afterwards, she reported that he did exactly as she had silently commanded. Bella Merlin describes a similar exercise, "Silent Commands," which she learned in her study at Moscow's State Institute of Cinematography in 1993. In this slightly easier version, the actors sit facing each other as they give and receive communications (2001:88). R. Andrew White encountered both standing and seated versions of these studies on "imanation and emanation" in his study at the Moscow Art Theatre Studio.[14]

Stanislavsky also takes from Yoga the obscure notion of the "superconscious," placing it next to and distinguishing it from the "subconscious." That the unconscious realm is the true seat of creativity, that this region is a vast territory, and that it can be activated through conscious means are ideas familiar to the Method. Unfamiliar, however, is Stanislavsky's division of the unconscious into two: psychology's subconscious and a superconscious from Raja Yoga (SS IV 1991:142; 2000:58).

As Ramacharaka explains, "The Oriental teachers have always held that [...] just as there was a field of mentation *below* consciousness, so was there a field of mentation *above* consciousness as much higher than Intellect as the other was lower than it" (1906:120). Moreover, Atkinson as Ramacharaka directly critiques

Western thinkers who assume a subconscious coextensive with the total unconscious realm, as does Strasberg. In Atkinson's opinion,

> The mere mention of the fact [that a superconscious exists] will prove a revelation to those who have not heard it before, and who have become entangled with the several 'dual-mind' [conscious/subconscious] theories of the recent Western writers. The more one has read on this subject, the more he will appreciate the superiority of the Oriental theory over that of the Western writers.
>
> (1906:121)

Appealing to the scientific bent of the West, he concludes that the subtler yogic view of the unconscious "is like the chemical which at once clears the clouded liquid in the test-tube" (1906:121).

While Stanislavsky sees the subconscious as an inner friend, working with the common phenomena of life, he defines the superconscious as a transcendent force that "most of all elevates a person's soul, and thus most of all must be valued and preserved in our art." Only with its help can the actor convey the "life of the human spirit." As he explains, "The subtler the feeling, the more unreal, abstract, impressionistic, etc., the more the superconscious, that is, the closer to nature [as in the tree visualization exercise above] and the further from [quotidian] consciousness." He concludes, "The superconscious begins where the real, or more properly speaking, the ultra-real ends" (SS IV 1994:140). The Soviet editors give this as a paraphrase from the 1914 Russian translation of Ramacharaka's *Raja Yoga* (SS IV 1957:496).

This statement testifies to the fact that the System also begins where the "real" ends. Through such statements, one begins to see how far the mature Stanislavsky had traveled from a standard conception of Realism in art and how unique his view of truth and creativity had become. The content of art, for Stanislavsky, is indeed emotion, but not only in a Western psychological sense, but in an Eastern transcendental one as well. Through his understanding of "experiencing" as a creative state that operates on a continuum of mind, body, and spirit and that taps equally the conscious, subconscious and superconscious layers of mind, Stanislavsky successfully leverages for theatre what he had learned from both Tolstoy and Yoga. A System based on the redefinition of "truth" as the experiencing of the performative moment and grounded in yogic practice can indeed encompass dramatic literature from different eras and cultures and in different aesthetic styles. One can finally understand the import of his aphorism which starts this book: "Human life is so subtle, so complex and multifaceted, that it needs an incomparably large number of new, still undiscovered 'isms' to express it fully" (SS II 1989:458).

Once the Eastern strand in Stanislavsky's thinking is identified, many passages, that look at first glance psychological, can be read at second glance through the prism of Yoga with the two systems of thought colliding in surprising ways. For example, Stanislavsky welds meditation with behaviorism: "It is important to realize that incorporeal reverie, lacking flesh and matter, can call forth genuine reflex actions in flesh and in corporeal matter. This ability plays a large role in our psychotechnique" (SS II 1989:142). When Stanislavsky explains that his

goal is "to teach [the student] the laws of correct breathing, the correct position of the body, concentration and watchful discrimination" (1980:116–17),
he implicitly refers to major tenets of Yoga: *pranayama* (the control of *prana*
through breath), *asana* (the familiar poses and balances) and *dharana* (meditation techniques) (Wegner 1976:87). He further stresses that these ideas pervade
every aspect of his practice when he follows the above list with the bald statement, "My whole System is based on this." As critic Tatyana Bachelis suggests,
Stanislavsky is more in tune with Yoga than psychology, more "mystic than
scientist" (Senelick 1988:23).

Stanislavsky creates rhetorical and literary structures in his books to support
his monistic view of the mind/body and body/spirit continua. On the one hand, he
continuously seesaws from internal issues to external ones. While any point may
theoretically provide entrée to the System, Stanislavsky begins with the mind,
and hence gives internal work apparent primacy. However, when one of Tortsov's
students seriously injures himself due to overzealous concentration on inner techniques, Tortsov responds by interrupting his planned curriculum and jumping ahead
to exercises on physical relaxation (SS II 1989:185). On the other hand, Stanislavsky
recreates a holistic experience for his readers by reiterating the same points for both
internal and external issues. Thus, when Stanislavsky discusses "truth" and "belief"
about half way through the first volume of his acting manuals, he introduces little
that is new. He appears merely to use new terminology for already familiar ideas.
While this rhetorical strategy successfully portrays a closed circle of ideas, it also
creates a false sense of redundancy that ultimately led to damaging abridgement of
the books in the United States.

The Russian text of *An Actor's Work on Himself, Part I* ends with a five page
passage in which Tortsov cautions his students that they have yet to acquire a holistic
system. They may now know how to induce belief in the given circumstances of
the play, they may now understand affective memory and imagination, they may
have encountered the "importance of the spiritual life in our kind of art," but they
have yet to meld these elements into a complete psychophysical technique. They
have yet to explore half of the equation: "the corporeal life of the actor." He boldly
calls their knowledge "incomplete" (SS II 1989:459). The deletion of this passage
from *An Actor Prepares* gave the English book a false sense of completion and
half the equation stood for the whole until the publication of *Building a Character*,
thirteen years later.

However much Stanislavsky tries, he never fully escapes Western dualism. He
is bound, as is Ribot, to a language that contains within it deeply dualistic assumptions. Despite the fortuitous Russian word that means both "emotional feelings" and
"physical sensations" and despite continuous reminders about the indissoluble link
between the psychic and physical, Stanislavsky creates an almost endless series of
oppositional concepts: inner/outer, emotion memory/muscle memory, mind/body,
spiritual/physical, truth/lie, invisible/visible, motion/lack of motion, unconscious/
conscious, subconscious/superconscious, etc. Whenever he turns from one to the
other, he unwittingly betrays hidden Cartesian elements in his thinking. "Until now,
we have worked with the process of *external, visible, corporeal communication* on

stage," he writes, "but there also exists another more important aspect: *internal, invisible, spiritual communion*" (SS II 1989:338). Stanislavsky herein implies that these two types of communication are not only separate realms, but have a hierarchical relationship. I think, therefore I am.

Moreover, by suggesting that the "conscious" can tap "the unconscious" (SS II 1989:293), and later in his career that the physical can trigger the action of the psyche, he continues to imply linguistically that there exists a causal relationship in what should ideally be psychophysical simultaneity. Ribot might very well have criticized Stanislavsky for his ultimate inability to escape his linguistic context like the Western psychologists, James and Lange.

One might, like Jonathan Pitches, see Cartesian and causal models in Stanislavsky's writings as firm evidence for an underlying Newtonian scientific paradigm in the System that brings consistency to the various stages of its development (1999:1–50). But one might also reflect on Ribot's criticism of language, and see Stanislavsky as merely trapped by words, unable to say what he intuits. Contemporary cognitive science seems to support the latter view. As Damasio proves in *Descartes' Error* (1994), reason and emotion are two sides of the same nonconscious psycho-physio-spiritual continuum that the System seeks to make a conscious part of the actor's technique.

Stanislavsky's effort to escape Western dualism, however flawed, represents his most successful attempt to describe the tacit dimension of acting. He recognizes in both Ribot's psychophysical monism and in Yoga's physiospiritual unity, an essential similarity to artistic practice as defined by Tolstoy. Although Stanislavsky favored different techniques at different times during his career, he sees each of the System's various elements as inextricably linked to all the others, in a tightly wound "knot" or "bundle" (SS II 1989:395, 417). In *An Actor's Work on Himself, Part II* he philosophizes, "How astounding a creation is our nature! [...] How everything in it is bound together, blended, and interdependent! Take, for example, the state of the actor on stage. The slightest dislocation in something planned destroys the whole." He concludes with a metaphor—like a musical chord, in which one false note creates disharmony, all elements of the system must work together in order to create a complete and harmonious performance (SS III 1991:314). This chord, like Yoga's chanted *om*, balances the whole.

Soviet censors attacked Stanislavsky's interest in Yoga heartily. Naturally as atheists they objected to any mention of the spirit and the soul; as Marxist materialists they criticized Hindu philosophy as "idealistic" despite its grounding in the biological world. No wonder that the word *prana*, which appears in first drafts of Stanislavsky's acting manual and in the 1935 version he sent to the US, disturbed them. While Hapgood retains the Sanskrit term once in her abridgement, the Soviet editors deleted it completely from the 1938 Russian edition. The term "superconscious," which was maintained in Stanislavsky's posthumously published books, proved no less a source of embarrassment to the Soviets. In 1957, the editor of the Russian-language *Collected Works* felt the need to explain that Stanislavsky had "borrowed this term uncritically from idealistic philosophy and psychology," a sin forgiven when he realized the error of his ways and switched to the more acceptable "subconscious" in the 1920s (SS IV 1957:495). In 1962, Soviet psychologist Pavel Simonov dismissed these terms as merely "unsuccessful" (1962:86).

Astonishingly, however, the atheistic Soviet censors left some quotations from Ramacharaka intact (usually those attributed by Stanislavsky to anonymous yogis), and sometimes the editors footnote the actual source, leaving a trail to Stanislavsky's subtext for the astute reader. Ironically, dismissive comments, taken together with the trail of references, allow us to understand that there are indeed yogic undertones in Stanislavsky's censored texts. Had the Soviets merely cut all references without comment, the Yoga in the System might have disappeared more entirely from the official publications and languished in unopened archives. Instead, they made it possible to find the Yoga between the lines.

Unlike sources in psychology, Yoga was embraced by the Method no more enthusiastically than it had been by the Soviets. Although accurately translated by Hapgood in *Creating a Role*, the term "superconscious" did not seize the American imagination. When unaware of Yoga in the System, it is easy to assume, as does John J. Sullivan, that "The term superconscious, which appears in Stanislavski's writing, is a genuine original. It does not appear in any well-established system of psychology" (Munk 1966:104). "Superconscious" could too easily be read as a mere synonym for "subconscious" or as a slip of the tongue. When Strasberg precedes his discussion of how Stanislavsky was "influenced by some of his previous interest in Hindu philosophy" with the editorial "unfortunately" (1987:60), he too helps erase Yoga's mark from Stanislavsky's work. Similarly, Strasberg cites psychology, but not Yoga, as Stanislavsky's source for the System in his *Encyclopaedia Britannica* article (1974:61). Strasberg further testifies to his differential treatment of the two key influences on the System in his book, *A Dream of Passion*. On the one hand, he explains that psychoanalytical techniques can help an actor "unblock" "unconscious inhibitions," so that "sensations begin to pour through and begin to lend toward a fullness and vividness of expression." On the other hand, perhaps referencing the same inward turning to which Grotowski would later object, Strasberg writes, "I have found that while individuals who practice Zen, Yoga, meditation, etc., are helped in their personal lives, such disciplines do not help them express themselves in their acting" (1987:139, 105). Thus, the Method actively embraced one source, imbibing Stanislavsky's psychology and imbuing it with a therapeutic mindset, while rejecting the other as had the Soviet censors.

In sum, Stanislavsky's plan for actor training, like Russian culture itself, blends East and West.[15] He drew from two sources equally—Ribot's psychology and Yoga's physicalized spirituality—to understand and express the content of dramatic art-emotion and human spirit. However, both Russian and American acting lore, for different reasons, erased Yoga from Stanislavsky's work and privileged psychology. While the System's Western underpinnings have been frequently examined, the Eastern aspects have not yet received their full due. Benjamin Lloyd explains this differential attention by noting that, "Few subjects in Stanislavsky's writing will make the theatre academic more squeamish than his relentless examination of the spiritual component in acting" (2006:73). Joining this "academic" in the US would be students of the Method and in the USSR Soviet actors, scholars, and censors who promulgated Marxist materialism. Lloyd locates their discomfort in the "well-intentioned effort to explain acting by exchanging the mysterious and spiritual for the scientific and psychological" (2006:74). I would also add that the Soviet necessity to comply with sanctioned, atheistic political thought came into play.

This differential treatment of Stanislavsky's sources actively distorts interpretations of the System. That Stanislavsky viewed affective memory in relation to the wider concept of experiencing remains hidden. That he strove to communicate transcendent, as well as personal, emotion through art becomes blurred. In the twenty-first century, despite a decade of new and uncensored information about the Soviet past, one still need only glance at a handful of English-language textbooks on acting to see that psychology and Realism continue to trump Stanislavsky's Tolstoyan, yogic, and non-realistic interests. Yet, these are the very interests that can revitalize Stanislavsky for the next generation of actors.

10 Action and the human body in the role

The USSR bias

While Strasberg concentrated on emotion, Soviet actors were focusing on another aspect of the System, physical actions, more suited to the Marxist mind set. This emphasis, like the US bias, disturbs the balance of mind, body, and spirit to which Stanislavsky dedicated his System. For Stanislavsky, both emotion and physical action, together with spirit, are equally important links in the unbroken chain that is theatrical art. If, as Tolstoy would have it, emotion is the content of art, then for Stanislavsky action becomes the theatrical language by which affective material is communicated, and the System, its grammar. "People on stage act and these actions—better than anything else—uncover their inner sorrows, joys, relationships, and everything about the life of the human spirit on stage" (Bancroft Typescript:165).

While Stanislavsky believes that the effort to convey emotion unites all the arts, action distinguishes theatre from the others. In this, Stanislavsky would agree with Aristotle who defined drama as an imitation of action. Stanislavsky often cites the etymology of "act" and "drama" as proof. He does so only three months before his death, after watching a student performance of Chekhov's *Three Sisters*. "Altogether our art is the art of action. The word 'act' comes from the Latin word 'actus,' which means action; the word 'drama' is of ancient Greek origin, also meaning 'action.'" He concludes by pointing to the very Russian words that describe a play's main divisions (*deistvii*, the acts) and its cast (*deistvuiushchye litsa*, the "acting persons") (Vinogradskaia 2000:496).[1]

This etymology informs Stanislavsky's terminology in the most essential way. He accepts "drama" as "doing." He rejects the usual Russian word to describe what the actor does on stage, *igrat'* ("to act," literally "to play"), replacing it with *deistvovat'* ("to behave," "to take action"), as if it were a Russian equivalent of the Greek *dran*. Stanislavsky makes his rejection explicit through an object lesson in his fictional classroom. Tortsov asks an actress to sit on stage awaiting further instructions, and then unexpectedly declares her work successful. When she protests, "I didn't act (*igrat'*) anything," she gets the point. "On stage," he tells her, "you must 'take action,' not 'act'" (SS II 1989:88). Moreover, he turns *igrat'* on its head, using it to label his students' unsuccessful work (SS II 1989:145). The traditional Russian term for acting has become his pejorative.

Stanislavsky's rejection of *igrat'* can easily be mistaken as an anti-theatrical restatement of Realism, as did director and playwright Nikolai Evreinov (1879–1953). One of Stanislavsky's staunchest critics, Evreinov saw theatre's value in its very divorce from reality; he embraced *igrat'* precisely because it emphasizes "artificiality." In his eyes, Stanislavsky "destroyed" the time-tested traditions and the very nature of theatre, by turning his back on *igrat'* (1912:37; 1938). Evreinov argues for the traditional word by pointing out that child's play (*igra*) and what the actor does on stage is essentially the same activity. He devotes an entire chapter in *Theatre for Oneself* to little Vera (whose name means "belief"). As she plays, she turns each of her five fingers into a character in a drama which she herself composes (1916:91–4). In *Theatre as Such*, he cites a new teaching method, allegedly invented in the US by a suspiciously named "N. Ticher," that uses dramatic situations to enhance children's learning (1912:55–6).

One can easily imagine Evreinov's ire in reading passages which reject his beloved *igrat'*. But, on closer analysis, his anger seems purely semantic. Had he forgotten that Stanislavsky too studied child's play to better understand adult theatre? Just as Evreinov had looked to Vera, Stanislavsky learned much about "belief" in imaginary circumstances from his six year old niece. Her "what if" games inspired his "magic if." In one improvisation, Tortsov encourages his students to play like children while they imaginatively create a snowy, desolate environment by using whatever comes to hand (SS II 1989:96, 119, 123). Stanislavsky's replacement of "playing" with "doing" does not reject the fictional level of acting so much as it focuses on theatre's special means of communication.

That actors speak through their actions becomes as important to Stanislavsky as what they say. If, as Ribot teaches, emotion cannot exist without motion however subliminal, and if, as Yoga professes, the mental and physical exist as an indivisible whole, then, Stanislavsky reasons, neither can emotional content be torn from its physical embodiment. In the System, "the life of the human spirit of the role" is continuous with "the life of the human body" on stage. In short, inner content (emotion) is inextricably linked to outer form (action).[2] From this point of view, even the physical act of speaking can be viewed as a mode of action, a notion that he would ask Maria Knebel to study in 1936 (Knebel' 1967:264). Contemporary Speech Act theory suggests that Stanislavsky's insight on "verbal action" was sound (Saltz in Krasner 2000:61–79).

Despite Stanislavsky's holistic sentiments, actors successfully tore the fabric of the System into halves, as they struggled to adapt it to their cultures. As surely as the US concentrated on emotional content, Marxist materialism favored the concrete physicality of form. While New York explored Affective Memory, Moscow took hold of the Method of Physical Actions. In 1963, when Harold Clurman visited the Soviet Union, he saw concrete evidence of this bifurcation. "The American actor (under forty-five)"—in other words the actor who grew up on the Method— "often goes through an agony of effort to give his acting emotional substance. In its extreme form this becomes a sweating sincerity." In contrast, Clurman marvels that "the Soviet actor takes feeling for granted. It is always present; he does not need to strain himself to achieve it." Moreover, Clurman explains that "the quietness and repose of most Soviet acting" originates in the "most basic truth of physical action—of look, movement, and relationship to immediate circumstances" (1966:219).

American Lee Norvelle (1962) and Russian Vasily Sakhnovsky (1988), whose articles mirror their respective cultures, reflect this bifurcation, not only in their treatment of emotion, but through action as well. Norvelle does not list action as a category at all. Sakhnovsky, in contrast, includes action in three out of nine key techniques, "the rule of action," "the through-line of action," and the "active 'as if.'" Teachers like Lee Strasberg and Soviet Vladimir Prokofev further demonstrate differential readings of the place of action within the System. While Strasberg accurately defines "action" in *A Dream of Passion*, he drops it from his catalogue of Stanislavsky's most important discoveries: relaxation, concentration, and affective memory (1987:75–8). In contrast, Prokofev cavalierly brushes aside affective memory in favor of "the method of physical actions, because it is the simplest and surest means to truth on the stage. The best approach" (Munk 1966:68). Strasberg had used nearly the same words in describing the power of Affective Memory.

A widespread interpretation of Stanislavsky's career, that presumes a radical change in his thinking during his last years, supports this bifurcation. As the story is told, Stanislavsky emphasized emotion in his early work at the First Studio, but later found Affective Memory too unreliable a technique and emotion too capricious and volatile to insure stable, repeatable performances. He therefore turned his attention to physical and hence more controllable techniques. The story ends when the Method of Physical Actions supersedes all other acting approaches, tested and rejected in the past. Émigré Russian actress and teacher Sonia Moore reflects this account when she writes, "With the Method of Physical Actions, Stanislavski reversed his earlier teachings" (1991:7). Leslie Irene Coger also captures it in the title of her article, "Stanislavski Changes his Mind" (Munk 1966:64).

This apparent about-face is usually explained through Stanislavsky's discovery of Ivan Pavlov's experiments in conditioning dogs (Chapter 8) and Ribot's similarity to the James/Lange theorem of emotion, which both assert that physical action provokes emotion as surely as emotion provokes physical action. Recalling anger, the actor might strike a fist on the table; but striking the table may just as readily provoke the actor's anger. Moore invokes this explanation when she rather exaggeratedly states that Stanislavsky "reversed more than his early belief. He reverses the very process of life itself" (1991:7). Coger, too, asserts that Stanislavsky "dispensed with emotional recall because the use of physical actions evoked the needed emotive content" (Munk 1966:64).

This interpretation of Stanislavsky's work in his last Studio encodes Soviet expectations as surely as Strasberg's emphasis on Affective Memory encodes the American therapeutic point of view. By privileging the body over the psyche, by relying on behaviorist theories and by regarding the actor's work on a play as "a dialectical process of analysis and synthesis" (Simonov 1962:70, 74), this story makes Stanislavsky's career palatable to Marxist materialism.

Furthermore, it allows Soviet critics to dismiss "errors" of Stanislavsky's youth as misguided experiments by investing the System with linear and teleological development. It supposes that Stanislavsky had sought all his life for the "correct" answer to a question he had posed in Finland in 1906: How can the actor control the moment of inspiration? While he experimented with many different techniques along the way, he ultimately found the "true" and "scientific" answer in a technique as incontrovertible as the laws of gravity. This account sweeps away the uncomfortable "idealism" in Stanislavsky's attraction to Yoga; it sweeps away, too, the psychophysical conception of action as simultaneously of the body and soul. Just as the Soviet view of history culminates in the creation of Communism, so too does the Soviet view of the System culminate in the Method of Physical Actions. Psychologist Pavel Simonov employs this kind of thinking when he calls Stanislavsky's last technique "the distinctive 'key,' the cornerstone" of the System, that incorporates Marxist "dialectical thinking," and allegedly proves that "the subconscious for Stanislavsky holds no hint of mysticism or transcendentalism" (1962:14, 72, 70).

In the US, critics of Strasberg could productively use the same viewpoint to dismiss the Method, arguing that the Actors Studio depends too much upon Stanislavsky's early work. Moore does so, when, in 1965, she upbraids the US for "accepting Stanislavski's early experiments as the Stanislavski System. It is time that our theatre experts become acquainted with what theatre schools and scientists in Russia acknowledge to be the heart of the Stanislavski System" (1991:11). Such arguments often rely on questionable sources from the USSR. While both Moore and Coger recognize Stanislavsky's integrative impulses toward mind and body (Moore 1965:29; Coger in Munk 1966:64), they also accept Soviet opinion as unquestionably reliable. Moore quotes Simonov at length, and Coger frequently cites Grigory Kristi who had edited Stanislavsky's Russian books under the guidance of a Soviet commission. Neither Moore nor Coger acknowledge that Simonov and Kristi had made it their jobs to adjust Stanislavsky to the powers-that-be.

This linear interpretation co-opts and distorts the System as certainly as popular Freudian attitudes do. While Strasberg asserts that great actors who claim that they do not use Affective Memory in their work either use it unconsciously or are in denial, Moore states that, "Since science has confirmed that the method of physical actions is based on physiological law [... it] must be the basis of every drama school" (1965:29). No wonder some astute US critics dismiss the Method of Physical Actions as a Soviet corruption, nothing more. Burnet Hobgood, for example, calls it a "red herring" (1973:147).

Just as it is "true" for Stanislavsky that action is central to theatre, so is it "true" that emotion is central to his System. Although apparently contradictory, both Soviet and American readings of the System can be argued persuasively. With Suler's help Stanislavsky did indeed explore emotion more directly in the First Studio than he did at any other time in his long career; at the end of his life he did indeed turn his attention to physical action, believing emotion to be too capricious. However, at the First Studio, Stanislavsky also taught that action proceeds from "the right selection of tasks, their composition, the right pattern, the execution of every task" (Markov 1934:147).[3] Nor did he abjure Affective Memory at the end of his life. Only three months before his death, Stanislavsky told his directing students that, "One must give actors various paths. One of these is the path of action. There is also another path: you can move from feeling to action, arousing feeling first" (Vinogradskaia 2000:498). Like the indivisible link between emotion and motion, the relationship between the content of drama and its language is best represented as a continuous circle of ideas, rather than as a line. Calling the Method of Physical Actions the culmination of Stanislavsky's work represents as much a simplification of his ideas as does the Method's technical treatment of Affective Memory. Stanislavsky's actual work as a practitioner always resists schematic interpretations.

Even the clear-sighted Knebel (1898–1985) admits falling into the interpretive trap. When she met Stanislavsky in 1935, she thought that his new ideas broke completely with what he had done before. However, "with the passage of the years, I understood [...] he did not cross out or discard, but rather summarized and brought together" all that he had discovered. She identifies "the novelty" of his later work in this merging of techniques (1968:47). Vasily Osipovich Toporkov (1889–1970), an actor in Stanislavsky's last project, agrees. "One cannot say that Stanislavski brought something completely new to his last work, something contrary to his previous concepts;" he merely "gave his system greater concreteness" (2002:171). In 1933, fearful of being misunderstood, Stanislavsky had told director Boris Zon the same: "My new method is a development of what has come before" (Zon 1955:453). Their remarks prove that the System operates through the mechanism of cumulative practice, not selective theory.

The Method of Physical Actions

From 1934 to 1938, Stanislavsky turned his political isolation at home (Chapters 2, 6) into productive work with selected actors from the Moscow Art Theatre in his last Studio, the Opera-Dramatic. While newspapers publicly hailed his early work as the inspiration for Socialist Realism on stage, he was privately examining aspects of drama unauthorized by the State. During these years, he was experimenting with a new rehearsal technique that he provisionally called "the method of physical actions."

The Studio's work was intense. Most of Stanislavsky's home was turned into rehearsal space. Actors and his assistants worked from early morning to late at night. Despite serious illness and even during his last days, Stanislavsky always appeared at lessons in a suit and tie with a fresh shirt and clean-shaven (Knebel' 1967:280–2). Knebel describes Stanislavsky's attitude toward their work in moving terms:

> He had never before held back, but in those years at the studio, his generosity in sharing his creative ideas took on a particular character. It struck me as courageous, tragic, and sublimely peaceful. It was as if he actually felt that death was close, and it engendered in him one desire—to give away everything while time still remained. I never heard him indulge in the grumbling of old age. He was deeply and joyously focused on the possibilities that our discoveries could offer to theatrical art.
>
> (1967:265)

But what exactly were they doing behind closed doors? Because Stanislavsky was rushing to write down the whole of his System, he wrote very little about this phase of his work. Information about his experiments depends almost entirely upon the eye-witness accounts of the Studio's members, whose reliability varies in relationship to their ideological points of view.

All agree that Stanislavsky was working out a new rehearsal technique based on the idea that a play, like a score of music, encodes actions, and that the words, like notes, suggest what and how the actors, like musicians, need to play. Moreover, this "score" is best discovered by the actor through an improvisatory approach to analysis, rather than through extended discussion at the table.

They also agree that he experimented by rehearsing opera, Gogol's comedy *The Inspector General*, Shakespeare's tragedies (*Othello, Romeo and Juliet, Hamlet*), and Molière's *Tartuffe*. Stanislavsky's choice of material for these workshops is significant. He had always feared being associated with only one theatrical style— psychological Realism. While it had been the style in which he had most productively directed, he wished to protect his System from such a limiting association. That his System be perceived as universally applicable became an obsession in his last four years. He turned to his acting manual as to an evangelical project, preaching the System with an overtly messianic attitude (Smeliansky 1990). In choosing opera, classics, and Shakespeare for his last experiments, he insists all the more on avoiding any endorsement of Realism. In 1936, mixing the language of behaviorism with that of Yoga, he writes, "we need the truth of physical actions and our belief in them not for the sake of Realism or Naturalism, but in order to stimulate an experiencing of the role's human spirit in us as a natural reflex." He further emphasizes that "the importance of the life of the human body" must not be "confused with the devices of Naturalism" (SS IV 1991:352). After working on Mikhail Bulgakov's biographical play about Molière in 1936, Stanislavsky had begun to consider directing something by the classic French playwright, who was generally considered unsuitable for the Art Theatre. What better to prove the "universality" of his System than *Tartuffe*—a seventeenth century comic play in verse? (Stroeva 1977:370)

All Studio members agree, as well, that while Stanislavsky had initiated the System with young, inexperienced actors, he now turned to seasoned members of the Moscow Art Theatre, challenging himself to inspire already formed actors with new ideas. He chose the loyal Marxist Mikhail Kedrov to serve as assistant director and play the title role in *Tartuffe* because of his "individuality" as an actor (Solovyova 2007:292). Rehearsals on Molière began in March 1936, ended on 27 April 1938 with Stanislavsky's death; a completed production opened to the public in December 1939 under Kedrov's direction. Stanislavsky also chose Maria Knebel, a character actor at the Moscow Art Theatre who had begun her study of acting with his First Studio protégé Michael Chekhov. At that time, she was also directing in small, alternative theatres around Moscow.

> In March 1936, Konstantin Sergeevich summoned me to him. I went to [his home on] Leontievsky Lane worrying, trying to figure out the possible

reasons behind the summons. He sat me down in a big, soft, armchair across from him, looked at me searchingly and affectionately, and then apparently satisfied with the fact that I was sufficiently perplexed and excited, finally asked "Have you heard of my studio?"

(1967:264)

This invitation to join surprised her no less than his appointment of her to head a group of actors, who were investigating the power of words to prompt action. Later, she also directed a group, who were attempting to develop a non-scripted performance by means of improvisations.

Accounts differ when members of the Studio begin to describe the principles behind Stanislavsky's new rehearsal technique.

Kedrov's version took a politically correct spin. Using Stanislavsky's often reiterated phrase, "The Method of Physical Actions," as label and *imprimatur*, Kedrov linked the Studio's work directly to behaviorism and taught that Stanislavsky had finally solved the problem of acting. Kedrov focuses on logical sequences of simple physical actions, more precisely activities; by discovering and listing these, the actor can anchor performance in material reality. In an escape scene, the actor walks forward, reaches out a hand, turns the knob, opens the door, and exits.

Missing from Kedrov's account is Stanislavsky's more complex understanding of "action" as psychophysical, simultaneously combining inner action of the soul with outer action of the body. Knebel's version retains this dimension. Thus, she promotes a subtler approach in which physical activities arise from a trajectory of intentional action. She teaches the actor to choose a psychophysical action that prompts all the physical activities in a given scene. In an escape scene, the character might strive to avoid an uncomfortable meeting, or save oneself from embarrassment, or beat a hasty retreat, or abscond, or cut and run, etc. The chosen action then conditions the physical activities of walking forward, reaching out a hand, turning the knob and opening the door in order to leave the room. The action is composed of the same sequence of physical motions but grounded in the character's rhythmic energy and trajectory of desire. Knebel called Stanislavsky's last work "Active Analysis" to differentiate it from Kedrov's overly simplified version.[4]

When Kedrov became artistic director of the Moscow Art Theatre in 1949, he fired Knebel, banishing her competing approach to Stanislavsky's last teachings (Chapter 6). But she did not abandon Active Analysis. She vowed to keep the "secret cult of knowledge" alive (1968:46). Her vow proved significant. In the years following Stanislavsky's death, arguments about the Method of Physical Actions in the USSR were as bitter as those about Affective Memory in the US. Kedrov and Knebel defined the poles of the debate, as did Strasberg and Adler in the US. He stood for the materialist, paternalistic Stanislavsky who had become the icon of Socialist Realism; she called this portrait of her mentor a Marxist "vulgarization" (1971:121–3). Of course, governmental oversight of theatres and actor training programs stacked the cards in favor of the Marxist Kedrov for many years.

Knebel found a haven for her views among the professional adult actors at Moscow's Central Children's Theatre. In 1950 she began directing there; in 1955 she became its artistic director. For a decade she staged fairy tales and Russian classics for children exclusively through Active Analysis. When political winds began to shift in 1960, she began writing and teaching full-time at the State Institute for Theatrical Arts (GITIS). She thus influenced three generations of theatre practitioners, including such notables as actor Oleg Efremov (who began acting under her direction in the 1950s and ended as artistic director of the Moscow Art Theatre in the 1970s) and director Georgi Tovstonogov (who studied with her in the late 1950s, directed in Leningrad for fifty-five years, and brought his work to the US in 1987). The well-known avant-garde director, Anatoly Efros, expresses the common sentiment about her when he baldly states that, having studied Stanislavsky for years, "I actually understood [him] in practice only when I came into contact with Maria Osipovna Knebel" (1993:139).

Despite Knebel's unflagging promotion of Active Analysis, Kedrov's fragmentary piece of the puzzle, the Method of Physical Actions, is still often taken for the whole in the US. Currently, as Bella Merlin points out, there remains "some disagreement among scholars and practitioners as to whether there actually is a difference between" the two (2007:196). While Jean Benedetti recognizes the Soviet reduction of Stanislavsky's late work, he uses "the Method of Physical Actions" to refer to the play's "active analysis on the rehearsal-room floor," thus combining the two into one. At the same time, to counter the Soviet interpretation he reminds his readers that "Physical action is the foundation on which the entire emotional, mental and philosophical superstructure of the ultimate performance is built" (1998:xiv–xv).[5] Merlin and I agree that there is a significant difference between the two. The Method of Physical Actions, even when practiced psychophysically, stops short of creating performance from a dynamic interplay of actions and counteractions (examined below). Going further than the Method of Physical Actions, Active Analysis taps "all the available avenues of investigation—mental, physical, emotional, and experiential—[which are] harnessed together holistically" (Merlin 2007:197).

Historically speaking, American readings of Stanislavsky's late work have varied with the availability and quality of information. Émigré teachers had no experience with Stanislavsky's last experiments. In the first English-language article about the System, Boleslavsky had written, "It is dramatic action that makes the theatre live" (1923:74). Yet, in exercises at the American Laboratory Theatre he and Ouspenskaya stressed other techniques (sense memory, concentration, animal exercises as an aide to characterization, etc.), which they had learned at the First Studio.

Furthermore, in his book, Boleslavsky treats action metaphorically, not concretely. Unlike Stanislavsky, who writes at length about how to break scenes into their component "bits," how to define a character's "problems" and select "tasks" that will impel action, how to connect all these bits, problems and tasks by means of a "supertask" and a "through-action," Boleslavsky simply likens the dynamic structure of a play to that of a tree. "Look at the trunk," he writes, "straight, proportioned, harmonious with the rest of the tree, supporting every part of it. It is the leading strain; 'leitmotif' in music; a director's idea of action in a play" (1933:56). In this metaphor, the First Studio's yogic underpinnings are felt, but the actor's practical work gets lost. Apart from explaining elsewhere that the actor must define action in verbs, Boleslavsky leaves the reader to puzzle out the application of his metaphor to performance.

Neither could Stella Adler adequately fill the gap in US knowledge. When she visited Stanislavsky in 1934, he had indeed begun to focus his efforts more directly on action. In her report to the Group Theatre, she spoke about its importance in relationship to the play's "given circumstances," thus stressing interpretation of the play, a key issue for Stanislavsky in his last years (Munk 1966:219). In this way she succeeded in bringing new attention to action. More than thirty years later, she explained that emotion "is only [used] as a frame of reference for the action itself. All the emotion is contained in the action." Thus, her information offered a viable alternative to Strasberg's teaching, which Sanford Meisner would later capture in his striking definition of acting as "the reality of doing" (Meisner and Longwell 1987:16).

However, Adler is as tongue-tied about action in her book, as is Boleslavsky. While he remains too abstract, she takes too technical an approach. Warning her readers, that "You must always be in action—as opposed to words," she offers many practical tips, but never sets them into a clear framework. Some of her advice is not so far from Strasberg's as one might expect. "Using an action from your past is the only way in which your personal past can be brought into the play," she explains. "Go back to the action and the specific circumstances you were in," she advises, "and remember what you did in those circumstances. If you recall the place, the feeling will come back to you" (1988:41, 47). Here she merely substitutes "action" for "affect" in the Method's central exercise. Additionally, her specific examples of "actions" echo Kedrov's focus on "activities" (getting dressed, reading a book, setting the table, etc.) rather than Knebel's insistence on psychophysical "actions" that embody trajectories of desire (urging, challenging, rejecting, etc.). Her approach will live more surely in the lore that surrounds her teaching than in her book.

Until the 1961 publication of *Creating a Role*, the US remained largely ignorant of the approach that had become so important to the Soviets. But *Creating a Role* does not succeed in closing the information gap. The book brings together unfinished drafts, which Stanislavsky penned from 1914 through 1937, for a projected third volume of his acting manual. Old and new materials thus appear as if contemporaneous. Furthermore, while Stanislavsky writes about a new "device for the approach to a role," his notebooks and drafts from 1936 and 1937 (SS IV 1991:371) merely tantalize practitioners with generalities. He says virtually nothing about practical applications.

Those who participated in Stanislavsky's final workshops (Mikhail Kedrov, Vasily Toporkov, and Maria Knebel, among them) developed Russian oral traditions about the Method of Physical Actions and Active Analysis. Such lore, so dependent upon Russian teachers, traveled to the West infrequently. In 1963, when the Moscow Art Theatre again toured the US, actors spoke about the Method of Physical Actions at the New School for Social Research in New York. I first learned of it from Sam Veniaminovich Tsikhotsky (Chapter 1). Knebel and her protégés at GITIS promoted this lore in Russia and Eastern Europe. With the dissolution of the Soviet Union, some of these, like Natalya Zverova and Leonid Kheifets, brought this work to the West.[6] I observed their classes in Moscow and Paris, and have adapted their work to my own. My analysis (below) of Stanislavsky's experiments draws upon these sources.

Active Analysis

In December 1936, Stanislavsky wrote a letter to his family:

> I am setting a new device *[priem]* in motion now, a new approach to the role. It involves reading the play today, and tomorrow rehearsing it on stage. What can we rehearse? A great deal. A character comes in, greets everybody, sits down, tells of events that have just taken place, expresses a series of thoughts. Everyone can act this, guided by their own life experience. So, let them act. And so, we break the whole play, episode by episode, into physical actions. When this is done exactly, correctly, so that if feels true and it inspires our belief in what is happening on stage, then we can say that the line of the life of the human body has been created. This is no small thing, but half the role.
>
> (SS IX 1999:655)

One of Stanislavsky's earliest assumptions reverberates in these words: that there exist indissoluble links between mind, body and spirit. Hidden within these words, however, are two other ideas: that physical action triggers an experiencing (*perezhivanie*) of the play, and that the text presents the actor not only with words but also with a structure of actions. These notions radiate out from another of Stanislavsky's key assumptions, that action distinguishes theatre from other forms of art. While Stanislavsky examined the mind–body–spirit continuum through psychology and Yoga, he used his final workshops to explore these two other ideas through the language of action.

The first of these presumes that "the passive state" on stage "kills theatrical action." Stanislavsky had always determined to activate actors, urging them "to depict [even] passive states on stage" by "conveying them actively" (SS IV 1991:99; 1961:49). In his earlier approach to the role, actors sat for long periods of time "around the table," examining every facet of the play in depth. They would study the play's manners, characters, era and artistic style. Then, they would begin to fantasize about what they had discovered in the play's world. They would imagine themselves walking through their characters' houses, meeting their relatives, having dinner, etc.[7] Drawing an association with affective memory, Stanislavsky called this approach affective cognition (*chuvstvennoe poznanie*), relying upon the ambiguous Russian word *chuvstva* which suggests simultaneously both emotion and sensation. Hapgood translates his phrase as "analysis of the feelings" (SS IV 1991:54, 57; 1961:8), emphasizing its emotional tenor.

This early approach taught actors, like those of the representational school, to activate themselves through fantasy; Stanislavsky also expected his actors, unlike others, to transfer imagined action into stage reality. In this transfer, he risked their enervation. After twenty years of working with this early approach, he complained that after analysis through affective cognition, "The actor comes on stage with a stuffed head and an empty heart, and can act nothing" (SS IV 1991:325–6). In his last workshops, he therefore replaces "analysis of feelings" with "Active Analysis" (*deistvennyi analiz*). He now demands that one begin to explore a play through improvisation, thus obviating the need to translate imagination into actuality.

Rather than walking mentally through your character's house, you would now walk through the rehearsal space, turning it into your house. Rather than depend upon your own fantasy, you could now create a collective one through "games," as Toporkov called them (2002:185), played by the whole cast. Merely juxtapose Stanislavsky's description of his work on Famusov (*Woe from Wit*) with Toporkov's description of his work on Orgon (*Tartuffe*). In the first case, Stanislavsky creates Famusov's house and its many rooms in his imagination, visualizing himself sitting in his study, sleeping in his bed, ascending the staircases. Thus, he creates a personal vision of himself in the role, much as Clairon did in her work on Agrippina (Chapter 7). In the second case, Stanislavsky asks the entire cast to turn their rehearsal space into Orgon's house. They locate each room, argue over which area would be better suited for dining, or sleeping undisturbed, or as servants quarters, etc. (SS IV 1991:69–74; Toporkov 2002:182–5).[8] Thus, they map out a collective and shared fantasy of the house. Such improvisations make the play and hence the actor's work more palpably present. "Here, today, now," resounds throughout Stanislavsky's writing from this period (SS IV 1991:331). As Knebel explains, improvisations "break down the wall between analysis and embodiment" (1971:53).

Whereas imaginative visualizations may create impressionistic outlines of action, the physical reality of improvisation allows the actor no gaps in the flow and logic of behavior; the actor explores the smallest and simplest physical details that make up our most complicated actions. What do we physically do (the physical activities) when we persuade someone, as does Iago, or challenge someone, as does Mercutio, or contemplate suicide, as does Hamlet (the psychophysical actions)? By persuading, challenging, or contemplating, the actor finds answers. In drafts from 1936 and 1937, intended for the third volume of his acting manual, Tortsov asks Nazvanov to analyze Khlestakov (the main character in Gogol's *The Inspector General*) through the physical actions necessary to him as he enters his hotel room after a discouraging day. Nazvanov takes several approaches. He inserts the key in the lock, opens the door, stands on the threshold deciding whether to enter or to retreat to the hotel restaurant. He then enters quickly with a light step. He repeats the entrance over and over again until he feels that he understands the "logic and consecutiveness" of Khlestakov's physical movements. As Stanislavsky explains, "the best way to analyze a play is to take action (*deistvovat'*) in the given circumstances" (SS IV 1991:332–3; Prokof'ev 1948:55). This is the period when Stanislavsky restates his basic analytical question. "What does your character *want* in the given circumstances?" becomes "What does your character *do* in the given circumstances?"

Stanislavsky also asks that his actors make lists of their physical activities. Like the rails along which a train travels, the "line of the life of the human body" keeps the actor on track in his creation of the "life of the human spirit" This listing, however, is not a new idea for Stanislavsky. He had called for the "score of vital, dynamic physical and psychological tasks" in 1916 (SS IV 1991:338, 348, 138; 1961:215, 226, 80).

"The Method of Physical Actions" incorporates all the above steps and, there-fore, these are familiar aspects of Stanislavsky's late work—improvisations to find and then list the logical sequence of physical activities.

Those aspects that link text to dramatic structure take us into Active Analysis and are generally less familiar in US lore. In early rehearsals for *Tartuffe*, Stanislavsky encouraged improvisations on any aspect of the play's story: how Orgon's family dines in the evening, how they play cards, Orgon's first meeting with Tartuffe, young Valère's courtship of Orgon's daughter, Mariane. These events do not occur in the play proper. But, as rehearsals continued, Stanislavsky limited his cast's imagina-tive leaps away from the play, and began to ask them to trace the exact structure of Molière's play in their improvisations. This is the point where the Method of Physical Actions becomes more precisely Active Analysis of text. This is the point where Stanislavsky's thinking becomes most radical, and simultaneously where his writings become frustratingly less and less specific, and lore more important.

At this stage of work, improvisations serve as successive "drafts" for future performances (Knebel' 1971:52). After relaxing and freeing body and voice, the actors read the play "with great care and admiration" (Prokof'ev 1948:52). They then begin to physicalize its key events using their own words, much as Stani-slavsky had described in his letter. In this kind of improvisation, actors recreate what Stanislavsky calls the "facts" of the play and the way in which the story unfolds. In short, actors learn the underlying structure of action before memo-rizing their lines. In Stanislavsky's opinion, echoed by Adler, this structure is more easily and quickly remembered than the words (SS II 1991:371). In short, Active Analysis fosters memorization of a text through a deep experiential understanding of the play's underlying dynamic structure.

A research study in cognitive science has found that most professional actors work precisely in this way. Helga and Tony Noice wanted to know how actors can routinely memorize "large amounts of dialogue" in order to speak it "in real time with complete spontaneity."[9] They found that "professional actors rarely acquire their roles by rote" even though actors themselves could not generally say how they learn. One actor told the Noices: "I memorize by magic." However, the Noices discovered that actors learn by a tacit "focus on communicating the meanings underlying the literal words" (2006:14–15). They coined a term for this cognitive process, "active experiencing," observing that the actors were using "all the physical, mental and emotional channels to communicate the meaning of material to another person" (2006:15). Their term could easily serve as a twenty-first century synonym for Active Analysis, suggesting, as does Stanislavsky, that an active, improvisatory state of mind and body can best induce the creative state of "experiencing."

If we were rehearsing Act II scene 3 of *Tartuffe* according to Stanislavsky's new "device,"[10] the actress who plays Dorine (Orgon's bright and crafty servant) would attempt to convince Mariane to stand up to her father and refuse an arranged marriage with the hypocrite Tartuffe. Using her own words, "Dorine" would try out strategies in order to do so: inspiring Mariane with enough courage to speak up to her father, giving her a shove in the right direction, frightening her with a picture of her bleak future in a loveless marriage, etc. "Mariane," in turn, would resist these arguments in any way she could muster: refusing to answer, pleading a daughter's duty to her father, crying to gain Dorine's pity, etc. In this way the two women would explore the dynamic potential of the scene they will eventually perform within its given circumstances, what Moore calls "analysis through action." As Toporkov explains, "That means we had to translate the scene into the language of actions, and the simpler the action, the better" (Toporkov 2002:175).[11] Notice that the verbs employed above are not merely physical, but psychophysical.

After each improvisation, the actors compare their work to the play, asking how their paraphrase differed from the playwright's text. If, in the play, Dorine conjures up a future nightmarish vision of Mariane's life as Mme. Tartuffe, and the actress has not done so, then however truthful her behavior on stage, she has not worked "exactly" or "correctly," as Stanislavsky put it to his family. Furthermore, if Molière's Dorine paints this vision with wit, and the cast's "Dorine" does so dourly, then she has still not succeeded. Knebel writes that these successive improvisations, checked for their textual accuracy, replace the "talking out about the play" with its "acting out" (Knebel' 1971:73).

Over the course of rehearsals, the actors' improvisations get closer and closer to the text. While at first the actors trace only the play's broadest outlines, as rehearsals progress, they assimilate more and more of the exact demands of the text: the images, style, and manner of writing. New, more detailed questions emerge. Why does Dorine speak so much and Mariane so little? Does each speak well or badly, fluently or haltingly? Why does Dorine choose to stress Tartuffe's florid complexion and his red ears in her portrait of him? Why does she rhyme her words with Mariane's lines more frequently than Mariane rhymes with hers? Does this indicate Dorine's mockery of Mariane, or her chiding of Mariane as if she were a child? In short, what do the images and metaphors, the rhythms and rhymes, indeed all the specific traits of the play's language reveal about the characters' actions and states of mind? In the next series of improvisations, the actors incorporate more and more of their answers to such questions, and in the process, more and more of the text.

Finally the cast needs the written text to get any more accurate a performance than they have achieved through paraphrase. Toporkov describes this moment in his work on *Tartuffe*. Once "the story of the Orgon family became clear to each of us in all its details," and once "we began to believe in it as in a genuine event, we wanted to embody it" (2002:182). This desire prompted us to "move on to the next stage in our rehearsals, the stage when we needed the words." The successive drafting of performance through paraphrase now "found greater expressiveness and completion in [the author's] thoughts and words. [...] This happened by itself, gradually as a result of our growing inner needs" (2002:197–8).

Stanislavsky's relationship to the play in this last stage of his work is wonderfully paradoxical. By stepping away from the text, the actor ultimately experiences a need for it. While the text initially gives the actors a sequence of episodic "events," each one generating a "score of physical actions" and an "order of thoughts" (SS IV 1991:326, 366, 329), the words finally allow the actor to express the full specificity of the character.

That Stanislavsky concerned himself with text is obvious in his choice of verse plays, which by their very nature force actors to pay greater attention to textual matters than would contemporary prose. Stanislavsky insisted that his actors grapple with every single word in Shakespeare's *Hamlet*, as well as with the musicality and tone of the verse (Prokof'ev 1948:52–4). Similarly, the rhythm of the verse in *Tartuffe* informed the rhythm of the actors' physical actions in performance (Toporkov 2002:198).

This last stage of Stanislavsky's work implies an approach to reading drama as surely as it teaches acting techniques. As one Russian critic put it:

> Almost all the basic tenets of Stanislavsky's "system" apply directly to drama. Stanislavsky speaks of "through-action" for the play as much as for the production, the drama's "supertask" as well as the actor's, the play's "tempo and rhythm" as well as the production's.
>
> (Osnos 1952:2)

While Hobgood dismisses the Method of Physical Actions as a Soviet corruption, he applauds Stanislavsky's approach to the role as a "systematic procedure in dramatic analysis," and as a "novel theory of dramatic construction, born of a concern to take tangible action as the medium of theatre and drama" (1973:147, 155, 157).

This implicit relationship to literary theory is one of the most fascinating, yet one of the most overlooked, aspects of the System. Stanislavsky was indeed known to be a poor judge of literature. His readings of Chekhov's plays are often used to prove his inadequacies in this regard. Nemirovich-Danchenko assessed his staging of Chekhov's *The Seagull* as having "scenic novelty" but lacking "the real Chekhovian lyricism; […] there was not yet in this anything of the aroma of the author's charm" (1936:161–2). Needless to say, Chekhov's own peevish protests about the staging of his plays have become common knowledge. Just months before his death, he wrote to his wife, complaining that "Stanislavsky has ruined my play [*The Cherry Orchard*]. Well, to hell with him!" (VII 1951:258). Fausto Malcovati, Stanislavsky's Italian translator, called him "*un peu aveugle*" in literary matters, and persuasively and humorously argued that he misunderstood playwrights as diverse as Blok and Bulgakov (5 November 1989).

Despite Stanislavsky's arguable talents in literary interpretation and his taste in literature, which tended toward the sentimental and melodramatic, he advanced a useful critical vocabulary for reading the text of a play as a score for dramatic performance, something that literary critics had failed to do. Scholar and Shakespearean director Bernard Beckerman writes that, Stanislavsky was one of the few who made "valuable" contributions through his System by developing "reliable tools for the analysis of dramatic form as it manifests itself in the theater" (1970:iii).

Stanislavsky reveals the key literary principles with which he approaches drama most clearly in his work on *Tartuffe*. He envisions the play as a "structure" of action. The words, style, literary images and rhythms of the text provide clues to its potential performance, just as a musical score implies an orchestra's sound. These he calls the "facts" of the play to which the actor must accommodate performance. "The idea of any artistic work is contained not only in its words, but in its structure, and in the very medium of art" (Kovshov 1983:86). In early drafts of *An*

Actor's Work on the Role, Stanislavsky speaks metaphorically about the "anatomy of the role and the play," the need to define a role's "skeleton and structure," its "arteries, nerves, pulse" (SS IV 1991:58, 131, 64, 135). Stanislavsky's metaphor reverberates in Martin Esslin's later foundational work on dramatic structure, *An Anatomy of Drama* (1976). It is this anatomy that Stanislavsky asks actors to discover in the text and to learn before memorizing the words. The Group retained this metaphor in their use of the word "spine" for defining the main thrust in a play or character.

Stanislavsky locates the basic structural element of drama in the "event" (*sobytie*). The play begins with "an inciting event" (*iskhodnoe sobytie*) and its "story" (*fabula*) is told through a sequence of events, each of which involves conflict. The various events can be prioritized by the actors and director as "main" or "incidental," depending upon their relative importance to the story. Each event occurs when an "impelling action"[12] collides with a "counteraction," producing conflict. The actions may connect directly, producing sharp conflict, or bounce off each other obliquely resulting in a subtler drama. The play's tone, quality, style, and thematic issues emerge from this interaction (Knebel' 1982). Like vector analysis in physics which describes the direction, force, and quality of motion, Active Analysis conceives of performance as a dynamic interplay of actions encoded by the playwright's score. In other words, performance is "structured as an uninterrupted chain of events infused with conflict" (Kovshov 1983:14–16).

Records of the rehearsals on *Tartuffe* show this type of structural analysis. Stanislavsky first divided the cast into two camps, one led by Tartuffe with Orgon and his mother in tow, another composed of Orgon's wife, daughter, brother-in-law and Dorine. Each camp's set of "tasks" were chosen to counteract those of the other camp. Stanislavsky then broke the entire play into twelve "bits," each one defined in terms of a struggle: "a protest against the oppression of Tartuffe," "Dorine's counteroffensive," "two skirmishes," "Orgon's counterattack by his promise to marry Mariane to Tartuffe," "Dorine's victory" (the scene analyzed above), "the battle of two giants" (Tartuffe and Elmire, Orgon's wife), "Tartuffe's victory and triumph," "a second battle," "the last battle and Elmire's victory," (in which Elmire exposes Tartuffe's lust), "Tartuffe's complete victory," "the panic of the defeated," and finally, the *deus ex machina* of the play, "by chance, Tartuffe's utter defeat and complete and all-embracing victory" (Stroeva 1977:374). The military terms that define each struggle and the war-like metaphors that underlie his analysis make his structural attitudes toward conflict very clear.

On an ironic note, Stanislavsky's presumption, that conflict defines drama, stands in stark contrast to one of the most absurd political lines of thought that developed in the USSR. By the 1940s Soviet critics would advance "conflictlessness" (*beskonfliktnost'*) as a necessary formula for drama. Against the most deeply ingrained dramatic traditions, writers were told that conflict was not good for drama. After all, if one lives in the best of all possible worlds, the only conflicts that exist are those between "better" and "best" (see Bown 1998). Such ideas deadened Soviet drama. Theatres, experiencing a crisis in their repertories, sought desperately for interesting new plays, but found only mediocre "potboilers" as Stanislavsky would have labeled them (Benedetti 1988:322). "The Method of Physical Actions" bled Active Analysis of its most central notion: that "actions" alone are insufficient; "counteractions" are crucial in the creation of dynamic performances.

In Stanislavsky's Active Analysis, once the play's structure is identified, the actors explore how each conflict arises through their specific, dynamic relationships to each event (SS IV 1991:327). A character either impels the conflict or resists. In Act II, scene 3, Dorine begins to develop her plan to oust Tartuffe through her manipulation of Mariane; she thus sets the scene in motion. Mariane, on the other hand, resists through her silence because she fears her father. As their tug of war proceeds, the actors vary their strategies. Dorine moves from persuasion to reverse psychology, Mariane from asking for Dorine's pity to asking for her help. By means of this dynamic push and pull, the characters discover "reversal points" (terms cited from Knebel' 1982; SS IV 1991:93–4, 307–8), which tip the balance of forces and thus move the story of the play forward. When Mariane agrees to fall in with Dorine's plan, the two actors have created "Dorine's victory," Stanislavsky's label for the main event in the scene. In short, they have uncovered the dynamics of "action" meeting "counteraction" (Toporkov 2002:181). Finally, the actors turn physical conflict into "verbal action" (Knebel' 1982:36). As Toporkov reports, when the actors in *Tartuffe* employed the text, "We had to engage the play's characters in an active verbal clash" (2002:98).

Stanislavsky's approach to text presents fascinating parallels with theories of the Russian Formalists, whose heyday roughly coincides with Stanislavsky's most sustained efforts to write his book. Formalism began in the teens, flourished in the twenties, and was snuffed out in the thirties by Marxist opposition; yet, as early theoreticians of structuralism and semiotics, Formalists left a widespread heritage in twentieth century critical thinking. Building upon a Symbolist assumption that literary form cannot be separated from content, they assert that a work of art is a self-contained system of signs, and that what we perceive as content is the result of artistic structure. As Victor Shklovsky wrote in 1921, "A work of literature is the sum-total of all stylistic devices *[priemy]* employed in it" (Erlich 1969:90). Stanislavsky's desire to make emotional content continuous with outer form in acting shows an affinity with the Symbolist premise.

Moreover, many of Stanislavsky's key words unexpectedly echo the Formalists' rhetoric. When Stanislavsky uses the word "device" (*priem*) in a positive way to describe his new approach to textual analysis, he brings to mind their "watchword" (Erlich 1969:190). Pavel Markov points out that Formalist rhetoric can be traced even to the First Studio, when he writes that one of the key tendencies at that time was "the 'laying bare' of the spiritual kernel of the play," echoing the Formalist idea of "laying bare of the device" (1934:25). Stanislavsky's positive usage of "device" in his last years contrasts strongly with his tendency to use the word negatively in talking about acting clichés.

When he labels the moment an actor suddenly perceives the world of the play in the same way that the character does as a "shift" (*sdvig*) (SS II 1989:101–2), he brings to mind another Formalist notion. Shklovsky felt that great literature disrupts the reader's usual perceptions of the world. By employing semantic and temporal "shifts" in form and plot, the author forces the reader to see familiar objects "as if for the first time" (Erlich 1969:76, 176–8). Not only does *sdvig* reverberate within the System; Stanislavsky's exhortation of the actor to create an illusion of the first time does so also.

Finally, Stanislavsky's dramatic schema recalls the Formalist distinction between "story" (*fabula*) and "plot" (*siuzhet*). While the story of any work of literature refers to the material from which it is made, the plot refers to the author's exact selection and arrangement of the story's elements. In this spirit, the play's "chain of events," through which the "story" is told, takes the place of "plot" in Active Analysis. On a more essential level, by presuming an archetypal dramatic structure of conflict, Stanislavsky views drama in a Formalist spirit, and this without example, since the Formalists, like most literary critics, concentrated on poetry and prose in generating their ideas. Like Vladimir Propp (1928), who studied Russian folktales for their remarkably common patterns of plot, Stanislavsky finds common patterns of structure through "action" and "counteraction" in dramatic literature. Only Sergei Balukhatyi (1927) used Formalism to illuminate plays in performance and his research involved a close comparison of Stanislavsky's production plan for *The Seagull* with Chekhov's text to determine how the structure of the performance supported the play.

Ironically, Stanislavsky's interest in Tolstoy's theory of art would seem to place him in opposition to the Formalists.[13] Although they had forged some of their most important ideas by studying the artistic writings of Tolstoy, Formalists had explicitly rejected his aesthetic philosophy. As Viktor Zhirmunsky wrote, "The material of poetry is neither images, nor emotion, but words" (Erlich 1969:175). In contrast, Soviet critics, who value a work for its ability to further social aims, appropriated Tolstoy. In fact, the Commissar of Enlightenment, Anatoly Lunacharsky (who had interceded with Lenin on Stanislavsky's behalf just after the revolution) quoted Tolstoy in a 1924 attack specifically directed against the Formalist position on art (Erlich 1969:105–6). Yet, as a practitioner and not a theorist, Stanislavsky was master at embracing apparently contradictory ideas when they suited his purposes. He saw no conflict in asserting both that emotion is the content of acting and that acting cannot be viewed as separate from its structural form in action.

Some aspects of Stanislavsky's late work had clearly trickled into the working methods of American actors. Ruth Nelson describes rehearsals at the Group Theatre with Harold Clurman in words that recall Stanislavsky's rehearsals on *Tartuffe*:

> We read the play once, each reading his or her own role. The improvisations began. That went on for weeks and weeks. After a very long time, we'd come back and read the play again. The improvisations got closer and closer to the situations in the play until we found ourselves using the words of the author.
>
> (Chinoy 1976:528)

After the publication of *Creating a Role*, some US teachers accurately represent various techniques from Stanislavsky's later work. Adler suggests that actors paraphrase dialogue, explaining that they can memorize the text best only after they understand its action (1988:102–3). Drawing upon her reading of Knebel, Moore knowledgably describes "analysis through action" as the process by which an actor "investigates the play through improvisation of action" (1965:71–3; 1991:8). More recently, Arthur Penn developed his own approach to directing that parallels Active Analysis. As he explains:

> [The actors] read the play each day, the entire play. And then I ask them to get up and do it. The next day they do the same thing. Sometimes they say, "Well, can't we just read the first act?" And I say, "All right. But don't take the play home. Don't study this text except here, just what we do on our feet." That's what the process is.
>
> (White 2005:46)

Nonetheless, English descriptions remain incomplete and fragmentary, when set against the tradition of Russia's lore.

The actor as artist

From the founding of the Moscow Art Theatre throughout rehearsals for *Tartuffe*, Stanislavsky consistently demands respect for the actor as a creative artist, independent of the author who wrote the play, the designers who envision it, and the director who stages it. While Stanislavsky initiated the System in 1906 to place the tools of creativity into the hands of actors, he advanced Active Analysis in the mid-1930s to make actors fully accountable for their creations. Perhaps he was attempting to counteract the growing importance of the director, who threatened to treat actors like pawns. Everything in Stanislavsky's last experiments throws greater and greater responsibility for the interpretation of the play onto the shoulders of actors. Physical actions make them aware of how their bodies create characters. Improvisations ensure that they encounter the play experientially. Asking actors to "list" and "score" their characters' actions and the play's "chain of events" enforces their direct interaction with the structure of the play. Paraphrasing takes away the usual crutch (recitation of the playwright's words), forcing them to think as the character. Indeed, memorizing the text of the play before its Active Analysis had occurred "was considered a sign of weakness in the actor." In contrast, actors attained "the highest achievement" when they could "reveal the scheme of a scene by means of purely physical actions and with a minimum of words" (Toporkov 2002:176). Such a feat served as proof that the actor had created the role with the freedom of an independent artist.

Even Kedrov extended Stanislavsky's impulse to "develop the actor's initiative." He began rehearsals by asking all cast members to tell the entire story of the play, thus insuring that every actor become intimately involved with the whole, not just with a single role. When asked why he did not begin in the usual fashion with actors reading their own roles, he answered, "Analysis of that sort is rarely profound" (Kovshov 1983:81–2). When émigré director Lev Vainstein staged my translation of *The Cherry Orchard* with graduate acting students at New York University (1980), I watched him do the same as Kedrov. Vainstein wanted the

American actors to take responsibility, not for their characters alone, but for the play as a whole. Thus rehearsals began with reading the play without casting it. The Americans rebelled against the Russian, each wanting to identify with a character and highlight the character's lines. And yet, Vainstein's approach spoke directly to Stanislavsky's driving respect for actors as artists.

Knebel tells an anecdote that further illuminates Stanislavsky's attitude toward the actor. When asked "what comes next" during a rehearsal of *The Inspector General*, he merely shrugged his shoulders and muttered, "I don't know." While this incident is often cited as proof of his disregard for or ignorance of the text, Knebel points out that Stanislavsky pretended ignorance in order to force the actor's independent decision. She called it his "pedagogical cunning" (1971:47–8). Such cunning, however, was easily misunderstood. In his notes on *The Inspector General* he tells actors, "I have thought up a play, I will tell you the story through its events, and you will play them [...] impromptu" (SS IV 1991:326). Such statements made in his final years were often mistaken as advice to dismiss the text. His subtler meaning—that in stepping away from the play the actor more surely finds the need for it—can easily get lost in this "pedagogical cunning." In her edition of *Creating a Role*, Hapgood begins the section on *The Inspector General* with the same unfortunate exaggeration. "'Here is my approach to a new role,' said Tortsov. 'Without any reading, without any confer-ence on the play, the actors are asked to come to a rehearsal of it'" (1961:213). Theatre historian Mel Gordon also seems unaware of Stanislavsky's "pedagogical cunning," when he republishes Stanislavsky's numerical "Plan of Work" from *Creating a Role* and creatively adds "But do not let them read the play until later" (1987:209), a sentence that appears neither in Hapgood's version, nor in the Soviet edition.

Stanislavsky's concern for the actor's autonomy as artist is the source of his concern with the person of the actor on stage. "Art begins," Stanislavsky said, "when there is no role, but when there is an 'I' in the given circumstances of the play" (Toporkov 2002:170). Within such a statement, two basic assumptions are made: that each actor can encompass all human experience, and that character is generated by reactions to specific circumstances. Knebel suggests how Stanislavsky sets up an interaction between these two premises when she writes:

> Actors must [...] work from their own individualities. That means, analyzing oneself as a human being/actor in the given circumstances of the play. But precisely because these circumstances are not at all those that formed the actor's personality in life [...] the actor learns what he must discard, what in himself he must overcome, which of his own personal traits can serve as "building material" for the construction of the character.
>
> (1971:87)

In other words, actors transform themselves into their characters by paying strict attention to all the minutiae of the circumstances, what Stanislavsky called the "facts" of the play. It is easy, however, to misunderstand this notion as a direc-tive to play oneself.

During my work with Tsikhotsky at the Actors Studio, the Method-trained cast often bristled when he criticized them for not playing their characters. When one actress protested that he had asked her to play herself, he reminded her that she had not considered how the circumstances of her character would modify her behavior. Her character wears a corset, when she does not. Her character was educated in a different system, grew up with values different than her own, lives in the Russian countryside, not in New York, etc. These circumstances, he said, would condition her behavior as surely as they had that of her character. Placing oneself in the role does not mean transferring one's own circumstances to the play, but rather incorporating into oneself circumstances other than one's own.

While Elia Kazan, Robert Lewis, and Cheryl Crawford had explicitly founded the Actors Studio to bring a "new sense of dignity" to acting (Garfield 1980:46), the Method, in contrast to the System, absolves actors from responsibility for the final artistic interpretation of the play. The actor remains accountable for the creation of an inner life, but the director answers for the elucidation of the play's dynamics. This division of labor can be detected in the way that each approach defines "logic" and "action."

While Stanislavsky had asked actors to think and behave as their characters would logically do in the circumstances of the play, Strasberg asks actors to think in any way (whether applicable to the play or not) that will prompt behavior needed by the scene or requested by the director. Thus for him, an actor's "logic" does not necessarily reflect the playwright's (LS A37:21 December 1965; 1987:84). Strasberg explained his understanding of logic especially clearly in a session at the Actors Studio in 1965 in response to Geraldine Page, who had performed the monologue in which Lady Macbeth receives a letter from her husband, telling her that the witches have promised him the crown. In an interview, Page explains that while she worked, she thought about how angry she becomes when her real life husband dismisses her compliments, but accepts them from others. This personal logic brought an unexpected anger to her scene (Munk 1966:249–50). In his commendation of her work, Strasberg admitted that he could not detect the logic she had employed, but added that such understanding of a scene is irrelevant to its appreciation. What takes place in her "private imagination" concerns him only in so far as it "serves the purpose of making the scene alive to her." Indeed, he advises her not to tell a director about her private logic. "You'll only confuse him" (LS 161:17 November 1961).

Active Analysis asks the actress playing Mariane in *Tartuffe* to examine the role of a daughter in a society where women's roles are radically different than in our own. How would I react if I were indeed subject to an arranged married? How would I feel, if I were in fact financially and legally dependent upon my father, with no possibility for making an independent living? How would I behave if I were actually frightened of my father's authority? By contrast, a Method actress playing Mariane asks a different series of questions. What exerts the kind of authority over me that Orgon does over Mariane? What do I fear as Mariane fears her father? On what or on whom am I as dependent as Mariane is on her father? In the first case, the actress recreates the logic of the play; in the second, she finds personal substitutions. While Active Analysis treats the actor as a springboard into the play, the Method treats the play as a springboard for the actor's personal substitutions.

While Stanislavsky saw action as the most essential tool on stage, Strasberg felt that actors need not necessarily concern themselves consciously with it. Although Strasberg writes that, "Any performance may be seen as a series of actions—as the score of the play—which must be carried out not simply physically, but logically and truthfully" (1974:62), he also explains that, "Actions are valuable only when they define areas of behavior which otherwise the actor would not create" (Hethmon 1991:136).

Strasberg's attitude takes "action" away from the actor and puts it in the hands of the director. While Stanislavsky taught actors to discover their actions from the "facts," like clues, set forth in the play, Strasberg saw actions as divorced from the text, having "nothing directly to do with the words of the scene." Rather they become the director's addenda to the script. While working on a scene from Noel Coward's *Private Lives*, he directs an actress to examine herself during the scene in order to discover whether she has changed over the years since her divorce. Strasberg explains to members of the Studio that the actress "would never play [this action] unless it were deliberately given to her because it is completely outside the words" (Hethmon 1991:136). Does Strasberg underestimate actors by assuming that they cannot imaginatively create an action so obviously implicit in the play? After stating that "it's almost frankly better if the actor doesn't know what the action is" but that "it is very important in production, directionally," he illustrates his statement with an anecdote about an overly emotional actress in the Group Theatre, whom he calmed down in a particular scene by giving her a simple physical "action," really an activity,—playing cards. When she resisted, telling him that no card game appears in the script, he countered, "I don't care, do it!" (LS 2:10 April 1956). In short, the director, he assumes, can manipulate an actor with or without their knowledge by assigning them actions. In contrast to Stanislavsky's sense of the actor's freedom as artist, Strasberg's attitude puts artistic control in the hands of the director.

Although Strasberg became familiar with Stanislavsky's late experiments, he was critical of them. As he put it, "Stanislavsky stressed [physical actions] a little too much at the end of his life" (LS 7:29 May 1956). After telling the Actors Studio about the "devices" that Stanislavsky worked out in his late years, Strasberg adds, "I don't think they work" (LS 161:31 December 1968). Indeed, Strasberg's redefinitions of logic and action serve important, practical functions by addressing the realities of working actors in the US. No commercial production can devote two years to probing a text, as did Stanislavsky on *Tartuffe*. Few directors allow actors the creative independence that Stanislavsky's ivory tower offered. Film, in contrast to stage, takes more and more control away from the actor. Scenes are not shot in consecutive order; in fact, the actor may not have the opportunity to read the full screenplay. Sometimes an actor's partner is not present during reaction shots and the actor must respond to a camera, not a person; the partner's work will be spliced in later. Sound and special effects may seem real to the filmgoer but must be imagined by the actor during filming; they too will be spliced in later. In short, by clever editing, directors can indeed create performances and effects on screen that never occurred in flesh. Strasberg's ideas help the actor cope with such work-a-day situations. Personal, "private" logic can be created without a script or partner and in the absence of a consecutive flow of story. Strasberg's sense of action adapts the actor to the reality of the director's growing power over the final product, especially so in film. Thus, while Stanislavsky proposed an ideal for artistic creation and focused on the control an actor on stage can reasonably exert, Strasberg adjusts to the contemporary business of acting and to film (Carnicke 1999; 2003).

Re-examining Stanislavsky's key notions about action—as the primary language of dramatic art and as the dynamic structures encoded in dramatic texts—makes him seem less a turn-of-the-century artist, and more contemporary in his approach to performance. Viewing him through this performative lens, he stands in an unexpected relationship to postmodern scholarship on performance. For example, when the leading French scholar Patrice Pavis proposes examining "a performance's lines of force," its "vectorization," (2003:16–17) he unknowingly follows Stanislavsky into Active Analysis. In turning to contemporary practice, Stanislavsky's support of the actor as artist reminds us as practitioners that respect entails taking responsibility.

Afterword

Stanislavsky on his own terms

While Stanislavsky has indeed informed acting theory and training throughout the world since his tours to the US, his ideas have been viewed through pervasive veils of assumptions. In the West, his System is still often mistaken for Strasberg's Method with its overemphasis on psychological Realism and therapeutic self-expression. In Russia, Soviet Marxism limited Stanislavsky to the physical world, behaviorist psychology, and Socialist Realism. These two cultural veils allowed features such as Realist styles and Western notions of "self" to be seen, but hid other aspects drawn from Tolstoy's aesthetics, Yoga, Symbolism, and Formalist attitudes toward texts. His gaze backward toward nineteenth and early twentieth century thought appears clearly through these veils. His pointing forward toward late twentieth century and twenty-first century conceptions remains in shadow.

Thus, acting lore envisions "Stanislavskian" actors either as those who seek genuine emotional truth through personal identification with their characters or as acolytes of a dogmatic approach to acting that has been scientifically verified. Both visions feature an unfocused image of Stanislavsky, who in fact saw the present moment of performance ("experiencing") as the actor's only truth, actors as a means for conveying to audiences human experience in all sorts of aesthetic styles, and acting as an embodied art, not science.

This blurred portrait was produced through a confluence of pressures, some subtle and accidental, others clearly articulated and deliberately imposed, most with ironic edges: linguistic and cultural translations and mistranslations; selective listening of zealous students in classrooms; political and economic climates in the US and USSR; the commercial basis of publishing and theatre in New York; censorship in Moscow; and the very nature of acting which is practical, personal, ephemeral, and difficult to describe, because it is tacit knowledge.

This fascinating, interdisciplinary collage erected monuments to Stanislavsky as a worldwide hero for theatrical art. By the mid-1950s his statue in the United States depicted a tyrannical patriarch of acting, whose piercing eyes could see into the psyches of psychologically naked actors. By the end of the 1930s the Union of Soviet Socialist Republics painted an icon of him as a scientist who had discovered the physical laws of acting. Such monoliths could not but tarnish and fade with the passing of time.

Despite the complexity of the transformative processes that conditioned our common understandings of Stanislavsky, neither of the two evolutionary branches that grew from his ideas remained as insistently dynamic and integrative as the trunk which unites them. Stanislavsky prophetically feared just such reductive appropriations of his System. Even before he had taken the first steps toward its creation, he had described a nightmarish vision of its future in his personal notebook. He imagines a typical acting student standing before a stern teacher, reciting the rules of the actor's grammar. The teacher checks his pupil's recitation against Stanislavsky's yet to be written acting manual. He sees himself as author, crying out in protest, "This is terrible, a fraud, the murder of talent [...]. Shred, burn the books, dismiss the students, and tell them I have committed a crime" (I 1986:209–10). His later fictional teacher, Tortsov, more soberly warns, that, "What is most dangerous for my device, for the whole 'system,' for its psychotechnique, and finally, for all art, is a formulaic approach to our complex creative work, a narrow, elementary understanding of it." And indeed, Tortsov sees such dogma everywhere among "exploiters of the 'system'" (SS II 1989:252). Using the special "pedagogical cunning" that Maria Knebel had identified (1971:47–8), Stanislavsky told Joshua Logan. "O, I see you've read my books. Well, [...] we have extended past that. Now that's for the bathroom" (1976:53).

Those who worked most closely with Stanislavsky rarely underestimated the complexity of his project to generate acting theory from practice. On 16 April 1936 actor Leonid Leonidov wrote in his diary, "How strange it is: thirty-four years with him, and you still don't get used to him. [...] We don't understand him, perhaps because he expresses his thoughts poorly. But there can be no doubt about the fact that he is right. Gulliver before the Lilliputians" (Kovshov 1983:41–2).

The only way to understand Stanislavsky on his own terms is to tear down the veils that still cloud our vision and bring down the monolithic monuments to him. I have brought Stanislavsky into sharper focus by examining all the disparate historical facts (those known and little known) in relationship to each other, thereby exposing the transformative processes that turned his ideas into two tradition-bound sets of lore. I have untangled the forces that converged to transform the System into the Method, traced how his ideas took a technical turn in the US, how the closed circle of interdependent concepts that he envisioned became a straight, teleological line in the USSR.

This detective work uncovers a dynamically new and newly relevant System for actor training and performance that can jolt us (actors, directors, teachers, and scholars) into taking another look at a man we thought we knew. The little-studied aspects of Stanislavsky's subtexts suggest more holistic, more complex, more elastic readings of his System than does our common knowledge. His previously overlooked conceptions of performance reinvigorate the

System by investing it with greater conceptual sophistication, disengaging it from a single artistic style, and propelling it forward into the future.

In short, Stanislavsky can still teach us, in the twenty-first century, something crucial about the embodied art of acting. His face, coming into focus, shows complexity and subtlety of detail. He smiles enigmatically, alluding to the dynamic project that delicately infuses the intractable world of acting practice with the elegance of theory.

The System's terminology:
a selected glossary

> My task is to speak to the actor in his own language. Not to philosophize,
> which I consider very boring …
>
> Stanislavsky (SS IV 1959:319)

This glossary is an alphabetized guide to key terms used in this book.[1] Each term
appears in my translation with alternative translations given where appropriate.
In practice provides brief guidelines to practical applications and samples of
historically based exercises from Russian-language documents and class work at
the Moscow Art Theatre Studio, the Russian Academy of Theatre Arts (formerly
GITIS) and the Bennett Lab.

To act/to play (*Igrat'*) The Russian word most commonly used to describe what
an actor does during performance can be translated both as "to act" and "to
play." Because normal Russian usage suggests the artificiality of stage convention (much as "to playact" does in English), Stanislavsky rejects this term for
his System. [See in contrast "To act/to take action"]

To act/to take action (*Deistvovat'*) The verb Stanislavsky uses to describe what
the actor does during performance. In choosing what action to take (from
the Russian "action," *deistvie*), he emphasizes that theatre communicates by
means of action. Therefore, the actor's essential function in performance is
"to take action." In advocating this verb for his System, Stanislavsky invokes
the etymology of "drama" from the Greek *dran* ("to do"). Common English
translations of *deistvovat'* include "to act," "to enact," and "to behave." [See
"Action"]

Action (*Deistvie*) What the actor does to solve the problem or fulfill the task set
before his or her character by the play. In the System, "action" is expressed as an
active verb (i.e. to beg for forgiveness, to take revenge, to coddle, to challenge, etc.).
Actions, in contrast to activities (*fisicheskie deistvii*), are psychophysical in that
they are simultaneously "mental"/"inner" (*vnutrennoe*) and "physical"/"outer"
(*fizicheskoe/vneshnoe*). The series of actions discovered through analysis of
the role creates "a score of actions" (*partitura deistvii*), which guides the actor
through his or her performance. Actions must be "apt" (*tselosoobraznye*) in relationship to the character's circumstances, and must follow each other "logically"
(*logichno*) and "consecutively" (*poslednovatel'no*). Stanislavsky places action

at the heart of his System; he believes that action distinguishes drama from all other arts, as does Aristotle. A great deal of confusion surrounds Stanislavsky's use of the word "action." Stanislavsky creates some confusion when he uses the same word to describe activities (*fizicheskie deistvii*) and actual psychophysical actions (*deistvii*). Distinguishing between the two becomes essential in differentiating the Method of Physical Actions from Active Analysis. Additionally, the American Method adds to the confusion by treating Stanislavsky's concept of *zadacha* ("problem" or "task") as equivalent to "action." This misunderstanding was solidified in Hapgood's translation of *zadacha* as "objective." [See "Active Analysis," "Counteraction," "Task/problem," "Through-action"] *In practice*: An action (whether "impelling" or "counter") propels the actor through the scene and is expressed through an active, doable verb (to convince, to get back, to instigate, etc.) that has both psychological and physical dimensions. To choose a verb for a scene, determine: (1) where in the play a new action begins; (2) what problem (an adjective or adverb) the character faces at that moment; (3) what the character might do (a strong verb) to solve that problem.

Active Analysis (*Deistvennyi analiz*)   Stanislavsky's late rehearsal method in which actors discover the underlying structures of actions and counteractions in a play before memorizing dialogue. Analysis is "active" because cast members examine the play "on their feet," through improvisations that test their understanding of how characters on the page relate to each other and confront each other in performance. The technique encourages deep communication between partners and spontaneity; it also fosters simultaneous activation of mind, body, and heart, which Stanislavsky sees as necessary in performance. The entire technique involves a paradoxical relationship to texts; by reading and then stepping away from the words, actors learn to value and need the words. [See in contrast "Affective cognition"] *In practice*: A scene begins whenever an impelling action moves the actors/characters toward an event and ends when an event causes the actors/characters to need new actions. For the Active Analysis of a scene: (1) Read the scene carefully to determine the main event—what must occur before the story can progress to the next scene. (2) Determine the impelling action—what force moves the scene toward the event. (3) Determine the counteraction—what force resists the forward movement of the scene. (4) Identify which characters play impelling actions and which play counteractions. (5) Improvise the scene in your own words but using the identified dynamics. (6) Reread the text of the scene and assess how closely the improvisation mirrors the scene. (7) Repeat this process until the actors have been able to perform the scene's dynamics precisely as in the text. During improvisations, actors may use whatever words, images, rhythms, and lines from the text that they remember. (8) After the improvisation comes close to the text, memorize the dialogue.

Activities (*Fizicheskie deistvii*)   The simple physical actions that set the context for the dynamic interplay of psychophysical actions and counteractions in plays and scenes. Examples: A mother and daughter might be setting the table (activity) as the daughter convinces (action) her mother that acting is a noble profession, while the mother in turn avoids (counteraction) the conversation by changing the subject. Two men are repairing an automobile (activity), as one bosses (action) the other around to show his knowledge, while the other fights back (counteraction) by bragging about his triumph at the last football game. [See "Active Analysis," "Action," "Counteraction"] *In practice*: Stanislavsky suggests exercising one's muscle memory by recreating familiar physical actions without the use of properties: sweep the floor with an imagined broom; catch an imaginary fish; drink an imaginary cup of tea; write a letter without real paper and pen; play with an absent cat; play an imagined piano, etc. (SS III 1990:398–9). Verify your physical memory by executing the same activity with real objects.

Actor/role (*Artisto-rol'*)   According to Stanislavsky, when the actor as artist creates a character successfully, the result is an entirely new being—the actor/role—composed partly of the actor's own spirit and flesh and partly of the playwright's conception. [See "Human being/actor"]

Adaptation (*Prisposoblenie*)   The actor's use of specific mental and physical adjustments in order to communicate an action or personality trait more clearly to one's partner(s) and audience. Adjustments to an action or role depend upon the circumstances in the scene (as given by both play and production), the envisioned personality of the character (in Russian *obraz*, "image"), and the person(s) with whom one communicates. Adaptations might involve conscious adjustments (as when you notice that your message is not being received properly and you adjust your tactic), or unconsciously (as when you are so fully invested in the action of the scene that you adjust automatically). For example, you might close a door differently to avoid a draft or to keep out a criminal (circumstances), whether you wish to portray a calm or nervous person (personality), or if you wish to let your scene partner know precisely how angry you are (an adjustment to your acting partner). [See in contrast "In general"] *In practice*: Adaptations most often appear in the little expressive details that an actor chooses for or discovers in performance: using a prop (clasping a purse close to one's chest in anxiety) or establishing a characteristic physical habit (jiggling one's knees whenever distracted).

Adjustment   [See "Adaptation"]

Affective cognition (*Chuvstvennoe poznanie*)   Also called "cognitive analysis" (*poznavatel'nyi analiz*) Stanislavsky's early rehearsal procedure for analyzing a play. This method teaches actors to discuss each element in the play at length and to imagine as concretely as possible all the details of the characters' lives in order to build understanding and empathy. It encourages extended sessions "at the table" (*za stolom*), where cast members talk about every aspect of the play. It also encourages actors to work individually by visualizing the conditions and details of the characters' lives. [See in contrast "Active Analysis"]

Affective Memory (*Affectivnaia pamiat'*)   A term, borrowed from French experimental psychologist Théodule Ribot (1839–1916), which refers to a human being's ability to remember previously experienced emotional states by recalling the accompanying physical sensations. Stanislavsky treats affective memory as a natural part of our sensory lives, like a sixth sense, that activates easily, in the same way as do our other senses. In other words, just as we listen to conversations with our ears, we also listen with our affective memories. Moreover, Stanislavsky assumes that audiences, like actors, possess affective memories that performances can stir. Spectators too listen both with their ears and affective memories. In the First Studio, Stanislavsky experimented with the active use of personal memories that present analogies with the play under rehearsal. However, he found (in consonance with Ribot) that conscious use of personal experience could disturb the actor's "mental hygiene" and distract from the play. Therefore, Stanislavsky shifted his attention to other sources of affective memory, notably imagination and "empathy" (*sochuvstvo*, a derivative of the verb "to feel"). He also stresses that art is best created from repeated, recollected, secondary (*povtornye*) hence controllable emotions, not primary, first-time (*pervichnye*) ones. Lee Strasberg turned the operation of affective memory into an acting exercise (in which a personal experience is revived via all the sensory memories that attach to it). The Affective Memory exercise has become the cornerstone of the Method. Hapgood translates the term as "emotion memory;" common usage calls it "emotional memory." [See "To feel/to sense," "Sense memory"] *In practice*: Stanislavsky taught that by going to museums, listening to concerts, seeing great theatre, opera and ballet, reading voraciously (newspapers, histories, novels, poetry, everything), and utilizing one's mind and empathies as broadly as possible, the actor can develop a store of affective memories.

Beat   [See "Bit"]

Bit (*Kusok*)   The analytical segment or "unit" (Hapgood's translation) into which the actor divides each scene in a play. A new "bit" begins whenever an action or counteraction shifts in manner of execution or in strategy based upon the mutual interaction of the scene's partners. In the US, this term has been transformed into "beats," which may derive from "bits" of the play strung together like "beads" on a necklace when pronounced with a Russian accent by émigré teachers. *In practice*: For Affective cognition, actors define their strategic shifts in action ("bits") through discussion and in private home work. For Active Analysis, actors discover these shifts as they occur during improvisations.

Character   There are three Russian terms for character. *Deistvuiushchee litso* ("the one who takes action," more literally "the acting face") denotes a character as given in a play's cast list; this term usually shows up in Stanislavsky's writings in regard to the casting of actors into a play's complement of roles. *Rol'* ("role") refers to the words in a play that provide an actor with the blueprint for performance; Stanislavsky consistently uses this term to define acting as an art that conveys "the life of the human spirit in the role." *Obraz* ("image") refers to a character as an artistic conception (whether in drama, acting or literature); "image" is the most commonly used word for "character" in Russian. Stanislavsky's frequent use of this last term makes his interest in visualization as a technique appear all the more essential. [See "Visualization"]

Cliché (*Shablon*, also *Shtamp*)   Any well-worn theatrical convention, used mechanically, lacking the "kernel" or "seed" (*zerno*) of true meaning. Stanislavsky's examples include a hand to the forehead to indicate shock or weakness, the wringing of a handkerchief to portray grief, jumping for joy, and clutching one's heart at the moment of death. [See "Craftsmanship," "Indicating," "In general," "Seed"]

Communication (*Obshchenie*)   Interaction among scene partners and between actors and audience. The Russian word suggests "communion," "sharing," "interacting," "relating," "being in contact." While communication implies the use of words, Stanislavsky also includes non-verbal means of communication. Influenced by his study of Yoga, he visualizes communication as the transmitting and receiving of rays of energy, much like psychic radio waves. He calls this exchange "emanation" (or "radiating") and "imanation" (or the "taking in of radiation") (*izluchenie* and *vluchenie*, from the root "ray," *luch*). [See "*Prana*"] *In practice*: (A) Some exercises sensitize actors to the existence and power of "rays." Two examples are: (1) Working in pairs, the "sender" sits opposite the "receiver," almost knee to knee. The "sender" communicates a simple command (remove your glasses, touch your nose, etc.) using only the eyes. The "receiver" attends closely to the "sender" and moves when a signal is felt (observed at the Moscow Art Theatre Studio, R. Andrew White). (2) The group forms two parallel lines, facing each other. Maintaining formation, each line walks through the other by passing through the gaps between people as if doors. They then walk backward into their original positions. As they walk, each person pays attention to the energy emanating from the others around him or her. The exercise is repeated many times, alternating eyes open and eyes closed, until the group can sense each other's presence and pass through the line easily and fluidly without the use of sight (observed at GITIS, S. M. Carnicke). (B) Other exercises apply radiation to short improvised scenes. Improvise one of the following scenes, first by using all possible means of communication (verbal, gestural, and rays) and then silently using only rays: a husband arguing with a wife today; the same argument in 1910; vendors selling their wares to customers (those with and without money) at a farmer's market; two people gossiping about their neighbors (SS III 1990:406–7).

Concentration (*Vnimanie*)   During performance, Stanislavsky expects actors to give their full spiritual/mental and physical attention (*vnimanie*), in other words their total concentration (*sosredotochnost'*), to the actions of the play, their scene partners, and the objects necessary to their work. He calls all these points of focus, whether animate or inanimate, the "objects" (*ob'ekty*) of attention. Successful concentration can foster a state of mind that appears to isolate actors from anything external to the world of the play, what he calls "public solitude" (*publichnoe odinochestvo*), but in a performance that breaks the fourth wall, the audience can become an "object of attention." Influenced by meditation techniques of Yoga, he trains concentration by defining "circles of attention" (*krugi vnimaniia*) that can be "small," "medium," or "large." Actors learn to control and limit their focus to only those "objects" within the defined circle. Émigré actress Vera Soloviova, who worked at Stanislavsky's First Studio, called this technique "getting into the circle." In Raja Yoga, Ramacharaka taught that one's power of concentration can be developed, as can a "physical muscle" through "mental drills" based in careful observation (1906:56). [See "Public solitude"] *In practice*: Exercises adapted from Yoga include: (1) Take a simple object (a pencil, a leaf, etc.) and observe it in relationship to the "thing itself," "the place from whence it came," "its purpose or use," "its associations," "its probable end" (Ramacharaka 1906:56). (2) Walk into an unfamiliar room and exit after a few seconds; write down everything you observed; and then re-enter the room to verify your recall (Ramacharaka 1906:73).

Conflict (*Konflikt*)   The clash produced when an impelling action meets a counteraction. Conflict may be direct (as in a fist fight) or oblique (as happens in the subtle plays of Anton Chekhov or in passive-aggressive encounters) [See "Active Analysis," "Action," "Counteraction"] *In practice*: Develop a group's sense of conflict by playing an embodied game of chess, with the room's floor marked as the chessboard and each person becoming a player (pawn, knight, castle, bishop, queen, king). As you play, pay attention to which moves are direct and which oblique (Stanislavskii II 1986:316).

Counteraction (*Kontrdeistvie*, also *Protivodeistvie*)   A term used in Active Analysis. An action that is "contradictory" (*protivorechivye)* to the impelling action in a scene is the counteraction. The clash of action and counteraction produces dramatic conflict. Moreover, just as an overall action ("through-action") can be identified in the play, so too can the actor find an overall "counter-through-action" (*kontrskvosnoe deistvie*), that extends throughout the play. [See "Action," "Conflict," "Through-action"]

Craftsmanship (*Remeslo*)   Professional acting, which operates primarily through technical means and relies upon well-worn theatrical conventions ("clichés"). Stanislavsky criticizes this type of acting as devoid of true art. While "craft" has positive connotations in English, Stanislavsky uses it pejoratively. [See "Cliché," in contrast "Experiencing"]

Creative idea (*Vymysel*)   Any fictional idea introduced into the rehearsal of a scene in order to activate the actor's imagination. When one finds oneself at a creative loss, such an idea can offer new impulses and a renewed approach. The Russian word can be translated as "creative idea," "fiction" as opposed to fact, anything thought up or imagined, a "notion." [See "Imagination," "Lure"] *In practice*: Creative ideas can be multiplied through active fantasy. Exercises to strengthen fantasy include: (1) One person suggests several words at random, and the group creates a story linking the suggested words. (2) Choose a few objects at random, and imagine a painting that includes them all. (3) Imagine a new circumstance, not yet given, for a scene that is already in rehearsal (SS III 1990:400–1).

Desire (*Khotenie*)   That which motivates a character or person to take action. The term has also been translated "want" and "motivation." Initially Stanislavsky felt that actors should begin working on a role by asking: What does my character *want* in the given circumstances? Later, he restated the question: What would my character *do* in the given circumstances? [See "Intention," "Will"]

Device (*Priem*)   Any specific exercise or method of procedure that facilitates the actor's art; a technique. For example, Stanislavsky calls the Method of Physical Actions and Active Analysis "devices." "Devices" represent "elements" (*elementi*) of the System. As watchword for the Russian Formalist school of literary criticism, "devices" are those discrete aspects of an artistic work, which create its structure (i.e. metaphors, rhythms of speech, repetitions and patterns in texts, etc.). Just as an author uses these building blocks to create a literary work, so does an actor build performance through the use of devices. Criticizing Formalism, however, Stanislavsky warns that all devices must be imbued with inner content and meaning; they should not become mere technical exercises.

Dual consciousness in acting   [See "Sense of Self"]

Dynamism (*Aktivnost'*)   The state of being in action, which, in Stanislavsky's eyes is the proper state for the actor in performance. [See "Action"]

Eidetic images (*Videniia*)   [See "Visualizations"]

Embodiment (*Voploshchenie*)   That phase in the actor's work that physicalizes character and story. For Stanislavsky, all performance entails embodiment, since "acting" refers to the art form that uses the actor's physical being as its medium. [See "Life of the human body in the role"]

Emotional memory   [See "Affective Memory"]

Étude   Stanislavsky uses the French word "étude" to refer to a non-scripted scene performed by actors, what in American usage is called "improvisation." He asked actors to perform études in their own words from scenarios that he would devise, or to paraphrase scenes from a text. He also employed "silent études," in which scenes unfold silently, through the exchange of energy rays and expressive physical gesture.

Event (*Sobytie*)   A term in Active Analysis that identifies the basic structural element of drama. An "event" describes anything that happens within the play brought about through the actions of the characters. The "inciting" (*iskhodnoe*) event sets the play in motion. A "main" (*osnovnoe*) event is one without which a scene could not conclude. "Incidental" events are of secondary importance to the play. Stanislavsky sees the play as a "chain (*tsep'*) of events" that runs from beginning to end, and by means of which the story (*fabula*) is told. This chain establishes the "skeleton" (*skelet*) of the play, which the actors flesh out. In Active Analysis, actors explore how the various events in the play affect the development of their roles. [See "Story"]

Experiencing (*Perezhivanie*)   The ideal kind of acting, nurtured by the System, in which the actor creates the role anew at every performance in full view of the audience; the actor's creative process itself. Such acting, however well planned and well rehearsed, remains essentially active and improvisatory. Stanislavsky uses this term to distinguish his theatre from all others. He had observed "experiencing" in one of his favorite actors, Tommaso Salvini (1829–1915), who believed that the actor feels what the character does during performance, and whom Stanislavsky directly quotes. Stanislavsky adapts the term itself, however, from *What is Art?* (1897), in which Lev Tolstoy argues that art communicates felt experience, rather than knowledge, "infecting" its audience with the artist's emotion. Stanislavsky also uses "to infect" in Tolstoy's sense; the actor "infects" the audience when a performance stirs the spectators' affective memories. The Russian root of "experiencing" conveys many different nuances: "to experience," "to feel," "to live through," "to survive." The System generates a synonym for "experiencing" in "I am" (*Ia esm'*), which stresses the actor's immediacy and presence on stage. [See "I am"] *In practice*: Any technique that fosters the actor's creative state and maintains the actor's dynamism can induce "experiencing." Stanislavsky saw his System as a compendium of such techniques and designed Active Analysis specifically to improve the actor's dynamism in performance. [See "Active Analysis," "Dynamism," "Lure," "System"]

Fact (*Fakt*)   A term in Active Analysis that refers to any detail, "fixed" by the playwright in the play or by the director and designers in the production. "Facts" are not open to interpretation by the actor, who must adapt performance to account for them. "Evaluation of the facts" (*otsenka faktov*), therefore, lays the foundation for rehearsing a role. "Facts" serve as essential clues to the play's action, and hence to performance. Facts, in and of themselves, are unimportant; their value resides in the actor's use of them "to evoke the life of the human spirit." [See "Given circumstances"]

To feel/to sense (*Chuvstvovat'*)   This Russian verb has many meanings: "to sense" (as in sensory perception), "to feel emotion," "to understand," "to become aware of," etc. Stanislavsky uses the word and its derivatives consciously to invoke this multiplicity. In the realm of "feelings" the System's actor works on all levels— physical, emotional, and intellectual—at once. When Stanislavsky wishes to limit his discussion of "feelings" to that of the physical, he uses "sensation" (*oshchushenie*). [See "Affective cognition," "Affective Memory," "Feeling," "Sense memory"]

Feeling (*Chuvstvo*)   One of the three initiators of the psychic life and of the creative process. The word refers equally to emotional feeling and physical sensation. Contemporary cognitive science calls "feelings" the subjective awareness of the bodily manifestations that are "emotions." [See "Mind," "Will," "To feel/to sense," "Psychotechnique"]

Given circumstances (*Predlagaemye obstoiatelstva*)   All the conditions, detailed by the playwright and implicit in the play's social and historical milieu, which determine characters' behavior. Stanislavsky also includes those circumstances set up for the actor by directors and designers during production. In the 1808 essay, "On National-Popular Drama," Alexander Pushkin wrote: "Authenticity of the passions, verisimilitude of feelings in the proposed (*predpolagamye*) circumstances, that is what our intellect requires of a dramatic author." Stanislavsky adapts this phrase to his needs by changing what is "proposed" by the playwright to what is "given" to the actor. [See "Fact"]

Human being/actor (*Chelovek-akter*)   Every actor is both an artist and a unique human being. According to Stanislavsky, actors always infuse their roles with their own individualities, because they use their bodies, minds, and spirits as their creative "instruments." Every actor who plays Hamlet differs from every other Hamlet by virtue of his or her very being. To describe this theatrical phenomenon, Stanislavsky coins the hybrid term, "human being/actor." In *An Actor's Work on Himself, Part I*, he writes, "There's no walking away from yourself [on stage]" (SS II 1989:294). [See "Actor/role"]

I am (*Ia esm'*)   The actor's sense of being fully present in the dramatic moment. A term that functions in the System as a synonym for "experiencing." Staniislavsky has two sources for the term. First, Yoga uses "I am" for a person's awareness of his or her place in creation (Ramacharaka 1906:1–2). Second, because contemporary Russian does not use a present tense form for the verb "to be," Stanislavsky borrows Old Church Slavonic, a language invented and used for liturgical purposes in medieval Russia. Hence, Stanislavsky's use of "I am" carries implicit spiritual overtones. [See "Experiencing"] *In practice*: All the elements of the System that relax the body and focus the mind in preparation for work can foster the state of improvisatory creativity that Stanislavsky calls "I am." Before rehearsing or performing, relax, establish a clear circle of attention, attend to all rays of communication, and invest yourself in your chosen action. As you work, be sure to move from moment to moment in the scene logically and specifically. [See "Relaxation," "Concentration," "Communication," "Action," in contrast "Indicating"]

Imagination (*Voobrazhenie*)   The actor's capacity to treat fictional circumstances as if they were real, to visualize the details of the character's life specifically and concretely, to daydream or fantasize about the events of the play. For Stanislavsky, training the actor's imagination is of utmost importance. [See "Creative idea," "Magic if," "Visualizations"]

Impelling action   [See "Action"]

Improvisation (*Improvizatsiia*)   [See "Étude"]

Indicating   Common in American usage. When an actor merely pretends to take action, but does not actually do so (when he pretends to see without looking, or when she hears without listening), the actor is said to be "indicating." [See "Cliché," "In general"]

In general (*Voobshche*)   When actors employ vague, generalized action with little adaptation to the specific circumstances of the scene (i.e. merely closing a door, rather than closing a heavy wooden door because there is a draft in the room), Stanislavsky says that they act "in general." [See "Indicating," in contrast "Adaptation"]

Inner monologue (*Vnutrennyi monolog*)   A term coined by Vladimir Nemirovich-Danchenko to describe the unspoken words that go through a character's mind during the course of a play. The actors of the Moscow Art Theatre craft their characters' inner monologues carefully in order to assist them with concentration. [See "Subtext"] *In practice*: Between the lines of your text, write the unspoken thoughts that prompt the spoken lines or that you imagine your character choosing to leave unspoken. Memorize these thoughts along with the lines. Perform both spoken and unspoken lines.

Inspiration (*Vdokhnovenie*)   Stanislavsky sees "inspiration" as a force from without, as a gift "sent from Apollo," hence, as something over which actors have no control. Stanislavsky therefore rejects this concept for his System, and teaches actors to look for their roles within themselves. [See "Subconscious"]

Intention   Used by Elia Kazan and generally in American actor training to identify what a character wants to achieve in a scene or play; motivation. The concept is akin to Stanislavsky's idea that a character's desire (or want) prompts action. The term itself may derive from his phrase, "the lines of intent" (*liniia stremleniia*), which describes the unbroken succession of "objects of attention," memories, fantasies, and "visualizations" that help an actor create a performance. [See "Concentration," "Desire," "Will"]

Justification of movement (*Opravdanie dvizhenii*)   Any motion on stage, however slight, should have logic and purpose. *In practice*: Exercises that strengthen an actor's ability to justify physical movement include: (1) Change your pose or position, and then imagine its justification (SS III 1990:447). (2) Run randomly through the rehearsal studio until the group leader calls "Stop!" Freeze your pose and allow your pose to suggest a story that has been unfolding. Shape the pose to fit the story more fully (as taught by Bennett). (3) Marble People: either singly or in groups, take a static pose; observers justify the poses they see and name the living statues (Stanislavskii II 1986:316).

Justification of text (*Opravdanie teksta*)   Stanislavsky expects actors to create the reasons, logic, and purpose behind all words spoken on stage. *In practice*: To justify your lines, use all the various "lures" in the System to make each word, phrase and image, along with the style and rhythms of the speech, express something specific: the intended meaning, a character's background or personality, the play's era, etc. The "lures" most helpful in justifying texts are "Magic if," "Inner monologue," associative or analogous experiences from "Affective Memory," "Creative ideas" suggested by your imagination, and "Visualizations."

Life of the human body in the role (*Zhizn' chelovecheskogo tela roli*)   The "outer" (*vneshnye*) and physical aspects of performance. In the embodiment (*voploshchenie*) of a character, the actor creates the "life of the human body in the role" by maintaining the logic and consecutiveness of physical actions. For example, in writing a letter, one first takes paper and pen, arranges the desk, thinks about what to say, and only then begins to write. The actor must also keep in mind nature's physical laws. For example, when looking out at the audiences as if to see a ship on the horizon, the actor needs to level his or her eyes in accord with physical reality, being careful not to look at the back wall of the auditorium. [See "Activities," "Embodiment"]

Life of the human spirit of the role (*Zhizn' chelovecheskogo dukha roli*)   Those aspects of performance that are "inner" (*vnutrennye*) as well as mental, psychological, spiritual and psychic (all potential translations of *dushevnye*, from the Russian *dusha*, "soul"). Throughout his career, Stanislavsky repeatedly states that the essential goal of theatrical art consists in the creation of "the life of the human spirit of the role" and its transmission on stage in "artistic form."

Logic (*Logika*)   For Stanislavsky, all stage action must make sense to the actor within the "given circumstances" of the play. If the play does not appear logical on the surface (as it might not in a Symbolist or absurdist play or for a character who goes insane), the actor seeks to create an inner logic (a "subtext"). For Stanislavsky, logic always begins with the evaluation of the "facts" of the text; inner logic then accounts for these facts. [See "Action," "Fact"]

Lure (*Manok*)   Anything that incites the actor to create, hence every technique in the System, is a "lure." Like a hunter who entices shy prey from under cover, the actor must gently induce a mood that allows for creative work by using such techniques as the "magic if," sets, props, and costumes that make the "given circumstances" of the play credible, "affective memory" or recollections analogous to experiences in the play, a "creative idea," etc. Anything that triggers the actor's imagination or entices the subconscious out of hiding can be considered a "lure." [See "Affective Memory," "Creative idea," "Magic if"]

Magic if (*Magicheskoe esli by*)   One of the techniques which inspire the actor's creative state. The actor asks: "What would I do if I found myself in this circumstance?" The answer should be an active verb ("the action" for the scene). For the American Method, Lee Strasberg rejected this formulation, adopting what he thought to be Evgeny Vakhtangov's modification: "What would motivate me, the actor, to behave in the way that the character does?" This question allows the actor to replace the play's circumstance with a personal one (called a "substitution"). [See "Lure"] *In practice*: Exercises for this technique include: (1) successively change your relationship to an object and treat it accordingly. What if this were a letter from my mother, from a close friend, from Stanislavsky, from a civil war soldier? (2) Pass an object around the room and imagine it to be other than it is. What if this stone were a diamond, radioactive, a carving from Ancient Egypt, etc. (SS II 1989:119)?

The Method   The various actor training approaches developed in the US by Stanislavsky's admirers, chief among them Lee Strasberg, Stella Adler, and Sanford Meisner. The term was coined by Strasberg when his interpretation of Stanislavsky was challenged by Stella Adler in 1934. The Method best represents the Americanization of Stanislavsky's ideas. [See in contrast "Method of Physical Actions," "The System"]

Method of Physical Actions (*Metod fizicheskikh deistvii*)   A rehearsal technique with which Stanislavsky experimented in the last part of his life, by means of which the actor develops a logical sequence of physical actions (activities) for his or her role through improvisation. For example, in *An Actor's Work on Himself, Part I*, Stanislavsky suggests that the actor who plays the character, Salieri (in Pushkin's *Mozart and Salieri*) murders Mozart first by choosing a wine glass, next by pouring the wine, next by dropping in some poison, and only then by handing the glass to his rival. While Stanislavsky cautions that physical actions serve as a threshold into the psychophysical, Soviet Marxists linked this method to behaviorism. They focused on the fact that emotional life can be more easily aroused and fixed for performance through work on the physical life of the role than through emotional recall and memory. Because this interpretation is based in the material body, Soviet interpreters advocated the Method of Physical Actions as Stanislavsky's most complete and scientific solution to acting. Therefore, the Method of Physical Actions best represents the Sovietization of Stanislavsky's ideas. [See "Activities," "Life of the human body in the role," in contrast "The Method," "System"]

Mind (*Um*)   One of the three initiators of psychic life and of the creative process. The actor's intelligent analysis of the play (either through Affective cognition or Active Analysis) is the first step toward creating a character. [See "Active Analysis," "Affective cognition," "Feeling," "Will"]

Moment-to-moment   An American phrase that describes work in which the actor is fully present on stage and within the immediate moment of the scene; acting in the "here and now." [See "Experiencing," "I am"]

Motivation   A term in American usage that defines what a character wants within the given circumstances of the scene, and more broadly, within the play. [See "Desire," "Intention," "Will"]

Objective   [See "Task"]

Objects of attention   [See "Concentration"] Whatever the actor pays attention to during performance. *In practice*: Exercise your concentration by establishing either mentally or physically (by walking) a small circle of attention, noticing what objects fall within it; next widen the circle to a medium area, and notice how many more objects fall within this larger circle; finally expand your attention to the largest circle of attention possible, and determine how many objects fall within this circle. As you attend to objects, use all your senses.

Physical actions   [See "Activities," "Method of physical actions"]

Prana   A Sanskrit word from Yoga to describe the energy that gives life to the body. While it may be translated as "life energy" or "vital energy," it usually does not appear in translated form. *Prana* is visualized as breath being carried through the body. Exercises that train breathing, called *pranayama*, use bodily function to control the metaphysical energy of life. Stanislavsky uses the Sanskrit word frequently in his writings, and relates it to rays of energy that facilitate communication. [See "Communication," "Psychotechnique," "Yoga"] *In practice*: Control of the breath best exercises *prana*. For example: (1) Relax completely. (2) Establish rhythmic breathing by inhaling for six heart beats, holding the breath for three, and exhaling slowly for six more heart beats. (3) Now breathe in and exhale, imagining that the breath travels through the bones of the legs, then through the bones of the arms, then into and out of the skull. (4) Turn your imagination to the vital organs of your body, with the breath entering and exiting each organ in turn. (5) As you mentally work through the bones and organs, become aware of the breath moving through your body as an energizing force (Ramacharaka 1904:166–8).

Primary feelings (*Pervichnye chuvstvovaniia*)   Emotions and sensations that arise in the immediate moment for the first time. Most feelings in real life are primary. For Stanislavsky, such feelings are uncontrollable and hence undesirable on stage. For example, an actor playing Romeo, who feels a "primary" flash of anger when he confronts the actor playing Mercutio may indeed cause real harm. [See "Affective Memory," "To feel/to sense," in contrast "Secondary feelings"]

Private Moment   An exercise developed by Lee Strasberg for the American Method that builds upon Stanislavsky's concept of the actor's "public solitude." In this exercise, the actor performs in front of others an action from personal life so private that he or she would never want to be seen doing it. [See "Public solitude"]

Problem   [See "Task"]

Psychotechnique (*Psikhotekhnika*)   Using the physical to tap the emotional and psychic. Stanislavsky grounds his System in Théodule Ribot's (1839–1916) psychophysical theories, which state that the mind and body are inseparable, and that emotions cannot be experienced without physical sensation. The psychophysical also extends into the spiritual realm for Stanislavsky, who borrowed exercises from Yoga in order to make the actor aware of the mind–body–spirit continuum of experience. As Stanislavsky writes in *An Actor's Work on Himself, Part I*, "In every physical action there is something of the psychological, and in the psychological, something of the physical" (SS II 1989:258). The term, "psychotechnique," which often identifies the work of the System, reflects that belief.

Public solitude (*Publichnoe odinochestvo*)   What the actor experiences when fully within a small "circle of attention." A sensation of intimacy and isolation is created by deep, creative concentration on objects within this small circle. During a moment of public solitude, the actor may appear unaware of the audience, but, nonetheless, the actor sends *prana* out into the auditorium, communicating the quality of the moment. [See "Concentration," "Communication," "Private Moment"] *In practice*: Exercises used by Stanislavsky to increase the actor's understanding of public solitude include the recreation of familiar events that need a small circle of attention: (1) Read a telegram about a relative's death. (2) Try to remember a song you once knew. (3) Look for a note with a very important telephone number on it, or an expensive opera ticket lost in your pocket. (4) Read in the paper about the death or the marriage of a friend (SS III 1990:402–3).

Rays (*Luchi*)   [See "Communication," "*Prana*"]

Relaxation (*Osvobozhdenie myshts*)   The release of excessive muscular tension. The System teaches the actor to recognize tension in any part of the body and to use the minimum muscular contraction required to perform any physical action. Stanislavsky agrees with Ramacharaka: "The person understanding Relaxation and the conserving of energy accomplishes the best work. He uses a pound of effort to do the pound of work" (1904:174). Since unnecessary tension impedes creative process, relaxation provides the necessary foundation for good acting. Hatha Yoga, which includes exercises in relaxation, balance, and bodily poses, influenced Stanislavsky's understanding of the body in performance. [See "Yoga"] *In practice*: (1) Lie down, or sit, and relax as fully as possible, allowing each muscle to give in to the force of gravity. Let your mind (what Stanislavsky calls your "internal monitor") wander through the body, from head to toes, identifying any area of tension. For each of these areas, take a deep breath and with the exhale command the tense muscle to relax. (2) When relaxed, raise each limb in turn (left arm, then right, left leg, then right) and let it drop into the floor. Feel the difference in the muscle as the limb lifts and then releases into the floor. (3) Now shift your attention to the floor (or floor and chair) that holds you up into the room. Find each point of contact between it and your body. Imagine the energy in the floor (or chair) that pushes up against your body to keep you in your static place (Ramacharaka 1904:180–6).

Representation (*Predstavlenie*)   Professional acting in which the actor creates a mental image of a character during rehearsals, and then consciously presents that image to the audience by reproducing it, usually in heightened style. In this school of acting, "experiencing" occurs only in rehearsal, while performance utilizes technical virtuosity. Stanislavsky employs the term "representation" to indicate that school of acting advocated by Coquelin the Elder (1841–1909), who wrote in *The Art of the Actor*, "Art is not identification, but representation." Coquelin likens the actor to the portrait painter, who represents the image of the model on canvas. While the Russian word has many nuances ("presentation," "performance," "enactment," a "show," even a "notion" or an "idea") "representation" best invokes the historical debate on acting that Stanislavsky joined. [See in contrast "Experiencing"]

Reversal points (*Povorotnye tochki*)   A term in Active Analysis that describes those places in the play where a character changes the direction of his or her action as a result of conflict. [See "Counteraction"]

Score of actions (*Partitura deistvii*)   [See "Action"]

Secondary feelings (*Povtornye chuvstvovaniia*)   Literally "repeated" feelings, secondary emotions and sensations are recollected rather than experienced for the first time. For Stanislavsky, such feelings prove useful on stage, because they can be harnessed for the benefit of the role and controlled in performance. [See "Affective Memory," "To feel/to sense," in contrast "Primary feelings"]

Seed (*Zerno*)   The core or kernel from which a character, performance, or play grows. Like the seed of a tree, which bears within it the idea of the future tree but does not yet look like a tree, the seed is a working hypothesis that begins to take shape and transform in rehearsals. This concept characterizes the Moscow Art Theatre tradition generally, and was probably coined as a term by Nemirovich-Danchenko.

Sense memory   The ability to recall sights, sounds, tastes, touches, and smells. For Stanislavsky, recall of the physical senses is one aspect of Affective Memory. (Note that the Russian word for "feeling" embraces both the physical and the emotional.) In the United States, sense memory generally serves as the foundation for emotional recall. At the American Laboratory Theatre, Richard Boleslavsky and Maria Ouspenskaya called sense memory "Analytical Memory." [See "Affective Memory," "Feelings"]

Sense of self (*Samochuvstvie*)   The state of mind and body necessary for the actor to create a performance. In *An Actor's Work on Himself, Part II*, Stanislavsky writes that "sense of self" combines two conscious perspectives: being on stage and being within the role. In other words, the "Sense of Self" is Stanislavsky's term for the actor's dual consciousness made familiar by the French philosopher Denis Diderot. He does not mean that the actor feels self-conscious. Rather, the sense of self is "proper to the stage" (*stsenicheskoe*), "inner" (*vnutrennoe*) in its concentration, "outer" (*vneshnoe*) in the actor's physical presence, and "creative" (*tvorcheskoe*). [See "I am"]

Sense of truth and belief (*Chuvstvo pravdy i vera*)   As actors create, they foster belief in the life of the play through their active imaginations, and take action as if the dramatic circumstances were true. In his notebooks, Stanislavsky cautions that theatre is not real life and that what is "true" on stage is whatever we believe to be true. In other words, performance is the actor's truth. [See "Magic if"]

Shift (*Sdvig*)   A sudden wrenching experience, in which the actor's perceptions seem suddenly new; a change or turn-around of perception. In rehearsal, a shift may occur when the actor suddenly sees the world through the character's eyes, or discovers the action that unlocks the puzzle of a scene. This word was popular among Russian avant-garde artists and the Formalists of the 1920s to refer to the way in which art makes familiar things appear to be seen "as if for the first time," another familiar phrase from Stanislavsky's System.

Song and Dance   An exercise developed by Lee Strasberg for the American Method as an aid to Affective Memory; intended to provoke emotional response. The actor sings, while the teacher calls out changes in rhythms and volume, as well as directions for physical movements (the dance) to accompany the song.

Soul (*Dusha*)   [See "Life of the human spirit of the role"]

Spine   [See "Through-action"]

Story (*Fabula*)   All incidents, histories, and events, whether given on stage or not, from which the action of a play is crafted. The story may include much that the playwright has not put into the play such as characters' biographies, actions that take place off-stage or at a prior time, etc. (In contemporary film, "backstory" expresses this concept.) In Russian Formalism, the "story" provides the creative material for the "plot" (*siuzhet*), which is the actual selection and arrangement of the story's elements. (For example, in Tennessee Williams' *A Streetcar Named Desire* the loss of the family plantation is in the story, but the auction does not appear as an event in the plot.) In Active Analysis, Stanislavsky substitutes the "chain of events" that takes place on stage for "plot." [See "Event"] *In practice*: In Active Analysis, begin by telling the story to each other as completely as possible. Next determine how this story will be told in performance by identifying the events that actually occur on stage. Which of these events "incites" (or begins) the drama, which are of "main" and of "incidental" importance? Next, establish the "chain of events" by specifying the exact order in which the events will occur during performance. (The order need not be chronological; some plays use flashbacks or flashforwards that disturb the story's natural chronology.) Give each event a brief title to help the cast focus on its function in telling the overall story. Rehearse by determining what actions and counteractions are necessary to make each event occur.

Subconscious (*Podsoznanie*)   One realm of the unconscious; an aspect of mental life within but hidden from the individual's consciousness. Stanislavsky envisions this realm as a "friend" to the creative process. One stated goal of the System is to arouse the subconscious through conscious means. Stanislavsky refers to the "ocean of the subconscious" to give a sense of its size and power. [See "Lure," "Unconscious," "Superconscious"] *In practice*: Stanislavsky, like Ramacharaka, tells actors that when they are puzzled by the work on the role they should "throw" their "bundle of thoughts" into the subconscious and allow the unconscious mind to do its work. The subconscious suggests solutions (Ramacharaka 1906:166; SS IV 1991:144 or 1961:82).

Substitution (also **Personal substitution**)   [See "Magic if"]

Subtext (*Podtekst*)   That which impels characters to speak; the inner life of a character in a play. "Subtext" may be inferred by identifying gaps in the text such as pauses, ambiguities in language, inconsistencies between what a person says and does, etc. [See "Inner monologue"]

Superconscious (*Sverkhsoznanie*)   Higher consciousness. For Stanislavsky, that realm of the unconscious that transcends the individual's experience and unites the one with the many; the spiritual realm. He takes the term from Yoga, where it describes the state reached through meditation. In his view, art taps this realm of being and thus can speak across cultures, eras, and individual differences. [See "Unconscious," "Subconscious," "Yoga"]

Superobjective (*Sverkhzadacha*)   [See "Task"]

System (*Sistema*)   Stanislavsky's preferred word for his compendium of lures and techniques for the actor. He saw his System as an actor's "guide" and an acting "grammar" that facilitates expressive communication from the stage, not a dogmatic or required curriculum. "My System should serve as a doorway into creative work," he writes (II 1986:193). From this point of view, he explains that his System is applicable for any performance in any style. "The System is not an artistic trend, not a style. It is like vocal training" (II 1986:254).

Task/problem (*Zadacha*)   The Russian word may be translated in two ways: (1) Stanislavsky speaks of fulfilling the "task" demanded by the given circumstances of the play's through-action. (2) He also writes that the actor resolves the "problem" posed by the circumstances via action. In the latter case, he compares the actor to a student who solves an "arithmetic problem." In both translations, the term relates "given circumstances" to "action." Hapgood translates it as "objective." Stanislavsky extends this concept into broader contexts. The moment-to-moment problems which the actor confronts throughout the play are unified by and subordinated to a larger problem, the "supertask" (*sverkhzadacha*, translated as "superobjective" by Hapgood). The supertask, in turn, suggests an overriding action that links together actions throughout the play, the "through-action." The "super-supertask" (*sverkhsverkhzadacha*) represents the actor's creative life-work. [See "Action," "Given circumstances"]

Technique   [See "Device," "Lure"]

Tempo-rhythm (*Tempo-ritm*)   "Tempo" refers to the internal rhythmic speed of an action; it includes the subjective awareness of time. A nervous person may move more quickly than a calm person. "Rhythm" refers to the external rhythmic speed at which the entire production unfolds. A farce moves more quickly than a tragedy. Stanislavsky uses this term to remind the actor of the need to balance internal and external pacing during performance.

Through-action (*Skvoznoe deistvie*)   Also "through line of action." A unifying, overall action that relates all moment-to-moment actions throughout the play to each other. Each character also has a "through-action" that links all his or her various actions throughout the play. "Through-action" helps keep the actor focused during performance. In the US, the Group Theatre used the term "spine" for this concept (i.e. "the spine of the play" and "the spine of the character"), drawing upon Stanislavsky's metaphor that compares the structure of a play to a "skeleton." [See "Action," "Event"]

Unconscious (*Bessoznatel'nyi*) That which in mental life is not available to the conscious mind. For Stanislavsky, this vast realm of being is divided into two: the "subconscious" (that lies within each person) and the "superconscious" (that transcends the individual). [See "Subconscious," "Superconscious"]

Verbal action (*Slovesnoe deistvie*) Stanislavsky points out that in life we speak in order to accomplish something through communication; hence, words are functional. On stage, the actor creates functionality for the fixed language of the play. The dramatist's words thus become part of the action in the play, and like all action, they must be "apt" to the circumstances, "logical" in terms of subtext, and follow a "consecutive" line of thought from beginning to end. [See "Action," "Subtext"] *In practice*: Play the scene "sitting on your hands," using only words to take action and connect with your partner(s) (Stanislavskii II 1986:317).

Visualizations (*Videniia*) Visualizations are images in the mind's eye that energize the actor's imagination. Stanislavsky's assistant, Maria Knebel, reminds actors that they must always see mental images as they speak. Stanislavsky's use of "visualization" may stem from both Raja Yoga and Quintilian, the classical Roman rhetorician who discusses the power of *visio* ("eidetic image," Latin) in his description of the orator's art. Stanislavsky suggests that the actor develop a "filmstrip" (*kinolenta*) of images to accompany the performance of every role. He trains "inner vision" (*vnutrennoe zrenie*) through exercises on imagination and meditation. Contemporary cognitive science supports Stanislavsky's emphasis on imagery in consciousness. [See "Imagination," "Yoga"] *In practice*: Examples of exercises adapted from Yoga include: (1) Close your eyes and imagine that you are a tree; specify the type, the age, etc. Utilizing all five senses, each in turn, imagine the specifics of what you feel (as the roots reach deep into the earth and the branches extend skyward), what you see (looking out into the environment), what you smell in the air (flowers, burning leaves, etc.), what you hear (birds, traffic, etc.). Finally imagine a story occurring underneath your leaves (a battle, a lovers' meeting, etc.) and allow the story to tap your affective memory (SS II 1989:133–6). (2) Choose several images at random and weave them into a story (SS III 1990:400).

Want (*Khotenie*) [See "Desire"]

Will (*Volia*) One of the three initiators of the psychic life and creative process. Willing, or more precisely the "desire" (*khotenie*), to solve the character's "problem" or fulfill a "task" (*zadacha*) in the scene propels the actor toward "taking action" (*deistvovat'*). [See "Desire," "Mind," "Feeling"]

Yoga Spiritual disciplines in the Eastern religions of Hinduism and Buddhism that are directed toward higher consciousness ("superconscious"). Two disciplines that most influenced Stanislavsky are Hatha Yoga and Raja Yoga. The first calms and relaxes the body by means of physical work on postures and balance (*asana*) and control of the breath (*pranayama*). Raja ("royal") Yoga works on mental control through concentration (*dharana*), visualization, observation, and meditation. [See "Concentration," "Visualizations," "*Prana*," "Relaxation," "Superconscious"]

Notes

Chapter 1

1   S. V. Tsikhotsky worked with M. N. Kedrov, one of Stanislavsky's last assistants (Chapters 5 and 9).
2   Part of this session is transcribed in Hethmon (1991:47–50), but this particular remark does not appear.
3   The lectures were published as *Method or Madness?* (1958).

Chapter 2

1   Senelick suggested to me in the 1990s that Gest had indeed "asked" for these productions as the Theatre's most famous.
2   For details on the tour's technical aspects, see the production stage manager's memoirs (Shverubovich 1990:417–612).
3   Pashennaia never felt accepted by the company and, thus, did not return to the States in 1924.
4   Belasco was Gest's father-in-law and helped promote the tour.
5   At the International Seminar on Stanislavsky in Translation, Moscow Art Theatre, Moscow, 14 May 1990, Smeliansky stated that Stanislavsky undoubtedly considered emigration.
6   In the US, Stanislavsky was treated as a "star," yet another irony of the tours (Shverubovich 1990:544, 570–1).
7   Mikhail Bulgakov presents a scathing parody of Stanislavsky's experiments in *Zapiski pokoinika: teatral'nyi roman* (1936, *Black Snow* in English).
8   Despite their differences, Stanislavsky showed his deep respect for his partner in 1933. Nemirovich-Danchenko was returning to Moscow from a financially disastrous stay in the US (Carnicke 2005). He did not have sufficient funds to make the last leg of his trip. Stanislavsky wrote to Stalin to request assistance for his partner, a man who played a "colossal role" in Russian theatre, giving "his energetic, talented, selfless work in the revolutionary years." Stanislavsky offered himself as guarantor (Smeliansky 1991).
9   In a letter dated 25 September 1994, Senelick wrote me that these anecdotes are "part of Soviet hagiography. […] Having Lenin praise Stanislavsky is like the faked photos showing Lenin seated next to Stalin."

Chapter 3

1   The Kachalov Group's history is detailed by Kachalov's son, the Art Theatre's production stage manager, V. Shverubovich (1990:178–391). Those who did not return to Moscow renamed themselves the Prague Group and continued to perform until the late 1920s.
2   The Guild traced its roots to the Washington Square Players, hence to the tributary

theatre of the twenties—the Little Theatre movement; the Guild produced many European plays and was considered far above the usual quality of Broadway.

3 The Moscow Art Theatre faced potential financial ruin in its first years. The young company, like the Group, was born in a capitalistic environment. Nemirovich-Danchenko describes his struggles to find funding: "Oh, what a nightmare! The most necessary thing of all: money, money, money" (1936:114). Of course, following the economic upheavals of the revolution, the Moscow Art Theatre became a fossilized Soviet institution heavily subsidized by the government.

4 The analogy breaks down in regard to Stanislavsky and Nemirovich-Danchenko, who brought a great deal more experience to their new project than did the founders of the Group, who were as untried as their actors.

5 This production garnered mixed reviews in New York and failed in London. For a full discussion of production at the Actors Studio, see Garfield (1980:214–47).

Chapter 4

1 Susan Strasberg told me in Paris, 6 November 1988, that her father's book was heavily determined by editorial decisions. Note also that Robert Lewis remains an exception among the Group Theatre actors, having published a number of books earlier in his career.

2 Boleslavsky's lectures are preserved in typescript as "The Creative Theatre," New York Public Library for the Performing Arts; some of Maria Ouspenskaya's classes were transcribed and published as "Notes on Acting with Maria Ouspenskaya" (October 1954–January 1955).

3 Method actor and teacher Robert Ellerman conveyed to me during the 1990s that in an interview with Roberts on 11 October 1975 Strasberg could not remember the terms "action-step/problem-step," which Boleslavsky linked to the issue of emotion in his classes.

4 Some of these translations were published in the Marxist journal *New Theatre* (1934, 1935) and in Cole (1974). Typescripts of Schmidt's translations of Markov's and Volkov's books are in the New York Public Library for the Performing Arts and Harvard University.

5 Stanislavsky mentions a precedent to Adler's visit in a letter to his co-director from 8 August 1930: "Not long ago, I gave myself a test in order to see whether I could still work with actors. An actress from the Theatre Guild in New York came to see me, and I worked with her for half an hour daily for two weeks. At first I was very tired and then I got used to it" (SS IX 1999:433). The actress was Beatrice Wood. Later that year, Eunice Stoddard, also of the Theatre Guild and later a member of the Group, followed suit (SS VIII 1961:545 n.). These sessions, however, attracted much less attention and exerted less influence on the US stage than did Adler's. Stanislavsky also recounts an anecdote about an anonymous actress who came to him for help that also recalls Adler's story (SS II 1989:418–9).

6 Strasberg donated these recordings to the Wisconsin Center for Film and Theater Research, An Archive of the University of Wisconsin, Madison, and the State Historical Society of Wisconsin, Madison. Selections were transcribed and edited by Hethmon (1991).

7 While working at the Actors Studio as Assistant Director and Interpreter for Tsikhotsky, I heard this analysis of Strasberg's speaking style from a lighting booth operator. I felt it apt.

Chapter 5

1 I borrow my use of "given circumstances" in this chapter from Vladimir Dybovskii's documentary history of *An Actor's Work on Himself* (1992).

2 In fact, Ribot is mentioned once in *An Actor Prepares* (1936:156).

3 My translation of the title, *Rabota aktera nad soboi* is literal. I have made two notable

decisions. Russian has no article; I chose "an actor" instead of "the actor" because the quasi-novel centers on the quest of a single student, Nazvanov. The singular self-referential *soboi* can refer to either gender; I use the masculine, again because the central character is a man.

4   Benedetti's new translations of Stanislavsky's *My Life in Art* and *Parts I* and *II* of the acting manuals, newly titled *An Actor's Work: A Student's Diary* (London: Routledge 2008), are the first to challenge the hegemony of translations by Robbins (*My Life in Art*) and Hapgood (*An Actor Prepares, Building a Character,* and *Creating a Role*).

5   For a full account of the creation of *My Life in Art* see Senelick (1981); the first English translation of Stanislavsky's revised variant was by G. Ivanov-Mumjiev and appeared in Moscow in the 1950s.

6   *Das Geheimnis des schauspielerischen Erfolges*, Alexandra Meyerburg, trans. (Berlin: Scientia Verlag, 1940). The publisher later moved to Zurich and republished this translation in 1945.

7   Reminiscence of critic A. P. Svobodin, at the International Seminar on Stanislavsky in Translation, the Moscow Art Theatre, Moscow, 18 May 1990.

8   Analyzed here are: the Typescript of Konstantin Stanislavskii, *Rabota aktera nad soboi, Chast' I, Okonchatel'nyi dlia Ameriki*, Moscow, 1935 (The New York Public Library for the Performing Arts); the English Constantin Stanislavski, *An Actor Prepares*, Elizabeth Reynolds Hapgood, trans. (New York: Theatre Arts Books, 1936); the 1938 Russian *Rabota aktera nad soboi, Chast' I* reprinted in SS II 1989). Chapter and page references to these editions in my analysis (Chapters 4 and 5) are given in brackets in the text.

Chapter 6

1   "Writing [so-called] Aesopian footnotes" could allow the "disenfranchised" scholar "to vent his frustration" in "notes [that] are read, understood, and translated into the rhetoric of resistance" (Jansen 1988:195).

2   In *Persecution and the Art of Writing* (Glencoe: Free Press, 1952), Leo Strauss coins this corollary to "reading between the lines" (Jansen 1988:248).

3   Born in 1902 in Russia, Moore was trained at Kiev's Solovtsov Theatre and at the Moscow Art Theatre's Third Studio with Evgeny Vakhtangov in early techniques of the System. She emigrated to the West in the early 1920s, thus before Stanislavsky's last experiments. When she moved to the US and saw that the System had been transformed into the Method, she decided to dedicate herself to promoting Stanislavsky in his Russian guise. She updated her knowledge by reading the latest Soviet books, many of which were smuggled out of the country for her by friends. Thus, she was strongly influenced by the Soviet version of the Method of Physical Actions. She experimented with information about Stanislavsky's last techniques with her own students. For a full discussion of her life and teachings see Suzanne M. Trauth and Elizabeth C. Stroppel, *Sonia Moore and the American Acting Training: With a Sliver of Wood in Hand* (Lanham: The Scarecrow Press, 2004).

Chapter 7

1   Throughout Chapter 6 page references to *An Actor Prepares* (1936) will be in brackets in the text.

2   In adopting *Ia esm'* ("I am") for *perezhivanie*, Stanislavsky describes an exercise in which Nazvanov visualizes himself in his room at night. When Nazvanov has imaginatively projected himself into the room, Tortsov identifies the state as that of *Ia esm'*. In the étude about the burned money, Tortsov states that he prefers this term to "inspiration" (SS II 1989:124; 432–3). However, while "I am" stresses the immediacy of the actor's experience on stage, it also implies a static state of being and hence semantically undermines Stanislavsky's notion of dynamic action as the basis of theatrical art.

This implication may derive from the term's use in Yoga as an inward turning of the mind as well as from the verb's intransitive form (Chapters 8 and 9).

3   In conversations with Inna Solovyova of the Moscow Art Theatre School I learned that the Sovremennik Theatre preferred *prozhivat'* ("to live").

4   By way of exception, Lloyd (2006) and Wain (2005) have recently examined *perezhivanie*.

5   Hobgood argues for "experience" because it invokes John Dewey's and Viola Spolin's definitions of the word (1973:149). Spolin's usage may bear further examination because her improvisatory work is also sympathetic with Active Analysis.

6   *Perezhit'* can also mean "to outlive" or "to survive." For example, a widow outlives her husband; a pilot survives a plane crash.

7   While Hughes analyzes the Tolstoyan influence on Stanislavsky (1993:39–48), he ignores Tolstoy's distaste of theatre and Sulerzhitsky's role as a Tolstoyan at the First Studio. Both Hobgood (1973:151) and Simonov (1962:7) also argue for Stanislavsky's source for *perezhivanie* in Tolstoy.

8   Stanislavsky left an undated typed draft of an acting manual in the US during the first Moscow Art Theatre tour. Because it is housed at the Bancroft Library, University of California, Berkeley, I refer to it as "Bancroft Typescript." Written some time in early 1923, it was sold to the University of California in 1968 by A. A. Koiransky, who accompanied it with a letter to librarian Fred Harris explaining its creation and history. The typescript includes over 200 pages on odd-sized scraps of paper with handwritten notes and addenda, some of which are all but illegible. Many passages and whole pages are crossed out. Some paragraphs exist in two versions. The organization and pagination are haphazard. Other drafts that grapple with the same theoretical content (1909–20) were assembled for publication in SS VI 1959:42–95. These passages were returned to the chronological notebooks from which they came in SS V Part 1 (1993) and V Part 2 (1994). There is an English translation of the 1959 assemblage by Olga Shartze, "On Various Trends in Theatrical Art" (Stanislavsky 1984:133–90).

9   Hughes exposes the fallacy in Tolstoy's assumption that the audience feels the same as the artist, by pointing to the fact that the spectator's feelings emerge from the totality of the play. Thus, one may indeed laugh, when a whiny character like Varya in Chekhov's *The Cherry Orchard* cries (1993:43–5).

10 In the letter which accompanies the Bancroft Typescript, Koiransky translates *remeslo* (normally "craft") as "trade" or "industry" in order to emphasize its commercial base and Stanislavsky's pejorative use of the word (Senelick 1983:127–30). Hobgood criticizes Hapgood for translating *predstavlenie* as "representation," which in his opinion inaccurately links this second trend of theatre to representational art, hence to Realism. He prefers "presentation" since it more accurately describes what this kind of actor does—i.e. presents planned and heightened images of characters to the audience (1973:148). Although I conceptually agree with Hobgood, conversations with Benedetti in the early 1990s convinced me that "representation" best reflects usage in nineteenth century acting debates known to Stanislavsky.

11 "Truth" remains a powerful word for postmodern actors as the title of Susan Batson's *Truth: Personas, Needs, and Flaws in the Art of Building Actors and Creating Characters* (New York: Rugged Land, LLC, 2007) proves.

12 Rokem examines this process in fascinating terms. Like a patient undergoing psychoanalysis who responds to the doctor as if to persons from his or her life, the actor responds with real feelings to the play (1987:175–84). Rokem's analysis recalls the Method's use of "substitution" in which a personal association is substituted for an element in the play. Hughes takes another approach by noting that a character is not an independently existing being and that the text furnishes only an "outline." Hence, the actor can "collaborate in the character's creation." "The responsibility for generating a fully realized character from the outline supplied by the text falls on the actor, [... and thus] makes a Stanislavskian approach possible" (1993:43).

13   Roach uses this passage from *Building a Character* to support his contention that Stanislavsky agrees with Diderot (1985:214). Relying upon Stanislavsky's usage of *perezhivanie* to argue for Stanislavskian dual consciousness, Kurtén also suggests that there is ultimately little difference between the theatres of "representation" and "experiencing," because, regarding dual consciousness "there is no difference on this point between the thinking of Stanislavsky and Diderot" (5 November 1989).

14   Russians use *perezhit'* colloquially to express feeling upset, or suffering through a terrible crisis. This meaning stems from an archaic usage of the word, both in English and in Russian. As Rayner writes, "suffering takes on its more archaic meaning in the sense of experiencing or letting something happen." She uses the word in this way when she writes, "For [drama] does not merely observe action as an object, it suffers the action as a whole" (1994:47, 37). In this meaning, all the most egregious transformations of the System into an emotionally self-indulgent method can find unfortunate support. As one of my acting teachers used to say tongue-in-cheek, the Method recreates only pain and anger.

15   I thank Anna Devere Smith for pointing this passage out to me.

Chapter 8

1   While Ribot believed that true memory of emotion always calls forth a physical response and hence is always emotional, Benedetti told me in the early 1990s that he objects to the commonly used phrase, "emotional memory," on the grounds that a memory of emotion need not be emotional. He therefore retains Hapgood's solution, and in so doing, its parallelism with "sense memory."

2   Strasberg points out that "effective" is also used in error in Stanislavsky's article on acting in the *Encyclopaedia Britannica* (1941:144).

3   Robert Ellerman conveyed to me on the telephone in the early 1990s that Vera Soloviova assured him that recalls at the First Studio were always conducted in private. Strasberg too could be said to practice the Affective Memory exercise in private in so much as he asked actors to go through all the steps of the recall without telling what specific experience they were reviving. In 2007, a student of mine who also studies at Chubbuck's studio assured me that there too actors are not expected to tell the source of their Personal Substitutions.

4   When considering the science in Stanislavsky's work, one should also consult Pitches (1999) who examines Stanislavsky and Meyerhold via Newtonian physics, Boleslavsky and the Americans via behaviorism, and Michael Chekhov and Anatolii Vasiliev via Goethe's Romantic science.

5   Stanislavsky adopts this image for the "subconscious" from Yoga (Chapter 8).

6   Schulman analyzes this psychological strand in the Method (1973).

Chapter 9

1   Roach also suggests another plausible source for Stanislavsky's concern with the spirit. The ancient Roman rhetorician, Quintillian, (whom Stanislavsky had read) saw the "spirit, the breath of life, the transmigration of what the Latins called *anima* or soul from one body to another [...] as a symbol of the oratorical or theatrical act of impersonation, the physical embodiment of one soul, its passions and its actions, by another." Roach links this ancient idea to Stanislavsky's concept of "inspiration." He does not consider, however, Stanislavsky's stated rejection of the word (1985:25, 217).

2   See also Ramacharaka 1906:1–7, 102, 107; White 2006:87–8; Wain 2005:36–8.

3   The influence between Stanislavsky and Demidov was mutual. The young man became fascinated with the System and he left medicine to study acting. He began at the First Studio, where he taught the group about Yoga. Over the years, Demidov assisted Stanislavsky with his study of psychology as well as Yoga. As an actor of the Moscow Art

Theatre, Demidov was interested in how emotion on stage stirs similar emotions in the audience (Stanislavskii II 1986:381, 180). His three volume interpretation of the System was published in Russia for the first time in 2007.

4 Stanislavsky also read and thought about the implications of Anthroposophy on the System (II 1986:201).

5 See McCartney (1978) for an especially clear exposition of the different schools of Yoga. Before R. Andrew White's article and the first edition of *Stanislavsky in Focus*, the only article in English to focus directly on Yoga in the System was Wegner (1976). Kramer (1991) also intuited its influence when he studied connections between the second century AD Sanskrit treatise the Natyasastra and the System. In 1990 when I was drafting the first edition of this book, actor Philip G. Bennett—a practitioner of Yoga, former assistant to émigré teacher Sonia Moore, and founder of the Bennett Lab in San Francisco—shared with me in conversation that he had sensed the Yoga in Stanislavsky's work. Ms. Moore had denied it in her discussions with him, however. Her denial accords with many of the Soviet sources she cites in her books.

6 Wain reports as undocumented that Aktinson may have co-authored his books with "Baba Baraga," a Brahmin (2005:33–4). Wain also explores Atkinson's place in "Western Orientalist discourse" (2005:31–2).

7 Stanislavsky names Suravardi as the Indian; Iu. K. Balturshaitis was the translator (SS VI 1994:488).

8 I am grateful to Mario Biagini, Associate Director of the Workcenter in Pontadera, Italy, for pointing out to me Grotowski's specific critique of Yoga in a personal conversation in 2006.

9 One year after Stanislavsky founded the First Studio, artist Mikhail Larionov proposed Rayonism in the visual arts, a style depicting reflected rays from objects by means of colored lines. Like Stanislavsky's brand of Rayonism, Larionov took inspiration actively from Eastern models as noted above. Regarding censorship, the Soviet *An Actor's Work on Himself, Part I* retains Stanislavsky's discussion of balance and poses, but drops his explicit reference to Yoga.

10 I thank White for drawing my attention to this passage. For more on this process of "subconsciousing," as Ramacharaka calls it, see White 2006:86 and Wain 2006:35.

11 Roach's discussion of Quintilian's *visiones* suggests another possible source for eidetic images. Quintilian, like Aristotle, believed that thinking occurs through mental pictures (1985:24–5).

12 Pitches mistakenly suggests that Stanislavsky and Sulerzhitsky "coin[ed] the Sanskrit term *prana*" (1999:92).

13 Pitches sees this drawing more mechanically as "charged electrical wiring feeding into the System's main cabling" (1999:42–3).

14 White by personal email, 25 May 2007.

15 Pitches identifies this blending in the 1909 rehearsals on *A Month in the Country* as "an uncomfortable fusion of Western proto-psychology and Eastern mysticism. [...] It is illustrative of Stanislavsky's eclecticism that he appropriated two divergent schools of thought without compunction" (1999:91–2). While the seasoned Moscow Art Theatre actors bristled at Stanislavsky's use of experimentation during rehearsals, I am not convinced that the marriage of East and West, so deeply imbedded in Russian culture, was itself at fault. Nor am I convinced that an artist should avoid mutually contradictory ideas, as must scholars and theorists.

Chapter 10

1 While the etymology of "drama" appears briefly in *Creating a Role* (1961:48), it is deleted from the 1936 *An Actor Prepares* (1936); it appears in the 1938 Russian version (SS IV 1991:98–100).

2 This notion is in sympathy with Russian Symbolists like poet Valery Bryusov, who had

served as literary advisor to Stanislavsky's 1905 Studio, and who rejected the dichotomy of sound and sense, assuming an organic unity of the two (Erlich 1969:34–5). Such connections illuminate Stanislavsky's interest in Symbolism as he developed the System.

3　Strasberg specifically echoes this premise when he said, "A scene is nothing more than a succession of problems," reflecting his use of the standard translation for *zadacha* as "problem." (LS 49:7 March 1958).

4　My next book will be a practical and theoretical guide to Active Analysis as taught by Knebel.

5　Benedetti's *Stanislavski and the Actor* (1998) is based upon the "factual, practical" core of *Uroki vdokhnoveniia* (1984) by Lidiia Pavlovna Novitskaia (whom he mistakenly cites as Irina). Novitskaia was also a member of Stanislavsky's last studio.

6　Zverova and Kheifets have taught in Paris for the international symposium, *Le Siècle Stanislavski*, Centre Georges Pompidou (November 1989) and under the auspices of ARTEL (Research and Traditions in Acting), established by Arriane Mnouchkin at *La Cartoucherie*.

7　Stanislavsky discusses this approach to the role in drafts from 1917 and 1918 for the third volume of his acting manual, using Griboedov's *Woe from Wit* as example. He had played one of its central characters, Famusov, a governmental bureaucrat and toady in 1906 and again in 1914.

8　Kovshov attributes the idea for this game to Kedrov (1983:48).

9　I thank my colleague Stacy Marsella for suggesting Helga and Tony Noice's research to me.

10　Analysis of this scene and the application of Active Analysis to it is mine. I base it and my discussion in this chapter on my observations at the Russian Academy of Theatrical Arts (formerly GITIS) in Moscow in 1989 and 1990.

11　Toporkov interpolates into his description the Marxist view when he later states that, "The exclusive goal of reading and re-reading the text was to determine the physical line [of actions]" (2002:176).

12　In the first edition of this book, I used "inciting action" for this term. I have since changed my translation to differentiate between the "impelling action" which drives a scene and the "inciting event" which kicks off the whole play. The Levins (1992) propose different translations for these terms by differentiating between the "leading" character and the one "led."

13　This association with Formalism is all the more ironic because Stanislavsky stated that he supported Stalin's campaign against them (Smeliansky 1996:43). Thomas sees Active Analysis as "a reduced type of Formalist Analysis" and suggests that "Action Analysis and Formalist Analysis are supposed to operate together to obtain the level of knowledge necessary for genuinely professional work" (2005:1). In my own classes, I have found Active Analysis not only sufficient, but capable of prompting fulfilled and sustained performances.

The System's terminology: a selected glossary

1　I thank Marten Kurtén for sharing with me his 1987 glossary for the System in Finnish and Swedish, Laurence Senelick and Jean Benedetti for their many conversations with me on Stanislavsky's terminology, and the Stanislavsky Center, Moscow, for organizing the International Seminar, *Stanislavsky in Translation* (Moscow, May 1990).

Bibliography

"*L'Actors Studio.*" (1989) Panel discussion at the International Symposium, *Le Siècle Stan-islavski*, Centre Georges Pompidou, Paris, 4 November 1989.

Adler, Stella (1988) *The Technique of Acting*, New York: Bantam Books.

The American Laboratory Theatre (1924–25) *Catalogue*, New York.

Archer, Jules (1975) *The Russians and the Americans*, New York: Hawthorn Books.

Autant-Mathieu, Marie Christine (2003) "Stalin and the Moscow Art Theatre," *Slavic and East European Performance*, 28(3):70–85.

—— (2005) "Système et contre-systèmes," in *Stanislavski, Tchekhov*, Paris: ARIAS:29–33.

Balukhatyi, S. D. (1927) *Problemy dramaturgicheskogo analiza: Chekhov*, Leningrad: Academia.

Barthel, Joan (1975) "The Master of the Method Plays a Role Himself," *The New York Times* (February 2).

Beckerman, Bernard (1970) *Dynamics of Drama: Theory and Method of Analysis*, New York: Alfred A. Knopf.

Beckwith, Sarah (1993) *Christ's Body: Identity, Culture and Society in Late Medieval Writings*, New York: Routledge.

Benedetti, Jean (1982) *Stanislavski: An Introduction*, New York: Theatre Arts Books.

—— (1990a) "A History of Stanislavski in Translation," *New Theatre Quarterly*, 23:266–78.

—— (1990b) *Stanislavski: A Biography*, New York: Routledge.

—— (1998) *Stanislavski and the Actor*, New York: Routledge.

Bentley, Eric (1962) "Who Was Ribot? Or Did Stanislavsky Know any Psychology?" *Tulane Drama Review*, 7(2):128–9.

Birman, Serafima (1959) *Put' aktrisy*, Moscow: VTO.

Bjornage, Kjeld (1989) Remarks at the International Symposium, *Stanislavsky in a Changing World*, USSR Theatre Union, Moscow, 9 March 1989.

Blair, Rhonda (2006) "Image and Action: Cognitive Neuroscience and Actor Training," in Bruce McConachie and F. Elizabeth Hart (eds), *Performance and Cognition*, London: Routledge.

—— (2008) *The Actor, Image, and Action: Acting and Cognitive Neuroscience*, London: Routledge.

Blyum, A. V. (1994) *Za kulisami "Ministerstva pravdy,"* St. Petersburg: Akademicheskii proekt.

—— (2000) *Sovetskaia tsenzura v epokhu total'nogo terrora*, St. Petersburg: Akademicheskii proekt.

—— (2003). *A Self-Administered Poison: The System and Functions of Soviet Censorship*, Oxford: Legenda.

Bohnen, Roman (1938*) Scrapbook*, The New York Public Library for the Performing Arts.

Bokshanskaia, Ol'ga Sergeevna (1945) "Iz perepiski s Vl. I. Nemirovichem-Danchenko (Evropa i Amerika 1922–1924)," *Ezhegodnik Moskovskogo khudozhevstvennogo teatra: 1943*, Moscow: MKhAT:485–584.

Boleslavsky, Richard (n.d.) "The Creative Theatre," unpublished typescript, The New York Public Library for the Performing Arts.

Boleslawski [*sic*], Richard (1923) "Stanislavsky: The Man and His Methods," *Theatre Arts Magazine*, 37:27, 74, 80.

—— (1933) *Acting: The First Six Lessons*, New York: Theatre Arts Books.

Bown, Matthew Cullern (1998), *Socialist Realist Painting*, New Haven: Yale University Press.

Braun, Edward (ed. and trans.) (1969) *Meyerhold on Theatre*, New York: Hill and Wang.

Brook, Peter (1968) *The Empty Space*, New York: Avon Books.

Brustein, Robert (1984) *Making Scenes: A Personal History of the Turbulent Years at Yale, 1966–1979*, New York: Limelight Editions.

Butova, T. V. (1997) *Amerikanskii teatr: proshloe i nastoiashchee*, Moscow: Gosudarst-vennii institut iskusstvovaniia.

Carnicke, Sharon Marie (1984) *"An Actor Prepares/Rabota aktera nad soboi*: A Comparison of the English with the Russian Stanislavsky," *Theatre Journal*, 37(4):481–94. [Early material for part of Chapter 5.]

—— (1989) *The Theatrical Instinct: Nikolai Evreinov and the Russian Theatre of the Early Twentieth Century,* New York: Peter Lang.

—— (1991) "Stalinslavsky: Stanislavsky's Final Years," *Theatre Three*, 10/11:150–63. [Early material for part of Chapter 2.]

—— (1992) "Boleslavsky in America," in Laurence Senelick (ed.), *Wandering Stars: Papers on Russian Émigré Theatre from 1900–1940*, Iowa City: University of Iowa Press:116–28. [Early material for part of Chapters 3 and 4.]

—— (1993) "Stanislavsky: Unabridged and Uncensored," *The Drama Review*, 37(1) (T 137):22–42. Revised and reprinted in Gabrielle Cody and Rebecca Schneider (eds) (2001) *Re-Direction: A Theoretical and Practical Guide*, New York: Routledge.

—— (1997) "Stanislavsky's Production of *The Cherry Orchard* in the US," in J. Douglas Clayton (ed.), *Chekhov Then and Now*, New York: Peter Lang:19–30.

—— (1999) "Lee Strasberg's Paradox of the Actor," in Peter Kramer and Alan Lovell (eds), *Screen Acting*, London: Routledge.

—— (2000a) "The Life of the Human Spirit: Stanislavsky's Eastern Self," *Teatr*, 1(1):3–14. [Early material for part of Chapter 9.]

—— (2000b) "Stanislavsky's System: Pathways for the Actor," in Alison Hodge (ed.), *Twentieth Century Actor Training*, New York: Routledge:11–36.

—— (2001) "Stanislavsky Enters the Twenty-First Century," *Slavic and East European Performance,* 21(1):49–56. [Early material for part of Chapter 3.]

—— (2003) "From Acting Guru to Movie Star: Lee Strasberg as Actor," in Martin Barker and Thomas Austin (eds), *Contemporary Hollywood Stardom*, London: Arnold:118–34.

—— (2005) *"Nemirovitch-Dantchenko aux Etats-Unis: Un héritage oublié et acculté,"* in Marie Christine Autant-Mathieu (trans. and ed.), *Le Rayonnement du Théâtre d'Art en Europe et aux Etats-Unis*, Paris:CNRS:255–74.

Chaikin, Joseph (1987) *The Presence of the Actor*, New York: Atheneum.

Chekhov, A. P. (1944–51) *Polnoe sobranie sochinenii i pisem*, 20 vols, Moscow: Khu-dozhestvennaia literatura.

—— (1971) *Izbrannye proizvedennia*, 3 vols, Moscow: Khudozhestvennaia literatura.

Chekhov, Mikhail (1955) "Lecture 10: Experience at the Moscow Art Theatre," unpublished audiotaped lectures recorded in Hollywood. The New York Public Library for the Performing Arts.

—— (1986, 2nd edn 1995) *Literaturnnoe naslestvie*, 2 vols, Moscow: Iskusstvo.

—— (1991) *On the Technique of Acting*, New York: Harper Perennial.

—— (2005) *The Path of the Actor*, London: Routledge.

Chinoy, Helen Krich (ed.) (1976) "Reunion: A Self-Portrait of the Group Theatre," A special issue of *Educational Theatre Journal*, 27(4).

Chubbuck, Ivana (2004) *The Power of the Actor: The Chubbuck Technique*, New York: Gotham Books.

Clayton, J. Douglas (1993) *Pierrot in Petrograd: The Commedia dell-Arte/Balagan in Twentieth-Century Russian Theatre and Drama*, Montreal: McGill-Queen's University Press.

Clurman, Harold (1957) *The Fervent Years*, New York: Hill and Wang.

—— (1958) *Lies Like Truth*, New York: MacMillan Co.

—— (1966) *The Naked Image: Observations on the Modern Theatre*, New York: MacMillan Co.

Cole, Toby and Chinoy, Helen Krich (eds) (1970) *Actors on Acting*, New York: Crown Publishers.

Crawford, Cheryl (1977) *One Naked Individual*, Indianapolis: Bobbs-Merrill.

Damasio, Antonio (1994) *Descartes' Error: Emotion, Reason and the Human Brain*. New York: Penguin.

—— (1999) *The Feeling of What Happens in the Body: Body and Emotion in the Making of Consciousness*, New York: Harcourt.

Derman, A. (1938) "Genii teatra," *Literaturnaia gazeta*, 45 (15 August):5.

Dewhirst, Martin and Farrell, Robert (eds) (1973) *The Soviet Censorship*, Metuchen: The Scarecrow Press.

Diderot, Denis (1957) *The Paradox of Acting*, New York: Hill and Wang, Inc.

Dixon, Leslie (1987) *Outrageous Fortune*, film directed by Arthur Hiller, Touchstone Pictures.

Dybovskii, Vladimir (1992) "V Plenu predlagaemykh obstoiatel'stv," *Minuvshee*, vol. 10. [All citations from typescript.]

Edwards, Christine (1965). *The Stanislavsky Heritage: Its Contribution to the Russian and American Theatre*, New York University Press.

Efros, Anatolii (1993) *Repetitsiia—liubov' moia*, Moscow: Panos.

Ekman, Paul (1980) "Biological and Cultural Contributions to Body and Facial Movements in the Expression of Emotion," in Amélie Oksenberg Rorty (ed.), *Explaining Emotions*, Berkeley: University of California Press:73–101.

—— (2007) *Emotions Revealed: Recognizing Faces and Feelings to Improve Communication and Emotional Life*, 2nd edn, New York: Owl Books.

Emeljanow, Victor (ed.) (1981) *Chekhov: The Critical Heritage*, Boston: Routledge and Kegan Paul.

Erlich, Victor (1969) *Russian Formalism*, The Hague: Mouton.

Ermolaev, Herman (1997) *Censorship in Soviet Literature: 1917–1991*, New York: Rowman and Littlefield Publishers, Inc.

Esslin, Martin (1976) *An Anatomy of Drama*, New York: Hill and Wang.

Evreinov, N. (1912) *Teatr kak takovoi*, St. Petersburg: Sovremennoe iskusstvo.

—— (1916) *Teatr dlia sebia, Chast' II*, St. Petersburg: Butkovskaia.

Evreinov, N. (1938) "K. S. Stanislavskii i ego teatr," *Sovremennye zapiski,* 67:325–33.

—— (1955) *Istoriia russkogo teatra s drevneishikh vremen do 1917 goda*, New York: Izdatel'stvo imeni Chekhova.

Ezhegodnik Moskovskogo khudozhevstvennogo teatra: 1946 (1948) Moscow: MKhAT.

Fergusson, Francis (1949) *The Idea of a Theater*, Garden City: Doubleday and Co.

—— (1957) *The Human Image in Dramatic Literature*, New York: Doubleday and Co.

Filippov, Boris (1977) *Actors Without Make-Up*, Moscow: Progress Publishers.

Garfield, David (1980) *A Player's Place: The Story of The Actors Studio*, New York: Mac-Millan Publishing Co.

Gelbard, Larry and Schisgal, Murray (1982) *Tootsie*, film directed by Sydney Pollack, Columbia Pictures.

Goleman, Daniel (1995) *Emotional Intelligence*, New York: Bantam Books.

Gordon, Mel (1987) *The Stanislavsky Technique: Russia*, New York: Applause Theatre Book Publishers.

—— (1989) "Nine Common Misconceptions about Stanislavsky and his System," *Soviet and East European Performance*, 9(2/3):45–6.

Gorelik, Mordecai (1962) *New Theatres for Old*, New York: E. P. Dutton and Co.

Gourfinkel, Nina (1972) "Repenser Stanislavski," *Révue de la Société d'histoire du théâtre*, 23(2):103–28.

Gray, Camilla (1962) *The Russian Experiment in Art: 1863–1922*, New York: Harry N. Abrams Inc.

Grigor'ev, A. (1938) "Tribun stsenicheskoi pravdy," *Trud*, 183 (10 August):3–4.

Grotowski, Jerzy (1968) *Towards a Poor Theatre*, New York: Simon and Schuster.

Guerney, Bernard Guilbert (ed.) (1960) *An Anthology of Russian Literature in the Soviet Period from Gorki to Pasternak*, New York: Vintage Books.

Gurevich, L. Ia. (1972) "Istoriia *Severnogo vestnika*," in S. A. Vengerov (ed.), *Russkaia literatura XX veka*, Munich: Wilhelm Fink Verlag:235–64.

Gus, M. (1938) "V bor'be za realizm," *Sovetskoe iskusstvo*, 6(412):3–4.

Hamlisch, Marvin and Kleban, Edward (1975) "Nothing," in *A Chorus Line*, New York: ASCAP/BMI.

Hapgood, Elizabeth Reynolds (n.d.) *Archive*, The New York Public Library for the Performing Arts.

—— (1961) "Translator's Note," in Constantin Stanislavski [*sic*], *Creating a Role*, New York: Theatre Arts Books.

—— (1963) "Stanislavski and the Moscow Art Theatre at the White House," *Players Magazine*, 39(7):198–9.

Harvard University (2000–1) *Institute for Advanced Theatre Training: 2000–2001 Catalogue*, online at <http://www.fas.harvard.edu.html>, accessed 11 January 2008.

Hecht, Leo (1989) "Stanislavsky's Trips to the United States," unpublished paper presented at the American Association of Teachers of Slavic and East European Languages Conference, Washington, DC, 30 December 1989.

Hethmon, Robert H. (ed.) (1991) *Strasberg at the Actors Studio*, New York: Theater Communications Group.

Himmelstein, Morgan L. (1963) *Drama Was A Weapon: The Left-Wing Theatre in New York 1929–1941*, New Brunswick: Rutgers University Press.

Hirsch, Foster (1984) *A Method to Their Madness*, New York: W. W. Norton.

—— (1986) "Still Savvy After All These Years," *American Theatre*, 2(11):12–15.

Hobgood, Burnet M. (1973) "Central Conceptions in Stanislavsky's System," *Educational Theatre Journal*, 25(2):147–59.

—— (1986) "Stanislavski's Books: An Untold Story," *Theatre Survey*, 27(1/2):155–65.

—— (1991) "Stanislavski's Preface to *An Actor Prepares* and the Persona of Tortsov," *Theatre Journal*, 43(21):219–32.

Hughes, R. I. G. (1993) "Tolstoy, Stanislavski, and the Art of Acting," *The Journal of Aesthetics and Art Criticism*, 51(1):39–48.

Hull, S. Lorraine (1985) *Strasberg's Method As Taught by Lorrie Hull*, Woodbridge: Ox Bow Publishing, Inc.

Iura, G. P. (1938) "Nasha gordost'," *Sovetskoe iskusstvo*, 6(412):3.

James, William and Lange, Carl (1967) *The Emotions*, New York: Hafner Publishing Co.

Jansen, Sue Curry (1988) *Censorship: The Knot that Binds Power and Knowledge*, New York: Oxford University Press.

Kalashnikov, Iu. (1938) "K vykhodu novoi knigi K. S. Stanislavskogo," *Teatr*, 9:57–63.

Kazan, Elia (1988) *A Life*, New York: Alfred A. Knopf.

Khailov, L. (1938) "Sozdatel' realisticheskogo teatra," *Sovetskoe Belorussiia*, 183 (9 August):2.

Knebel', M. O. (1967) *Vsia zhizn'*, Moscow: VTO.

—— (1968) "Vysokaia prostota," *Teatr*, 9:46–9.

—— (1971) *O tom, chto mne kazhetsia osobenno vazhnym: Stat'i, ocherki, portreti*, Moscow: Iskusstvo.

—— (1982) *O deistvennom analiza p'esy i roli*, Moscow: Iskusstvo.

Komar'skaia, N. (1957) "U istokov," *Sovetskaia kul'tura*, 148 (14 November):2.

Kovshov, Nikolai (1983) *Uroki M. N. Kedrova*, Moscow: Iskusstvo.

Kramer, Richard E. (1991) "The Natyasastra and Stanislavsky: Points of Contact," *Theatre Studies*, 36:46–62.

Krasner, David (ed.) (2000) *Method Acting Reconsidered: Theory, Practice, Future*, New York: St. Martin's Press.

Kulesza, Marek (1989) *Ryszard Boleslawski: Umrec w Hollywood*, Warsaw: Panstwowy Instytut Wydawniczy.

Kurtén, Martin (1989) "Emotion and Action," paper delivered at the International Symposium, *Le Siècle Stanislavski*, Centre Georges Pompidou, Paris, 5 November 1989.

Lazebnick, Philip (1991) *Devil's Due*, episode of *Star Trek: The Next Generation*, directed by Tom Benko.

Lewis, Robert (1958) *Method Or Madness?*, New York: Samuel French, Inc.

—— (1962) "Emotional Memory," *The Tulane Drama Review*, 6(4):54–60.

—— (1984) *Slings and Arrows: Theater in My Life*, New York: Stein and Day Publishers.

Levin, Irina and Igor (1992) *Working on the Play and the Role: The Stanislavsky Method for Analyzing the Characters in a Drama*, Chicago: Ivan R. Dee.

—— (2002) *The Stanislavsky Secret: Not a System, Not a Method, but a Way of Thinking*, Colorado Springs: Meriwether Publishing, Ltd.

Liadov, V. I. (ed.) (1998) *O M. O. Knebel'*, Moscow: no publisher.

Liubomudrov, M. (1989) "Vse dolzhno idti ot zhizni …." in Vl. I. Nemirovich-Danchenko, *Rozhdenie teatra*, Moscow: Izdatel'stvo Pravda:5–36.

Lloyd, Benjamin (2006) "Stanislavsky, Spirituality, and the Problem of the Wounded Actor," *New Theatre Quarterly*, 22(1):70–5.

Logan, Joshua (1976) *Josh: My Up and Down, In and Out Life*, New York: Delacorte Press.

MacGowan, Kenneth (1923) "And Again Repertory: The Moscow Art Theatre and Shakespeare Divide New York," *Theatre Arts Magazine*, 7(2):89–104.

Magarshack, David (1980) "Introduction," in David Magarshack (ed.), *Stanislavsky on the Art of the Stage*, Boston: Faber and Faber:11–87.

Malcovati, Fausto (1989) Remarks delivered at the International Symposium, *Le Siècle Stanislavski*, Centre Georges Pompidou, Paris, 5 November 1989.

Mamet, David (1999) *True and False: Heresy and Common Sense for the Actor*, New York: Vintage Books.

Markov, P. A. (1934) *The First Studio*, typescript of translation by Mark Schmidt, The New York Public Library for the Performing Arts.

Marowitz, Charles (2007) "Getting Stanislavsky Wrong," *American Theatre*, 29(3):56–9.

Marsella, Stacy C., Carnicke, Sharon M., Gratch, Jonathan, Okhmatovskaia, Anna, and Rizzo, Albert (2006) "An Exploration of Delsarte's Structural Acting System," *Intelligent Virtual Agents 2006*, LNAI 4133, Berlin: Spinger-Verlag:80–92.

Martel, Jay (1988) "Why Johnny Can't Act," *Spy* (December):91–100.

McCartney, James (1978) *Philosophy and Practice of Yoga*, Romford: L. N. Fowler and Co, Inc.

McFarren, Cheryl (2003) *Rethinking Affective Memory: Background, Method, and Challenge for Contemporary Actor Training*, unpublished dissertation, University of Colorado at Boulder. [Forthcoming with Mellen Press]

McGaw, Charles (1980) *Acting is Believing*, 4th edn, New York: Holt, Rinehart, and Winston.

McLauchlan, Russell (n.d.) *"The Cherry Orchard* with Two Bright Stars," *Clippings*, The New York Public Library for the Performing Arts.

Meierkhol'd, V. E. (1913) *O Teatre*, St. Petersburg: Prosveshchenie.

Meisner, Sanford and Longwell, Dennis (1987) *Sanford Meisner on Acting*, New York: Vintage Books.

Merlin, Bella (2001) *Beyond Stanislavsky: The Psycho-Physical Approach to Actor Training*, New York: Routledge.

—— (2003) *Konstantin Stanislavsky*. New York: Routledge.

—— (2007) *The Complete Stanislavsky Toolkit*, Hollywood: Drama Publishers.

Mirsky, D. S. (1958) *A History of Russian Literature From its Beginnings to 1900*, New York: Vintage Books.

Mokul'skii, S. (1957) "Primer sotsialisticheskogo teatra," *Teatr*, 10:135–40.

Moore, Sonia (1965) *The Stanislavski System*, New York: Viking Press.

—— (1991) *Stanislavski Revealed: The Actor's Guide to Spontaneity on Stage*, New York: Applause Theatre Books.

Munk, Erika (ed.) (1966) *Stanislavski and America*, New York: Hill and Wang.

Nemirovitch-Dantchenko [*sic*], Vladimir (1936) *My Life in the Russian Theatre*, London: Geoffrey Bles.

Nemirovich-Danchenko, V. I. (2003) *Tvorcheskoe nasledie*, 4 vols., Moscow: Moskovskii khudozhestvennyi teatr.

—— (2005) *Pis'ma O. S. Bokshanskoi*, 2 vols., Moscow: Moskovskii khudozhestvennyi teatr.

Noice, Helga and Tony (2006) "What Studies of Actors and Acting Can Tell Us About Memory and Cognitive Function," *Current Directions on Psychological Science*, 15(1):14–18.

North, Stephen M. (1987) *The Making of Knowledge in Composition: Portrait of an Emerging Field*, Upper Montclair: Boynton/Cook Publishers, Inc.

Norvelle, Lee (1962) "Stanislavski Revisited," *Educational Theatre Journal*, 14(2):29–37.

Odets, Clifford (1979) *Awake and Sing!* in *Six Plays of Clifford Odets*, New York: Grove Weidenfeld:33–102.

Osnos, Iu. (1952) "Teoriia dramy i uchenie Stanislavskogo," *Sovetskoe iskusstvo*, 42:2.

Ouspenskaya, Maria (n.d.) *Clippings*, The New York Public Library for the Performing Arts.

—— (1954–5) "Notes on Acting with Maria Ouspenskaya," *The American Repertory Theater Magazine*, 2(1–4).

Pashennaia, Vera (1954) *Iskusstvo aktrisy*, Moscow: Iskusstvo.

Pavis, Patrice (2003) *Analyzing Performance: Theater, Dance, and Film*, Ann Arbor: University of Michigan Press.

Perkins, David (1964) *Wordsworth and the Poetry of Sincerity*, Cambridge: Harvard University Press.

Pitches, Jonathan (1999) *Science and the Stanislavsky Tradition*, New York: Routledge.

Plamper, Jan (2001) "Abolishing Ambiguity: Soviet Censorship Practices in the 1930s," *The Russian Review*, 60:526–44.

Polanyi, Michael (1966) *The Tacit Dimension*, Garden City: Doubleday and Co., Inc.

Poliakova, Elena I. (2006) *Teatr Sulerzhitskogo: Etika. Estetitka. Rezhissura*, Moscow: Agraf, Ltd.

Prokof'ev, V. L. (1948) "Na poslednykh repetitsiiakh K. S. Stanislavskogo," *Teatr*, 1:49–56.

Propp, V. I. (1928) *Morfologiia skazki*, Leningrad: Academia.

Radishcheva, O. A. (1997) *Stanislavskii i Nemirovich-Danchenko Istoriia teatral'nykh otnoshenii: 1897–1908*, Moscow: Artist, Rezhisser, Teatr.

—— (1999a) *Stanislavskii i Nemirovich-Danchenko Istoriia teatral'nykh otnoshenii: 1909–1917*, Moscow: Artist, Rezhisser, Teatr.

—— (1999b) *Stanislavskii i Nemirovich-Danchenko Istoriia teatral'nykh otnoshenii: 1917–1938*, Moscow: Artist, Rezhisser, Teatr.

Ramacharaka (1904) *Hatha Yoga; or The Yogi Philosophy of Physical Well-Being,* Chicago: Yogi Publication Society. [Translated into Russian by V. Singh, St. Petersburg: n.p., 1909.]

—— (1906) *Raja Yoga; of Mental Development*, Chicago: Yogi Publication Society. [Translated into Russian by V. Singh, St. Petersburg: n.p., 1914.]

Rayner, Alice (1994) *To Act, To Do, To Perform: Drama and the Phenomenology of Action*, Ann Arbor: University of Michigan Press.

Ribot, Théodule (1897) *The Psychology of Emotions*, London: Walter Scott, Ltd.

—— (1910) *Problèmes de psychologie affective*, Paris: Félix Alcan.

Roach, Joseph (1985) *The Player's Passion*, Newark: University of Delaware.

Roberts, J. W. (1981) *Richard Boleslavsky: His Life and Work in the Theatre*, Ann Arbor: UMI Research Press.

Rokem, Freddie (1987) "Acting and Psychoanalysis: Street Scenes, Private Scenes, and Transference," *Theatre Journal*, 39(2):175–84.

Rozik, Eli (2002) *The Roots of Theatre*, Iowa City: University of Iowa Press.

Sakhnovskii, V. G. (1988) "Vechnye zakony tvorchestva," *Teatr*, 1:77–92.

Schechner, Richard (2006) *Performance Studies: An Introduction*, 2nd edn, New York: Routledge.

Schechner, Richard and Wolford, Lisa (eds) (1997) *The Grotowski Sourcebook*. New York: Routledge.

Schiffman, Jean (2001) "Method Man," *Back Stage West* (November 15): 4–5.

Schnitzler, Henry (1954) "Truth and Consequences of Stanislavsky Misinterpreted," *Quarterly Journal of Speech*, 40(2):3–15.

Schulman, Michael (1973) "Backstage Behaviorism," *Psychology Today* (June):51–4, 88.

Senelick, Laurence (1981) "Stanislavsky's Double Life in Art," *Theatre Survey*, 26(2):201–11.

—— (1983) "New Information on *My Life in Art*," *Theatre Survey*, 24(1/2):127–30.

—— (1988) "The Stanislavsky Colloquium at the *Théâtre de Chaillot*," *Soviet and East-European Drama, Theatre and Film*, 7(2/3):22–6.

—— (ed.)(1992) *Wandering Stars: Russian Émigré Theatre, 1905–1940*, Iowa City: University of Iowa Press:9–12.

—— (2007) "Before Stoppard: Merezhkovsky's Bakunin Play," *Slavic and East European Performance*, 27(1):41–54.

Shapiro, Adol'f (1999) *Kak zakryvalsia zanaves*, Moscow: Novoe literaturnoe obozrenie.

Shklovskii, Viktor (1921) *Rozanov*. Petrograd: Opoiaz.

Shverubovich, V. (1990) *O starom Khudozhestvennom teatre*, Moscow: Iskusstvo.

Simonov, Pavel Vasil'evich (1962) *Metod K. S. Stanislavskogo i fiziologiia emotsii*, Moscow: Akademiia nauk.

Sinitsyna, Olga (1999) "Censorship in the Soviet Union and Its Cultural and Professional Results for Arts and Art Libraries," *INSPEL*, 33:35–42.

Skatershchikov, V. (1976) "Lenin i otnoshenie k talantu," *Sovetskaia kul'tura*, 32:2.

Slonim, Marc (1967) *Soviet Russian Literature: Writers and Problems 1917–1967*, New York: Oxford University Press.

Smeliansky, Anatoly Mironovich (1989a) *Mikhail Bulgakov v Khudozhestvennom teatre*, Moscow: Iskusstvo.

—— (1989b) Untitled paper delivered at the International Symposium, *Stanislavsky in a Changing World*, USSR Theatre Union, Moscow, 27 February 1989.

—— (1990) Untitled paper delivered at the International Seminar, *Stanislavsky in Translation*, the Moscow Art Theatre, Moscow, 14 May 1990.

—— (1991) "The Last Decade: Stanislavsky and Stalinism," *Theater*, 12(2):7–13.

—— (1992) "In Search of El Dorado: America in the Fate of the Moscow Art Theatre," in Laurence Senelick (ed.), *Wandering Stars: Russian Emigré Theatre, 1905–1940*, Iowa City: University of Iowa Press:44–68.

—— (1996) "Assimilation: How Stalin, the Moscow Art Theatre Founder Stanislavsky and the Playwright Bulgakov Got Along or Didn't," *The New Theater Review*, 15:41–5.

Solovyova, Inna Natanovna (1999) "The Theatre and Socialist Realism: 1929–1953" in Robert Leach and Victor Borovsky (eds), *A History of Russian Theatre*, Cambridge: Cambridge University Press:325–57.

—— (2007) *Khudozhestvennyi teatr: Zhizn' i prikliucheniia idei.* Moscow: Moskovskii khudozhestvennyi teatr.

Stanislavskii, K. S. (n.d.) Unpublished typescript of an early draft of an acting manual with handwritten notes, Bancroft Library, University of California at Berkeley.

—— (1919–20) "Zapisnye knizhki i dnevniki Stanislavskogo," KS No. 833, 79, unpublished typescript with handwritten notes. The Stanislavsky Archive, MKhAT Museum, Moscow.

—— (1925) *Moia zhizn' v iskusstve*, Moscow: no publisher.

—— (1935) *Rabota aktera nad soboi, Chast' I: Okonchatel'nyi dlia Ameriki*, unpublished typescript, The New York Public Library for the Performing Arts.

Stanislavski [*sic*], Constantin (1936) *An Actor Prepares*, Elizabeth Reynolds Hapgood (trans.), New York: Theatre Arts Books.

—— (1938) *Rabota aktera nad soboi, Chast' I*, Moscow: Khudozhestvennaia literatura.

—— (1940) *Das Geheimnis des schauspielerischen Erfolges*, Alexandra Meyerburg (trans.), Berlin: Scientia Verlag.

—— (1949) *Building a Character*, Elizabeth Reynolds Hapgood (trans.), New York: Theatre Arts Books.

Stanislavskii, K.S. (1954–61) *Sobranie sochinenii*, 8 vols., Moscow: Iskusstvo. [Abbreviation SS]

Stanislavski [*sic*] Constantin (1961) *Creating a Role*, Elizabeth Reynolds Hapgood (trans.), New York: Theatre Arts Books.

Stanislavsky, K. (1980) *Stanislavsky on the Art of the Stage*, David Magarshack (trans. and ed.), Boston: Faber and Faber Ltd..

—— (1983) *Rezhisserskie ekzempliary K. S. Stanislavskogo*, vol. III, Moscow: Iskusstvo.

—— (1984) *Selected Works*, Moscow: Raduga Publishers.

—— (1986*) Iz zapisnykh knizhek*, 2 vols., Moscow: VTO.

—— (1988–99) *Sobranie sochinenii*, 9 vols., Moscow: Iskusstvo, 1988–99. [Abbreviation SS]

Strasberg, Lee (1941) "Acting and the Training of Actors," in John Gassner (ed.), *Producing the Play*, New York: Holt, Rinehart, and Winston:128–62.

—— (1956–69) "The Actors Studio," Sound Recording No. 339A, 1956–69, Wisconsin Center for Film and Theater Research, An Archive of the University of Wisconsin, Madison, and the State Historical Society of Wisconsin, Madison. [Abbreviation LS]

—— (1966) "Letter to the Editor," *Tulane Drama Review*, 11(1)(T 33):234–9.

—— (1974) "Acting," *Encyclopaedia Britannica*, 15th edn, I:59.

—— (1989) Interview, "Lee Strasberg: A Double Life in the Theatre," *Village Voice* (June 26).

—— (1987) *A Dream of Passion: The Development of the Method*, Boston: Little Brown and Company.

Stroeva, M. N. (1973 and 1977) *Rezhisserskie iskaniia Stanislavskogo*, 2 vols., Moscow: Izdatel'stvo Nauk.

Sulerzhitskii, L. A. (1970) *Povesti i rasskazy. Stat'i i zametki o teatre. Perepiska. Vospominaniia o L. A. Sulerzhitskom,* Moscow: Iskusstvo.

Svobodin, Aleksandr Petrovich (1990) Remarks at the International Seminar, *Stanislavsky in Translation*, Moscow Art Theatre, Moscow, 18 May 1990.

Tagore, Rabindranath (2004) *Sadhana*, New York: Doubleday.

Theatre Arts Books Archives, accessed in the offices of Routledge Publishers, New York, in 1989–90. [Former editor, William Germano, told me in July 2005 that these archives are now lost.]

Thomas, James (2005) *Script Analysis for Actors, Directors, and Designers*, 3rd edn, Boston: Focal Point.

Tolstoi, L. N. (1964) *Sobranie sochinenii*, vol. XV, Moscow: Khudozhestvennaia literatura.

Toporkov, V. O. (2002) *K. S. Stanislavskii na repetitsii*. Moscow, AST Press, Skd.

Trilling, Lionel (1972) *Sincerity and Authenticity*, Cambridge: Harvard University Press.

Vendrovskaya, Lyubov and Kaptereva, Galina (eds) (1982) *Evgeny Vakhtangov*, Moscow: Progress Publishers.

Vernadsky, George (1969) *A History of Russia*, New Haven: Yale University Press.

Vineberg, Steve (1991) "Emotional Insurgents," *American Film* (June):40–5.

Vinogradskaia, I. (ed.) (2000) *Stanislavskii repetiruet: Zapisi i stenogrammy repetitsii*, Moscow: Moskovskii khudozhestvennyi teatr.

—— (ed.) (2003) *Zhizn' i tvorchestvo K. S. Stanislavskogo: Letopis'*, 4 vols., Moscow: Moskovskii khudozhestvennyi teatr.

Vladimirova, Z. V. (1991) *M. O. Knebel'*, Moscow: Iskusstvo.

Vol'kenstein, Vladimir (1922) *Stanislavskii*, Moscow: Shipovnik.

Volkov, Solomon (2004) *Shostakovich and Stalin*, New York: Knopf.

Wain, Ashley (2005) *Acting and Essence*, unpublished dissertation, University of Western Sydney, Australia.

Weales, Gerald (1967) "The Group Theatre and Its Plays," in *American Theatre*, New York: St. Martin's Press:67–85.

Weaver, John A. (1923) "A 100 per cent American Speaks," *The Literary Digest* (3 March).

Wegner, William H. (1976) "The Creative Circle: Stanislavski and Yoga," *Educational Theatre Journal*, 28(1):85–9.

White, R. Andrew (2005) "A Director Rehearses," *New England Theatre Journal,* 16:43–59.

—— (2006) "Stanislavsky and Ramacharaka: The Influence of Yoga and Turn-of-the-Century Occultism on the System," *Theatre Survey*, 47(1):73–92.

Wiles, Timothy (1980) *The Theater Event*, Chicago: University of Chicago Press.

Winerman, Lea (2005) "The Mind's Mirror," *Monitor on Psychology*, 38(9):48.

Worrall, Nick (1989) *Modernism to Realism on the Soviet Stage: Tairov, Vakhtangov, Okhlopkov*, Cambridge: Cambridge University Press.

Worthen, William W. (1983) "Stanislavsky and the Ethos of Acting," *Theatre Journal*, 35(1):32–40.

Yogananda, Paramahansa (1993) *Autobiography of a Yogi*. Los Angeles: Self-Realization Fellowship.

"Zadachi RAPP na teatral'noi fronte" (1931) *Sovetskoe iskusstvo*, 136(64/65):2.

Zaechner, R. C. (1968) *Hinduism*, New York: Oxford University Press.

Zhirmunskii, Viktor (1928) "Zadachi poetiki," *Voprosy teorii literatury*, Leningrad: Academia.

Zon, B. V. (1955) "Vstrechi s K. S. Stanislavskim," in *K. S. Stanislavskii: Teatral'noe nasledestvo*, vol. I, Moscow: Akademii Nauk SSSR:444–91.

Index

Theatre Arts on Acting

Edited by Laurence Senelick

"The successful leading players of today stand on an uneasy bridge between two extremes of theatrical development. Behind us lie the glories of tradition, the grand manner, the star system … Before us lie the fear of convention and imitation, the demand for novelty, the restless, impatient craving for easy success …"

John Gielgud

"I hate actors who bump into the furniture, or stand where they seem to be goosed by an armchair, or are frightened by tables, beds, lamps, doors and the surroundings in general."

Hume Cronyn

During its fifty year run, *Theatre Arts Magazine* was a bustling forum for the foremost names in the performing arts. Renowned theatre historian Laurence Senelick has plundered its archives to assemble a stellar collection of articles on every aspect of the theatrical life.

Contributors include:

Konstantin Stanislavski on Character Building; Stark Young on Illusion in Acting; Edith Isaacs on Typecasting; Lee Strasberg on Past Performances; Cedric Hardwicke on The Moribund Craft of Acting

… as well as articles by and about Michael Chekhov, John Gielgud, Fred Astaire, Richard Boleslavsky, Shelley Winters, Laurence Olivier, Bette Davis, Alastair Cooke and Vivien Leigh

Laurence Senelick is Fletcher Professor of Drama and Oratory at Tufts University, and winner of the George Jean Nathan award for Dramatic Criticism. He is the author of over 20 books on theatre history and dramatic theory and a practicing actor, director and translator.

ISBN13: 978-0-415-77492-5 (hbk)
ISBN13: 978-0-415-77493-2 (pbk)

eBooks – at www.eBookstore.tandf.co.uk

A library at your fingertips!

eBooks are electronic versions of printed books. You can store them on your PC/laptop or browse them online.

They have advantages for anyone needing rapid access to a wide variety of published, copyright information.

eBooks can help your research by enabling you to bookmark chapters, annotate text and use instant searches to find specific words or phrases. Several eBook files would fit on even a small laptop or PDA.

NEW: Save money by eSubscribing: cheap, online access to any eBook for as long as you need it.

Annual subscription packages

We now offer special low-cost bulk subscriptions to packages of eBooks in certain subject areas. These are available to libraries or to individuals.

For more information please contact webmaster.ebooks@tandf.co.uk

We're continually developing the eBook concept, so keep up to date by visiting the website.

www.eBookstore.tandf.co.uk